watching Wildlife

Southern Africa

South Africa, Namibia, Botswana, Zimbabwe, Malawi, Zambia

WATCHING WILDLIFE SOUTHERN AFRICA
2ND EDITION
Published September 2009
First published January 2002

Published by
Lonely Planet Publications Pty Ltd ABN 36 005 607 983
90 Maribyrnong St, Footscray, Victoria 3011, Australia

LONELY PLANET OFFICES
Australia
Head Office
Locked Bag 1, Footscray, Victoria 3011 ☎ 03 8379 8000,
fax 03 8379 8111 talk2us@lonelyplanet.com.au
USA
150 Linden St, Oakland, CA 94607 ☎ 510 250 6400,
toll free 800 275 8555 fax 510 893 8572 info@lonelyplanet.com
UK
2nd fl, 186 City Rd, London EC1V 2NT ☎ 020 7106 2100,
fax 020 7106 2101 go@lonelyplanet.co.uk

ISBN 9781741042108

Photographs
Front cover photograph: Zebra, Martin Harey/Getty Images.
Cover flap photographs: Leopard, (Emily Riddell/Lonely Planet Images),
elephant; (Craig Pershouse/Lonely Planet Images), lion (Ariadne Van
Zandbergen/Lonely Planet Images), hippopotamus (Ariadne Van Zand-
bergen/Lonely Planet Images), African wild dogs (Ariadne Van Zandber-
gen /Lonely Planet Images)
Back cover photographs (from left to right): cheetah (Alex Dissanayake/
Lonely Planet Images); hornbill (Karl Lehmann/Lonely Planet Images);
Black Rhino (Douglas Steakley/Lonely Planet Images)Many of the images
in this guide are available for licensing from Lonely Planet Images: www.
lonelyplanetimages.com.

Printed by Markono Print Media Pte Ltd, Singapore.

CONTENTS

AUTHORS

MARY FITZPATRICK
South Africa

Mary is from the USA, where she spent her early years in Washington, DC – dreaming, more often than not, of how to get across an ocean or two to more exotic locales. After finishing graduate studies, she set off for several years in Europe. Her fascination with languages and cultures soon led her further south to Africa, where she has spent the past 15 years living and working all around the continent, including in Tanzania and South Africa. She has authored and co-authored many guidebooks and articles on the continent, and heads off on safari at every opportunity.

MATTHEW D. FIRESTONE
Coordinating Author

Matt is a trained biological anthropologist and epidemiologist who is particularly interested in the health and nutrition of indigenous populations. His first visit to Southern Africa in 2001 brought him deep into the Kalahari, where he performed a field study on the traditional diet of the San hunter-gatherers. Unfortunately, Matt's promising academic career was postponed due to a severe case of wanderlust, though he has relentlessly travelled to over fifty different countries in search of a cure.

NANA LUCKHAM
Zimbabwe, Zambia & Malawi

Born in Tanzania to a Ghanaian mother and an English father, Nana started life criss-crossing Africa by plane and bouncing along the roughest of roads. She first made it to Southern Africa in 1994, when she spent six months living in Zimbabwe, and went on her very first game drive at Hwange National Park. After time spent as an editor and a United Nations press officer she now works as a full-time travel writer, and has visited and written about national parks all over Southern and Eastern Africa. She has contributed to several Lonely Planet titles including their *Southern Africa*, *Africa*, *Algeria* and *South Pacific* guides.

KATE THOMAS
Botswana & Namibia

Growing up in an English seaside town, Kate would sit on the pebbly beach contemplating life on the other side of the sea. After finishing her studies in Paris and London, she flew to Melbourne, returning by cargo ship, road and rail. When she took a job on the foreign desk of a British newspaper, she pinned a map of Africa above her desk. It soon became torn and tattered and she knew she had to see the real thing. For the past few years she's been writing from Africa, where she's watched mountain gorillas in DR Congo and tried to find pygmy hippos in Liberia.

Watching Wildlife Southern Africa **was first published in 2001. It was researched and written by:**

LUKE HUNTER
With an Honours zoology degree from Monash University, Luke embarked on his PhD at the University of Pretoria's Mammal Research Institute, where he spent seven years (including a post-doctoral stint at the University of Natal) working out methods for reintroducing cheetahs and lions into areas where humans had wiped them out. Luke wrote and photographed a small book on cheetahs, and continued his work on wild cats in South Africa based from Monash University.

SUSAN RHIND
A wildlife biologist, Susan ventured to Africa for a break following the completion of her PhD, and spent nearly two years working and travelling around seven of Africa's countries. Susan has scientifically studied dolphins, monkeys and Australian marsupials.

DAVID ANDREW
David created *Wingspan* and *Australian Birding* magazines; edited *Wildlife Australia* magazine; and among other jobs has been a research assistant in Kakadu NP, a birding guide for English comedian Bill Oddie and an editor of Lonely Planet guides.

MEERKAT, KGALAGADI TRANSFRONTIER PARK

INTRODUCTION

More than any other continent, Africa is synonymous with wildlife and there are two truly exceptional regions here for viewing it. For many, East Africa has traditionally been 'classic' safari country but Southern Africa now outranks it in terms of numbers of foreign visitors (and, of course, most of them come for the wildlife). While the diversity and density of species here is exceeded in some forests of Central Africa and South America, there is nowhere else on earth where such a variety of wildlife is so visible. Even a week's tour of the parks here guarantees sightings of dozens of mammal species and hundreds of birds, as well as sundry reptiles and smaller fry. For the wildlife devotee, Southern Africa will probably deliver the safari of a lifetime.

This book aims to assist and enhance the process. For the first-timer, we cover the basic 'how-to' information for planning a visit, specifying the best times, the various safari options, suitable equipment and clothing, the best places to see particular species and so on. Then, for everyone from the complete novice to the wildlife specialist, we detail how to extract the most once you're here. The most productive reserves of Southern Africa are reviewed in detail, providing information on the specific wildlife attractions of each destination and the finer points of finding them. We cover a range of different parks and reserves, including everything from the largest national parks to lesser-known attractions noted for a particular species that's hard to find elsewhere.

Additionally, we've gone for diversity over dupli¬cation, so that coastal, desert, fynbos and wetland reserves appear alongside the typical savanna-grassland ones for which Africa is so well known. The book does not aim to cover every reserve – there are over 500 of them in Southern Africa – but you will find the very best of them here.

To help with identification, our Wildlife Gallery illustrates over 270 species most likely to be seen, all of them in colour photographs. But more than that, the Gallery also provides a little interpretation of animal behaviour and ecology. Beyond simply ticking species off a list, Southern Africa offers exceptional opportunities to truly observe animals, whether it's interpreting the vocalisations of vervet monkeys, unravelling the chain of command among different vulture species or perhaps even anticipating where and when a kill might happen. We hope you'll find this book provides the clues for that extra insight.

Above all, we hope it inspires you to keep on watching wildlife. Whether it encourages and aids your first trip, a return visit or even just an armchair safari, we want the book to increase your enjoyment of wildlife. Money from wildlife-¬watching tourism is very much the main form of revenue for conservation in Africa. However you decide to go on safari, keep on doing it! And if your stories enthuse a friend, encourage them to do likewise; if this book has helped you at all, pass it on to someone else who is thinking of going.

HIGHLIGHTS & ITINERARIES

WHAT TO SEE AND WHERE TO SEE IT

LIONS ON THE HUNT
KRUGER NATIONAL PARK, SOUTH AFRICA

SEE LION **P202**, KRUGER NP **P60**

You'll commonly spot lions on the hunt in Kruger National Park, though that doesn't mean that they're common by any means. On that contrary, lions are one of nature's most perfect predators, and to catch them on the hunt is to have a front-row seat to the drama of life and death.

HIGHLIGHTS

RECLUSIVE LEOPARDS
SOUTH LUANGWA NATIONAL PARK, ZAMBIA

SEE LEOPARD **P203**, SOUTH LUANGWA NP **P178**

Topping the wish list of most safari-goers and Big Five seekers is the leopard, the most reclusive of Africa's big cats. In South Luangwa National Park, a hot spot for these masters of stealth and ambush, you can revel in the excitement of spotting a leopard lounging on a branch in the treetops.

CHEETAHS IN FLIGHT
NXAI PAN NATIONAL PARK, BOTSWANA

SEE CHEETAH **P204**, NXAI PAN NP **P128**

You have to look quick if you want to catch a cheetah in flight – these graceful but deadly felines have been clocked at speeds of more than 110km/h, and can leap more than 7m in a single bound. In the Nxai Pan, you can indulge in the guilty pleasure of watching prey meet a brutal demise after being knocked off balance and dispatched with a lethal bite to the throat.

WHITE RHINOCEROSES
HLUHLUWE-IMFOLOZI GAME RESERVE, SOUTH AFRICA

SEE WHITE RHINOCEROS **P218**, HLUHLUWE-IMFOLOZI GR **P64**

HIGHLIGHTS

The more commonly spotted of Africa's two rhinoceros species, the near-threatened white rhino has made a spectacular comeback from the brink of extinction. Tracking these surprisingly gentle giants through the velds of Hluhluwe-iMfolozi is a chance to test your safari skills.

BLACK RHINOCEROSES
ETOSHA NATIONAL PARK, NAMIBIA

SEE BLACK RHINOCEROS **P219**, ETOSHA NP **P100**

With a quick temper (and a heaving bulk to match), black rhinos were dubbed one of the Big Five dangerous game by early hunters on foot. On the salt flats of Etosha – and in the safety of your car – you can bath in adrenalin while you stare down this formidable but charismatic beast.

ELEPHANT HERDS
ADDO ELEPHANT NATIONAL PARK, SOUTH AFRICA

SEE AFRICAN ELEPHANT **P216**, ADDO ELEPHANT NP **P76**

HIGHLIGHTS

Weighing in at more than 6000kg, and reaching heights of more than 3m, African elephants are the largest terrestrial animals on the planet. At Addo, huge herds can quickly surround a vehicle and make you feel positively diminutive, though it's the old and solitary bulls that command the most respect.

HYENAS ON THE PROWL
KRUGER NATIONAL PARK, SOUTH AFRICA

SEE SPOTTED HYENA **P201**, KRUGER NP **P60**

Highly evolved predators with killer instincts and massive jaws, hyenas can hold their own alongside larger cats, and bring down prey as they please. As the sun drops over Kruger National Park. you will feel chills run down your spine as their haunting but distinctive calls echo through the African bush.

HORNBILLS
WATERBERG PLATEAU PARK, NAMIBIA

SEE HORNBILLS **P272**, WATERBERG PLATEAU PARK **P113**

Easily identified by their enormous but highly specialised bills, and impossible to forget once you've heard their noisy yet engaging call, hornbills are true safari staples. Watching these distinctive birds glide along the thermals above the Waterberg Plateau is an enchanting sight.

HIGHLIGHTS

AFRICAN WILD DOGS
MOREMI GAME RESERVE, BOTSWANA

SEE HUNTING DOG **P210**, MOREMI GR **P132**

Botswana's Moremi Game Reserve protects a healthy number of these endangered pack animals, which are protected by strong conservation measures. Although they're surprisingly playful, you'll squirm and cringe if you catch sight of the pack disembowelling their hapless prey.

NILE CROCODILES
NORTH LUANGWA NATIONAL PARK, ZAMBIA

SEE NILE CROCODILE **P292**, NORTH LUANGWA NP **P181**

Spotting a crocodile in the wild is a mixed blessing, and your reaction usually depends on the distance between you and the lizard. Indeed, crocs are best given a healthy berth, though it's difficult not to stare in awe at this prehistoric predator. In the waterways of North Luangwa, don't unpack the swimsuit – crocs congregate in the thousands!

HIGHLIGHTS

CAPE FUR-SEALS
CAPE CROSS SEAL RESERVE, NAMIBIA

SEE CAPE FUR-SEAL **P215**, CAPE CROSS SEAL RESERVE **P110**

It's not easy being 350kg of blubbery fat and muscled protein, especially when you're the favourite food of the ferocious apex predator that is the great white shark. At the Cape Cross Seal Reserve, an enormous colony of these hulking mammals overwhelms the eyes, the ears and even your nose!

JACKASS PENGUINS
TABLE MOUNTAIN NATIONAL PARK, SOUTH AFRICA

SEE JACKASS PENGUIN **P243**, TABLE MOUNTAIN NP **P95**

Although their somewhat unfortunate moniker makes them the laughing stock of the birding world, jackass penguins are surprisingly elegant birds that dart through the icy seas with power and grace. At Table Mountain National Park you can hear them bray like angry jackasses, so you might want to pack earplugs alongside your binoculars.

HIGHLIGHTS

GEMSBOK IN THE DESERT
ETOSHA NATIONAL PARK, NAMIBIA

SEE GEMSBOK **P233**, ETOSHA NP **P100**

There is no shortage of striking antelope species in Southern Africa, though few are as dramatic as the gemsbok or oryx, a supremely adapted desert dweller with a massive pair of rapierlike horns. Set against a backdrop of harsh and forbidding scrubland, a herd of oryx in Etosha is reminiscent of a fleeting mirage.

HIGHLIGHTS

HIPPOPOTAMUS
ISIMANGALISO WETLAND PARK, SOUTH AFRICA

SEE HIPPOPOTAMUS **P223**, ISIMANGALISO WETLAND PARK **P80**

With the infamous (but questionable) reputation of being the number-one people killer in Southern Africa, hippos are best given a healthy distance and an equal amount of respect, both in the water and on the land. However, assuming you've found a comfortable spot from which to view these river pigs, there are few animals more amusing to watch.

HIGHLIGHTS

CLASSIC SOUTHERN AFRICA
THREE WEEKS TO ONE MONTH/JOHANNESBURG TO LILONGWE

Southern Africa is one of the world's top destinations for wildlife, and this classic route will highlight the best that the region can offer. Starting off in the South African capital of Johannesburg, your first port of call is Kruger National Park (p60), one of the finest safari parks on the continent, and one of the few places where you're almost guaranteed to spot the Big Five. Heading northwest into Botswana, spend a good amount of time in Chobe National Park (p120), where enormous elephant herds will make you and your safari vehicle feel positively inadequate. Hugging the Zimbabwean-Zambian border, Victoria Falls & Zambezi National Parks (p156) are fuelled by the continent's most famous waterfall, and populated by all manner of water-loving wildlife. On the Zambian side, South Luangwa National Park (p178) floods in the wet season, creating a rich riverine habitat for thirsty creatures. Your final stop is Lake Malawi National Park (p166), Southern Africa's signature Rift Valley lake ecosystem. This itinerary ends in the Malawian capital of Lilongwe, a low-key city where you can swap travel stories over a few rounds of cold beer.

In order to immerse yourself in the classic Southern Africa experience, it's good to take an entire month to fully explore the extents of this incredible collection of safari parks. However, if you're a bit short on time, or if you want to cut down on the long cross-country driving distance, you can always take an internal flight or two.

DESERT EXPLORER
TWO TO THREE WEEKS/GABORONE TO WINDHOEK

While the savanna often steals the spotlight in Southern Africa, the deserts of Botswana and Namibia cradle impressive concentrations of wildlife that are living in near complete isolation. Starting off in the Botswanan capital of Gaborone, head northwest to the Central Kalahari Game Reserve (p124), which lies at the heart of the expansive stretch of sand that is the Kalahari. With your GPS in hand, head west to the Kgalagadi Transfrontier Park (p68), a peaceful park between Botswana and South Africa where you can easily spot herds of nomadic antelopes searching for nourishment among the scrub. Crossing into Namibia, you'll soon reach Namib-Naukluft Park (p104), a seemingly inhospitable landscape of towering red dunes that miraculously supports supremely adapted wildlife. Turn north along the coastal highway to access the Skeleton Coast National Park (p108), a veritable hellscape clinging to the shores of the frigid South Atlantic. Finish your exploration in Namibia's crown jewel, Etosha National Park (p100), which protects the country's largest offering of large animals including a healthy complement of predators. Wind things down in the Namibian capital of Windhoek, where you can study the map and plan your next safari over some hearty German cuisine.

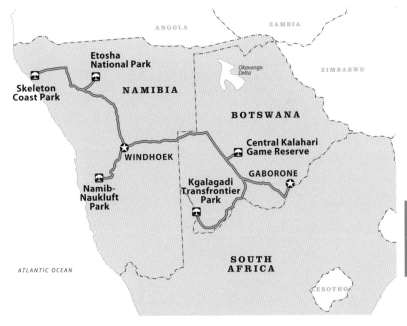

ITINERARIES

The going can be a bit slow at times, though Botswana and Namibia are two countries where the journey is often more invigorating than the destination. Depending on how much time you spend in Gaborone and Windhoek, a few weeks is all you need to escape the tourist trail and check out these up-and-coming parks.

ROUGH & RUGGED
THREE WEEKS TO ONE MONTH/WINDHOEK TO HARARE

While some safari parks are at times saturated with trains of tourist vehicles, this rough and rugged itinerary is perfect for anyone who wants to leave civilisation – and the paved road – behind. Starting in Windhoek, jump head first into your wilderness adventure with a visit to the Kaudom Game Reserve (p111), an incredibly challenging terrain criss-crossed by 4WD tracks. The going gets tougher when you cross into Botswana and reach the Moremi Game Reserve (p132), a boggy oasis that is famous for its furry felines and wild dogs. Enjoy the abundance of water as your next two stops are the Makgadikgadi Pans & Nxai Pan National Parks (p128), which are centred on seemingly endless saltpans inhabited by only the hardiest of wildlife. Things really start to get extreme inside the borders of Zimbabwe, where you're going to have to keep an eye on the petrol as you navigate Hwange National Park (p142), which is roughly the size of Northern Ireland. Finally, leave behind your wheels and take to a canoe as you paddle through the floodplains of Mana Pools National Park (p150) on an aquatic safari. In keeping with the theme of the itinerary, finish things off in the occasionally tense but always dynamic Zimbabwean capital of Harare.

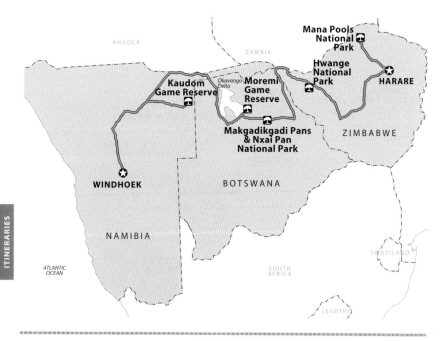

This itinerary takes in large stretches of poorly developed roads and remote wilderness, which means that you're going to need time and patience to tackle whatever gets thrown in your way. However, your reward will be a brief but impossible-to-forget glimpse at some of Southern Africa's wildest game parks.

UP-AND-COMING SOUTHERN AFRICA
TWO TO THREE WEEKS/LUSAKA TO LILONGWE

While their bigger and more famous neighbours tend to steal the regional spotlight, both Zambia and Malawi are up-and-coming players on the safari circuit; here you can seek out wildlife while leaving the crowds behind. Starting off in the Zambian capital of Lusaka, head west to Kafue National Park (**p182**), which is bisected by a remote highway, and supports sprawling herds of antelopes that number in the thousands. After backtracking through Lusaka, continue east to the Lower Zambezi National Park (**p184**), which is back on the map with a new conservation mandate to preserve its vital wetland areas. For a decidedly different take on the safari experience, cross the border and visit Liwonde National Park (**p168**) in southern Malawi, where you stand a decent chance of spotting both sable antelopes and black rhinos in the wild. While down south, be sure to check out nearby Lengwe National Park (**p172**), which protects an eclectic assortment of buffalo herds, samango monkeys and even Nile monitors. Finish your trip in Lilongwe, where you can pick up a different trail and set out for the next wildlife adventure.

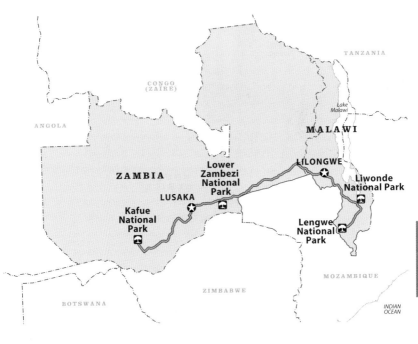

If you have the time to spare, a safari in Zambia and Malawi pairs wonderfully with destinations in Southern Africa. While it takes two to three weeks to follow the itinerary above, you can alternatively choose just one or two wildlife parks, and tack them onto your trip to make a custom-tailored itinerary.

CAPE TO CAPE

TWO TO THREE WEEKS/CAPE TOWN TO CAPE CROSS

The treacherous and unforgiving coastline of Southern Africa has a long and torturous history of claiming ill-fated captains, but fortunately you can stick to the land while following this famous seafarers' route. Pry yourself away from the Mediterranean climes of Cape Town, round the Cape of Good Hope, and arrive at the **De Hoop National Reserve** (**p88**) in search of rare antelopes on land and whales and dolphins in the sea. Heading inland into the bushveld, you'll soon arrive at **Karoo National Park** (**p84**), where you can scour the plains for Cape mountain zebras and klipspringers. En route to the Namibian border, make a brief stop at **Augrabies Falls National Park** (**p78**), which is a renowned haven for klipspringers as well as desert-dwelling black rhinos. Continuing onwards to Namibia, don't miss the **Waterberg Plateau Park** (**p113**), a veritable lost world of high-dwelling wildlife including both roan and sable antelopes. Finally, press on to **Cape Cross Seal Reserve** (**p110**) along the infamous Skeleton Coast, where you can get up close and personal with bleating colonies of Cape fur-seals. While there is no accommodation in the reserve, you can bed down in the nearby tourist-friendly town of Swakopmund.

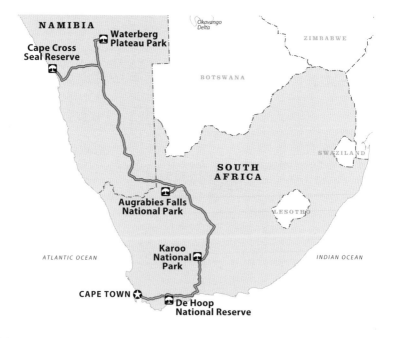

Africa's southwestern tip can be traversed in a couple of well-paced weeks, which means you'll have plenty of time to check out the wildlife that thrives in the unique environment lining the coast. If you have a bit more time, you can lengthen this itinerary with a few of the top national parks in South Africa and Namibia.

SOUTHERN AFRICAN BIRDING
ABOUT ONE MONTH/JOHANNESBURG TO LILONGWE

Southern Africa is regarded as one of the world's top birding destinations, which means you don't have to look too hard to spot African standards, regional specialities and rare endemics. Starting in Johannesburg, your first stop on the birding tour is the iSimangaliso Wetland Park **(p80)**, one of the most vitally important wetlands on the continent. Further inland, the extinct volcano that frames Pilanesberg National Park **(p72)** is most famous for the Big Five, though you can also spot the kori bustard, the world's largest flying bird. On a brief detour into Zimbabwe, pay a visit to Gonarezhou National Park **(p146)**, which boasts a total avian count of more than 400. Next you'll need to transit Botswana to reach Namibia's Caprivi Strip – here lies Mamili National Park **(p112)**, which hems the Linyati Swamp and is home to flocks of migratory birds. Northeast in the heart of Zambia is Kasanka National Park **(p187)**, a marshy landscape where you can quickly add two dozen endemics to your count. The last stop on the birding tour is Nyika National Park **(p170)**, Malawi's largest protected area that is famous for its rare subspecies. Just in case you need some time to update your checklists with your travel companions, this trip conveniently ends in Lilongwe.

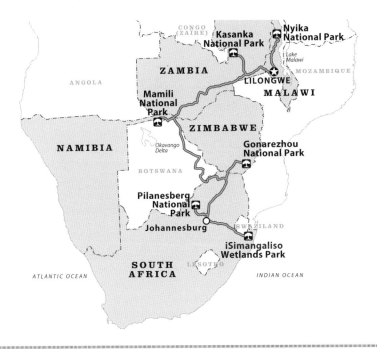

Patience is a virtue, especially when it comes to birdwatching, which is why you should give yourself plenty of time to explore some of Southern Africa's most famous birding spots. Truth be told, virtually every national park in the region is home to rare endemics worth seeking out, though the parks mentioned here are some of our favourites.

ENVIRONMENT & CONSERVATION
UNDERSTANDING THE LAND AND ITS HISTORY

Southern Africa, an enormous plateau with escarpments on both sides and a great rift down the middle, is a region of primeval natural splendour and untamed rawness that is both geographically and environmentally diverse. Boasting one of the world's most impressive collections of national parks, Southern Africa is defined by its rich concentration of wildlife, which has been fostered through generations of increasingly comprehensive conservation measures.

THE SOUTHERN AFRICAN ENVIRONMENT

NATURAL HISTORY

Africa was once joined to South America and Australia as part of the supercontinent Gondwana, which broke up between 270 and 200 million years ago. For another 30 million years Africa and Eurasia were periodically linked by land bridges, which enabled the spread of mammals between the two continents. Even today, Africa remains a refuge for the great Pleistocene fauna that perished elsewhere around the world. While Australia, North America and South America lost more than 75% of their mammalian megafauna in the last 100,000 years, Africa's deficit was only around 15%.

Climatic changes caused by ice ages in the northern hemisphere caused the expansion and contraction of African habitats. During glacial periods, the climate at lower altitudes was drier than present, enabling savannas to expand and restricting forests to isolated pockets. Between ice ages, wetter conditions prevailed, forests spread and drier habitats retreated. Africa never knew the great ice blankets that cloaked other continents, and its climatic constancy is thought to be part of the reason so many species persisted.

Even today, the Southern African environment is far from stable, and is constantly reshaped by complex elements. For example, fire has long swept through coarse grasslands during the dry season, promoting new growth. In the absence of fire and grazing animals, woody growth dominates until elephants open it up and it reverts to grasslands. Now, however, it is humans that are the main shaper of the landscape, forming high population densities while destroying habitats at unsustainable rates.

WILDLIFE

There is no place comparable to Africa for its range and density of large mammals, and they are merely the most conspicuous members of one of the richest wildlife communities on the planet. Be it large mammals, small ones, birds, reptiles, fish or invertebrates, the continent is a sanctuary for an astonishing diversity of life. Despite this richness in wildlife, relatively little of it has African origins, at least at the group level. Among the mammals, only a few groups actually arose in Africa; the rest poured in about 30 million years ago when Africa suddenly emerged from millions of years of isolation by colliding with Europe.

Truly African mammalian groups include the primates, elephants and hyraxes, bats, insectivores, elephant shrews

ENVIRONMENT

and aardvarks. Some of them, such as the monkeys and elephants, flooded out of Africa to colonise other parts of the globe. Groups that travelled the other way and populated Africa from outside include most of the carnivores, ungulates, hares, squirrels and many rodents. Even so, that's not to say most African mammals are not African. Land bridges seeded Africa with new groups of mammals, but most contemporary species arose from that founding stock for the first time here. Gazelles, giraffes, zebras, lions, leopards and cheetahs are among the suite of modern species that evolved in Africa from immigrant ancestors. Birds, reptiles and amphibians are far more ancient inhabitants of Africa. The fossil record for birds is meagre, but by 35 million years ago most African groups were already established or, like today's Palaearctic migrants, commuting regularly from other continents. Similarly, most reptiles and amphibians have an African ancestry that has run unbroken for tens of millions of years, and even hundreds of millions in the case of crocodiles.

HUMANS & WILDLIFE

As the birthplace of our species, Africa has hosted humans and their precursors longer than any other continent. For much of hominid evolution, our progenitors were probably forager-scavengers rather than outright predators, but there is evidence to suggest that we've actively hunted for at least two million years. Intelligent, organised and omnivorous, these early humans would have been given a wide berth by most species, and our hunting ancestry is probably the reason most wild animals still flee when they see modern people on foot.

Even so, it's very unlikely hominids had a widespread effect on wild-animal populations for millions of years. Until very recently in our evolution, we were vulnerable to the same population checks and ecological constraints that have prevented global dominance by a single species. Early humans may have depleted populations of some species, and perhaps even contributed to the occasional extinction, but hominids were just as susceptible to the same forces. Indeed, we modern humans are the sole surviving line of at least 12 different hominid species, some of them perhaps coexisting at the same time. We may never know what destroyed these other attempts at humanity: environmental catastrophe, predation, disease or perhaps competition with a more successful species – very possibly our ancestors.

Regardless, it's important to remember

ENVIRONMENT

PERTURBATIONS

Southern Africa experiences regular ecological disturbances, described by ecologists as 'perturbations', which create both opportunity and adversity for wildlife. For many species, drought, flood and fire usually create little hardship – the animals simply move away. Those unable to do so furnish predators with an easy meal, at least until the supply runs out. Lions, hyenas and jackals feast on drought-weakened grazers, crocodiles gorge on carcasses washed down by floods, and storks, kites and kestrels patrol the leading edge of fires for fleeing reptiles and rodents. For plants, perturbations may be equally life giving. Fresh grasslands burst to life after fires clear away old growth and many protea species only disgorge their seeds after a scorching; both provide herbivores of all sizes with a glut of new food. Similarly, the silt deposited by floods creates fertile beds for new growth, and trees destroyed by fire or floodwaters provide nutrients for seedlings and thousands of invertebrate species.

that extinction is a natural process that has been going on since life began. But only very recently has the activity of one species, modern *Homo sapiens,* caused extinction on a scale estimated to be between 100 and 1000 times the natural rate. And although the most devastating effects came with the arrival of the Europeans, the process had already begun with the indigenous people of Southern Africa.

THE UTOPIA MYTH
It's tempting to think that, prior to the Western invasion, Africa's human population lived in complete harmony with its wildlife. Compared with the destruction wrought by Europeans, this may seem reasonable, but it ignores the fact that Southern Africa's indigenous people had advanced, organised societies in which wildlife was utilised. Hunting was a daily fact of life, and there is considerable evidence to suggest that where human numbers were high, wildlife populations either moved away or were depleted. In addition to subsistence hunting, powerful feudal cultures like the Zulus conducted ceremonial hunts in which thousands of animals were killed to display the king's power and benevolence. Some modern reserves like South Africa's Hluhluwe-iMfolozi Game Reserve were once royal hunting grounds for this explicit purpose.

Our 'ecological footprint' was further exacerbated by livestock. The popular notion of pastoralism in Africa sometimes assumes indigenous Africans endured as hunter-gatherers until contact with Europeans. But herding in sub-Saharan Africa is at least 3500 years old, probably originating in northeast Africa and spreading gradually southwards. By the first millennium AD, livestock ownership was widespread in Southern Africa, with significant effects on wildlife. Livestock competed with indigenous ungulates for grazing, and modified habitats to the extent that naturally rare species may have been edged towards extinction. The first historically recorded

African mammal to disappear, the blue antelope, was already in decline as a result of this competition long before Europeans shot the last of them. Similarly, predators have long been killed in defence of herds, and even today pastoralists using traditional weapons to make short work of large carnivores.

There were two important differences between Africans and Europeans in their exploitation of wildlife. First, African religious beliefs lacked the three-tiered hierarchy of monotheistic religions – God, Man, Nature – which held that the natural world existed solely for people to exploit. Most African religions are grounded in the belief that humans exist as part of an indivisible entity that includes the gods and all aspects of the natural world. It's a system that traditionally accorded far greater tolerance of and respect for wildlife than the European view. The other fundamental difference lay in technology. Southern Africa's people simply did not have the technological means to further exploit the natural world. Had gunpowder and firearms been an African innovation, it's certain at least some of the ecological damage we associate with European colonisation would have occurred centuries earlier.

THE PILLAGING OF AFRICA
Speculation aside, the last 400 years have seen successive waves of Europeans exert unrivalled dominion over Southern Africa's wildlife resources. Even before the Portuguese, Dutch, British and Germans formally divvied up the region as their own, European hunters were carving out personal fortunes based on ivory. The same routes that transported slaves and gold from inland Africa to trading settlements, ports and ultimately Europe and the Americas, also carried the tusks of hundreds of thousands of elephants. Other wildlife was shot for skins and meat or simply because it was there and could be.

With permanent European settlement,

the environmental destruction spread and intensified as people cleared wildlife to make way for livestock. Settlers also transported the European notion of sport hunting to Africa, so that where wildlife was too abundant to utilise, it was shot for amusement. Surprisingly, very few species were exterminated; the blue antelope was lost by 1800 and the quagga, a uniquely marked zebra subspecies, by 1878. But extinctions are merely the most dramatic symptom of a relentless process of attrition at the hands of Europeans, which now sees wildlife restricted largely to protected areas. With the same degree of dedication that once annihilated wildlife, conservationists are now scrambling to preserve it.

CONSERVATION

PARKS AND RESERVES

The cornerstone of wildlife conservation in Southern Africa has historically been national parks and other reserves declared under colonial governments. Management problems notwithstanding, these continue to provide the highest level of official protection to wildlife and ecosystems across the region, and remain the focus for most wildlife tourism

despite the fact that many were created with no regard for preserving biodiversity. On paper at least, national parks protect all wildlife from exploitation such as hunting, and prohibit cultivation, settlement and all other disturbances.

The establishment and maintenance of protected areas in each country is handled by a national body, but in practice, law enforcement and reserve management are hampered by lack of funding and other chronic problems. Conservation is a low priority when resources are thinly spread, though fortunately NGOs such as the International Union for Conservation of Nature (IUCN) and the World Wide Fund for Nature (WWF) maintain a permanent presence in the region under the UN Environment Program (UNEP). Other big players include the UN Educational, Scientific and Cultural Organisation (Unesco), the Flora and Fauna Preservation Society (FFPS), the African Wildlife Foundation (AWF) and the Wildlife Conservation Society (WCS).

High-profile mammals such as elephants and rhinos presently benefit from intensive study, donor aid and funding from tourism, though the threats facing their survival are very real. Black rhinos were nearly wiped out in the space of 30

ENVIRONMENT

WILDLIFE'S UNLIKELY GUARDIAN

Believe it or not, the tsetse fly is one of the primary reasons why such considerable areas in Africa are still given over to wildlife. The fly is the vector for sleeping sickness or 'nagana' as it's known in Southern Africa (from the Zulu word *uNakane,* meaning 'the pest'). Nagana is actually caused by a trypanosome (a microscopic blood parasite), but it's the fly's blood-sucking habits that infect people and animals. Africa's indigenous wildlife is immune to the disease, but livestock and people are not. Infected humans and cattle develop malaria-like symptoms, which can ultimately be fatal. For African peoples and colonising Europeans alike, that was reason enough to keep out of tsetse-infested areas, allowing wildlife to persist by default. This century, spraying with insecticides like DDT cleared many areas of the parasite by the 1960s (but also resulted in untold environmental damage). Even so, nagana is still widespread, especially in conservation areas, though old habits die hard as regional governments occasionally revive the idea of dumping proven poisons on ecologically sensitive areas.

SOUTHERN AFRICAN ENDANGERED SPECIES

ANIMAL	CONSERVATION STATUS	BEST PLACE TO SEE
AFRICAN WILD DOG (P210)	ENDANGERED	MOREMI GR (P132), KRUGER NP (P60)
BLACK RHINOCEROS (P219)	CRITICALLY ENDANGERED	ETOSHA NP (P100), PILANESBERG NP (P72)
RIVERINE RABBIT (P197)	CRITICALLY ENDANGERED	KAROO NP (P84)

years – from an estimated 70,000 in 1960 to about 2500 in 1990 – which vaulted the issue of conservation to the international stage. Today, Southern Africa has an abundance of protected areas, but it continued to suffer from grave environmental scourges.

POACHING & CULLING

The most notorious environmental issue in Southern Africa is arguably poaching, which occurs throughout the region. In one sense, it's not difficult to see why: a kilogram of elephant ivory is worth as much as US$1000 wholesale, and rhino horn is valued at thousands of dollars per kilogram. This amounts to tens of thousands of dollars for a single horn, or more than 100 times what the average Southern African earns in a year. Poaching is also difficult to control due to resource and personnel shortages and the vastness and inaccessibility of many areas.

Entrenched interests have also been a major contributing factor, with everyone from the poachers themselves (often local villagers struggling to earn some money) to ivory dealers, embassies and government officials at the highest levels trying to get a piece of the pie. Reports of widespread corruption in regards to illegal poaching increased during the 1960s and 1970s, and journalists and environmental watchdogs such as the WWF have documented widespread abuses across the continent.

In 1989, in response to the illegal trade and diminishing numbers of elephants, a world body called the Convention on International Trade in Endangered Species (CITES) internationally banned the import and export of ivory. It also increased funding for anti-poaching measures. When the ban was established, world raw ivory prices plummeted by 90%, and the market for poaching and smuggling was radically reduced.

Although elephant populations recovered in some ravaged areas, human populations continued to grow, and another problem surfaced. Elephants eat huge quantities of foliage, but in the past herds would eat their fill then migrate to another area, allowing time for the vegetation to regenerate. However, an increasing human population pressed the elephants into smaller and smaller areas – mostly around national parks – and the herds were forced to eat everything available. In many places, the bush began to look as if an atom bomb had hit.

POPULATION CONTROL

Increasingly across the region, park authorities are facing elephant overpopulation. Proposed solutions include relocation (where herds are permanently transplanted to other areas) and contraception. The only other alternative is to cull herds, sometimes in large numbers; this seems a bizarre paradox, but illustrates the seriousness of the problem. In the West people generally hold a preservationist viewpoint, that elephant herds should be conserved for their own sake or for aesthetic reasons. However, the local sentiment maintains that the elephant must justify its existence on long-term economic grounds for the benefit of local people, or for the country as a whole.

This is an issue sure to generate much debate, with proponents citing the health of the parks, including other wildlife and the elephants themselves, while organisations such as the International Fund for Animal Welfare (IFAW) are appalled at such a solution, which they claim is cruel, unethical and scientifically unsound. IFAW believes aerial surveys of elephant numbers are inaccurate, population growth has not been accurately surveyed, and that other solutions have not been looked at carefully enough, including more transfrontier parks crossing national borders.

Furthermore, there is much dispute about whether controlled ivory sales should be reintroduced, with countries with excessive elephant populations and large ivory stockpiles pushing hard for a relaxation on the ban. Some argue that countries with large tracts of protected land are paying for the inability of other African countries to properly manage and protect their wildlife. Indeed, it remains to be seen whether a lift on the ban will occur, but meanwhile debate about the ivory trade, and the culling solution to overpopulation, rages on.

ECOLOGICAL DEGRADATION

Parks and reserves are now effectively islands in a sea of cultivation, ranches and humanity, and many priority areas for conservation still lie outside this system. At present, Southern Africa includes some of the poorest and resource-stressed nations in the world. The population of the region has doubled in the last 20 years, and is predicted to multiply another three times in the next 20 years. To conserve human communities – and the region's wild areas and ecosystems – most experts agree that population

growth must be contained by improving education (especially for women) and raising living standards by fostering economic growth.

Ecological degradation is a serious regional problem; about one quarter of Southern Africa's land is considered to be severely degraded. In former Southern African homeland areas, years of overgrazing and overcropping have resulted in massive soil depletion. This, along with poor overall conditions, is pushing people to the cities, further increasing urban pressures. Water is another issue, and droughts are common in the region. To meet demand, rivers have often been dammed or modified. While this has improved water supplies to some areas, it has also disrupted local ecosystems and caused increased silting.

Just as worrisome as overpopulation is deforestation, with Southern Africa's forest areas today representing only a fraction of the region's original forest cover. Deforestation brings with it soil erosion, shrinking water catchment and cultivable areas, and decreased availability of traditional building materials, foodstuffs and medicines. It also means that many birds and animals lose their habitats, and local human populations risk losing their resources, especially their water.

Deforestation is particularly disastrous when indigenous trees are replaced by more aggressive introduced species; at present, these present a real threat to Southern African ecosystems. There are more than 700 alien plant species in the region, and about 10% of these are classed as invasive aliens – that is, they thrive to the detriment of endemic species. For example, Australian wattle trees and Mexican mesquite flourish by sinking their roots deeper into the soil than indigenous trees, which then suffer from lack of nourishment. The Australian hakea shrub was introduced to serve as a hedge, and is now rampant, displacing

ENVIRONMENT

ENVIRONMENT

native trees and killing off smaller plants. Areas such as South Africa's unique Cape fynbos floral kingdom are threatened by Australian acacias, which were introduced for their timber products or to stabilise sand dunes.

THE SOLUTIONS?

For years, the conservation 'establishment' regarded human populations as a negative factor in environmental protection, and local inhabitants were often excluded from national parks or other protected areas because it was assumed that they damaged natural resources. A recent example is that of the San, who were forced from parts of their traditional lands around the Central Kalahari Game Reserve for the sake of conservation and tourism.

Fortunately, governments and NGOs are now aware that policies shaped without local participation inevitably lead to local opposition. Community conservation projects encourage local involvement, leading to a strong sense of ownership and benefits such as crop protection, and health and education funding. Indeed, 'community-based conservation' has become a critical concept as tour operators, funding organisations and others recognise that Southern Africa's protected areas are unlikely to succeed in the long term unless local people can obtain real benefits. If there are tangible benefits for local inhabitants – benefits such as increased local income from visitors to wilderness areas – then natural environments have a much better chance of evading destruction.

TRAVELLING SUSTAINABLY

As one of the world's most iconic destinations, Southern Africa spoils visitors with a never-ending assortment of wildlife-watching activities. At the same time, the greatest challenge to responsible travellers in the region is preserving the purity of the environment for future generations. Quite simply, each of us bears the responsibility to minimise the impact of our stay, and to travel in the most sustainable way possible.

The continuous growth of the travel industry has brought incredible economic success to parts of Southern Africa. However, this growth has also placed enormous stress on both biological and cultural habitats, and threatens to destroy the very destinations that tourists are seeking out. In recent years, the term 'sustainable tourism' has emerged as a buzzword in the industry, and refers to striking the ideal balance between travellers and their surrounding environment.

One of the most important tenets of sustainable tourism is the notion of respecting local communities, and community preservation is one area where travellers can make the biggest individual difference. While in Southern Africa, talk to locals, and ask them about their customs and traditions. An eagerness to learn on the part of the traveller may reassure a local that others value their customs, even if everything is changing around them.

An immediate benefit of tourism is a strong financial boost to the local economy, which certainly needs it. (It's worth remembering that regardless of whether you're shoestringing or living it up in five-star hotels, international travel in any capacity is a luxury that most people here will never be able to enjoy). So if the opportunity arises to spend money at a locally run business or vendor arises, don't hesitate to give a little back.

One of the simplest things you can do before embarking on a trip to Southern Africa is to learn about pressing conservation and environmental issues, which are highlighted throughout this chapter. Keeping these issues in mind, do your best to do business with and support hotels, lodges, tour operators and environmental groups that promote conservation initiatives, and have public long-term management plans.

VOLUNTEER TOURISM

There are large numbers of volunteers in Southern Africa, which is certainly cause for celebration as 'voluntourism' is a great way to travel sustainably while simultaneously reducing the ecological footprint of your trip. It's also an amazing forum for self-exploration, especially if you touch a few lives and meet a few new friends along the way.

Volunteer projects cover a wide spectrum ranging from wildlife conservation and environmental protection to community outreach and education.

Some general places to start your search include **Volunteer Abroad** (www.volunteerabroad.com), **Frontier** (www.frontier.ac.uk), **Working Abroad** (www.workingabroad.com), **Global Volunteers** (www.globalvolunteers .org) and **Volunteer Africa** (www .volunteerafrica.org), well-organised online directories of volunteer placements. There are also various volunteer holiday opportunities included in the online listings of **ResponsibleTravel.com** (www .responsibletravel.com) and **Camps International** (www.campkenya.com).

For more long-term placements, consider **Voluntary Service Overseas** (**VSO**; www.vsointernational.org), the largest independent (nongovernmental) volunteer organisation in the world, the US-based **Peace Corps** (www.peace corps.gov), and the Unesco-sponsored **Coordinating Committee for International Voluntary Service** (www .unesco. org/ccivs).

If you have professional skills, and are looking for more specific wildlife-related volunteer or even work placements, consider the following organisations:

African Wildlife Foundation (**AWF**; www.awf.org)

HUNTING – ANIMAL WELFARE VS ECONOMICS

In some parts of Southern Africa, areas of land are set aside for hunting, and hunters are charged 'trophy fees' to shoot animals. This is abhorrent to many people – especially in Western countries.

On the one hand it is argued that trophy or sport hunting is a form of tourism that stimulates local economies and thereby fosters 'conservation-minded' attitudes. Paradoxically, the financial benefits of hunting encourages the management and protection of these animals and their environment. Hunting, it is argued, provides an enticement to landowners to maintain the natural habitats that provide a home for the hunted animals.

On the other hand, killing an animal for fun is simply morally and ethically wrong to many people. It's argued that slaughtering wildlife in order to raise conservation funds to save it is a twisted way of thinking. Furthermore, if improperly managed, trophy hunting can have seriously detrimental effects on wildlife, especially threatened and endangered species.

Although conservation organisations do not agree on policy towards hunting, the World wide Fund for Nature (WWF) has a pragmatic attitude, stating that 'for endangered species, trophy hunting should only be considered when all other options have been explored…and that trophy hunting, where it is scientifically based and properly managed, has proven to be an effective conservation and management method in some countries and for certain species'.

Flora and Fauna Preservation Society (FFPS; www.fauna-flora.org)

International Fund for Animal Welfare (IFAW; www.ifaw.org)

International Union for Conversation of Nature (IUCN; www.iucn.org)

UN Environment Program (UNEP; www.unep.org)

UN Educational, Scientific and Cultural Organisation (Unesco; www.unesco.org)

Wildlife Conservation Society (WCS; www.wcs.org)

World Wide Fund for Nature (WWF; www.panda.org)

HABITATS

THE ARID LANDS

Encompassing western South Africa, much of Namibia and most of Botswana, the great dry tract known as the South West Arid Zone is worthy of the overused adjective 'unique'. Climatically desolate, this area is actually one of the region's richest centres of endemism. With rainfall averaging between 125mm and 250mm, it's correctly known as semidesert, but in the far west where it merges with the true desert of the Namib, annual falls rarely top 50mm. While lacking the ecological abundance of wetter habitats, the arid lands distinguish Southern Africa from the rest of the continent probably more than any other habitat. To get a real sense of Southern Africa, and tick off many species found nowhere else, the arid lands are a must.

If there is a single unifying characteristic of the region, it is sand. In fact, the largest expanse of sand in the world occurs here. Resting on a vast ancient basin of rock, it extends from South Africa's Orange River through the entire southern subregion, and peters out just shy of the equator. As rainfall increases along a northern gradient however, vegetation becomes more lush, and you wouldn't know it actually sits on a sandy bed. In the south where rainfall is least, desert grasses and shrubs are comparatively sparse, leaving the sand exposed.

This is the Kalahari. For hundreds of kilometres, continuous rows of small dunes covered in sand-binding grasses create a landscape of parallels. With no permanent lakes or water, a handful of river beds are the point of convergence for ephemeral rainfall and for the desert's wildlife. Arid-adapted springboks, gemsboks and elands extract vital moisture from their diet, and can go their entire lives without drinking. But drinking makes sense when water is available, and they join water-dependent species like blue wildebeests in the river beds. Unlike true arid-adapted species, wildebeests lack dense, reflective coats, and narrow muzzles for selecting the most succulent forage, so they have to work harder to survive here.

Their predators follow – big cats, spotted and brown hyenas – as do little endemic hunters like Cape foxes, black-footed cats, meerkats and yellow mongooses. The body fluids of their prey free carnivores of the need for free-standing water, though like everything here, they drink daily when possible. The open landscape provides relatively few niches for birds, but for ground-living species like sandgrouse, larks and bustards.

THE DESERT OF ROCKS

Where the southern extreme of the Kalahari peters out, it blends with a stony semidesert called the Karoo, which then heads northwest in a rocky band through central Namibia until it finally becomes the Kaokoveld and Damaraland. At first glance the vegetation is monotonous, but it's rich in unique succulents, desert grasses and dwarf shrubs providing food for klipspringers, Hartmann's mountain zebras and, in the far north, black rhinos.

In South Africa, where a vast grassy plateau dominates the landscape, Karoo grazers – springboks, black wildebeests and Cape mountain zebras – occur alongside more widespread species like elands and mountain reedbucks. Less obvious but only found in the Karoo are riverine rabbits, a handful of rare rodents, and endemic larks, warblers and korhaans. In the northwest, where the Karoo is called Namaqualand, intense spring flushes of desert flowers trigger a flurry of breeding activity for specialised endemics like Karoo bush rats, dassie rats and pygmy rockmice. As well as nectar-lovers like monkey beetles, bees and sunbirds, the floral bounty attracts human admirers by the busload.

Technically outside the boundaries of the South West Arid Zone, but merging with it at its extreme west, the only true desert in Southern Africa lies along Namibia's coast. Stretching over 2000km from the South African border well into Angola, the gravel plains and sienna dunes of the Namib are home to life that depends on fog. The Atlantic Ocean's freezing Benguela Current cools the coastal air as it flows towards Namibia, forming moisture-laden fogs that are blown up to 80km inland. Fog-basking beetles, trench-digging beetles and zebra-striped tenebrionid beetles harvest the condensing fog and provide the keystone for life. White lady spiders, small geckos and the rapacious Namib dune beetle feed on the fog gatherers and are in turn hunted by predators like the blind Namib golden mole, a miniature sand-swimmer known as the 'shark of the dunes'.

Devoid of flora, the dune faces are shunned by larger life, but in the broad alleys between dunes, dormant grass seeds respond to rare cloudbursts. As little as 10mm of rain reanimates the seeds and turns the low-lying sand into meadows. Fresh grass, insects and seeds provide a bounty for larks, chats and warblers in the thousands, as well as korhaans, ostriches and desert-adapted antelopes. As the sandy flats dry out, these species disperse back out onto the stony plains, tracking the unpredictable inland thunderstorms that provide patchy relief.

SEE IT AT...
» **Kgalagadi Transfrontier Park** (p68)
» **Central Kalahari GR** (p124) » **Namib-Naukluft Park** (p104)

GRASSLANDS

The most distinctive and homogeneous grasslands in the region occur on

South Africa's central plateau, known locally as the 'highveld'. Being at high altitudes, these plains experience frosty, dry winters with occasional snow, then endure a drenching from brief but violent storms – which you could just about set your watch by on summer afternoons. Combined with regular grassfires, the battering regime ensures the plains remain mostly treeless except for protected gullies and rocky ridges. Summer fires and rain see the grasslands cloaked in green regrowth, but for most of the year they vary in colour from saffron through golden-yellow. They're probably at their most impressive towards the end of winter when tall, straw-coloured strands are buffeted by cold highveld winds.

Hardy, coarse grasses dominate, and most of them are sour tasting, like the appropriately named turpentine grass and yellow thatching grass. Local farmers call this habitat 'sourveld', though it hasn't stopped them saturating it with livestock. But even prior to the influx of domestic species, the bitter, nutrient-poor grasslands never carried the diversity and density of herbivores sustained by East Africa's sweetgrass plains. They are, however, notable for the endemic ungulates that once formed massive herds here. A couple of them are now extinct. The quagga (pronounced kwokka after its braying call) was a lightly marked subspecies of Burchell's zebra which died out in the wild before 1900. The blue antelope, a relative of sable and roan antelopes, disappeared a century earlier.

Other highveld grazers came close to a similar fate, but tiny pockets, protected mostly by interested private citizens, have ensured their persistence. Bonteboks, black wildebeests and mountain zebras have now been restored to much of their former range, which they share with more widespread Southern Afri-can endemics like springboks. Large carnivores are mostly absent, except for isolated populations of the adaptable leopard, but smaller hunters including mongooses, black-footed cats and Cape and bat-eared foxes are abundant, if mostly difficult to spot. Ostriches are the most conspicuous avian inhabitants of the highveld, but at ground level, and often hidden by the long grasses, many different species of longclaws, pipits, widows, bishops, larks and korhaans forage for the teeming seeds and insects.

ISLANDS OF GRASS

Far more widespread than the highveld are the grasslands scattered throughout the woodland-plains mosaic that makes up savanna. These patchy open areas are distinct from the unique highveld grasslands, and they usually have a moderate scattering of trees and thickets. They also lack the highveld's most characteristic species, but because they occur in more fertile, low-lying regions, they sustain a much greater variety of wildlife in far higher concentrations. Black wildebeests are replaced by the more common blue wildebeests, the same species that undertakes legendary migrations in the Serengeti; in Southern Africa they are more sedentary, but readily undertake mini-migrations in search of grazing in the savanna patchwork. Red hartebeests and tsessebes fill the bontebok's niche, hartebeests preferring the dry grasslands in the northwest, while the tsessebe is found in better-watered habitat to the northeast.

The richer grazing also sustains 'bulk grazers', ungulates, which by virtue of their size require huge quantities of palatable grass. Most conspicuous, white rhinos and buffaloes are invariably accompanied by an entourage of cattle egrets opportunistically snapping up disturbed insects. Other insectivorous aeronauts like rollers, whydahs and black-shouldered kites are very common, and the rich herpeto-fauna (reptiles and amphibians) attract snake eagles and secretary birds. Mammalian predators, particularly pursuit hunters like cheetahs and African wild dogs, also thrive in the richness of the savanna grasslands, particularly pursuit hunters like cheetahs and African wild dogs. Low in the predator hierarchy, they avoid areas used by the dominant carnivore here, the lion. Spotted hyenas are common on the plains, and their less widespread cousins, the brown hyenas, occur in drier areas. Aardwolves, honey badgers, servals, white-tailed mongooses and jackals are widespread, some being more obvious than others.

SEE IT AT...
» **Kruger NP** (p60) » **Pilanesberg NP** (p72) »
Mountain Zebra NP (p90)
» **Moremi GR** (p132)

SAVANNAS

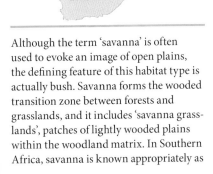

Although the term 'savanna' is often used to evoke an image of open plains, the defining feature of this habitat type is actually bush. Savanna forms the wooded transition zone between forests and grasslands, and it includes 'savanna grasslands', patches of lightly wooded plains within the woodland matrix. In Southern Africa, savanna is known appropriately as 'bushveld', and is the dominant vegetation type of the region. It covers a vast expanse, beginning as a broad band across the northern reaches of Namibia, Botswana and South Africa and extending though most of Zimbabwe, Zambia and Malawi. Collectively, savanna is the most widespread habitat on the continent, and is also by far the richest for its variety and its abundance of wildlife.

Savanna composition varies markedly across its enormous range, but common to all is the thorn tree. At least 25 different species of thorn tree, all members of the genus *Acacia*, make up the different savanna communities of Southern Africa. Among these, the umbrella thorn is easily the most recognisable. Its unmistakable flat-topped crown appears in countless African wildlife documentaries, but don't let the cliché deter you; they really are beautiful trees, and when you see one against a setting sun with attendant browsing giraffes, it's only the fussiest of photographers who can keep the lens cap on.

Umbrella thorns and another acacia, the knobthorn, with its characteristic knob-covered trunk, are typical of 'sweet' savannas, which maintain high nutritional quality well into the dry winter. This makes them extremely attractive to large concentrations of browsing ungulates such as giraffes, greater kudus, impalas, black rhinos and elephants. Scattered thickets of buffalo-thorns provide refuges for smaller browsers, like grey duikers and bushbucks, as well as a great variety of birdlife including drongos, shrikes, flycatchers and louries. Predators abound here, especially lions, leopards and spotted hyenas, as well as many hard-to-see smaller species like civets and mongooses.

On the poorer soils of northern Namibia, Zimbabwe, southern Zambia and northwest South Africa, where seasonally high rainfall leaches out nutrients, savannas are less nutritious and don't sustain such high wildlife concentrations. However, this creates niches for a number of specialised ungulates that thrive at low densities (sables, roans, Lichtenstein's hartebeests and both types of reedbucks), and are preyed upon by African wild dogs, leopards and the ubiquitous lion. As with the sweet savannas, a great ensemble of arboreal as well as ground-roosting birds occur here, such as korhaans, francolins, hornbills and larks.

TREES OF LIFE

Compared with the relatively homogeneous landscape of grasslands and desert, savannas provide a terrific array of niches for an equally diverse fauna. One of the most distinctive savanna trees, the mopane, is a good example. The leaves are highly nutritious, and sought out by browsers ranging from the diminutive steenbok to herds of elephants, which uproot the shallow-rooted mopane to reach the valuable canopy. For less pushy feeders – such as ground-based browsers like greater kudus, impalas and duikers – mopane is still readily accessible because the distinctive butterfly-shaped leaves retain their nutrients after they've fallen to the ground.

Baboons and vervet monkeys forage in the trees themselves, though they often ignore the leaves and search instead for a leaf resident. A small psyllid insect secretes a tiny, honey-coloured shelter made of waxy scale where the larva develops. Primates turn leaves over and carefully collect the sweet-tasting scale one by one, and no doubt also eat the larvae inside. As well as offering food and safe perches for primates and hundreds of bird species, mopane trees provide sheltering holes for woodpeckers, barbets and hornbills as well as tree squirrels, tree rats and bushbabies. These in turn attract nocturnal preda-

tors like owls and genets. On poor soils with limited rainfall, mopane forms a scrubby savanna rarely higher than 3m. But where conditions are particularly favourable, 25m-high trees create a mopane forest, and it's difficult to believe you're still in savanna country.

SEE IT AT...

» **Kruger NP** (p60) » **Chobe NP** (p120)
» **South Luangwa NP** (p178)
» **Moremi GR** (p132)

FORESTS

Like a series of tree-covered stepping stones, Southern Africa's high-altitude forests run in a chain of relict patches starting on South Africa's southern Cape coast, and petering out on Malawi's Nyika Plateau. But regardless of location, they're all similar enough to tropical Africa's upland forests to be tagged with the same 'Afro-montane' label. Indicating true African mountain forest (rather then the dense woodland that creeps onto the lower slopes), Afro-montane vegetation usually grows on high, steep slopes that intercept moisture-laden ocean air. Dense mists and heavy rains are a regular feature, creating a humid, lush environment where everything is damp, from the rotting leaf litter underfoot to the moss- and fungus-covered trunks of 25m-high forest trees.

Unlike equatorial forest, the understorey is usually quite sparse, but glades of ferns and forbs choke patches of ground where the canopy admits beams of light. Here, Southern Africa's smallest antelope, the blue duiker, finds refuge and browses the shrubs. A miniature cleaner of the forest floor, it also eats fallen leaves, fruit and flowers, and seeks out monkeys and fruit-eating birds like louries, barbets and parrots in the canopy above (they invariably dislodge and discard fruits to the floor below where the duiker mops them up). Anything the duikers miss quickly rots down to become part of the rich cushion of detritus on the forest floor, a breeding ground for thousands of different insect species. Elusive bug-hunters including elephant shrews, two endemic forest shrews and the rare giant golden mole sniff them out but all are very difficult to spot. Fortunately for birdwatchers, avian insectivores like flycatchers, shrikes, robins and bulbuls are hard to miss.

Also conspicuous, the placid samango monkey is the only primate of the southern Afro-montane forests; vervets and baboons venture in from surrounding habitat, but neither are forest specialists. Samangos share the canopy with three species of indigenous squirrel, all of which sunbathe on exposed branches on winter mornings, the only time it's relatively easy to spot them. Even more elusive are the tree civet and tree dassie – you'll need a spotlight to see these two entirely nocturnal canopy residents. Both spend the day asleep in high tree hollows, but once night falls, the civet can sometimes be seen foraging on the forest floor for insects, small mammals and fruit. The tree dassie rarely ventures to the ground, but its characteristic latrines at the base of huge yellowwoods, teaks or milkwoods are good clues to look up.

FORESTS IN THE SAND

With an almost completely unbroken canopy, and a thick understorey of shade-tolerant shrubs and lianas, the region's coastal forests are denser then their montane counterparts. Also known as lowland forest, they cloak parallel rows of ancient dunes, which, over time, have developed a fertile detritus layer. Even so, the soil may be very porous, and digging a few centimetres reveals the sandy substrate. Consequently, trees maximise their water intake with deep roots that for a few species are spread in huge, spoke-like buttresses. Some of them are the tallest trees in the region and the canopy here can top 35m.

Samango monkeys and tree squirrels are common, and coastal forests are more rewarding sites than the mountains to look for forest mammals. They also shelter a few species with a distinctly tropical feel like Delegorgue's pigeons, African broadbills and the perfectly camouflaged Gaboon viper, its skin a living reflection of the forest floor's leaf litter.

At the forest edges, where the understorey thins out, bushbucks, bushpigs and black rhinos overlap with the blue duiker, and forest birds mingle with savanna and woodland species. Red duikers, sunis and a Southern African endemic, the nyala, are also more easily spotted here, and attract the only large forest carnivore, the leopard. If the innate shyness of these forest inhabitants doesn't make sighting one enough of a challenge, then the lushness of the habitat will. Where the detritus is sparse, such as around puddles, moist walking trails through forests are an excellent canvas for their tracks and the signs of many other forest creatures.

SEE IT AT...
» **iSimangaliso Wetland Park** (p80)
» **Maloti-Drakensberg Transfrontier Area** (p89) » **Mkhuze GR** (p86)
» **Nyika NP** (p170)

FYNBOS

Lying in the extreme southwest of the region between southern Namaqualand and Port Elizabeth is a habitat found nowhere else on earth.

ENVIRONMENT

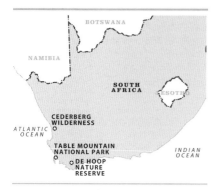

Named after the fine-leaved shrubs that predominate, South Africa's fynbos (Afrikaans for 'fine bush') is one of the richest floral regions in the world. With over 8600 plant species, 70% of them endemic, only a few tropical rainforests can match fynbos for variety, which is sufficient to qualify it for classification as one of the world's six floral kingdoms. A region of cold winter rains and desiccating summers, the heathlike fynbos is resistant to both fire and frost. Often described as Mediterranean or 'macchia' after the scrubby hard-leaved shrubs of Spain, it is far more diverse than any similar European habitat, with characteristically African proteas and cycads alongside hundreds of different sedges, reeds, ericas, lilies and irises.

Fire is the key to fynbos diversity. The plants here use different strategies to cope with the frequent fires that sweep through in the dry summer and autumn. Likewise, different fires, or even different stages of the same fire, favour species differently. Many proteas and the tall mountain cypress protect their seeds in heat-resistant flowerheads that spring open to disgorge their seed bounty in the relatively cool fires of autumn. Other species have hard-coated seeds that lie dormant in the soil until an intense summer fire triggers their germination. Because the timing and interval between fires is always changing, no single species dominates.

While fire maintains fynbos diversity, ants seem to actually increase it. Over 1400 species of fynbos plant rely on ants to disperse their seeds, a relationship called myrmecochory. The plants 'bribe' ants with elaiosomes, fleshy extrusions on the seeds rich in protein, fats, sugars and vitamins. The ants carry the seeds back to their nests to eat the elaiosomes, and then abandon the seeds, which germinate safely below ground where they're protected from seed-eating rodents. In addition, ant dispersal may actually isolate seedlings from their parent species. Most myrmecochorous plants are pollinated by insects flying very short distances, so germination may be restricted to just a few plants in a very localised area. Over time, this genetic isolation can lead to entirely new species, and may explain why some have such restricted ranges; for many fynbos plants, the entire world population occupies an area less than the size of a football oval.

UNKNOWNS & ENDEMICS

With such an abundance of floral riches, fynbos swarms with eaters of nectar and pollen. Many thousands of insects occur only here, and most of them are still unknown to science. A few such as the protea beetle and carpenter bee are fairly obvious visitors to the flowers, but by far the most striking pollinators are the birds. With their vividly coloured bracts (hard, outer petal-like leaves) enclosing a tightly clustered mass of nectar-bearing flowers, the proteas probably evolved to attract birds, and most dazzling of them all are the sunbirds. Like Africa's answer to hummingbirds (to which they are not closely related), sunbirds have tubelike beaks, a brush-tipped tongue for mopping up nectar and jewel-like metallic plumage. At least seven different species occur in fynbos; one of them, the orange-breasted sunbird, can be seen nowhere else. Other endemic birds include the Cape sugarbird, a much larger nectar-eater belonging to a unique South African family, as well as Protea canaries, Cape francolins and Victorin's warblers.

Unlike the nutrient-rich flowers, most fynbos plants are fibrous, nutritionally poor and loaded with unpalatable compounds like tannins. As a result, the mammalian fauna is not nearly as diverse as elsewhere, but there are a few notable species which characterise the fynbos. The uncommon and timid Cape grysbok browses fynbos with a narrow muzzle, selectively cropping the new growth where indigestible compounds are less dense. With the proliferation of vineyards in the southwest Cape, they also turn readily to grapes and vines. Far more likely to be seen, the bontebok is another fynbos specialist, though it can't subsist on the heath itself, and seeks out the open plains known as grassy fynbos scattered throughout the scrub. Cape mountain zebras and grey rhebucks are other distinctive mammals, and although leopards were once common here, the role of top predator is now largely occupied by the caracal. Mammals aren't especially abundant or diverse in fynbos, but reptiles and amphibians are prolific; collectively there are about 30 species found nowhere else.

SEE IT AT...

» De Hoop NR (p88) » Table Mountain NP (p95) » Cederberg Wilderness Area (p94)

THE HIGH POINTS

Lying along a colossal crescent that starts in central Namibia and dwindles in western Mozambique, the mountains and hills of Southern Africa rise abruptly from the surrounding jigsaw of savanna, grassland and semidesert. Technically, mountains are too diverse to qualify as a discrete habitat, and they harbour a number of distinctive vegetation types including high grasslands, montane forests and mountain fynbos. But whether it's snow-covered summits, stony massifs or the little rock outcrops that dot the countryside, mountains and their hilly offshoots host characteristic fauna and flora worth looking for. Heading to the hills (or in some places, even just scanning them with binoculars from the lowlands) promises a few species found nowhere else, and at the very least increases the chances of spotting some more widespread wildlife which is difficult to find in other habitats.

The mountainous spine of Southern Africa's highlands (and by far the highest section), the Drakensberg Mountains form a jagged border between South Africa and Lesotho, which the Zulus call 'uQathlamba' – the Battlement of Spears. At its highest point the range is just under 3500m high, out of reach for most wildlife except for hovering bearded vultures and hardy little ice rats (the highest-living mammal in Southern Africa). Slightly lower down and extending along the escarpment from the Cape fold mountains to the Chimanimani highlands in Zimbabwe, black eagles hunt rock dassies, klipspringers and occasionally rock-dwelling reptiles like rock agamas and adders. Leopards and caracals also hunt here, and where the rock gives way to grass-covered slopes they prey on highland antelopes including oribis, mountain reedbucks and elands.

Both rock- and grass-covered slopes sustain a liberal scattering of proteas and aloes, attracting sunbirds and sugarbirds

ENVIRONMENT

as well as baboons, which are equally at home on the steep cliffs, rocky hillsides or grassy slopes. Typical grassland birds like whydahs, warblers, widows and larks are common on the lower slopes and, far more difficult to see, rodents and rodent-hunters like servals and grass owls are also found.

LITTLE HEADS OF ROCK

Like rocky islands, koppies (derived from the Afrikaans for 'little head') can be found in almost any habitat but they provide the greatest contrast, both scenically and biologically, where they jut out of flatlands – the plains, savannas and deserts. Obligate rock-dwellers (those that only live in rocky habitats) like , rock dassies and flat lizards occur in little pockets, isolated from one another by the surrounding habitat and only occasionally running the gauntlet to cross to a neighbouring koppie. Rocky recesses provide root-holds for *Euphorbia* trees and rock figs and also give shelter to rodents, rock agamas and snakes.

If they're high enough to include a few sheer cliffs, koppies also attract ledge-nesting birds like bald ibises, rock kestrels and rock martins. Invariably, the rock specialists share these outcrops with occasional visitors from the encircling habitat. Lionesses venture into them to give birth, and elands and greater kudus move onto the lower slopes to feed. In the past koppies were equally as important to humans, and on a few koppies the evidence still remains. Scattered throughout Southern Africa are rock paintings of elands, sables and other antelopes that are thought to have been left by the San people around 4000 years ago.

SEE IT AT...

» **Maloti-Drakensberg Transfrontier Area** (p89) » **Nyika NP** (p170) » **Pilanesberg NP** (p72) » **Namib-Naukluft Park** (p104)

AQUATICA

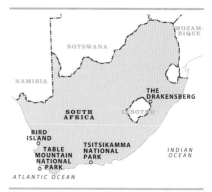

Every habitat relies on water to sustain life. For some Southern African habitats, water is scarce enough that its arrival brings about a transformation and even well-watered habitats here endure a dry season. But for some species, water is a daily feature. Indeed, they depend on a continuous supply and would perish without it.

INLAND

Hugely variable in character and configuration, inland waters include everything from rivers to lakes, marshes and ponds. Surrounding many a wetland or river, water-loving trees like wild figs, fever trees and jackalberries give away the presence of water even before you see it. Trees mean food and shelter, and with water so close, they become a fertile focal point for wildlife congregations. Weaver birds and foam-nest frogs nest in the branches overhanging the water, perhaps as insurance against land-based predators, but it's not enough to deter snakes and genets. Constantly available fruit in sycamore fig trees attracts fruit-eaters on every level: barbets, hornbills and monkeys in the branches, duikers, bushpigs and civets below, and even fruit-eating fish and terrapins in the water. Like a floating tree raft, another species, the water fig, provides nest sites for storks and cormorants, and cover for hippos, Nile crocodiles and sitatungas. Elephants even wade in to browse its leaves.

Other water plants from the prolific reed family are generally less palatable, but provide perches and 'bolt-holes' for kingfishers, herons and grebes. Marsh mongooses, servals and Nile monitors hunt among them for crabs, frogs, wetland rodents and tiny musk shrews. Waterbucks, lechwes and reedbucks take refuge in the reeds while, high above them, African fish eagles find a high waterside perch to wait for barbel (catfish) to venture near the surface and they occasionally even take ducks, dabchicks or flamingos.

THE COAST
Where the land meets the sea, plants and animals have to endure a constant pattern of inundation and evaporation. But the ocean's warm shallow waters ensure a daily delivery of rich planktonic soup to the shore inhabitants. Sparking an entire food web, the plankton supports marine worms, limpets, mussels and crabs, which themselves sustain battalions of shorebirds like sandpipers, greenshanks and stints as well as Cape clawless otters. Coastal fishers like noddies, gulls, terns and jackass penguins vie with fur-seals just offshore and jostle for space on the beach to breed. Their colonies attract the hunters and the scavengers; great white sharks patrol the shallows, and beachcombing brown hyenas and jackals look for lost seal pups and carcasses spewed up by the waves. After dark, smaller predators like mongooses, honey badgers and monitor lizards search for the eggs of shorebirds and marine turtles. Female leatherbacks and loggerheads lay their eggs along the east coast and then abandon them to their fate; many will be discovered by the beachcombers long before hatching.

ESTUARIES
Immutably linked to the coast, some inland waterways also receive a twice-daily deluge of salt water. Known as estuaries, the waters here experience a constant seesaw in salinity levels. This regular mixing of freshwater and saltwater gives rise to a nutrient bounty, but also provides constant challenges for wildlife. Water temperature fluctuates enormously, and the soup of suspended sediments restricts the penetration of light for photosynthesis, and clogs up gills and filter-feeding apparatus. This means that wildlife is constantly moving around, seeking the best balance for its requirements. Flamingos follow the mobile waves of algae and zooplankton, and kingfishers, herons and terns hunt for fish. Nile crocodiles prefer fresh water, but make occasional excursions into the estuarine zone, and, more unexpectedly, Zambezi sharks sometimes make the opposite trip.

A few species always stay put in the region between high and low tide. Mangrove trees use tendril-like buttress roots for support in the erratic muddy floor, and a few species grow snorkel-like roots clear of the mud for 'breathing'. Mudskippers, fiddler crabs and mangrove snails shelter among the roots and emerge at low tide to forage on the algae-coated mud, never straying far from a burrow; jackals, otters, marsh mongooses and aerial predators also move in as the water recedes.

OCEANS
Even if you're not a diver, watching the open ocean can boost your species count. There are more than three-dozen species of whale and dolphin here, many of them visible from shore or on short boat trips. Likewise, pelagic (seagoing) birds like albatrosses, petrels and shearwaters abound though none of them breed in the region. Small islands off the southern coast reveal huge breeding colonies of Cape gannets, cormorants, gulls and jackass penguins as

ENVIRONMENT

well as the most visible great white sharks in the world. The warmer, eastern coastline is home to many easily seen marine attractions, including whale sharks by the dozen, and nesting sea turtles. Far less likely to be spotted despite its preference for shallow waters, the dugong is now one of the most threatened denizens of Southern African waters.

SEE IT AT...
» Table Mountain NP (p95) » Maloti-Drakensberg Transfrontier Area (p89) » Bird Island NR (p94) » Tsitsikamma NP (p95)

OTHER HABITATS

While we tend to think of Southern African habitats as forests, savannas and grasslands (to name a few), there are many other, less obvious habitats that animals use – some of which overlap the boundaries of our own 'habitats'. And there are good reasons for animals to partake of human hospitality: our endeavours provide extra sources of food, shelter and breeding sites for creatures equipped to make the transition from natural to human-designed environments. But not all of these habitats are human-engineered, and some are simply overlooked.

VILLAGES, TOWNS & CITIES
Although generally bereft of large animals, urban environments are utilised by some species opportunistically, and in a few cases are the habitat of choice. Into the latter category fall various rodents, but birds fare better than mammals as a rule, because the latter are often sought for food and discouraged as competition or carriers of disease. What this means for the visitor is that large city parks can support at least some living things, such as squirrels, roosts of bats and even troops of monkeys.

Opportunistic birds such as pied crows and black kites swoop for scraps near markets; starlings and sparrows nest in buildings where the vertical faces are effectively cliffs; and marabou storks perch like sentinels overlooking savanna and city squares alike. Several species of weaver build large colonies of nests right in the middle of settlements, and fruit-bats also may roost in towns, both probably because the risk of predation is less – although raptors hunt above city streets through the 'canyons' created by buildings.

AGRICULTURE & CULTIVATION
Where land is cleared for cultivation, the end result is comparatively poor in both plants and animals. Most large animals quickly desert following these changes, or if they're unable to move far, they die out – and others are hunted to local extinction. When elephants, absent for months in other parts of their range, return along traditional migration routes to find crops and dwellings in their way, conflict with people inevitably develops. Similarly, the fencing of fields across wildebeest migration routes causes the animals to change course.

Nonetheless some animals, particularly birds and small mammals such as mongooses and genets, readily adopt agricultural land as an extension of their natural habitat. While driving along highways, you can expect to see various weavers and sparrows, doves, and blossom-feeding sunbirds; the ubiquitous common bulbul; and orchard-raiding hornbills, crows and starlings. Watch for secretary birds, bustards and storks picking over burnt fields, cattle egrets among livestock, and shrikes perched on overhead wires. Ironically, when agriculture does benefit a species, it can be to such a degree that animals such as rats, normally held in check by natural predators, become a major pest. Thus baboons are expanding their numbers and range at the interface between cultivation and savanna, and red-billed queleas can descend on crops in millions, causing widespread damage.

THE AIR UP THERE

Habitat is usually described in terms of objects, but, for a vast number of animals, the main event is actually the space above or between objects, and 'habitat' in the conventional sense is just a backdrop (albeit one to which all creatures ultimately must return at some time or other). Although generally transparent, air is not just empty space. It behaves like other matter except that it's much lighter than most, and there's a lot more of it. It stands still and moves – sometimes very quickly or in circles. Air heats up and cools down (sometimes rapidly and in quick succession), bumps into things and fills voids such as great caves. It also acts as an agent of dispersal, carrying the seeds of plants and the young of spiders and insects over many kilometres.

All these factors are exploited by a few mammals, a myriad insects, and most birds. To them it is a dining room, highway, playground, courtship arena or observation post. Air can communicate the presence of food: thunderheads on the horizon stimulate termites to hatch – millions drift upward like plumes of smoke, attracting birds and mammals alike, and swifts move ahead of the storm front to feast on the bounty. Vultures take advantage of thermals as they look for a kill; their volplaning is a clear signal to predators to move onto a kill themselves. And smoke, often visible from kilometres away, signals a grassfire to which bustards, raptors and jackals are drawn in their search for a meal.

TERMITE MOUNDS

Termite biology and behaviour is itself fascinating, but the earthen mounds of these silent armies play an important role in the life cycles of many other creatures. At various stages, termitaria form important refuges for other animals. For example, monitor lizards lay their eggs and various birds dig nest tunnels in mounds, aardvarks and pangolins dig out shelters in abandoned mounds, and animals ranging from small bats and snakes to warthogs, ratels, porcupines and jackals use hollow mounds as shelters and nurseries. Topis and cheetahs use mounds as vantage points, and elephants and rhinos rub against them for a scratch.

Termite mounds also help to shape the environment by encouraging the growth of certain plants. For example, mounds on floodplains become islands during wet seasons that plants colonise – in turn sheltering more plants and animals, and encouraging the growth of thickets. It's pretty hard to miss termite mounds on the savanna, but look also for arboreal termitaria – in which kingfishers excavate nest tunnels – and the distinctive mushroom-shaped structures made by some termite species.

ENVIRONMENT

MINIATURE MUSHROOM FARMERS

Termite mounds are a wonder of natural engineering. Alone, these insects are helpless, but somehow colonies cooperate to build protective fortresses by cementing together grains of earth with saliva. Inside, the temperature and humidity remain more or less constant, regulated by ventilation shafts and chimneys; other passages serve as brood chambers. The hub of the colony is the queen, whose main task in life is to squeeze out millions of eggs. Most eggs hatch into workers, who tend the queen, forage for food, and build and repair the mound; others become soldiers that defend the nest. A mound's inhabitants can consume tonnes of vegetation annually; once chewed, the vegetation is deposited in storage chambers in the mound where it sprouts a fungus that is consumed by the termites. Pretty impressive so far, but consider this: during the rains, termites of several species spread the fungus on the ground outside, where it sprouts edible mushrooms that set spores, which the termites gather to renew their underground supply. Not bad for tiny, blind insects.

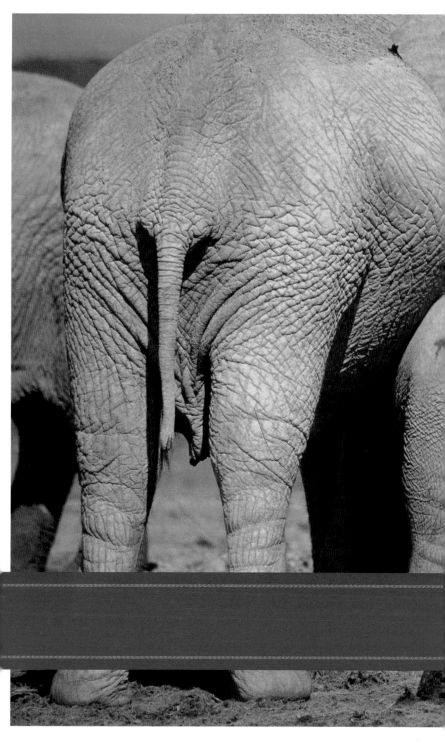

DESTINATIONS

SOUTHERN AFRICA'S TOP WILDLIFE SPOTS

SOUTH AFRICA

CAPITAL PRETORIA **AREA** 1,233,404 SQ KM **NATIONAL PARKS** 21 **MAMMAL SPECIES** APPROX 300

World-class wildlife-watching, cosmopolitan cities, stunning panoramas and vibrant cultures combine to make South Africa sub-Saharan Africa's most visited destination. Kruger – the country's flagship park – is just a start. Take time to sample more of its many other protected areas.

THE LAND Dominated by interwoven mosaics of woodland, savanna and the dry, rocky shrublands known as the Karoo, most of South Africa looks very different from the iconic grasslands many people associate with Africa. Indeed, the largest diversity and density of South African wildlife occurs not on open plains but in the woodlands of the north and east, known locally as bushveld or 'the lowveld'. The country's premier reserve, Kruger National Park, protects an expanse of bushveld the size of Israel or Wales, and is also where the main populations of large mammals occur, including the eminently viewable Big Five. One of them, the rhino, owes

its existence to South Africa: there are more white rhinos here than in the rest of Africa combined, and Kruger protects just under half the continent's black-rhino population.

Away from the bushveld, wildlife is thinner on the ground, but a further 20 national parks and countless provincial parks offer a huge variety of wildlife habitats, a few of which shouldn't be missed. The Kalahari Desert experiences seasonal congregations of nomadic herbivores and is also excellent for seeing predators, both mammalian and avian. The far more temperate uKhahlamba-Drakensberg mountain area is also known for raptors, including the region's only population

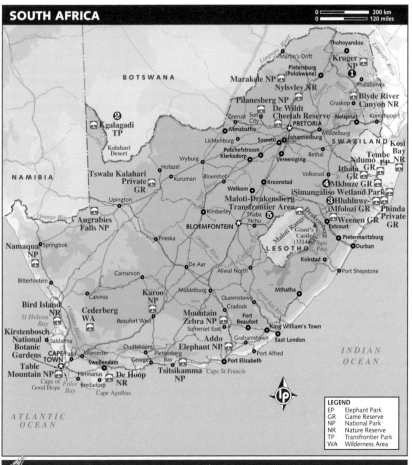

SOUTH AFRICA

0 ——— 200 km
0 ——— 120 miles

LEGEND
EP Elephant Park
GR Game Reserve
NP National Park
NR Nature Reserve
TP Transfrontier Park
WA Wilderness Area

SOUTH AFRICA

⭐ TOP SPOTS

1. KRUGER NATIONAL PARK
(p60) Good facilities, superb
birding and high wildlife diversity
– including the Big Five plus many
more –combine to make Kruger
South Africa's flagship park.

**2. KGALAGADI TRANSFRONTIER
PARK** (p68) This wild area offers
stark semi-desert scenery,
prowling predators, raptors
galore and impressive seasonal
congregations of springboks and
other antelopes.

**3. HLUHLUWE-IMFOLOZI
GAME RESERVE** (p64) With its
evocative landscapes, abundance
of rhinos, elephants and buffalos,
and network of wilderness trails,
Hluhluwe-iMfolozi is justifiably
popular and makes a fine contrast
with Kruger.

4. MKHUZE GAME RESERVE (p86)
Mkhuze remains something of an
insider's tip, with a rich blend of
habitats ranging from grasslands

to rivers and sand dunes, 400-plus
bird species, and excellent wildlife
watching, including both rhino
species and large herds of zebras.

**5. MALOTI-DRAKENSBERG
TRANSFRONTIER AREA** (p89)
Prime viewing opportunities for
the bearded vulture plus superb
highland scenery and hiking
are the hallmarks of this rugged
mountain area.

of bearded vultures. Other uKhahlamba-Drakensberg specialities include increasingly rare antelopes such as mountain reedbucks, grey rhebucks and oribis. Where the mountains give way to the highveld grasslands and the Karoo, endemic black wildebeests, Cape mountain zebras and dozens of bird rarities can be seen.

South Africa also harbours unique smaller attractions and is the only country on earth to have one of the world's six floral kingdoms entirely within its boundaries. The southwest Cape's fynbos has the highest concentration of plant species on earth, more than two-thirds of which are endemic. Fynbos wildlife is not as diverse, but this is the only place to see bonteboks, Cape grysboks, and six endemic bird species including Cape sugarbirds, orange-breasted sunbirds and Protea canaries.

Most significant wildlife populations in South Africa are enclosed behind fences, intended to prevent conflict with the substantial human communities that now abut most parks. But don't let this deter you; many parks are vast and you'll only see fences when you drive through the gates. Rest assured, the animals within are wild and everything from weavers fashioning their intricate nests to a leopard feeding on its tree-cached kill can be spotted.

WHEN TO GO South Africa can be rewardingly visited for wildlife at any time of year. Summer (late November to March) brings rain, mists and – in the lowveld – some uncomfortably hot days. Winter (June to September) is cooler, dry and ideal for hiking. Because vegetation is less dense, and thirsty animals congregate around rivers and other permanent water sources, winter is also optimal for wildlife-watching.

School holidays can be an even more important consideration than the weather. From mid-December through January, and again around Easter, national-park accommodation is heavily booked and prices can more than double.

WILDLIFE HIGHLIGHTS

» Feeling the spray from breaching southern right whales off the Cape coast (p88 & p110) » Watching klipspringer lambs play-chasing with their parents among the rocks of the Karoo's Nuweveld Mountains (p84) » Calling narina trogons with taped playback in Zululand's humid sandforest (p91) » Watching a cheetah in a 100km/h sprint after a springbok along the Auob riverbed in the Kalahari (p68) » Swimming among little jackass penguins at Boulders Beach in Table Mountain NP (p95) » Watching black rhinos from a hide at dawn in KwaZulu-Natal's Hluhluwe-iMfolozi GR (p64)

GEMSBOK, KGALAGADI TRANSFRONTIER PARK

SOUTH AFRICA ITINERARIES

1. THE BIG FIVE From Jo'burg head to **Kruger National Park** (p60), where you could easily spend a week or more exploring its diverse habitats and unrivalled species

diversity. **Pilanesberg National Park** (p72), another easy jaunt from Jo'burg, has a wide variety of species, including the Big Five, plus rich birdlife. For combining wildlife-watching with luxury, few places can beat **Phinda Private Game Reserve** (p92), known for its cheetahs, Big Five and general wildlife, and its impeccable standards. Much more rugged, **Marakele National Park** (p94) offers the Big Five, plus the world's largest Cape vulture colony.

SOUTH AFRICA

2. BIRDER'S DELIGHT From Durban, make your way to **Mkhuze Game Reserve** (p86), with over 400 bird species, including a unique mix of temperate and tropical species. The

nearby **iSimangaliso Wetland Park** (p80) is ideal for wetland species. Also readily accessible from Durban, **Hluhluwe-iMfolozi Game Reserve** (p64) is known for its general birdlife, including its raptors, and **Kosi Bay Nature Reserve** (p94) is one of the best destinations for spotting palmnut vultures. Further inland, the **uKhahlamba-Drakensberg Area** (p89), with its reliable spottings of bearded vultures and fine overall birding, is not to be missed. From Cape Town, **Bird Island Nature Reserve** (p94) offers excellent viewing, including various migrant species.

3. COAST, DESERT & MOUNTAINS Set aside as much time as possible to sample South Africa's wide diversity of habitats. **Kruger National Park** (p60) and **Kgalagadi Transfrontier Park** (p68) are essential stops, and

offer starkly contrasting landscapes, with the Kgalagadi's semidesert panoramas a particular highlight. Along and around the coast, you can spend several days exploring **Namaqua National Park** (p95) or hiking in **Table Mountain National Park** (p95) before moving on to **De Hoop Nature Reserve** (p88), **Tsitsikamma National Park** (p95) and **Addo Elephant National Park** (p76), and from there on to **iSimangaliso Wetland Park** (p80). Finish off with several days hiking in the **Maloti and uKhahlamba-Drakensberg ranges** (p89), or in the **Cederberg Wilderness Area** (p94).

SOUTH AFRICA

LOCATION Skukuza is 462km east of Pretoria. Sealed roads accessible year-round, but Crocodile Bridge Gate can be underwater during the summer.

FACILITIES 800km of wildlife-watching roads, hides, disabled facilities, Elephant Hall at Letaba, cultural heritage sites throughout the park. Guided day and night drives available at most camps. Several camps, including Skukuza, Berg-en-Dal and Letaba offer specialist 'bush drives'.

ACCOMMODATION 12 main rest camps, plus bushveld camps, bush lodges and lodges on privately run concessions. Park accommodation types include guest houses, chalets, bungalows, camping grounds and caravan sites.

WILDLIFE RHYTHMS During summer many herbivores drop their young, and birding is at its richest with the influx of summer migrants, particularly insect-eaters. March through May is the period when impalas, blue wildebeests and warthogs rut and their vulnerability to predators increases. During winter (May to October) visibility is best and wildlife concentrates at water sources.

CONTACT South African National Parks (SanParks or SANP) Central Reservations (☎ 012-428 9111; www.sanparks.org), Kruger NP administration office (☎ 013-735 4000).

KRUGER NATIONAL PARK

South Africa's largest and most diverse reserve is also one of its oldest. Free from persecution for more than a century, the animals are often extremely accepting of vehicles and Kruger offers exceptional opportunities for close-up wildlife-watching. Almost the size of Israel, it has a diversity of species unmatched elsewhere in South Africa, drawing more international tourists than any other destination in the country. Its popularity has led to inevitable development, often criticised by the purists. Kruger has about two-dozen camps and the most extensive road network of any Southern African national park, but don't let this put you off: it is justifiably famous for very regular viewing of the **Big Five** as well as rarer highlights such as **cheetahs** and **African wild dogs**. Most visitors will see 30 mammal species in a three-day visit (particularly if you join one of the excellent guided night drives) and **birdlife** is prolific, with more species recorded here than in any other park in South Africa. For many people, the key to enjoying Kruger is simply to avoid the main roads as far as possible.

SOUTHERN KRUGER: EASY ACCESS & ABUNDANT WILDLIFE Almost all visitors begin exploring Kruger at the southern end of the park (the most accessible section). With the highest rainfall in the park, the vegetation here can be correspondingly dense, particularly in the rainy months (October to March) when new growth makes wildlife-watching difficult. But this is also the best region to look for both **rhino** species, and **elephants** and **lions** are abundant. Base yourself at Lower Sabie Camp for almost assured viewing of lions and their main prey species, **buffaloes**. The Lower Sabie Rd (H4-1) heading towards Skukuza is justifiably nicknamed 'Lion Drive' and the thorn thickets lining the eastern side of the road are the favoured habitat of **black rhinos** as well as **bushbucks** and **grey duikers**. If you don't find any **lions** yourself, book a guided night drive at Lower Sabie (or any of the major camps) for a chance

WILDLIFE HIGHLIGHTS
» South Africa's richest park with more mammal and bird species than any other in the country » Frequent Big Five sightings » Good chances of spotting cheetahs, African wild dogs, roan antelopes, sables and nyalas » Guided night drives – ideal for viewing small carnivores, owls, nightjars, and a chance of seeing big cats hunting » Prolific birdlife

of seeing lions on the hunt, plus **small carnivores**, **owls** and **nightjars**.

Giraffes are most common in the south, readily seen along a narrow band of open savanna between Crocodile Bridge Gate and Lower Sabie Camp (take the S28). **Burchell's zebra**, **blue wildebeests** and **tsessebes** are also common here, especially in the dry winter when migratory herds from further north swell the resident herbivore populations. Rarer species concentrate in the woodlands of Kruger's southeastern corner. The mountain bushveld around Berg-en-Dal Camp is the only place in the park where you can see **mountain reedbucks**. Their slightly larger cousins, **southern reedbucks**, occur on the moist grasslands between the hills. Their Zulu name, Mziki, mimics their distinctive high-pitched alarm whistle: if you hear it, search the hills for **leopards**. **White rhinos** are also common on these grasslands. Along the H2-2 (near Pretoriuskop Camp), chances are very good for **sable antelopes** and for one of the rarest mammals in the park, **Lichtenstein's hartebeest**. They were reintroduced from Malawi when Kruger's indigenous population became extinct, and this is the only

national park in South Africa where you can see them. This area is also known for good **African wild dog** sightings. During peak periods, the main routes can be very busy, so if seeing other cars bothers you, take the less travelled, unsealed roads

---

⦿⦿ WATCHING TIPS

Some terrific views of animals can take place at camps and picnic areas where otherwise shy species have become used to people. At Letaba Camp, for example, very tame bushbucks wander between the chalets and even females with lambs approach to within touching distance (but don't!). Check the disused termite mound at Afsaal picnic area for a very tame colony of dwarf mongooses. Any eating areas in the main camps will attract tree squirrels, glossy starlings, hornbills and crested barbets looking for scraps. Dams, viewpoints and picnic spots close to the camps make ideal spots to prolong the afternoon before heading back before gate-closing time. Sunset Dam is only two minutes away from Lower Sabie Camp, and offers excellent close-up viewing and photo opportunities of birds such as kingfishers, African darters and storks. Nwanetsi lookout point overlooking the central plains is less than 2km from Nwanetsi Camp and is one of the best viewing sites in Kruger.

SOUTH AFRICA

IMPALA, KRUGER NATIONAL PARK

such as the S114, the S21 and the S128. Or consider taking a guided day drive: these access areas closed to self-drive visitors and the guides are generally excellent.

CENTRAL KRUGER: THE BIG FIVE

The geographical centre of the park is also the heart of its best wildlife-watching and you can be reasonably sure that a few days spent here will be rewarded with sightings of all the **Big Five** (though **rhinos** are scarce; try the S36). Grasslands, which begin as a ribbonlike strip on the southern boundary, fan out here across open basalt plains, providing excellent visibility for spotting numerous grazers and the predators that follow them. Take the main H1-3 road or the gravel S35 and S41 for a good chance of seeing **cheetahs**, rare in the park due to the very high densities of **lions** and **spotted hyenas**. Rich sweetgrass savanna along the road between Satara Camp and Orpen Gate is another excellent area to search for them. You'll see **impalas** by the hundreds (Kruger has more than 100,000) – spend extra time

PRIVATE RESERVES

Like all reserves in South Africa, Kruger is entirely enclosed, but along its western boundary 100km of fences have been removed to merge it with numerous adjoining privately owned reserves. While the wildlife is the same as Kruger's, the private reserves offer a very upmarket wildlife experience in which viewing of the Big Five and other 'specials' is virtually guaranteed. Unlike Kruger, visitors don't drive themselves and the guided wildlife drives leave the roads, following predators on the hunt or moving in on rare species to have a closer look. The guides (called rangers) work very hard at habituating animals to vehicles so that viewing of normally elusive species such as leopards, cheetahs and African wild dogs is unsurpassed. Such superb sightings come at a price though, and a night at a luxury lodge in one of these reserves can cost 10 times as much as Kruger. The experience, however, is unforgettable.

watching them on these open areas, particularly during the rut in April and May. Where there are impalas there are **cheetahs** and **leopards**, and the intense social activity of the breeding season distracts the antelopes from their normal vigilance, making them vulnerable to predators.

Keep a lookout on the plains for **red-billed queleas**, which arrive in vast swarms during the summer to nest in stunted thorn tree thickets dotting the savanna (December to April). With as many as 500 nests in a single tree, hundreds of the nestlings fall to ground, attracting **raptors**, **snakes**, **monitor lizards** and small carnivores such as **slender mongooses**. Drive the Old Main Rd (S90) between Satara and Olifants Camps – also excellent for **secretary birds**, **white storks** and plains **antelopes**.

Wildlife-watching along Kruger's numerous rivers can be excellent, and one of the best routes in the entire reserve follows the Timbavati River (the S39). Check large riverine trees for snoozing **leopards** (sometimes a dangling leg or tail gives them away) that cache their kills among the branches to avoid losing them to other predators. **Elephants**, **buffaloes** and numerous herbivores are common along the rivercourse, and during the winter you can wait at Piet Grober Dam for superb views of animals congregating at the water. Early in the morning, **vervet monkeys** and **chacma baboons** warm up on sunlit trees along the rivercourses. In particular, spend some time watching sycamore figs, which fruit all year round: in addition to primates, they attract **tree squirrels**, fruit-eating birds such as **purple-crested louries** and **African green pigeons**, and insect-eaters like **chinspot batises** and various **starlings** drawn to the swarms which feed on the figs. If you miss them on the drive, Letaba Camp is rich in fig trees and their attendant fauna.

NORTHERN KRUGER: ELEPHANTS, ANTELOPES & BIRDS
Kruger's northern section is the driest part of the park and wildlife is best along the rivers and at

MAKULEKE CONTRACT PARK

The heart of Kruger's far north is Makuleke Concession, a beautiful and geologically ancient area consisting of a 24,000-hectare wedge of land rimmed by the Limpopo and Luvuvhu rivers. In 1969, South Africa's apartheid government forcibly removed the local Makuleke people from the area in order to incorporate their traditional lands into Kruger National Park. In the late 1990s the land was returned to the Makuleke, who in turn agreed not to resettle it but to use it for ecotourism purposes. A 'contract park' was created, in which the land is administered and managed environmentally as part of Kruger park, with tourism developments owned by the Makuleke. Both geographically and in ambience, it is set well apart from Kruger's network of park-run camps and, for the moment at least, is very much a secluded, upmarket experience. Elephants favour the area during the winter months; buffaloes, hippos, lions, leopards and nyalas are present year-round; and birding is excellent.

waterholes. Leave the main tarred road (H1-7), which follows the rivers only for brief intervals and take gravel roads such as the S52 and S56, which explore alluvial plains near Shingwedzi Camp. The north is dominated by mopane trees, a favourite browse of **elephants**; if you haven't already encountered them further south, you will see them here. Baobab trees also become common as you head north, many of them showing the destructive mark of elephants, which gouge out their water-rich bark and inner wood to eat, particularly during the very dry winter.

The aridity of the north makes it less attractive to common herbivores such as **Burchell's zebras** and **blue wildebeests**, which tend to be seminomadic or migratory here. This creates a refuge for rarer antelopes including **Lichtenstein's hartebeests** (the only place other than the far southeastern corner where they may be seen), **roan antelopes**, **sables** and **elands**; the area around Bateleur Bushveld Camp is an excellent place to look. This is the best part of the park to search for **nyalas**, particularly along the Luvuvhu River at the very northern tip of Kruger, also renowned for excellent birdwatching: notable specials include **Pel's fishing owls, silvery-cheeked hornbills, narina trogons, broad-billed rollers** and **swallow-tailed bee-eaters**. The mopane shrubveld along the H1-8 between Punda Maria Camp and Pafuri Gate is the only place in South Africa you're likely to see **three-banded coursers**.

The far north area is also well-known for **African wild dogs** which, like the rare herbivores that prosper here, find a retreat from dominant species. Lions – their main predator – are fewer, making the north ideal for denning. Termite mounds are worth a second look: dogs use them as dens when they pup during May to July, the only time they are resident in an area for any length of time. If you see them, take lots of photos: Kruger researchers rely heavily on tourist photos to monitor numbers and distribution of wild dogs, and run yearly competitions for the most valuable submissions.

LUVUVHU RIVER, KRUGER NATIONAL PARK

HLUHLUWE-IMFOLOZI

SOUTH AFRICA

LOCATION 250km northeast of Durban. Sealed road accessible year-round.

FACILITIES 200km of wildlife-watching roads, guided day and night drives (book at park office), lookout points, hides, self-guided trails, guided day walks.

ACCOMMODATION Chalets sleeping two to six, tented camps, private bush camps, luxury lodges.

WILDLIFE RHYTHMS Summer is very hot and also the main rainfall period; widespread water and lush bush make wildlife-watching difficult. It is, however, when seasonally breeding herbivores such as impalas and blue wildebeests drop their young. June to October is the dry period when animals are generally more visible, particularly at waterpoints.

CONTACT KZN Wildlife (☎ 033-845 1000; www .kznwildlife.com).

HLUHLUWE-IMFOLOZI GAME RESERVE

Once the private hunting grounds of King Shaka Zulu, Hluhluwe-iMfolozi is the largest big-wildlife reserve in KwaZulu-Natal and, along with sections of the iSimangaliso Wetland Park, jointly the oldest park in Africa. The permanent water of the Hluhluwe and the Black and White iMfolozi Rivers combined with an abundance of high-quality vegetation sustains large populations of **giraffes**, **blue wildebeests**, **Burchell's zebras**, **impalas**, **nyalas**, **greater kudus** and many other herbivores. Additionally, it's the only reserve in the province with a full complement of the 'Big Six' – **lions**, **leopards**, **elephants**, **buffaloes** and both **rhino** species. While the cats are infrequently seen, Hluhluwe-iMfolozi is an excellent reserve to view elephants, buffaloes and the **white rhino**, a species which owes its existence to the park.

RHINO SANCTUARY Hluhluwe-iMfolozi was set aside with the specific purpose of protecting Africa's tiny relict population of **southern white rhinos**, an action which saved the species from certain extinction. In the sanctuary of this single location, white rhino numbers have blossomed; from only 25 at the end of the 19th century, there are now over 9000 in South Africa alone, all of them descended from Hluhluwe-iMfolozi stock. Hluhluwe-iMfolozi itself is home to 1800 – far more than the combined total of all other African countries – and visitors are virtually guaranteed to see some. They are more or less evenly distributed throughout the reserve, favouring low-lying wooded grasslands and vleis (seasonally flooded wetlands) rather than the park's many hills and high points. Among the best spots to look are the chain of grassland waterholes along the main route from Memorial Gate to Hilltops Camp (in the Hluhluwe section).

Elephants and **buffaloes** are also easily seen. Try the Sontuli, Ngolotsha and Okhukho Loops in iMfolozi. The loops follow the course of the Black iMfolozi River, often

WILDLIFE HIGHLIGHTS

» The rhino capital of Africa, optimal also for spotting elephants and buffaloes » Increasingly common spottings of African wild dogs » Guided night drives – offering, with luck, the chance to see lions, leopards, spotted hyenas and small carnivores » Large numbers of giraffes, Burchell's zebras, blue wildebeests, nyalas, greater kudus, impalas, chacma baboons and vervet monkeys » Prolific birdlife (425 species), including many raptors used as a highway by elephants moving in their regular pattern between iMfolozi and Hluhluwe. The lookout points along the rivers are productive spots to wait for them with binoculars, particularly towards sunset when they are more active: sometimes the main breeding herd of more than 100 animals passes beneath the patient observer. Buffaloes, particularly bulls in small bachelor groups or alone (known in South Africa as 'dagha boys') also use the rivercourses. During the heat of the day, dagha boys take refuge among the reeds and African date palms lining the river banks: keep watch for them when driving through river crossings such as those along the Hippo Pools Rd (in Hluhluwe) and along the main circular road in iMfolozi.

HIDES, HILLS & HIGH PLACES The dense bush and widespread waterways make viewing of less conspicuous wildlife more of a challenge. Most of the common herbivores – **giraffes, blue wildebeests, Burchell's zebras, waterbucks, impalas, nyalas, greater kudus** and **warthogs** – can be seen anywhere in the reserve but the

hides are probably the most rewarding way to observe them. The dry season (between June and October) when the rivers are low is the best time to invest effort in the hides – assuming they have water (ask staff members at the camp reception desks before setting out). Thiyeni Hide (in Hluhluwe) is probably the best and is situated ideally for early-morning photography. It's also a favourite site for **rhinos** to wallow in the

SOUTH AFRICA

RHINOCEROSES, HLUHLUWE-IMFOLOZI GAME RESERVE

mud and take advantage of the scratching post on the opposite bank – two activities which play an important role in controlling ticks and other external parasites. **Warthogs** and **buffaloes** indulge in the same behaviours. It pays to make a brief reconnaissance trip to the waterholes on nearby Seme Loop; if there is plentiful water around, waiting at the hide is far less productive.

iMfolozi is more prone to water shortages than the Hluhluwe section and in very dry periods, Mphafa Hide may be the only water source between the White and Black iMfolozi Rivers. As well as visits from the large browsers and grazers, it sometimes delivers sightings of **lions**, more abundant in iMfolozi than Hluhluwe. Carnivores can survive for long periods without drinking because the body fluids of their prey satisfy their requirements, but most cats will drink daily if water is available. Lions usually drink early in the morning or late in the afternoon but they readily spend the entire day sleeping near waterholes. Look carefully under bushes and trees around waterpoints: sometimes, only the flick of an ear or tail-tip reveals their presence. If you don't see any, book a guided night drive at any of the camps to search for hunting lions, as well as **leopards**, **spotted hyenas** and small carnivores including **large-spotted genets** and **white-tailed mongooses**.

There are many high points and lookout points in the reserve, another fruitful tactic for spotting wildlife. From the lookout points near Hilltops Camp, you are likely to see **buffalo** herds and enjoy excellent viewing of many raptors, including **jackal buzzards**, **martial eagles**, **crowned eagles** and various **vultures**, which ride the thermals in their search for prey and carcasses. The spotting scope in front of the Hilltops restaurant is well worth the nominal fee. The lookout points along the Hluhluwe River near Sisuzu are the most likely points to see **hippos** (which only occur in Hluhluwe), and **bushbucks** can be found in the tall reeds along the river banks.

NEW ADDITIONS The **African wild dogs** in iMfolozi are the only protected population in the province. Although they were once reduced to single figures in the region, a reintroduction project initiated in 1998 offered new hope, and there are currently about 80 individuals – a more than tenfold increase. Wild dogs can move enormous distances in a day and only localise their movements when there are young pups in the den. Your best chance of seeing them is to ask about recent sightings at camp reception or else look out for the marked wild-dog research vehicle; researchers radiotrack them daily and are happy to provide tips about places to look. They may also have information on **cheetahs**, another species whose numbers have been recently replenished and whose movements are difficult to predict. The open low-lying areas in Hluhluwe near Memorial Gate are good cheetah habitat.

OSTEOPHAGIA

It's little known and perhaps surprising, but many herbivores occasionally gnaw on bones. Known as osteophagia, the behaviour arises among animals whose diets are deficient in phosphorus, calcium or other trace elements. It is particularly common where there are sandy soils which, being very permeable, are poor at retaining minerals. As a result, 'sandveld' plants tend to be low in vital elements and herbivores are forced to seek them elsewhere. Winter is the most likely time to observe osteophagia: as plants on poor soils ripen and dry they translocate minerals to the roots, leaving the above-ground foliage with as little as one-tenth the normal level of phosphorus and calcium. Animals resorting to bone-chewing may satisfy their nutritional requirements, but the behaviour carries a high cost. Bones often harbour the bacterium which causes botulism, a disease which results in paralysis of all the muscles and eventual death.

FEVER TREES

Clustered wherever there are well-watered soils (along rivers, around pans and on floodplains), the yellow-barked *Acacia xanthophloea* is better known by its common name, the fever tree. So convinced were early explorers that the tree's powdery, yellow-green bark harboured malaria, that men would cover their faces with handkerchiefs as they passed the trees. In fact, the fever tree's peculiar bark is harmless and its unusual colour arises from photosynthetic pigments rather than pathogens. Even so, it does have an association with malaria, albeit a blameless one. Fever trees grow best in a moist humid environment, the same conditions that the malaria-carrying *Anopheles* mosquito relies on for breeding. So wherever people encountered malaria at its worst, fever trees were typically abundant. Today, except for rare and isolated cases, Hluhluwe-iMfolozi is largely free of malaria but the beautiful fever tree is still widespread.

IMPALAS, HLUHLUWE-IMFOLOZI GAME RESERVE

SOUTH AFRICA

LOCATION 920km west of Johannesburg. Entry from South Africa, Namibia or Botswana. Namibian routes involve at least 300km of gravel as does the final 60km from the South African side, but are negotiable by 2WD. All Botswanan routes require 4WD.

FACILITIES Guided night drives, information centre at Twee Rivieren, Predator Information Centre at Nossob.

ACCOMMODATION Three permanent camps (Twee Rivieren, Mata Mata and Nossob), with a variety of accommodation on the South African side, plus wilderness camps and a luxury lodge. Botswanan side has four basic camp sites (Two Rivers, Rooiputs, Polentswe and the Game Scout Camp in the Mabuasehube section) with no facilities.

WILDLIFE RHYTHMS Wildlife congregates in the riverbeds following rain (February to May). December to January marks the birth peak of the springboks, attracting a great variety of predators. This is also the period when some small carnivores have their litters.

CONTACT South Africa: SANP Central Reservations (☎ 012-428 9111; www.sanparks .org), Kgalagadi park office (☎ 054-561 2000). Botswana: Department of Wildlife & National Parks (☎ 03-918 0774; dwnp@gov.bw).

KGALAGADI TRANSFRONTIER PARK

Comprising the Kalahari Gemsbok National Park on the South African side and the Gemsbok-Mabuasehube complex in Botswana, this was the first Southern African peace park. Most tourism activity happens on the 2WD-friendly South African side but if visitors have a 4WD and are entirely self-sufficient, they can stay on the Botswanan side. Take note though, aside from a three-day 4WD wilderness trail (advance bookings essential), the road network on the Botswanan side is undeveloped, except in the Mabuasehube section. Logistical constraints aside, the aridity of the Kalahari forbids intensive human occupation, resulting in one of the most pristine areas in Southern Africa. Excellent visibility and wildlife congregations along the relatively fertile riverbeds provide some of South Africa's most rewarding viewing, and it is a favourite park for wildlife photographers and other visitors seeking moments of action and interaction.

ABUNDANT LIFE AMONG THE DUNES Despite its inhospitable appearance, the enduring presence of arid-adapted vegetation ensures there is abundant life. In the central and eastern areas of the park, extensive duinriet grasslands bind the sand, providing a firm foundation for low bushes and ground-hugging shrubs such as the brandy bush and tsama melon. With little available cover, the few large acacia trees scattered among the dune vegetation are worth a closer look. They provide much-needed shade for Kalahari animals (look carefully – during the heat of the day, animals usually lie down and are easily missed), and in some cases also harbour important food sources. Most common of the dune trees, the widely dispersed shepherd's tree with characteristic pale whitish-grey bark bears highly nutritious leaves year-round, attracting **antelopes** which also relish the flowers. Look near the trees for the **eland** (males weigh up to 900kg), predominantly a browser and able to feed

WILDLIFE HIGHLIGHTS
» Excellent for aerial and terrestrial predators; lions, spotted hyenas and brown hyenas are readily sighted, and the Auob riverbed is excellent for cheetahs » Cape foxes, African wild cats and numerous other small carnivores are exceptional » Unparalleled chances to view birds of prey, with 52 raptor species » Impressive summer congregations of antelopes – springboks, blue wildebeests and gemsboks – along the riverbeds

on leaves beyond the reach of other antelopes. Restricted almost exclusively to the dunes and rarely seen in the riverbeds, their herds may number in the thousands where there is a high concentration of browse.

The dunes are most productive for wildlife-watching from June through to the first rains in February, but the large herds tend to be widely dispersed. During this period, rather than driving long distances, it is often more rewarding to wait at dune waterholes: try Vaalpan, Moravet and Kielie Krankie. The largest Kalahari resident, the **giraffe**, has recently been reintroduced and the small herd appears to have settled around the Craig Lockhart waterhole near Mata Mata Rest Camp.

LIFE ALONG THE RIVERBEDS Less scenic than the dunes, the two main riverbeds of the park – the Nossob and the Auob – are the real focal points for wildlife-viewing. The rivers rarely flow but deep groundwater allows long-rooted blackthorn trees, raisin bushes and other desert plants to persist year-round. Drivers usually hurtle past them on their way to waterholes, but each is a mini-ecosystem in itself. Small clusters

WATCHING TIPS

Don't be afraid to sit and wait in the Kalahari. In winter, wildlife is drawn to the numerous pans and artificial boreholes (with attendant windmills), particularly the 'sweetwater' waterholes – as opposed to the brackish, less palatable ones. Good places to try include Leeuwdril, Kij Kij, Rooiputs, Union's End, Cubitje Quap, Kwang and Kannaguass in the Nossob, and most windmills in the Auob. Ask at the camp offices which waterholes are active. Smaller attractions abound in the camps. Nossob Rest Camp is one of the best places to see Cape foxes, which hover around the camping ground at night, while ground squirrels will come running at the sound of an opening food packet at all the camps. Twee Rivieren Rest Camp has extremely tame scaly-feathered finches.

of **pale chanting goshawks**, particularly when perched low on bushes or fallen trees, usually indicate a small hunter on the prowl. Most often it will be a **honey badger**, frequently active during the day, particularly when it is cool. The goshawks follow the badger, gathering around as it digs for rodents or reptiles and snapping up anything that escapes the badger's notice. Occasionally the solitary **slender mongoose**, distinctive with its rich ruddy-brown fur and black-tipped tail, attracts the goshawks' opportunistic attention.

SOUTH AFRICA

LION ON THE CREST OF A DUNE, KGALAGADI TRANSFRONTIER PARK

Aside from the goshawks, the riverbeds are excellent for raptor-viewing, including **bateleur** and **martial eagles**; **secretary birds**; **lanner, red-necked** and **pygmy falcons**; and **white-backed** and **lappet-faced vultures**.

During the rainy season, usually between February and May, a spectacular eruption of flowering and growth in the riverbed plants draws animals in from the surrounding dunes where they spend the dry winter searching for sustenance. Large aggregations of the nomadic antelope species – **springboks, gemsboks, red hartebeests** and **blue wildebeests** – converge on the riverbeds in this season of plenty. Breeding males often remain in the riverbed year-round, defending their territories in anticipation of the arrival of the herds; this is contrary to the popular belief that they have been evicted from the herd, and explains why single male springboks, blue wildebeests and red hartebeests are found spaced evenly along the riverbeds, often with no other antelopes in sight. With the arrival of immigrants from the dunes, they attempt to herd females into their patch and mate with any that are receptive, while also driving off challenging males. The 'rut', as it is known, is a period of intense activity sometimes restricted to only one to two weeks. The timing is never predictable, but it generally happens following the rains – a rich time to visit.

PREDATOR TERRITORY The bounty of prey species in the riverbeds inevitably attracts their predators, most conspicuously **lions**. The absence of dense, thorn-ridden vegetation frees their coats of the burrs, scars and knots inflicted on their bushveld cousins, and Kalahari lions are often considered the most beautiful of their species. **Leopards** (easily missed unless one looks carefully) use the tangled camelthorns along the riverbeds to cache their kills, while **cheetahs** hunt **springboks** establishing their breeding territories following the rains. Clans of **spotted hyenas** are here – usually seen on early-morning visits to waterholes. Their largely solitary cousin, the **brown hyena**, is restricted to Southern Africa's semiarid regions and the Kalahari is one of the best places to see them.

Less obvious predators are easily viewed here also. During early summer, **black-backed jackals**, **Cape foxes** and **bat-eared foxes** den along the riverbeds, providing excellent opportunities to see newly emerged pups playing outside their sandy retreats. The Kalahari is also a haven for the **African wild cat**. This progenitor of the domestic cat is threatened by interbreeding with its tame cousin, and it is only in very isolated regions where the pure African wild cat persists. Look carefully among the calcite ridges lining the riverbeds (especially along the Nossob near the picnic area south of Dikbaardskolk waterhole): wild cats and other small hunters are readily seen searching the little caves and crannies for prey.

TSAMA MELONS & GEMSBOK CUCUMBERS

In a land of so little water, two unusual plants provide the inhabitants of the Kalahari with vital moisture. The fruits of the watermelon-like tsama and the deep-rooted gemsbok cucumber comprise 95% water and are sought out by many Kalahari creatures. Birds such as glossy starlings, grey hornbills and pied crows eat the flesh, as do desert rodents which consume the nutrient-rich seeds. Large herbivores in the Kalahari also eat the fruit and even consume the cucumber's extremely bitter roots in their efforts to gain moisture. When water is particularly scarce, even meat-eaters may resort to frugivory (eating fruit), and hyenas, honey badgers and occasionally large cats devour tsamas during the dry winter. Even when eaten, a discarded tsama melon can be a source of water. Dried, eaten-out tsama shells act as mini-reservoirs for rainwater – a bounty in a place where puddles seldom form.

THE SPRING IN SPRINGBOK

If you spend any time watching springboks, particularly youngsters, you'll probably see them stotting. This is the name given to the stiff-legged, bouncing gait adopted by a number of antelope species, apparently when they spot predators. In the springbok, stotting is raised to spectacular heights in which they arch the back and bounce on all four legs at once in gymnastic 3m-high leaps. Completing the display, they flare the white, erectile dorsal crest known as the 'pronk', which is why South Africans call the behaviour 'pronking'. Terminology aside, what function does it play? The most commonly cited theory says that stotting signals to a predator that it's been seen and that the stotter is too fit and agile to bother wasting energy trying to catch. But while predators do elicit the display, springboks pronk at almost anything that causes tension or excitement. A wave of pronking often ripples through a springbok herd as it approaches water and young animals pronk repeatedly in exuberant play with one another or perhaps simply to gain bearings on unfamiliar surroundings. Even distant thunder and lightning heralding a brewing storm can be enough to set off a chain reaction of bouncing springboks.

SPRINGBOKS, KGALAGADI TRANSFRONTIER PARK

SOUTH AFRICA

SOUTH AFRICA

PILANESBERG NATIONAL PARK

The entire boundary of this national park is formed by the rim of an extinct 1300-million-year-old volcano. Rising 600m above the flat bushveld plains, concentric rings of mountains, created when the volcano collapsed inwards, provide the setting for one of South Africa's most diverse and accessible reserves. Founded in 1979, the park is the site of one of Africa's largest wildlife restocking efforts – almost 6000 animals were translocated here in a venture called Operation Genesis in the 1970s. The project was highly successful and today Pilanesberg is not only one of the best places in South Africa to see wildlife, it is also a source of animals for capture and translocation to other young reserves.

LOCATION Approximately 110km northwest of Pretoria. All access routes are tarred, internal roads are tar or well-maintained gravel.

FACILITIES Over 180km of wildlife-watching roads, guided night drives, guided and self-guided walks, lookout points, hides, bird aviary at Manyane Complex, sunken hide at water level at Kwa Maritane Lodge.

ACCOMMODATION Various chalets, cottages and lodges. Camping ground and caravan site at Manyane and Bakgatla. The Sun City Complex with hotel accommodation for hundreds is located on the southern boundary.

WILDLIFE RHYTHMS Between September and November, a flush of new growth following annual burning produces excellent wildlife-watching in the open areas. Over summer (November to January) the grass is longer but many herbivores drop their young and the birding is excellent with the arrival of many migratory bird species.

CONTACT Bookings office (☎ 014-555 1600/5356).

WHERE DESERT & BUSHVELD MERGE Lying at the confluence of two major vegetation zones, Pilanesberg contains fauna that is an unusual combination of the arid-adapted inhabitants typical of Kalahari thornveld and the bushveld species occurring in moist woodland savanna. The wide valleys between the concentric mountains provide excellent vistas for spotting a wide diversity of species. This is one of the few parks in South Africa where **springboks** (an arid-zone species) and **impalas** graze in mixed herds or where **gemsboks**, **greater kudus**, **elands** and **sable antelopes** share the gentler hillsides; rockier hills are home to **mountain reedbucks** and **klipspringers**.

In the summer (November to January), low-lying areas in the valleys receive abundant water, giving rise to nutrient-rich 'sweetveld' grasslands that attract many grazing species. Large congregations of **Burchell's zebras** (one of the most abundant ungulates in the park), **blue wildebeests**, **red hartebeests**, **tsessebes** and **warthogs** collect in the valleys, particularly in the central area around Mankwe Dam. By winter, these areas tend to be overgrazed and animals disperse onto the

WILDLIFE HIGHLIGHTS
» High wildlife diversity, with a mixture of arid and moist woodland species, including over 20 species of ungulates, all readily viewable » Rewarding Big Five viewing, though buffaloes are uncommon – found mostly in out-of-the-way areas » Chance to see cheetahs and African wild dogs, plus frequent sightings of brown hyenas » Over 300 recorded bird species, representing a combination of arid-zone and bushveld species

hillsides – still easily seen but in smaller, less conspicuous herds.

A PLETHORA OF BIRDS Pilanesberg's range of environments also provides suitable habitat for diverse bird fauna. The world's heaviest flying bird, the **kori bustard**, shares the grasslands with **ostriches**, **secretary birds** and many smaller species such as three species of whydahs (**pin-tailed**, **shaft-tailed** and **paradise**) and the similar-looking but not closely related **long-tailed** and **red-collared widows**. **Lesser masked weavers** and vivid **golden** and **red bishops** inhabit vleis (seasonally flooded wetlands) while **masked weavers** build their nests in trees overhanging the water (there's a good example of this at Tilodi Dam).

At Mankwe Dam, a hide built out over the water provides viewing of **hippo** pods and **waterbucks**, and sightings of **waterbirds** are excellent. A dozen species of the **heron** and **egret** family have been recorded here as well as ubiquitous **African fish eagles**, **hamerkops**, **white-faced ducks** and **Egyptian geese**. **Pied**, **giant** and **pygmy kingfishers** also occur and if you're very early in the morning you might see **Cape clawless otters** from the hide. Other notable birds among the

---

👁 WATCHING TIPS

Stop every so often and scan the rocky hillsides with binoculars, particularly along Nkakane and Dithabaneng Drs. Lions use high points to search the valleys for prey, and leopards are most often seen in the hills. Other inhabitants of rocky hills, including caracals, klipspringers and black eagles, are very easily missed unless you spend a bit of extra time searching. Fascinating research projects on lions, rhinos, African wild dogs, cheetahs and elephants are conducted at Pilanesberg. Look for the research vehicles with distinctive 'Ecological Monitoring' stickers and ask the researchers for information; they are very approachable and a great source of recent sightings.

300-odd species total include four species of **francolins**, (**Natal**, **Swainson's**, **crested** and **coqui**), all readily seen along the roadside, and **blue cranes**, **chinspot batises**, **pearl-spotted owls** and **Kalahari robins**.

RHINOS & ELEPHANTS Really big wildlife is easily spotted; aside from the large parks of KwaZulu-Natal, Pilanesberg is one of the finest places to view both rhino species. The largely solitary and retiring **black rhino** is the more difficult to find, favouring gully thickets (dense forests growing where two hillsides meet) and the thick vegetation along the base of

HERD OF ZEBRAS, PILANESBERG NATIONAL PARK

the hills during the day. They are readily seen in more open habitat at night – book a guided night drive. The more common **white rhino** is abundant here and it is not unusual to see upwards of 20 in a single day, particularly if you spend an entire day driving during the mild winter when they are more active on the open grasslands.

Elephants are a common sight anywhere in the park; stop at the lookout points (particularly along Lenong View) with some good binoculars, and scan the wooded savannas if you don't encounter them while driving. Pilanesberg is unusual in that some male elephants occasionally form associations with rhinos – extraordinary to observe but apparently the undesirable result of the historical translocations.

PILANESBERG'S PREDATORS Large carnivores are well represented at Pilanesberg, though some are fairly recent arrivals. **Lions** reintroduced from Namibia's Etosha National Park have only been resident since 1994 but have thrived since their re-establishment. The pride territories meet around the wildlife-rich central region; check the large dams (Mankwe, Makorwane, Lengau, Malatse and Batlako), especially during the dry months (April to October). Rangers post recent sightings at the Manyane Gate and Pilanesberg Centre, and in the early morning territorial roars can help pinpoint their location. Far less vocal, **leopards** are

abundant at Pilanesberg. The red rocks at the junction of Mankwe Way and Kubu Dr produce the most consistent sightings – stop and scan with binoculars. Leopards can be difficult to spot during the day, but night drives (available at all camps) see them frequently, and another nocturnal predator, the **brown hyena**, is virtually guaranteed. Brown hyenas also regularly visit the Scavenger Hide at Mothata and there has been an active den in the rocky hillside along Ntshwe Dr for a number of years. Another hyena species, the entirely insectivorous **aardwolf**, is often seen among the clustered termitaria (termite mounds) near the junction of Nkakane and Tshepe Drs and along Mankwe Way.

Night drives reveal other rarely seen species. **Lesser bushbabies** perform extraordinary acrobatics on the tips of thorn trees in their efforts to capture insect prey. They readily hunt moths and other insects attracted to the glow of spotlights but rarely sit still for long: branch tips, while good for hunting, are exposed and they risk attack from **spotted eagle owls** and two **genet** species, the **large-spotted** and **small-spotted** (distinguishable by their tail tips, which are black and white respectively). **Cape porcupines**, the largest rodents in Africa, are frequently seen, and stocky **Jameson's red rock rabbits**, rarely spotted elsewhere, are common in the rocks along the road up to the Fish Eagle picnic area overlooking Mankwe Dam.

PACHYDERMS AS PEACEMAKERS

As with numerous other South African reserves re-establishing wildlife, most of Pilanesberg's founding elephants were juveniles when released and they matured without the normal social interactions of complete herds. Lacking the stabilising influence of mature dominant bulls, young males reach sexual maturity prematurely and occasionally display aberrant behaviour misdirected at rhinos. Often the bulls simply associate with them but in a number of incidents – at least 40 were recorded – they attacked and killed rhinos. Today, improved drugs and capture techniques enable the translocation of fully grown elephants – impossible when the first Pilanesberg introductions were made two decades ago. In a fascinating experiment aiming to establish a normal dominance hierarchy and suppress the young males' unruly behaviour, six huge males that towered above Pilanesberg's juveniles were captured in Kruger National Park and released in Pilanesberg in 1998. Following the arrival of the 'peace keepers', the rhino-killing stopped.

NIGHT SIGHTS

Pilanesberg's guided night drives provide excellent chances of observing nocturnal predators on the prowl. To spot them, the rangers will be looking for eyeshine. Eyeshine is created by a reflective layer of cells called the tapetum lucidum which rebounds 'missed' light to the retina for a second grab at imaging. Many diurnal species, including most antelopes, have a tapetum layer (don't be fooled by eyeshine alone when spotlighting!) but it's best developed in night-time hunters like the cats which have as many as 15 layers of the mirrored, tapetum cells. No one has tested exactly how effective it is in wild species, but the humble domestic cat can see six times better in darkness than people.

Even more basic than the reflective refinement of the tapetum, good night vision requires rhodopsin or 'visual purple', a light-sensitive compound produced with vitamin A. But the best source of vitamin A is in plants and tubers like yams, beyond the dietary reach of most meat-eaters. So they rely on herbivores to process vitamin A into conveniently accessible packages stored in the liver, lungs and other tissues. By doing so, the prey unintentionally equips the predator with its nocturnal advantage.

SOUTH AFRICA

RED-BILLED OXPECKER ON A GIRAFFE'S BACK, PILANESBERG NATIONAL PARK

SOUTH AFRICA
ADDO ELEPHANT NATIONAL PARK

LOCATION 72km northeast of Port Elizabeth. Sealed road accessible year-round. Internal roads are well-maintained gravel.

FACILITIES 75km of wildlife-watching roads, lookout points, hide at Spekboom waterhole, 12km walk in botanical reserve, waterhole, birdwatching hide, guided night drives.

ACCOMMODATION Variety of huts and cottages sleeping two to six, bush camp, camping ground, caravan site and luxury lodges.

WILDLIFE RHYTHMS The spring flush of flowers (September to November) creates unforgettable scenes of elephants grazing in fields of daisies. Birding is best from September to April when summer migrants arrive.

CONTACT SANP Central Reservations (☎ 012-428 9111; www.sanparks.org), Addo park office (☎ 042-233 8600).

●●● WATCHING TIPS

Spend time around the main reception complex and waterhole hide for some excellent birding opportunities. Malachite, black and double-collared sunbirds feed on flowering aloes from May to September while the summer months (November to February) bring breeding Cape weavers and red bishops to the reeds around the pan. Others such as African sedge warblers, malachite kingfishers, spotted-backed weavers and black-crowned night herons are regularly seen at the waterhole.

ADDO ELEPHANT NATIONAL PARK

As its name suggests, **elephants** are the great attraction of this park, home of the last remaining population in the Eastern Cape. Largely devoid of tall trees, Addo's low-canopy forest of thornbush and succulent shrubs affords excellent viewing prospects for the park's namesake as they browse on densely clustered spekboom – the dominant plant and the elephants' main food source. The park also protects the world's largest breeding population of **Cape gannets**, and its second-largest breeding population of **African penguins**, although these areas are not under direct park management and are not usually accessible to the general public.

SANCTUARY FOR MEGA-HERBIVORES Originating from only 11 animals – the survivors of intense persecution by ivory hunters and farmers – Addo's **elephants** can probably recognise every other individual in the population, creating remarkable opportunities to observe social interactions at key points. In the summer, waterholes (especially Hapoor Dam) attract family after family, which meet in a kind of social 'congress' and take their turn at the water. From near-extinction earlier this century, there are now more than 450 elephants in Addo, making it one of the densest populations in South Africa: on a hot afternoon, you could easily see half the entire population in two to three hours at the pans.

Other Cape mammals reduced to relict populations find refuge here. The **buffalo** is usually a grazer, but in the spekboomveld thicket it survives largely by browsing the thick bush. Unlike the huge herds seen on open plains elsewhere, Addo buffaloes form small, matriarchal family groups periodically joined by the largely solitary males. Look out for nocturnal visits of these unusual social groups at the spotlit waterhole near the main reception complex at the rest camp. This is also a good site for watching endangered **black rhinos**. Originally reintroduced from Kenya in the 1960s, modern genetic analysis

WILDLIFE HIGHLIGHTS
» Near-certain close-up viewing of elephants » Common sightings of ostriches, secretary birds, Burchell's zebras, red hartebeests and meerkats; black rhinos and buffaloes occur but are shy » Bushbucks, yellow and small grey mongooses and many unusual reptiles – including Southern dwarf chameleons and the endemic Tasman's girdled lizard » The best place in Africa to view unique flightless dung beetles

revealed them to be a distinct subspecies and the population is gradually being replaced with Namibian rhinos – genetically identical to the 'Cape' rhino originally inhabiting this area until the last one was shot in 1853. Other mammals to look out for are the very tame **meerkats** easily seen along the Woodlands-Harpoor Loop. The Gorah Loop grasslands are scenically dull but home to **Burchell's zebras**, **elands**, **red hartebeests**, **bat-eared foxes** and **black-backed jackals** as well as **ostriches**, **secretary birds**, and South Africa's national bird, the endangered **blue crane**.

Addo's dense, hedgelike bush includes over 500 species of plant, best experienced on the Spekboom Trail. Established as a botanical reserve, the trail was fenced off from elephants, rhinos and buffaloes in the 1950s. Freed from browsing pressure for over 40 years, the vegetation here looks quite different to the rest of the park. The walk also reveals some smaller residents, easily missed when driving. Look out for the **flightless dung beetle** and **giant golden orb-web spiders**, whose unruly webs span the bush paths in the early morning – the female spider is 10 times the size of the male and most likely to be seen. Addo is rich in tortoises and while the 15-to-20kg **leopard tortoise** is readily seen from vehicles, check the herbaceous ground cover for less conspicuous **angulate tortoises** and the tiny **parrot-beaked tortoise**. At head height,

the canopy shelters other secretive reptiles including **southern dwarf chameleons** and endemic **Tasman's girdled lizards**. Walk quietly to improve your chances of encountering **yellow** and **small grey mongooses** and elusive, small antelopes including **bushbucks** and **grey duikers**.

SOUTH AFRICA

ROLLING IN IT

Once widespread in South Africa, the unique flightless dung beetle or scarab *(Circellium bacchus)* is now restricted to a few scattered populations in the Eastern Cape; the largest is at Addo. The only scarab that has lost the power of flight, it thrives in Addo, which lacks flying competitors. They eat mainly elephant dung but prefer the more pliable droppings of buffaloes for 'brood balls'. The female constructs and rolls the ball (with the male following) to a suitable site where it is buried and subterranean mating follows. A single egg is laid and following hatching, the larva feeds in the dungball for four months until it emerges as an adult. Elephants readily walk along the roads and drop large deposits of dung – irresistible to the beetles. Flightless dung beetles are endangered and one of their main enemies is people – in cars! Please heed the signs and avoid driving over beetles or the dung which may harbour dozens of them.

ELEPHANTS CHASING A BLACK-BACKED JACKAL FROM A WATER HOLE, ADDO ELEPHANT NATIONAL PARK

SOUTH AFRICA

LOCATION 130km west of Upington. Sealed road accessible year-round.

FACILITIES Wildlife drive network, lookout points, three-day hiking trails, short walks. Combined canoe/cycling/walking excursions and guided night drives (book at park office at the rest camp).

ACCOMMODATION Chalets sleeping two to four, camping ground and caravan site.

WILDLIFE RHYTHMS The falls are most spectacular following the rains in January to April – also when most plants flower, attracting pollen and nectar-eating birds.

CONTACT SANP Central Reservations (☎ 012-428 9111; www.sanparks.org), Augrabies Falls park office (☎ 054-452 9200).

👀 WATCHING TIPS

The gorge near Echo Lookout has had a resident pair of black eagles nesting for some years. They are readily seen if you wait patiently at the lookout. The breeding season (April to June) is particularly rewarding as they make frequent passes at eye level carrying nesting materials. Check the camping ground shower blocks at night for a giant of the gecko family – Bibron's thick-toed gecko.

AUGRABIES FALLS NATIONAL PARK

The original human inhabitants of this area, the Khoi people, called the Augrabies Falls 'Akoerabis' (the place of great noise). This applies only to the 56m-high Main Falls themselves; otherwise this is a park where silence dominates. The isolation and rocky desert environment makes Augrabies one of South Africa's most peaceful locations, and it is worth a visit even just to enjoy the total quiet at Oranjekom or Arrow Point lookouts with their spectacular dawn and dusk views.

KLIPSPRINGERS & MORE Tourism activities centre on the Orange River Gorge – 18km of steep-sided canyons and ravines that can be seen from various lookout points or explored more closely by canoe. Wildlife congregates along the rivercourse though you are more likely to see it from the wildlife-watching roads that traverse numerous small tributaries on the southern side of the gorge. This area is one of the finest sites in South Africa for viewing **klipspringers**, rivalled only by Karoo National Park. These stocky little antelopes mate for life, so when you see one it's virtually certain that its mate is nearby. Early mornings, especially when they lamb in spring and early summer (September to January), reveal them to be surprisingly playful. **Pale-winged starlings** often perch on the klipspringers, using their long beaks to probe ears and under tails for ticks.

Springboks, ostriches and **giraffes** (the last is recently reintroduced) are also frequently seen along the roadside close to the rest camp and create some unique photo opportunities against the moonscape-like backdrop. Take the drive over the scorched-looking Swartrante Hills to Echo Corner and Fountain Lookout for a chance to see **elands** and **gemsboks**. Augrabies is also home to the 'desert' **black rhino**, largest of the four black rhino subspecies and adapted for extreme aridity.

The main viewing area around Main Falls offers smaller but no less rewarding attractions. It's worth spending an hour or two at the numerous **rock dassie** colonies on the paths between the reception complex and the Main Falls.

WILDLIFE HIGHLIGHTS
» Excellent for tame (ie used to vehicles) klipspringers
» Frequent sightings of giraffes, elands, springboks, rock dassies and black eagles » Leopards present, although seldom seen » The camping ground is visited by Cape ground squirrels and small grey mongooses while the falls area crawls with Augrabies flat lizards.

Small grey mongooses hunt among the reeds here, subsisting largely on small rodents such as **striped mice**, seen darting across the paths. However, they also make regular forays into the dassie colonies, presumably looking for unguarded youngsters born around December. Adult dassies, however, are vigorous defenders of their offspring and have modified incisors which act as defensive tusks – more than a match for any mongoose. If a mongoose is discovered in the colony, dassies band together and chase it furiously, an extraordinary scene sometimes played out in front of the main restaurant.

In winter, the bright-yellow flowers of the quiver tree (kokerboom) attract a rich variety of birds including **lesser double-collared sunbirds**, **dusky sunbirds** and **scimitar-billed woodhoopoes**. Also in and around the camp, Augrabies' reptile fauna is best seen during the short self-guided walks. Apart from very conspicuous **Augrabies flat lizards**, most species are shy but walkers occasionally encounter **sand snakes** and **black-necked spitting cobras**. **Puff adders**, **horned adders** and **Cape cobras** may also be seen, particularly on cold mornings when they are sluggish and sun themselves on the rocks. The short Dassie Trail between the rest camp and Moon Rock crosses numerous reed-lined streams where **Nile monitors** up to 2m long are sometimes seen.

AUGRABIES FLAT LIZARDS

With its spectacular colouring and existing at one of the highest densities recorded for any lizard in the world, the Augrabies flat lizard (*Platysaurus broadleyi*) is impossible to miss. Easily overlooked once their sheer abundance no longer surprises, the apparent lizard chaos at the falls is actually a complex society based on 'dear enemies' and discriminating females. The flamboyant males establish territories where the black fly (their main food source) emerges from the river in swarms. Territories are fiercely contested but males don't waste energy confronting neighbours who can maintain the status quo – the 'dear enemy'. Instead, they continually repel intrusions by 'floater' males – individuals without a territory. Flashing them with a vivid orange, sometimes yellow, abdomen indicates their dominant status and floaters are wise to retreat or risk being attacked. And the reason territories are so important? Females, of course. They congregate where flies are most abundant, so males with good territories inevitably attract more mates.

GIRAFFE, AUGRABIES FALLS NATIONAL PARK

LOCATION 245km north of Durban. Sealed road accessible year-round: beware of hippos on the R618 tar road after dark.

FACILITIES Wildlife-watching roads, guided ferry trips, turtle drives, lookout points, five-day self-guided hiking trails, many short walks, Crocodile Centre.

ACCOMMODATION Numerous camps within the park offering a full range of huts, cottages, camping grounds and caravan sites.

WILDLIFE RHYTHMS Late spring through summer (October to March) is best for humpback whales, whale sharks and nesting turtles.

CONTACT KZN Wildlife (☎ 033-845 1000; www .kznwildlife.com).

●● WATCHING TIPS

The camping ground and cabins at Cape Vidal are excellent for viewing samango monkeys; they often enter huts looking for food (even while people are inside), so lock up. Similarly, the camp site at Sodwana Bay attracts very tame troops of banded mongooses looking for hand-outs. Just north of St Lucia town on the road to Cape Vidal, the Crocodile Centre has detailed information and feeding displays about iSimangaliso's top predator – it's worth a look.

ISIMANGALISO WETLAND PARK

Actually comprising 10 separate protected areas linked to the 60km-long St Lucia estuary, iSimangaliso Wetland Park (formerly Greater St Lucia Wetland Park) is one of Southern Africa's most important coastal wetlands. The administrative boundaries are inconsequential to visitors as there are no fences and wildlife moves freely over the entire park. The reserve protects diverse land and water habitats, all interlinked but each with distinctive faunal attractions.

FROM REED BEDS TO CORAL REEFS Of the discrete land ecosystems surrounding Lake St Lucia, the richest in wildlife are the Eastern Shores where the highest vegetated dunes in the world tower over adjacent swamp and grassland. The dune forest is home to **Tonga red squirrels,** who often reveal their presence by extraordinary tail-flicking displays and trilling contact calls. Occasionally they accompany 'bird parties'. Generally a winter phenomenon, bird parties comprise some local specials: **Knysna louries, Woodward's batises, puffbacks, wattle-eyed** and **blue-mantled flycatchers, Natal robins, white-eared barbets, tambourine doves** and others. **Black rhinos, buffaloes, Burchell's zebras, waterbucks, greater kudus, nyalas, bushbucks, warthogs** and the largest population of **southern reedbucks** in Southern Africa also occur on the Eastern Shores. The best way to explore is on the Emoyeni Trail, a five-day hike starting at Mission Rocks. Those with less time can choose from a series of circular day hikes on the self-guided Mziki Trail.

Only 15km away, the Western Shores of the lake receive less than half the rainfall, so the vegetation is dominated by dry woodlands and savannas. Wildlife is less prolific but easier to see. Patches of sandforest are sanctuary to **Neergaard's sunbirds, African broadbills, green coucals** and at least 111 species of **butterfly. Sunis** and **red duikers** are common and frequently seen around the

WILDLIFE HIGHLIGHTS
» Excellent for shy sandforest specials including red duikers, samango monkeys, sunis and Tonga red squirrels
» Abundant hippos, Nile crocodiles and wetland birds in the estuary » Prolific birdlife » Frequent sightings of nyalas, warthogs and southern reedbucks; Burchell's zebras, buffaloes and black rhinos can also be seen

camp sites at False Bay Park – also where **nyalas** were first described to science over 150 years ago.

Lake St Lucia itself is home to 800 **hippos** and at least 1000 **Nile crocodiles** over 1m long, most of them congregating in the Narrows and along the eastern shore of the estuary. You can hire boats in St Lucia town or else join a guided launch with KZN Wildlife. The launch is also the best way to view iSimangaliso's abundant birdlife including **black egrets** (with their 'canopying' feeding display), **black-crowned night herons, goliath herons, woolly-necked storks, African fish eagles, greater flamingos, African spoonbills** and **eastern white pelicans**.

The estuary is linked to the offshore St Lucia Marine Reserve which, with the adjoining Maputaland Marine Reserve, forms one of the largest coastal reserves in Africa. The reefs here offer spectacular diving, best experienced at Sodwana Bay. Apart from the profusion of vibrant **reef fishes** and abundant coral, the warm water also attracts **humpback whales** and **whale sharks**. Sodwana Bay is also a key nesting site for **loggerhead** and **leather-back turtles**. On night drives, **honey badgers** and **side-striped jackals** are sometimes seen raiding their nests.

THE YAWN CHORUS

Apart from physiological reasons, hippos use yawns to intimidate one another. Yawning is a ritualised threat which displays massive recurved canines – capable of inflicting serious damage. Despite living in close social groups, hippos value their own small 'personal space' and constantly yawn and grunt at one another to maintain it. If the yawning display is ignored, the conflict may escalate and it occasionally ends in death, particularly when territorial bulls fight. Hippos also yawn at other threats, humans included. At iSimangaliso the hippos are very used to the high amount of water traffic and rarely pay much attention to boats. However, when they emerge to feed along the obvious paths surrounding the lake, they are extremely dangerous. Short-sighted and nervous on land, they are quick to attack and their massive jaws are quite capable of biting a human in two. If you find yourself the recipient of a hippo yawn, retreat!

SOUTH AFRICA

BLUE DUIKER FORAGING FOR FOOD

ITHALA GAME
RESERVE

SOUTH
AFRICA

SOUTH AFRICA

LOCATION 400km north of Durban. Sealed road accessible year-round.

FACILITIES 80km of wildlife-watching roads, short 4WD trails, lookout points, self-guided nature trails, waterhole hide, short guided walks, guided day and night drives.

ACCOMMODATION Chalets sleeping two, four and six, luxury lodge, three private bush camps and camping ground (no caravans).

WILDLIFE RHYTHMS High winds are a feature of winter (June to August), driving animals to seek cover and generally be less visible. The warm spring and summer months tend to be more productive and are when most young herbivores are born (November to January).

CONTACT KZN Wildlife (☎ 033-845 1000; www .kznwildlife.com).

● ● WATCHING TIPS

Ithala is one of the few big reserves in South Africa where you are permitted to leave your vehicle (but stay in its vicinity). Use this privilege to stop and regularly scan the expansive scenery for wildlife, using binoculars. The marked 'auto-trail' (a booklet is available from the curio shop) along Ngubhu Loop indicates some valuable points of interest, such as an active black eagles' nest.

ITHALA GAME RESERVE

Extremely rugged and scenic terrain is Ithala's hallmark, and its steep mountain roads are the closest two-wheel drivers can come to the feeling one gets from four-wheel driving. It is also an important reserve for high-altitude grasslands, which are heavily affected by intensive agriculture and forestry and now survive in a handful of protected areas. Grasslands and mountains alike extend far into the distance here, and a pair of binoculars will greatly enhance your chances of spotting wildlife from the numerous lookout points.

MOUNTAIN GRASSLANDS Ithala's high plains give sanctuary to a rich assemblage of grazers, ranging in size from the numerous and easily seen **white rhinos** down to the slender **oribi**. This little orange-brown antelope has disappeared from much of its range where habitat-clearing for crops and plantations has destroyed its habitat. Easily alarmed and considered the fastest of the small antelopes, they are not easy to see: scan the grasslands around the airstrip and along Bergvliet Loop with binoculars and watch for the characteristic rocking-horse running motion. Grassfires usually laid towards the end of winter provide new growth which they find irresistible. If you miss them in the park, the small Vryheid Hill Nature Reserve near the town of Vryheid (70km to the west) is a good place to look for them.

Tsessebes also occur in Ithala; it's the only population in KwaZulu-Natal, at the extreme southern limit of their range. They spend most of their time on the plains, near the airstrip. **Blue wildebeests**, **Burchell's zebras**, **elands**, **red hartebeests** and **southern reedbucks** can be seen on the plains, and look for pairs of **secretary birds** striding through the long grass in search of snakes, lizards and small rodents. In the early morning, you might be lucky enough to catch **servals** or **African wild cats** out hunting. They readily walk on roads, probably because these are noiseless and improve their chances of hearing rodents and ground birds in the grass. By keeping your speed below 20km/h, you are less likely to happen upon them suddenly and startle them into cover. Also keep a lookout for their prey including seven **cisticola** species, **Cape** and **bully canaries** and two **longclaw** species

WILDLIFE HIGHLIGHTS
» Very good for viewing both rhino species » Frequent spottings of giraffes, Burchell's zebras, blue wildebeests, impalas, red hartebeests and tsessebes » Local specialities include oribis, nesting bald ibises and black eagles » Excellent birdlife, with 400 recorded species

(**orange-throated** and **yellow-throated**).

Providing protection from the frequent winds that buffet the plains, both the high cliffs and wooded valleys of the Ngubhu Basin and Dakaneni Loop can be rewarding for big wildlife-watchers. **Elephants** and **buffaloes** favour the watercourses deep in the Basin and are best spotted from the lookout points along the Ngubhu Loop. **Black rhinos** occur here, one of the few species that can safely utilise poisonous *Euphorbia* (candelabra) trees. Look for discarded segments of the cactus-like stems for signs of recent feeding activity: if they are still oozing the toxic, white latex-like sap, it means a black rhino isn't far away. Candelabra trees are prominent near the junction of Ngubhu Loop and the 2WD road to Thalu Bush Camp, along the descent into the Dakaneni Loop and above Ntshondwe Camp. Other inhabitants of the Basin, **greater kudus**, **impalas** and **giraffes** (Ithala's emblem), are common among the sweet-thorn woodlands lining the valleys.

High above, the cliffs of the Basin are home to rare **southern bald ibises**. Restricted to a narrow band of montane grasslands in eastern South Africa, they form breeding colonies of up to 100 birds on the safety of steep mountainsides. During July to October look for their untidy, platform-like nests clustered on ledges and in clefts. Also seen on the cliffs, **chacma baboons** make excellent sentries. Their booming alarm bark carries widely in the mountains and usually means one of two things – intrusion by another troop or a sighting of a **leopard** (Ithala's top predator is most often seen along the Ngubhu Loop).

ALOES

Favouring rocky soils and abundant on mountainsides, the mountain aloe (*Aloe marlothii*) is an important source of food during Ithala's lean winters. Unlike most plants, aloes flower from June to August, producing prodigious amounts of nectar and pollen when other food sources are barren. Vervet monkeys and over 40 species of bird are attracted to the plants – the monkeys' orange pollen-coated faces bear testament to the aloes' bounty. The Zulu people are well aware of its value during the lean period and, in addition to delighting in the nectar (the orange faces of children will greet you along the road to the park in winter!), they fashion delicate snares of goat-hair tied to the flowers to trap feeding birds. They also pound the dead, dried leaves to make a potent snuff and use the spiny 'trunk' to make kraals (enclosures) for livestock. Aloes are protected from human utilisation within Ithala's boundaries but are well worth watching for visits from other inhabitants.

GREATER KUDUS, ITHALA GAME RESERVE

SOUTH AFRICA

LOCATION 4km southwest of Beaufort West. Sealed road accessible year-round.

FACILITIES 70km of wildlife-watching roads, 4WD day trails, guided night drives, birdwatching hide, information centre and two interpretive nature trails including one equipped for wheelchairs and blind visitors.

ACCOMMODATION Chalets sleeping three and six, 12-bed huts, camping ground and caravan site.

WILDLIFE RHYTHMS Spring to early summer (September to December) marks the lambing peak for many Karoo herbivores and is also when most Karoo bushes and plants bear their flowers, attracting birdlife.

CONTACT SANP Central Reservations (☎ 012-428 9111; www.sanparks.org), Karoo park office (☎ 023-415 2828/9).

SOUTH AFRICA

WATCHING TIPS

Some of the more wary herbivores spend the daytime in the mountains and only emerge around sunset. Allow a little extra time to make it back to camp before gate-closing and look out for elands, grey rhebucks and Cape mountain zebras in the foothills close to the rest camp.

KAROO NATIONAL PARK

As one of the last protected vestiges of the Great Karoo plains, this park is an excellent site for viewing large herbivores that formerly existed here in huge migratory herds. Most of these representative Karoo species can be seen on the grasslands in the southeast of the park (take the Lammertjiesleegte Loop). Mixed herds of **springboks**, **Burchell's zebras**, **red hartebeests**, **elands**, **Cape mountain zebras** (the second-largest remaining population) and **black wildebeests** as well as **ostriches** give some idea of the sight that must have greeted early European hunters and explorers – though, sadly, at a much reduced scale. Birdlife, however, is largely undiminished, and aside from many species of **raptors** and all three Southern African **bustards** (**kori**, **Stanley's** and **Ludwig's**), it includes Karoo endemics such as the **Karoo korhaan** and **Sclater's** and **Karoo larks**.

KLIPSPRINGERS & RAPTORS IN ABUNDANCE

For those interested in mammals, the greatest attraction here is the ease with which you can view normally timid **klipspringers**. Monogamous and territorial, pairs of these extraordinarily sure-footed antelopes dot the scree slopes of the 150-million-year-old Nuweveld Mountains. Driving along the well-named Klipspringer Pass as it heads to the Middle Plateau of the Nuweveld, watch out for them browsing the scrubby anchor Karoo bushes and young sweet-thorn trees. Although unusually tame here, they have a habit of freezing as cars approach and are easily missed, so drive slowly. Small family groups of **mountain reedbucks** also occur; however, they are not nearly as confident as klipspringers and often only announce their presence with a shrill alarm whistle and by flashing the white underside of their tail – a danger signal which, if you're very fortunate, might reveal the presence of a hunting **caracal**.

Raptors are often seen up on the Middle Plateau, and the gorge beneath the Rooivalle Lookout is frequently occupied by **black eagles** using the ravine currents to hunt their main prey species, the **rock dassie**. **Peregrine**

WILDLIFE HIGHLIGHTS

» A great place for watching klipspringers » Common sightings of black wildebeests, red hartebeests, springboks and mountain reedbucks » Home to the second-largest remaining population of the Cape mountain zebra » Buffaloes and black rhinos – though spottings are rare » Rewarding birding, with over 20 breeding pairs of black eagles and numerous Karoo endemics

THE RIVERINE RABBIT

Alternatively classified by early naturalists as a hare (due mostly to its prominent, elongated ears) or a rabbit, modern genetic analysis confirms the riverine rabbit is a true rabbit and also one of South Africa's most endangered mammals. Never widespread (it has always been restricted to the central Karoo region), the species has lost over half its original range to farming and now numbers less than 1500. Breeding projects have reintroduced the species to Karoo National Park, the only protected area open to the public where it can be seen. Just as important, projects outside the park with local farmers are fostering awareness of the species' rarity and pride in those property owners with rabbits on their farms.

falcons, **lanner falcons** and three species of **kestrels** (**rock**, **greater** and **lesser**) also favour the rocky cliffsides, as do **rock martins**, cruising effortlessly at 80km/h in the canyon below as they search for insect prey. They are often seen flying in mixed flocks with members of the similar but separate swift family. Five species – **European**, **black**, **white-rumped**, **little** and **alpine swifts** – inhabit the gorge. Book a 4WD trail at the reception office (rest camp) to venture further onto Middle Plateau for a chance to see **black rhinos** and **buffaloes**.

NIGHT SIGHTS Even before colonisation by European farmers, large carnivores were never plentiful in the relatively barren Karoo, and today only the adaptable **leopard** still persists here. Guided night drives are well worth taking for a chance (albeit very slight) to spot these elusive cats. Smaller hunters, however, are regular sights. On the grasslands **bat-eared foxes** and diminutive **Cape foxes** hunt for small rodents and the seven species of **shrews** and **elephant shrews** that occur here. The endemic **black-footed cat** is a special nocturnal find but you need to be alert to thwart its habit of squatting low in the grass and slinking off when detected. Occasionally, the presence of **owls** perched on low bushes or in the grass gives them away. Owls sometimes follow the cats as they forage, opportunistically taking small birds that the hunters flush from their night-time roosts in the Karoo grass.

Aardwolves, the smallest member of the hyena family, are most abundant where there are congregations of termite mounds; despite their carnivorous ancestry, they subsist entirely upon termites, consuming up to 250,000 each night. Sometimes they can be spotted trailing another nocturnal termite specialist, the **aardvark**. With their long tubular snout, oversized ears and tapered tail, aardvarks resemble no other mammal and use their prodigious strength and bearlike claws to rip open termite mounds. Aardwolves mop up afterwards, lapping the exposed insects from the soil surface.

Spotlighting is the only way you're likely to see the most endangered mammal in the park, the **riverine rabbit**. They are entirely nocturnal and solitary, and favour the dense riverine scrub lining the Karoo's seasonal rivers – all conspiring to make a sighting a rare and special event.

SOUTH AFRICA

KLIPSPRINGER

MKHUZE GAME RESERVE

SOUTH AFRICA

LOCATION 309km north of Durban. Sealed roads except final 25km – call ahead after heavy rain.

FACILITIES 100km of wildlife-watching roads, hides, Fig Forest Walk, guided night drives, bird walks and game walks (book at park office).

ACCOMMODATION Various bungalows, cottages and tented camps. Camping ground and caravan site at entrance gate.

WILDLIFE RHYTHMS Wildlife-watching from the numerous hides is best between June and October. Wildlife is more widely dispersed during the rainy season (November to February) and is less likely to be seen from the hides (however birdlife is more varied).

CONTACT KZN Wildlife (☎ 033-845 1000; www .kznwildlife.com).

MKHUZE GAME RESERVE

Forming part of a vast coastal expanse called the Mozam-bique Plain, Mkhuze lies in a rich transition zone where northern tropical species mix with temperate forms from further south. The park protects the southern fringes of the Makatini Flats, an extensive floodplain formerly home to large numbers of **elephants** and **migratory herbivores** making their seasonal movements into Mozambique. Bounded by the Mkhuze River in the east and the Leb-ombo Mountains in the west, a rich blend of habitats in-cluding grasslands, acacia woodlands, ancient sand dunes, rivers and pans, and two rare types of forest, are home to an equally varied fauna.

LAST STAND OF THE TROPICS If you imagine the Mozambique Plain 'squeezed' between the Lebombo Mountains and the coast, Mkhuze lies at the narrowest end of the funnel. Suitable habitat for many tropical species is suddenly telescoped down and many tropical species, particularly birds, have their southernmost distribution here. Rare birds you won't see further south include **Jameson's firefinches** (look for them in the foothills of the Lebombos near the Emshopi entrance gate), **purple-banded** and **Neergaard's sunbirds**, **yellow white-eyes**, **Woodward's batises** and **purple rollers**. Some species migrate from Mozambique to breed here including **grey-hooded kingfishers**, which nest from February to April, and flocks of up to 30 **broad-billed rollers** which are visible during September until December.

One particularly productive habitat here is sycamore fig forest, a very rare forest type under intense pressure from habitat destruction for farming. The fig trees attract a great variety of species and there is a very rewarding self-guided walk (Fig Forest Walk) you can take to look for them. It begins where the Mkhuze River flows into Nsumo Pan (near the Nsumo picnic site) – itself prime habitat for birds including many different **herons**, **ducks**, **waders**, **flamingos** and a breeding colony of **pink-backed pelicans**, as well as **hippos**. The fig trees along the river are home to

WILDLIFE HIGHLIGHTS
» A birdwatcher's paradise, with over 400 bird species, including tropical species at the southern limit of their distribution » Significant populations of both rhino species, plus elephants (which have been reintroduced) » Nyalas, impalas, blue wildebeests, warthogs and Burchell's zebras numbering in the thousands » Hippos, sunis, and both grey and red duikers, and reasonably good chances of spotting leopards

Pel's fishing owls, **African fish eagles** and at least five species of **kingfisher**, which perch on the branches to search for fish, frogs and crustaceans. **Crowned eagles**, with talons powerful enough to crush a man's arm, hunt in the forest canopy for **vervet monkeys**, while shy and secretive **southern banded snake eagles** fly from tree to tree searching for reptile prey. The calls of **purple-crested louries**, **green-spotted doves**, **trumpeter hornbills** and **red-billed woodhoopoes** (to name just a few) are constant companions during the walk. The lush canopy makes them difficult to spot but their calls assist greatly, particularly if you choose a spot to sit and wait.

Birds aside, Mkhuze is home to a rich community of mammals, best seen from the numerous hides. Between sunrise and midday Kumasinga Hide is very productive and virtually guarantees sightings of **white rhinos**, **nyalas**, **red** and **grey duikers** and **greater kudus**, particularly during the dry winter (June to October). **Blue wildebeests**, **Burchell's zebras**, **impalas** and **warthogs** are very common and shy **bushbucks** and **sunis** also drink at Kumasinga. If you are extremely lucky, the reserve's top predator, the **leopard**, might come for an early morning drink. Mkhuze is a sanctuary for **black rhinos**, which outnumber the less threatened **white** rhino here. They are sometimes seen along the Loop Rd and the drive to Enxwala viewpoint, also good sites to search for Mkhuze's small population of reintroduced **elephants**.

THE FIG BOUNTY

One of the rarest forest types in Southern Africa, the sycamore fig forest at Mkhuze is the largest remnant in KwaZulu-Natal and home to hundreds of mammals, birds and insects. The key to its richness is a year-round abundance of fruit. The sycamore produces fruit at least twice a year and different individual trees bear figs in different months. This dependable food supply attracts a tremendous variety of fruit-eating species: in the canopy, vervet monkeys, baboons and tree squirrels compete with African green pigeons, louries and brown-headed parrots for the ripest fruits. Fallen figs are eaten by bushpigs, porcupines and red duikers, and even fish feed on fruits dropping into the Mkhuze River. Insects literally infest the figs which, in turn, attract avian and mammalian insect-eaters alike, including paradise and blue-mantled flycatchers, various bats and four-toed elephant shrews, which search for prey among the leaf litter and fallen fruits.

WARTHOGS, MKHUZE GAME RESERVE

SOUTH AFRICA

DE HOOP
NATURE
RESERVE

LOCATION 50km east of Bredadorp.

FACILITIES Wildlife-watching roads, education centres, mountain-biking trails (book ahead), coastal and wetland walking trails.

ACCOMMODATION Self-catering cottages, camping ground and caravan site, restored manor house.

WILDLIFE RHYTHMS Most southern right whale calves are born in August, also the wettest and windiest month.

CONTACT CapeNature (☎ 021-659 3500; www .capenature.org.za).

SOUTH AFRICA

DE HOOP NATURE RESERVE

At first glance the heathlike fynbos of the Southwest Cape appears rather drab, but this region has the highest concentration of plant species in the world, many of which are found nowhere else on earth. Under tremendous pressure from surrounding agriculture, there are few intact stands of this diverse floral kingdom remaining. De Hoop protects one of the largest and gives sanctuary to a unique community of coastal wildlife.

With its very high tannin content and tough texture, fynbos is unpalatable to many antelopes but a few species thrive here. The largest remaining population of **bonteboks** inhabits the grass-covered plains running from the limestone hills at the entrance gate to the coastline. Once reduced to only 17 individuals, all bonteboks in the world originate from the nearby Bontebok National Park (only 60km from De Hoop, it's well worth a day trip) and reintroduced populations are ensuring the species' survival. Another rare antelope, the **grey rhebuck**, occurs at De Hoop – one of the few reserves where these normally shy South African endemics are visible. The waterhole on the road to the office is an excellent place to wait for other plains game, including **elands**, **greater kudus**, **ostriches** and endangered **Cape mountain zebras**.

With 40km of coastline, an offshore marine reserve and a major wetland, De Hoop also protects a very different fauna to that seen on the coastal plain. **Southern right whales** swim inshore during July to October when they arrive to give birth and to mate – Cape Infanta at the eastern end of De Hoop is one of the most important calving grounds. Small family groups of **Bryde's whales** are a special sight, sometimes surrounded by **common** and **bottlenose dolphins**. The permanent wetland De Hoop Vlei attracts over 100 species of **waterbird** – take the 5km Vlei Walking Trail and binoculars to view rare **African black oystercatchers**.

WILDLIFE HIGHLIGHTS
» Excellent for rare Cape 'specials' including bonteboks, Cape mountain zebras and grey rhebucks » Thirteen marine mammal species, including southern right whales » 260 bird species, including African black oystercatchers and blue cranes

👀 WATCHING TIPS

This region is home to the greatest numbers of endangered blue cranes in the world. If you don't see any on the grasslands near Potberg Centre, look for them on the agricultural lands just outside the park boundaries.

MALOTI-DRAKENSBERG TRANSFRONTIER AREA

MALOTI-DRAKENSBERG TRANSFRONTIER AREA

SOUTH AFRICA

Renowned for its stunning panoramas, hiking and recreational opportunities, this area encompasses several parks and reserves in and around the Maloti (Maluti) and uKhahlamba-Drakensberg ranges in South Africa and Lesotho. In the Golden Gate Highlands National Park (and adjoining Qwa-Qwa Nature Reserve) in the Maloti range, there is a road network where visitors can view **black wildebeests, Burchell's zebras, blesboks, elands** and **mountain reedbucks** by car. Wildlife is not prolific, but aside from the magnificent setting, there are some special attractions. There are a few sites where bones are set out to provision the rare **bearded vulture** (or lammergeier). At Giant's Castle Game Reserve, in the uKhahlamba-Drakensberg's Central Berg area, visitors can hike from the main camp to a specially constructed stone hide, one of the few places in the world where sightings of lammergeiers are almost certain. Nearly always accompanied by scavengers such as **house crows** and **white-necked ravens**, these unusual-looking birds have an unusual feeding strategy: they drop bones onto a favourite rock (called an ossuary) until they shatter and the birds can reach the marrow inside. **Cape vultures, black eagles, yellow-billed kites** and **jackal buzzards** are also regular diners at the 'vulture restaurant'. Golden Gate Highlands National Park also has a vulture hide, about 2km from Brandwag Camp, where raptors (mostly Cape vultures but also some lammergeiers) may congregate in the hundreds.

In one of the most beautiful sections of this wild area, a hike along the Tugela (Thukela) River in the Royal Natal National Park in the Northern Berg passes through grasslands and forested gorges where **mountain reedbucks, oribis, pin-tailed whydahs, Gurney's sugarbirds** and many species of **widows, cisticolas, pipits, warblers** and larks are readily seen. In the summer, look out for **puff adders** and **Berg adders** sunning themselves on the paths. Both species are very placid and bite only if highly provoked (such as when trodden on!). At Tendele and Mahai Camps, **chacma baboons, grey duikers, helmeted guineafowl** and **red** and **golden bishops** are common visitors. Main Camp in Giant's Castle has regular visits from very tame **large-spotted genets**.

LOCATION Golden Gate Highlands National Park and Qwa-Qwa Nature Reserve: 330km south of Johannesburg. Royal Natal National Park: 270km north of Durban. Giant's Castle Game Reserve: 190km north of Durban.

FACILITIES Bearded vulture viewing hides, wildlife-watching roads and hiking trails.

ACCOMMODATION A great variety.

WILDLIFE RHYTHMS Summer (December to March) is best for birdlife. In winter (June to August), wildlife concentrates on the lower slopes. The lammergeier hide at Giant's Castle is only open on weekends from May to September (book far in advance at ☎ 36-353 3718).

CONTACT Golden Gate Highlands: SANP Central Reservations (☎ 012-428 9111; www.sanparks.org); Giant's Castle and Royal Natal National Parks: KZN Wildlife (☎ 033-845 1000; www .kznwildlife.com).

WILDLIFE HIGHLIGHTS

» Reliable site for viewing bearded vultures » Good chances of spotting mountain reedbucks and oribis » Chats, cisticolas, warblers, pipits and raptors are well represented

● ● WATCHING TIPS

At Golden Gate Highlands National Park, the eastern loop road encompasses the home range of a female African wild cat.

SOUTH AFRICA

MOUNTAIN ZEBRA
NATIONAL PARK

LOCATION 280km north of Port Elizabeth.

FACILITIES 42.5km of wildlife-watching roads; also lookout points and walking trails. Horse-riding trail and three-day hiking trail (book at park office).

ACCOMMODATION Chalets sleeping four and six, camping ground and caravan site.

WILDLIFE RHYTHMS Most Cape mountain zebra foals are born between October and March. Mares with newborns are extremely protective of their offspring, leading to intense social activity in the herd during the birth season.

CONTACT SANP Central Reservations (☎ 012-428 9111; www.sanparks.org); Mountain Zebra park office (☎ 048-881 2427).

MOUNTAIN ZEBRA NATIONAL PARK

Like many parks of the Cape Province, this reserve was established as a sanctuary for an endangered endemic mammal (after which the reserve is named). The surrounding slopes of the Bankberg Mountains create a natural amphitheatre in which to view the largest remaining population of the **Cape mountain zebra**, which was once reduced to 91 individuals. Mountain Zebra National Park has one of only three naturally surviving populations and this is the best place to see them.

DWELLERS OF THE HIGH PLATEAUS The Rooiplaat Loop in the north takes you through a scenic pass onto the best wildlife-watching areas. In spring and summer (September through March) most **Cape mountain zebras** congregate on these grassy plateaus, favouring their palatable grasses. Although nonterritorial, stallions violently defend their harems from challenging males, and Rooiplaat's open plains offer excellent chances to view the clashes. Naturally migratory, they tend to move into the mountains in winter when grazing on the plains is poorest. The Rooiplaat Plateau also shelters herds of **common elands**, **red hartebeests**, **black wildebeests**, **blesboks** and **springboks** as well as **bat-eared foxes**. **Ostriches** and **blue cranes** are seen on the plateau as well as dozens of grassland bird species including **quail finches**, **pin-tailed whydahs**, **Cape canaries** and **southern ant-eating chats**.

CARACALS Deep valleys running into the seasonal Wilgerboom River provide habitat for a very different fauna to that seen on the plains. Set out along Kranskop Dr as early as possible for the best chance to see the park's top predator, the tuft-eared **caracal**. The chattering bark of **rock dassies** and the alarm screams of resident **black eagles** act as valuable cues to stop and scan the rocky slopes for this cat. Highly adaptable, caracals also live in densely wooded watercourses where the herbivores range from the tiny (**grey duikers**) to the huge (**buffaloes**). But cat-spotters occur everywhere: **greater kudus**, **klipspringers** and **mountain reedbucks** live on the lower slopes and their respective alarm calls (a booming bark, a trumpetlike whistle and a shrill nasal whistle) usually mean 'caracal!'.

● ● ● WATCHING TIPS

White-browed sparrow-weavers, pale-winged starlings and fiscal shrikes are virtually guaranteed visitors to the chalets if you take meals on the verandah.

WILDLIFE HIGHLIGHTS
» The best reserve for spotting Cape mountain zebras
» Excellent for red hartebeests, springboks, black wildebeests and ostriches » Visible predators include bat-eared foxes, four mongoose species and caracals » Bird highlights include black eagles, blue cranes and many small grassland species

NDUMO GAME RESERVE

Lying at the confluence of the Pongolo and Usutu Rivers, Ndumo is favoured with year-round water and prolific wetland habitat. Indeed, during the wet season (October to March) the northeast corner of the reserve resembles a mini Okavango Delta where the two rivers meet in a swamp of channels and pans. A mosaic of dense ma-hemane bush, open floodplains and riverine forests of fig trees, fever trees and ilala palms provides habitat for many subtropical species that are difficult to see else-where in Southern Africa.

NYALAS, CROCODILES & BIRDS

Large mammals tend to be shy and difficult to spot but **nyalas** number in the thousands, forming unusually large herds. They rarely venture far from the protection of thick bush but with relatively few predators here, they congregate on the floodplain to graze the rich grasses. The hides overlooking Nyamithi Pan in the early morn-ing and evening offer the best chance for viewing large aggregations as well as numerous **giraffes**, **greater kudus**, **waterbucks**, **impalas**, **bushbucks** and **red duik-ers**. Late in the afternoon, **bushpigs** sometimes appear in their small family groups known as sounders. Primarily nocturnal, they occasionally venture out at sunset when they wallow in mud to remove parasites and regulate their temperature – particularly during the summer. Some 700 **Nile crocodiles**, larger than 2m, and over 300 **hippos** inhabit the rivers and pans and cannot be missed from the hides.

Most visitors are attracted to Ndumo for its prolific birdlife. **African fish eagles**, **Pel's fishing owls**, **palmnut vultures**, **southern banded snake eagles** and **pygmy geese** are plentiful around the pans. Many **kingfisher** species also occur including **giant**, **brown-hooded**, **woodland**, **malachite** and **pied**, the last distinctive for their hovering hunting patterns. Patches of threatened sandforest are home to rare trees and rare birds alike. Among huge Lebombo wattles, wild mangoes and Mo-zambique coffee trees, look for **narina trogons**, **African broadbills**, **broad-billed rollers**, **pink-throated twin-spots** and **yellow-spotted nicators**. Ndumo has 85% of the bird species found at Kruger National Park yet it is only 0.5% the size.

WILDLIFE HIGHLIGHTS

» One of Southern Africa's finest birding sites, with 420 species » Abundant hippos, nyalas, impalas and Nile crocodiles » Bushpigs, red duikers, bushbucks and sunis are all common but can be difficult to see

LOCATION 409km north of Durban. Tarred all the way except for the last 15km – check ahead after heavy rains.

FACILITIES Wildlife-watching roads, guided wildlife drives, guided walks, numerous hides and viewing towers.

ACCOMMODATION Camping ground, caravan site and rustic huts; wilderness camp (closed at the time of research).

WILDLIFE RHYTHMS The mild, dry winters (March to October) when water levels are lowest are best for wildlife-watching on the floodplain. Birding is excellent year-round, but reaches its peak in summer.

CONTACT KZN Wildlife (☎ 033-845 1000; www .kznwildlife.com).

● ● WATCHING TIPS

Accompanied walks are perhaps the best way to spot tiny suni antelopes. They're abundant here but freeze at the sound of footfall and are difficult to spot in the dense bush. They constantly flick their tails – a giveaway if you watch for it.

PHINDA PRIVATE
GAME RESERVE
SOUTH
AFRICA

LOCATION 300km north of Durban. Access for 2WD but call ahead in the rainy season (December to February).

FACILITIES Guided wildlife drives and walks, bird hide, boat cruises, river canoeing, scuba diving and snorkelling (off-site).

ACCOMMODATION Four luxury lodges.

WILDLIFE RHYTHMS Winter is the dry season when undergrowth is sparse; the best time for clear sightings. Summer is when migrant birds arrive and many antelopes give birth.

CONTACT CCAfrica (☎ 011-809 4314; www.phinda.com).

PHINDA PRIVATE GAME RESERVE

Among the finest of South Africa's many privately owned reserves, Phinda is adjacent to Mkhuze Game Reserve but about 10 times as expensive to visit. The wildlife is essentially the same (though Phinda has **lions** and lacks black rhinos) but in contrast to Mkhuze's self-drive experience, Phinda's rangers promise exceptional guided sightings. If your list is missing a few 'lifers' (species you have never seen in your life) like **cheetahs**, **sunis** or **African finfoots** and you've got the cash, Phinda virtually guarantees them.

RETURN OF THE WILDLIFE Phinda's full name, Phinda Isilwane, is Zulu for 'the return of the wildlife'. Prior to 1990, the most abundant large mammal here was the domestic cow but, along with miles of barbed wire fencing, Phinda's owners removed them and restored the full complement of KwaZulu-Natal mammalian megafauna. As well as over 1000 head of various **antelope** species, **elephants** and more **white rhinos** than remain in most African countries, they reintroduced the top predators. Today, **Big Five** sightings are standard wildlife-drive fare and this is one of the few reserves in Africa where **cheetahs** are a certainty. Their numbers are modest but like most big cats here, the cheetahs are indifferent to safari vehicles, and permit terrific chances for watching behaviour – mothers with cubs are exceptionally viewable.

BUCK & BIRDS Local herbivorous specials include the **suni**, tame **red duikers** (keep an eye out for them on the paths of Forest Lodge) and **nyalas** in abundance as well as more widespread species like **blue wildebeests**, **Burchell's zebras**, **impalas**, **greater kudus** and **giraffes**. Although the wildlife drives invariably focus on mammals, ask the rangers to show off their considerable birding knowledge. There are more than 360 species here and some people come to Phinda for the birdlife alone. If you're a birder, be sure to tell reception when you check in and they'll make sure you get time with specialist birding guides who can show you rare species like **narina trogons**, **African finfoots**, **black coucals** and sandforest specials like **African broadbills** and **Neergaard's sunbirds**.

WATCHING TIPS

Phinda's rangers and trackers will find everything for you but ask about guided day trips (which they call 'adventures') to wildlife attractions nearby, including black rhino walks in Mkhuze Game Reserve, diving on the east-coast coral reefs and guided flights over iSimangaliso Wetland Park.

WILDLIFE HIGHLIGHTS

» The best place in South Africa to see cheetahs
» Excellent Big Five and good general wildlife, including easily seen subtropical antelopes like nyalas, red duikers and sunis » Prolific birdlife, including species favouring an extensive patch of rare sandforest habitat

TEMBE ELEPHANT PARK

Established to protect the survivors of intense poaching in neighbouring Mozambique, Tembe is sanctuary for about 200 **elephants**. Formerly ranging freely over the border, their seasonal migrations carried them through the crossfire of Mozambique's civil war until elephant-proof fences restricted them to the protected South African side. After a decade in safety, Tembe's elephants are beginning to relax, but combined with the scars of AK-47 fire (still visible on some individuals) the years of persecution have left them nervous, aggressive and prone to charging with little provocation. Although there are many places in Southern Africa where elephants are easier to see, Tembe's war refugees are truly wild and dangerous – if you see them, leave the engine running and treat all charges as genuine.

ELEPHANT WILDERNESS All Tembe's roads are 4WD and only 10 vehicles per day are admitted, so you may not encounter another vehicle in the course of a day's exploration. And with the possibility of a belligerent elephant just around the next corner, Tembe really conveys a sense of wilderness. Except for the Tembe Elephant Park Lodge, there is at present nowhere to stay and self-driving visitors have to leave Tembe before the sun sets. Nonetheless, a day trip can be rewarding, particularly if you use nearby Ndumo Game Reserve (35km away) as a base. The thick subtropical bush makes wildlife-watching difficult from vehicles, especially in the lush summer, and time is best spent at hides. Ponweni Hide overlooking Muzi Swamp is an excellent (and safe!) place for spotting **elephants**, particularly during the driest period, May to October, when they share the limited water with herds of **nyalas**, **buffaloes**, **waterbucks** and **impalas**. Rare elsewhere, **red duikers**, tiny **suni** and **crested guineafowl** are abundant; they are often seen on the enclosed Ngobozana Sandforest Trails near the main gate, but you need to walk quietly and look deep into the undergrowth. The trails are also excellent for birdlife including **African broadbills**, **narina trogons**, **Neergaard's sunbirds** and, a very occasional visitor, the **blue-throated sunbird**.

LOCATION 415km north of Durban. Entrance road is tarred but all internal roads are 4WD.

FACILITIES Self-guided sandforest walks, hides, picnic area, viewpoint tower.

ACCOMMODATION Private luxury camp (Tembe Elephant Park Lodge, www.tembe .co.za). Nearby Ndumo Game Reserve offers alternatives.

WILDLIFE RHYTHMS Although wary, elephants (and most other large mammals) are readily seen at waterholes in the dry season (May to October).

CONTACT KZN Wildlife (☎ 033-845 1000; www .kznwildlife.com), park officer (☎ 035-592 0001).

SOUTH AFRICA

WILDLIFE HIGHLIGHTS

» Home of South Africa's wildest elephants » Nyalas, impalas, waterbucks and red duikers are easily seen » Southern Africa's largest population of suni » Abundant birdlife similar to that at Ndumo but not as diverse; the blue-throated sunbird is a notable speciality

●● WATCHING TIPS

For day trippers who have to leave before sunset, maximise your visit by ending at the viewing tower – 4km, or just a five-minute drive, from the main gate. It's an excellent site for watching antelopes and birdlife at sunset.

OTHER SITES

AUSTIN ROBERTS BIRD SANCTUARY
This small sanctuary in Pretoria's eastern suburbs is home to 170 bird species, with virtually guaranteed viewing of South Africa's national bird, the blue crane. Entry is free, but it's open only on weekends and holidays. Guided walks available with a month's notice.
☎ *012-440 8316; www.tshwane.gov .za/austinroberts.cfm; Boshoff St, New Muckleneuk, Pretoria*

BIRD ISLAND NATURE RESERVE
Scattered along the west coast are mostly inaccessible islands of seabird breeding colonies. About 5000 pairs of Cape gannets nest on Bird Island (the easiest to reach) between October and December; year-round are cormorants, jackass penguins, Hartlaub's gulls and Cape fur-seals. A gannet observatory enables superb viewing. Only 10km south is Wadrif Saltpan, where masses of flamingos, terns, waders and ducks congregate.
☎ *021-659 3500; www.capenature.org.za; Lambert's Bay*

BLYDE RIVER CANYON NATURE RESERVE Conveniently located on the way to Kruger National Park's Orpen Gate, this stretch of the Drakensberg is famous for rugged scenery, waterfalls and cliffs. All five Southern African primates live here with good populations of antelopes such as rhebucks, Sharpe's grysboks and oribis. The birdlife is excellent.
☎ *013-759 5300; info@mtpa.co.za; 130km north of Nelspruit*

CEDERBERG WILDERNESS AREA
South Africa's only reserve specifically for leopards, Cederberg is best known for its scenery. A network of hiking trails (limited road access) traverses South Africa's largest remaining patch of montane fynbos, where Cape grysboks, grey rhebucks, grey duikers and chacma baboons can be seen. Spring

brings sunbirds and sugarbirds. Klipspringers, black eagles and rock dassies as well as San paintings occur among the rocks.
☎ *021-659 3500; www.capenature.org.za; 210km north of Cape Town*

DE WILDT CHEETAH RESEARCH & BREEDING PROJECT A breeding project for endangered wildlife, De Wildt is known for finding the key to breeding captive cheetahs, and was also the first to breed 'king' cheetahs. Guided tours also view captive African wild dogs, brown hyenas, caracals, riverine rabbits and various raptors, including visitors to a very well-patronised 'vulture restaurant'.
☎ *012-504 1921; www.dewildt.org.za; 65km northwest of Pretoria*

KIRSTENBOSCH NATIONAL BOTANIC GARDENS If you miss the other, larger fynbos reserves, be sure to stop at these gardens. Over 9000 indigenous plant species at the eastern base of Table Mountain attract orange-breasted sunbirds, Cape sugarbirds, Klaas' cuckoos, Cape francolins and more.
☎ *021-799 8783; www.sanbi.org; Constantia, Cape Town*

KOSI BAY NATURE RESERVE A series of four estuarine lakes, Kosi Bay is surrounded by dune forest, raffia palms, mangroves, swamps and fig forest, best explored by the guided four-day Kosi Trail. Hippos inhabit the lakes, and the thick coastal bush has vervet and samango monkeys as well as bushbucks and red and blue duikers. Birdlife is prolific and the raffia palm forest is probably the best place to see palmnut vultures.
☎ *KZN Wildlife 033-845 1000, reserve office 035-592 0234; www.kznwildlife.com; 450km north of Durban*

MARAKELE NATIONAL PARK One of South Africa's least developed

national parks, Marakele is ideal for the self-sufficient traveller (and you'll need a 4WD). Wildlife includes the Big Five (except for lions) and over a dozen antelope species. The world's largest Cape-vulture colony nests in the Waterberg Range; almost 300 other bird species have been seen here.
☎ 014-777 1745;www.sanparks.org /marakele; 240km northwest of Pretoria

NAMAQUA NATIONAL PARK As well as hosting a spring wildflower flush that draws visitors from around the globe, Namaqua protects a rich diversity of endemic desert life: many succulents, lizards, tortoises, mole-rats, bees and scorpions are found nowhere else. More conspicuous life includes ostriches, korhaans, larks and arid-adapted antelopes.
☎ 027-672 1948; www.sanparks.org /namaqua; 550km north of Cape Town

NYLSVLEI NATURE RESERVE A summer visit guarantees superb bird-viewing. In good seasons 60,000 wetland birds of 100-plus species have been recorded; 300-odd more species live in the surrounding bushveld. Mammals aren't abundant, but tsessebes, southern reedbucks and roans are among the normally elusive species seen fairly often.
☎ 014-743 1074, 014-736 4328; www .golimpopo.com; 130km north of Pretoria

TABLE MOUNTAIN NATIONAL PARK An easy day trip from Cape Town, with coastal fynbos and Cape mountain zebras, bonteboks, elands and red hartebeests. Chacma baboons are extremely tame (but heed the warning signs) and birdlife is good. Between June and November, you can see southern right whales across False Bay, and there's also hiking, cycling, fishing and windsurfing. Take Simon's Town Rd back and stop at The Boulders to swim with jackass penguins.
☎ 021-701 8692; www.sanparks.org; 57km south of Cape Town

TSITSIKAMMA NATIONAL PARK Its challenging 46km Otter Trail takes you though prime otter habitat but is mostly renowned for its scenery and the chance to glimpse dolphins offshore – otters are extremely shy and you'll need to be out early and keep very quiet for a chance to spot one. Tame rock dassies, small grey mongooses and sunbirds frequent the camp sites, and short walks through beautiful indigenous Cape forest hold a chance for blue duikers and Knysna louries. Tsitsikamma is very busy on weekends and holidays.
☎ 042-281 1607; www.sanparks.org /tsitsikamma; 56km east of Plettenberg Bay

TSWALU KALAHARI PRIVATE GAME RESERVE The largest privately owned reserve in Southern Africa, Tswalu is as expensive as it is huge, but for people wanting a luxury Kalahari experience, it's unrivalled. Typical desert species like springboks, gemsboks and red hartebeests are here (as well as others that don't belong, such as roan and sable antelopes) and, most notably, the desert race of the black rhino. Guided night drives offer excellent chances for spotting many of the Kalahari's rich carnivore community, from Cape foxes to lions. Birdlife is excellent, with raptors, bustards, finches, queleas and weavers.
☎ 011-274 2299; www.tswalu.com; 300km northwest of Kimberley

WEENEN GAME RESERVE Rolling terrain lightly covered in thornveld and grasslands ensures good visibility of a surprisingly rich mammal fauna. There's nothing here you can't see in the larger KwaZulu-Natal reserves, but usually you're free to hike without guides in search of wildlife that includes both rhino species, buffaloes, giraffes, elands and mountain reedbucks. Birdlife is very good and there's a vulture feeding site.
☎ KZN Wildlife 033-845 1000, reserve office 036-354 7013; www.kznwildlife.com; 180km northwest of Durban

NAMIBIA

CAPITAL WINDHOEK **AREA** 825,000 SQ KM **NATIONAL PARKS** 18 **MAMMAL SPECIES** 192

The driest country in the Southern African region, Namibia has rocky canyons, shimmering salt pans and sunburned savannas that provide a dramatic backdrop for wildlife-watching. Though the terrain can be challenging, easy sightings of lions, desert elephants and black rhinos make it a rewarding Big Five hotspot.

THE LAND Namibia is a land of extremes. From the Skeleton Coast, shingled with the sun-bleached bones of southern right whales, to hot arid savannas and acacia woodlands, wildlife-watching opportunities abound. Despite desolate landscapes and a climate that can be harsh, Namibia has some of the world's grandest national parks, ranging from the desert plains of the Namib-Naukluft Park to the salt flats of Etosha, where big cats and elephants are easily spotted.

The country can be divided into four main topographical regions: the Namib Desert and coastal plains in the west; the eastward-sloping Central Plateau; the Kalahari, along the borders with South Africa and Botswana; and the densely wooded bushveld of the Kavango and Caprivi regions. Wildlife is most abundant in the north where the most fertile habitats lie, ranging from the seasonally inundated Etosha National Park to the relatively lush reserves along the Caprivi Strip. For 'big wildlife' watchers, there are really only three significant areas in Namibia: Kaokoland, where elusive desert elephants and black rhinos follow the river courses running to the Skeleton Coast; the isolated and rarely visited Kaudom, where Namibia's last African wild dogs find refuge; and Etosha National Park, one of the world's finest wildlife reserves.

Further south is the largest game reserve in Africa, the Namib-Naukluft

NAMIBIA

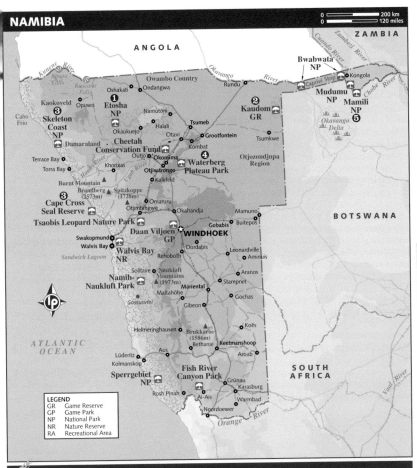

TOP SPOTS

1. ETOSHA NATIONAL PARK
(p100) Undoubtedly one of the world's best wildlife reserves; a day at its waterholes can see an endless procession of thousands of animals, from banded mongooses to big cats and elephants.

2. KAUDOM GAME RESERVE
(p111) One of Namibia's most challenging parks, home to a population of lions, packs of wild dogs and colourful birds.

3. SKELETON COAST NP & CAPE CROSS SEAL RESERVE (p108)
Rocky cliffs host metropolises of fur-clad seals, offset by miles of saffron-coloured landscapes and half-moon sand dunes.

4. WATERBERG PLATEAU PARK
(p113) This protected tabletop refuge is home to a variety of rare species, including roan and sabre antelope, alongside birds of prey and giraffes.

5. MAMILI NATIONAL PARK
(p112) Expansive floodplains foster large populations of hippos, Nile crocodiles and birdlife, including wattled cranes, herons and swamp boubous.

Park, which covers an astonishing 6% of Namibia. Much of it is true desert and large mammals occur in extremely low densities, though local specials include Hartmann's mountain zebras as well as more widespread Southern African endemics like springboks and gemsboks. For aficionados of smaller life, the Namib is an endemism hotspot: on the dunes, Gray's larks, dune larks, slip-face lizards and fog-basking beetles are found, while the scattered rocky plateaus host long-billed larks, rockrunners and Herero chats.

The severe Namibian coast is no place to expect abundant big wildlife though it's the only spot in the world where massive fur-seal colonies are patrolled by hunting brown hyenas and black-backed jackals. The coast also hosts massive flocks of summer waders including sanderlings, turnstones and grey plovers, while Heaviside's and dusky dolphins can often be seen in the shallow offshore waters. In 2009 the Namibian government opened the Sperrgebiet, a vast 16,000-sq-km expanse of land that's home to the threatened desert rain frog, dramatic rock formations and disused diamond mines. Namibia's haunting beauty, shimmering salt pans and saffron-coloured sand dunes provide one of the world's most dramatic backdrops for adventurous wildlife-watchers.

WHEN TO GO Namibia stretches over 825,000 sq km and temperatures can vary dramatically. The driest parts of Namibia are best visited during the summer rains (November to March) when large pools form in the desert, attracting unusually large congregations of all forms of desert wildlife. Conversely, the best time to visit Etosha is during the winter (May to September) when the air is dry and thirsty animals gather at waterholes. The best time for birdwatching is between December and the end of March.

WILDLIFE HIGHLIGHTS

» Being woken by the sound of distant lion roars at Etosha's Okakuejo Camp (p100)
» Catching glimpses of the thirsty baboons of the Namib at the arid Namib-Naukluft Park (p104) » Meeting monogamous pairs of Damara dik-diks on the trails at Waterberg Plateau Park (p113)
» Listening to the endless chatter of 80,000 fur-seals at Cape Cross (p110) during the birthing period » The flash of colour provided by flamingos numbering in the millions when Etosha Pan (p100) is filled » Following the tracks of lumbering desert elephants along the dry Hoanib and Hoarusib riverbeds (p108)

BABOONS GROOMING

NAMIBIA ITINERARIES

1. SAFARI Etosha National Park (p100), with its sweetgrass plains, shimmering salt pan and teeming waterholes, is arguably Namibia's biggest draw. With this in mind, start in

Windhoek, stop at **Okonjima** (p115) on the way and arrive at the park in time to bunker down for a good night's rest. Even one day at a waterhole can produce literally thousands of animals. Then 4WD east to remote **Kaudom Game Reserve** (p111), second only to Etosha in terms of wildlife sightings.

2. COAST Explore the otherworldliness of the **Skeleton Coast** (p108), using Swapok-mund as your base. Head north to **Cape Cross Seal Reserve** (p110), where there's a

good chance of spotting black rhino and the elusive desert elephant, and then go south to the **Namib-Naukluft Park** (p104). The intrepid could continue further to the dry and desolate **Sperrgebiet** (p115).

3. BIRDWATCHER'S PARADISE Namibia has some of the best birding opportunities in Southern Africa. In summers of high rainfalls, head to the flooded **Etosha Pan** (p100),

where flocks of salmon-coloured flamingos and eastern white pelicans gather. The intrepid might consider attempting the boggy marshes of **Kaudom** (p111) in the extreme northeast, where over 70 migratory species, including dwarf bitterns, African crakes and open-billed storks, converge in the summer months. Return to Windhoek via the dizzying heights of **Waterberg Plateau** (p113).

LOCATION 435km north of Windhoek on sealed roads.

FACILITIES Extensive network of lookout points, spotlit waterholes and wildlife drives.

ACCOMMODATION Mix of basic and luxury camps. Lodges at Onguma Treetop Camp skim the night sky.

WILDLIFE RHYTHMS Peak viewing time is between July and September, when temperatures are high, rain is scarce and waterholes are teeming with animals. The best birding is in summer (December to February).

CONTACT Ministry of Environment and Tourism (☎ 061-236975; reservations@iwwn.com .na), Namibia Tourism (☎ 061-2906000; www .namibiatourism.com.na).

ETOSHA NATIONAL PARK

With little more than a low stone fence separating you from the surrounding white plains, and with your thermos of early-morning coffee and cameras ready, there are few places that can match the wildlife prospects of dawn at Etosha's Okaukuejo waterhole. The jewel in Namibia's wildlife crown, Etosha National Park is undoubtedly one of the best reserves in the world. Although the stark Etosha Pan occupies almost a third of the park and gives the reserve its name, it's the surrounding sweetgrass plains and mopane woodlands that sustain large numbers of wildlife. A network of artificial waterholes and naturally upwelling springs scattered along the southern boundary of the pan ensure large congregations of wildlife, and even one day at a single waterhole such as Okaukuejo can produce literally thousands of animals.

WEALTH AT THE WATERHOLES Once the bed of a vast inland lake, Etosha is now bone dry for much of the year: indeed, the bleached calcite soils and emaciated thorn trees give winter a still, skeletal air. However, this is when waterholes are at their most productive, drawing in prolific wildlife from the dry plains. Perhaps more so than anywhere else in Southern Africa, Etosha's waterholes during the dry season assure exceptional sightings. In the morning, arrive as early as possible at a waterhole and wait. Milling around in the pre-dawn shadow, throngs of **blue wildebeests**, **Burchell's zebras**, **giraffes**, **springboks**, **gemsboks**, **elands** and others wait for first light. Coming down to water is dangerous even when visibility is good, and herbivores try to avoid nocturnal drinking when predators have the advantage of night. Virtually the moment the first splinter of sun appears above the horizon, the procession begins. Row upon row of animals move down to the water, most taking their fill quickly and then moving off into the surrounding scrub, inevitably to be replaced by another herd.

The dense concentration of animals invites constant activity around the water. **Zebra** stallions herd their small

WILDLIFE HIGHLIGHTS
» Encountering hundreds, or even thousands, of large animals (including lions and elephants) at waterholes
» Watching herds of blue wildebeests, zebras, springboks and gemsboks race through the park » Crossing paths with pairs of Damara dik-diks on the trails » Easy sightings of four of the Big Five, including leopards, black rhino, lions and big cats » Birdlife includes flamingos, European migrants and birds of prey

NAMIBIA

harems when another group appears, and opposing males sometimes clash in furious bouts of kicking and biting in defence of their mares. Young male antelopes, typically springboks and gemsboks, lock horns and spar, practising the skills which one day may win them dominance. Flocks of **Cape turtle doves, red-eyed doves** and three species of **sandgrouse (Namaqua, Burchell's** and **double-banded)** circle constantly, attracting raptors such as **pale chanting goshawks, Ovambo goshawks, lanner falcons, bateleurs** and **martial eagles**; the chances of seeing an aerial kill are high at the waterholes. Everything makes way when **elephants** arrive, particularly if there's a bull in sexual readiness. Known as 'musth' and obvious by the copiously oozing temporal gland on the temples, bulls in this state are aggressive and intolerant. Other drinkers are chased and vehicles should keep their distance.

THE EARLY BIRD CATCHES THE CATS

The waterhole procession continues for most of the morning so, although the

---

WATCHING TIPS

While sitting on the benches around Okaukuejo waterhole at night, keep an eye on the large camelthorn trees that line the path along the stone wall. Arboreal black-tailed tree rats emerge at night to forage on young shoots, buds and the outer tunics of seedpods. Shine with a flashlight into the trees to show up the distinctive white belly. Occasionally, small-spotted genets can be seen hunting the rats and other nocturnal denizens such as Bibron's thick-toed gecko, also readily seen on the chalet walls at night. Close to the spotlights, watch the branch tips for lesser bushbabies and fork-tailed drongos as they snatch moths and other insects from the air. At Namutoni Rest Camp, huge numbers of red-billed queleas roost in the reedbeds near King Nehale waterhole. Watch them from the fort tower as the flocks return from the plains at sundown, so dense that they resemble smoke clouds.

---

best light for photography is in the early morning, you won't be disappointed if you arrive late, as an entire day can pass at a waterhole without a lull in activity. Take note though, that except for ubiquitous **black-backed jackals** trotting nimbly

NAMIBIA

GEMSBOK WITH ZEBRAS AND SPRINGBOKS, ETOSHA NATIONAL PARK

among the herds, the chances of viewing predators at the pans are better early in the day, particularly with shy species such as **leopards**, which seek cover as it warms up. **Cheetahs** also drink early, though they are rare in Etosha despite the suitable habitat and high numbers of **springboks**, their main prey. Competition from **lions**, which also concentrate heavily on springboks, keeps cheetah numbers low: most sightings are around Namutoni, Andoni and Charitsaub. Like other cats, **lions** generally drink early or towards sundown but they readily rest near waterholes throughout the day. With no natural enemies aside from other lions they can relax at waterholes, which also provides excellent chances for an ambush. Waterholes with suitable cover around them are worth a second look – try Chudop, Kalkheuwel (also very good for **leopards**) and the Salvadora-Charitsaub-Sueda triangle in between Halali and Okaukuejo. Okondeka near Okaukuejo Rest Camp is a focal point for the Okondeka pride.

Other productive waterholes are Klein Namutoni and Twee Palms (both are excellent for afternoon photography), Aus and Gemsbokvlakte. However, you needn't even leave camp to enjoy the waterholes. All the rest camps have a waterhole within walking distance; perhaps the best of them is the famous floodlit waterhole at Okaukuejo. Apart from very regular visits by **elephants** and most of the **antelope** species, this is an excellent site for **black rhinos**. Virtually assured during winter if you sit up during the night, you can see more black rhinos in a single sitting than the numbers surviving in most other African countries.

FLOODS & FLOCKS In a region with such little water, Etosha is transformed during the short, wet summer. Most rain falls between January and March, arriving in violent, thunderous squalls and filling much of Etosha Pan with a shallow, life-giving layer. This is one of the most important breeding grounds of **greater** and **lesser flamingos** (the latter more striking in its pinker plumage and dark-

LIONESS AND HER CUBS, ETOSHA NATIONAL PARK

red bill) which arrive at the pan in the thousands. Huge numbers are attracted to the shallow water of Fischer's Pan near Namutoni where they build their conical mud nests on the mudflats. In summers of particularly high rainfall, up to a million flamingos may spread themselves across the pan and the colonies are sometimes raided by **spotted hyenas** and **black-backed jackals**. Large numbers of **eastern white pelicans** also breed here in good years.

For many Palaearctic migrants, the flooded Etosha Pan provides an opportune stopover, so they tend to be visible at the start of summer rains (November) and towards the end (March to April). Waders such as **sanderlings**, **Caspian plovers**, **grey plovers** and **marsh sandpipers** join breeding migrants from equatorial Africa including rare **dwarf bitterns** and nonbreeding intra-African visitors such as **Abdim's storks** and **open-billed storks**. Migratory birds of prey including **steppe buzzards**, **African hobbies**, **Montagu's** and **pallid harriers**, **western red-footed falcons** and **lesser kestrels** swell the raptor species count; in all, 35 species are known from the park. Less reliant on rainfall for their life cycles, raptors can be sighted all year due to the constant supply of carcasses.

NEW LIFE Water everywhere means that other wildlife is not tied to the waterholes and disperses to utilise grasslands which are unproductive during the winter. With so much water around there isn't much point waiting at waterholes, and summer is best spent driving in search of animals. Large herds of **blue wildebeests**, **springboks**, **gemsboks** and **Burchell's zebras** move to the sweetgrass plains to the north and west of Okaukuejo. This is where summer breeders such as springboks and blue wildebeests drop their young, and the plains near Okondeka waterhole and at Grootvlakte (head west from Okaukuejo Rest Camp as far as permitted – beyond the Ozonjuiti m'Bari waterhole is only open to registered tour operators) are usually excellent for seeing herds with newborn young. The birthing flush attracts large numbers of predators and this is probably the best time to see **cheetahs** on these plains. Opportunistic **jackals** are everywhere, searching relentlessly for unattended young or dogging larger hunters in the hope of a kill. **Honey badgers**, **bat-eared foxes** and troops of **banded mongooses** search among the new grass for newly emerged frogs and insects attracted to the flush of wildflowers. Endemic **black-faced impalas** also drop their young at this time (late December and January), though the largest concentrations occur far to the east near Namutoni Rest Camp.

Summer days can be extremely hot and, more so than in winter, it is important to be looking for wildlife at the crack of dawn (when the gates open) or late in the afternoon. Once the day begins to heat up, most animals take cover and even if you do spot something, it's unlikely to be doing much more than resting.

ETOSHA'S ENDEMIC ANTELOPES
Etosha is home to two **antelopes** which occur only in northwestern Namibia and across the border in Angola (where the prolonged civil war has left their populations uncertain). Both are easily overlooked – one because it seems familiar, the other due to its diminutive size. At first glance, the **black-faced impala** looks no different from the common impala, but it is a unique subspecies with slightly darker colouring and a purplish-black facial blaze. Very difficult to see outside Etosha, it is common around Halali and Namutoni Rest Camps. Also near Namutoni, one of Africa's smallest antelopes, the **Damara dik-dik**, occurs at densities of 90 every square kilometre – one of the densest concentrations of any small antelope in Africa. Along Dikdik Dr (Bloubokdraai) they ignore vehicles, making this one of the best places to observe the monogamous pairs; they mate for life, so if you see one cross the road, be sure to wait for its partner to appear.

NAMIBIA

NAMIBIA

NAMIB-NAUKLUFT PARK

Africa's largest park is also one of the most arid, and much of the Namib-Naukluft appears to have no life at all. However, coastal fogs (born when moist Atlantic air meets freezing Antarctic currents) provide critical moisture and allow wildlife to persist in barren, moonscape-like conditions. Nowhere in this vast wilderness is wildlife abundant, but there are few places on earth where the sense of life's persistence is as palpable. From the vast central dune sea, of which the northward progress over the gravel plains is checked only by occasional flows down the Kuiseb River, to the relatively lush Naukluft mountain plateau, the Namib's wildlife requires patience and insight to enjoy.

GRAVEL PLAINS & WATERY HAVENS Bordered by the Swakop and Kuiseb Rivers, the Namib section of the park is the most accessible and the scenic Welwitschia Plains Dr provides an excellent introduction (permits available at Swakopmund or Windhoek, and ask for the informative brochure). Life is hardly noticeable here, but look around the base of drought-resistant dollar bushes and ink bushes for signs of **beetles**, **spiders** and the **Namaqua chameleon**, top predator of the shrub mini-ecosystems. Don't be surprised if inquisitive **tractrac chats** suddenly appear from nowhere at the designated stopping points: in this place of extremes, people are a profitable source of easy pickings. Less confident are endemic **Gray's larks**. Small and stone-coloured, they crouch when alarmed and are extremely difficult to see. Search the gravel with binoculars: they frequently hide close to the road until the disturbance of a vehicle has passed. North of the Swakop River, the plains are strewn with ancient **welwitschia** plants which, by absorbing condensation from coastal fogs, can survive any drought and live for thousands of years.

More conspicuous wildlife congregates along the two riverbeds. The Kuiseb Bridge camp site allows explora-

LOCATION Multiple entry points, some accessible by 2WD. Sesriem park entrance is 65km from Sossusvlei.

FACILITIES Numerous walks in the Naukluft section including short walks and day trails. The self-guided Naukluft Hiking Trail winds through stunning scenery but is very challenging (allow four to eight days and book well ahead).

ACCOMMODATION Wide choice of camps in the Namib section. Basic and luxury options near Sossusvlei and Naukluft. No accommodation at Sandwich Lagoon. Good Tok Tokkie walking trails (www.namibweb.com/tok .htm).

WILDLIFE RHYTHMS The rains are often unpredictable but usually occur in summer (December to February), if at all, transforming parts of the Namib (particularly the dunes at Sossusvlei where wildlife congregates). September to October onwards is best for birds at Sandwich Lagoon.

CONTACT Ministry of Environment and Tourism (☎ 061-236975; reservations@iwwn.com.na).

WILDLIFE HIGHLIGHTS
» Encountering arid-zone endemics, including Hartmann's mountain zebras and dune larks » Sightings of unusual desert species, including the baboons of the Namib » Home to Namibia's only population of wild horses » Gemsboks, springboks and ostriches are common » Rare reptiles include Peringuey's adders, dune-plated lizards and web-footed geckos

tion of the canyon, home to **klipspring-ers**, **steenboks** and small troops of arid-adapted **chacma baboons**. The canyon walls are home to cliff-breeding birds such as **black eagles**, **black storks** and **rosy-faced lovebirds**, while the compara-tively lush vegetation of the riverbeds at-tracts **swallow-tailed bee-eaters**, **cardinal woodpeckers** and **brubrus**. **Lappet-faced vultures** nest in large camelthorn trees from May to September.

On the coast and accessible only by 4WD, Sandwich Lagoon was formerly Namibia's most important coastal wet-land for seabirds and shorebirds. The sheltered lagoon once attracted an estimated 200,000 birds but increased siltation of the wetland is forcing birds elsewhere. September and October still see the arrival of Palaearctic waders such as **Arctic terns**, **curlew sandpipers**, **sanderlings**, **little stints**, **turnstones**, and **bar-tailed godwits** (albeit in reduced numbers). Flocks of **greater** and **lesser flamingos**, **eastern white pelicans**, **black-necked grebes**, **chestnut-banded plovers** and **Hartlaub's gulls** also occur. Check the MET offices in Swakopmund

WATCHING TIPS

An artificial waterhole on the gravel plains near Ganab camp site attracts Hartmann's mountain zebras, springboks, gemsboks and ostriches. Other waterholes, Zebra Pan and Hotsas, are further afield from camp sites but still worth visiting. Found throughout the Namib, the barking gecko unleashes its squeaking vocal repertoire just as the sun is setting. Wait patiently with a flashlight near the source of the 'barks', particularly in the Sesriem camp site.

for updates on the birdlife before you decide to make the trip.

MOUNTAIN OASIS Rising unexpectedly from the flat gravel plains in the east, the Naukluft Massif is a high plateau cut by narrow gorges, waterfalls and freezing mountain pools. This is the richest area of the Namib for wildlife, though even here it is widespread and scarce. You are almost certain to see **Hartmann's mountain zebras**, a distinct race restricted to western Namibia and southern Angola; this section of the park was proclaimed for them. The largest of the three races of zebras

MEERKAT AND HER PUPS PLAY

NAMIBIA

BABOONS OF THE NAMIB

Making their home in the most arid region in the world to be inhabited by any primate (aside from humans), the chacma baboons of the Namib live a perilous existence. Water is so scarce here that they may go without drinking for months (116 days is the record) – people would perish after about a week. To be able to survive here, the Namib baboons have learned a unique suite of adaptive behaviours. Showering themselves with shaded, cool sand from under trees, taking single bites from poisonous but moisture-filled plants and limiting social activity to the cool hours of the early morning all serve to lower a baboon's body temperature. Even so, their temperature may vary 5°C to 6°C in a day, regularly topping 42°C. While this would ultimately prove fatal for humans, overheated baboons simply lie down with splayed arms and legs, passively dissipating heat until it is cool enough to resume foraging.

occurring in Southern Africa, they are most active early in the morning and after 3pm; on cold mornings, look for them on east-facing slopes where they sun themselves. Ubiquitous **gemsboks** and **springboks** occur on the plateau flats, while **klipspringers**, **greater kudus** and **grey duikers** inhabit the wooded gorges. **Leopards**, **caracals** and numerous other carnivores occur but most are very rarely seen. Colonies of **meerkats** and **yellow mongooses** are the most visible predators, often sharing their burrow systems with **Cape ground squirrels**.

The massif's varied habitats are rich in birdlife, marking the transition zone between the Namib's gravel plains and less arid Karoo savanna to the southeast. February is usually the best month, when rains on the plateau attract **African black ducks**, **Karoo robins**, **pin-tailed whydahs** and **cinnamon-breasted warblers** along with **Rüppell's korhaans** and rock dwellers such as **long-billed larks**, **Herero chats**, **rockrunners**, **Monteiro's hornbills** and **chestnut weavers**. The well-vegetated valleys are home to **swallow-tailed bee-eaters**, **long-billed crombecs**, **Layard's titbabblers**, **golden-tailed woodpeckers** and **lesser honeyguides**; above in the cliffs, look for **black eagles**, **lanner falcons** and **augur buzzards**.

DUNE DWELLERS Probably the most recognisable icon of the Namib, the

apricot dunes of the vast central dune sea harbour a very different fauna. In contrast to the epic scenery of the dune surrounds, the wildlife here is inconspicuous and cryptic. Reliant on the coastal fogs, the dune community engages in unique moisture-collection rituals. **Fog-basking beetles** line up on dune crests, their posteriors raised skywards to intercept the incoming fog, which condenses on their smooth carapace. **Button beetles** have a different tactic, excavating neat, parallel trenches which act as fog-traps from which they drink their fill. **Web-footed geckos** also rely on condensation, using their long tongue to collect moisture beads from the head and snout. They're most likely to be seen in the early morning, when you can follow their tiny, fig-leaf tracks. You may also encounter their main predator, **Peringuey's adder**, which submerges itself beneath the sand, leaving only its face protruding – keep an eye out for its distinctive side-winding track. Appropriately named dune endemics, **dune-plated lizards**, **slip-face lizards** and **dune larks** are other specialities to watch out for.

The fauna of the dunes is probably best seen at Sossusvlei, where a huge clay-bottomed pan can hold water for months following good rainfall (in summer, if it does occur), attracting larger game such as **gemsboks**, **springboks** and **ostriches**. Further south, the windmill at Garub is the only source of water for **wild horses**. Probably descended from mounts kept by occupying German troops in the late 1800s, the horses are a unique component of the Namib. Watch for them along the tarred road between Lüderitz and Aus and pay particular attention at night: after droughts, road deaths are the main cause of mortality to the desert horses.

NAMIBIA

NAMIB-NAUKLUFT PARK

SKELETON COAST NATIONAL PARK & KAOKOLAND

NAMIBIA

LOCATION 200km north of Swakopmund (Ugab River Gate) or 170km west of Khorixas (Springbokwasser Gate). Salt/gravel road accessible year-round

FACILITIES Travel by 4WD, wildlife-watching from a hide at Uniab Delta.

ACCOMMODATION Largely camps and luxury tents.

WILDLIFE RHYTHMS October to May is consistently sunny with clear skies. Migratory birds arrive between September and February. During winter (April to May), a time of dense fogs and cold westerly winds, most wildlife tends to seek cover.

CONTACT Ministry of Environment and Tourism (☎ 061-236975; reservations@iwwn.com.na).

Named not only for the many mariners who perished here, but also for the numerous shipwrecks and whale remains that litter this desolate stretch of northern Namibian coastline, the Skeleton Coast is one of Southern Africa's most remote parks. Stretching almost 500km from the Ugab River mouth to the Angolan border in the north, the barren coastal desert forbids large congregations of wildlife, and this is not a place to expect encounters with teeming herds. However, the arid-adapted wildlife inhabits surroundings unlike any other, and for those prepared to invest some extra effort there are unique viewing and photographic opportunities here.

LIFE AT THE OASIS A few kilometres north of the Torra Bay camp site, the mouth of the Uniab River spreads out into a series of reed-fringed freshwater pools where wildlife seeks respite from the arid desert. Small groups of **springboks**, **greater kudus** and flocks of up to 50 **ostriches** are drawn from the gravel plains to the pools, while the permanent water permits normally nomadic **gemsboks** to occur here year-round.

However, more rewarding than occasional sightings of large wildlife is the birdlife of the delta. Large aggregations of **flamingos**, **black crakes**, **Egyptian geese**, **Cape shovelers**, **Cape teals**, **avocets** and **purple gallinules** are commonly seen from the elevated parking area above the fifth delta. During the summer, **little stints** and **wood** and **curlew sandpipers** occur while residents of the arid plains such as **tractrac chats**, **black korhaans** and **Gray's larks** (a Namibian endemic) make regular visits. Around sunset, flocks of **Namaqua sandgrouse** arrive daily from as far as 60km away to drink and, in the case of the male, to soak their absorbent belly feathers to carry water back to the chicks. A 6km self-guided trail takes walkers along a narrow canyon of the Uniab towards the coast where you should watch out for rare **Damara terns** on their nests (little more than a shallow scrape in the gravelly soil). From September through to May, tens of thousands of Palaeartic migrants such as **sanderlings**,

---

WILDLIFE HIGHLIGHTS

» Cape fur-seals form massive, noisy colonies on the coast » Home of the much-publicised desert elephants » Prolific wetland birdlife at Uniab Delta » Sightings of bird species include rufous-tailed palm thrushes and parrots » Good chance of ostrich sightings turnstones and **grey plovers** congregate on the beach.

WILDERNESS WITHIN THE WILDERNESS The entire northern section of the park (starting 14km north of Terrace Bay) has been set aside as a wilderness area and is closed to self-driving tourists. However, organised tours enable visitors to explore the region by guided walks and 4WD tours. The huge **Cape fur-seal** colony at Cape Frio is the main wildlife attraction, but all along the coast beached seal carcasses attract **brown hyenas** and **black-backed jackals**. The only seal-hunting **lions** in the world occur along the Skeleton Coast, even preying on the bulls – which may weigh as much as 350kg – as well as scavenging the occasional beached **whale** or **dolphin**. Nobody is sure if lions still occur as far north as Cape Frio but there is a large pride just outside the park boundary between the Hoanib and Uniab riverbeds in the south. Privately owned Palmwag Lodge (☎ 061-259293) is in the pride's territory.

Although not abundant, other big wildlife occurs in the wilderness area and outside the park in Kaokoland. The much-publicised desert **elephants** use the Hoanib and other major rivercourses to move between patches of vegetation and water. Scarce and capable of covering large distances daily, they are difficult to find. The best chance of seeing them is probably with a tour by the very experienced Skeleton Coast Fly-in Safaris (www.skeleton coastsafaris.com). **Black rhinos, giraffes, chacma baboons**, and **klipspringers** inhabit the tree-lined watercourses as well as many small birds including **mountain chats, rockrunners, titbabblers, white-backed** and **red-faced mousebirds** and **Rüppell's parrots** (the range of the last is restricted to Kaokoland and neighbouring southern Angola). The tours camp on the Kunene River, the only place in Southern Africa with recorded sightings of **rufous-tailed palm thrushes, Cinderella waxbills** and **grey kestrels**.

AMPUTEES FOR FREEDOM Kaokoland (and adjoining Damaraland) is home to the world's last free-ranging population of **black rhinos** (all other populations live in protected areas) but its isolation leaves them vulnerable to poachers from neighbouring Angola and Zambia. Beginning in the late 1980s, the Ministry of Environment and Tourism embarked on a program aimed at removing the incentive for killing rhinos by sawing off their horns – a strategy also used on white rhinos elsewhere. Rhinos are darted from helicopters and both horns are removed just above the bone, using a small chainsaw. Released with an antibiotic coating of Stockholm tar on the stump, the rhinos apparently suffer no ill effects – but their calves might. Researchers found that although dehorned rhinos forage and interact with other rhinos normally, mothers were probably less capable of defending calves from predators. The fact that horns also regrow as much as 6cm a year – necessitating frequent and expensive trims – meant the controversial scheme was eventually abandoned.

SEAL COLONY

NAMIBIA

LOCATION 115km north of Swakopmund. Compacted salt road accessible year-round to all vehicles.

FACILITIES Sealing museum.

ACCOMMODATION Cape Cross Lodge has luxury rooms. An hour's drive away, Swakopmund has a good mix of options.

WILDLIFE RHYTHMS Short birthing period runs from late November to early December.

CONTACT Ministry of Environment and Tourism (☎ 061-236975; reservations@iwwn.com.na).

CAPE CROSS SEAL RESERVE

The only pinniped (which encompasses seals, sea lions and walruses) that breeds on continental Africa, the **Cape fur-seal** is restricted to about 25 colonies. Most occur on inaccessible islands, but a handful of extremely large mainland colonies provide extraordinary viewing opportunities. En route to the Skeleton Coast National Park lies one of the most accessible, Cape Cross. Between 80,000 and 110,000 fur-seals live here in a dense, seething mass. Unlike some seal species which huddle closely, Cape fur-seals vigorously defend their own small personal space. They wage a perpetual growling, bleating battle for resting spots, creating a staggering din that never subsides. Combined with the colony's pungent aroma, the effect is truly breathtaking.

There is endless activity and interaction in the colony – adults fighting for space, lost pups looking for mothers, yearling seals playing in the surf – so visiting at any time is fruitful. However, the social bedlam reaches a violent high during the breeding season when adult males begin arriving in mid-October to stake out territories. Their patch may only be a few metres wide but they defend it fiercely from other males and clashes are occasionally fatal. Territories are constantly disputed, peaking in mid-November when pregnant females 'haul out' to look for birth sites. Males gain mating 'rights' with females that pup in their territories, so their arrival at the colony intensifies the already high levels of aggression.

Like males disputing territories, females fight over pupping sites – each prefers a position close to the water. But despite the female's strong maternal bond and vigorous defence of her offspring, unattended pups are vulnerable to predation from **brown hyenas** and **black-backed jackals** (active early in the morning and late afternoon). This, combined with abandonment and being crushed by adults – particularly bulls in the frenetic defence of their harem – means that over a quarter of pups die in their first year. Please do not contribute to pup deaths by walking among the seals and creating a stampede. If you get tired of seal-watching, scan the water with binoculars for various seabirds including **white-breasted** and **Cape cormorants** and **Arctic** and **common terns**.

WILDLIFE HIGHLIGHTS
» **Close-up viewing of a sprawling Cape fur-seal colony**
» **Predators such as black-backed jackals and brown hyenas** » **Flocks of white-breasted and Cape cormorants**
» **Common terns are regularly seen off-shore** » **Breeding and birthing season of the pinniped can be as dramatic as a human soap opera**

●●'● WATCHING TIPS

Rather than walking the length of the viewing wall expecting to see something different, choose a spot and sit for a while: no matter where you are, there is constant interaction and interesting behaviour.

KAUDOM GAME RESERVE

Probably Namibia's richest wildlife area after Etosha National Park, Kaudom is also one of the most challenging. Deep sandy roads criss-crossed by fossil river valleys (called omiramba), which become boggy marshes during the wet season, restrict access to 4WD only and vehicles must travel in pairs. There are few places in Southern Africa that evoke such a sense of wilderness, and for the adventurous wildlife-watcher, Kaudom has much to offer.

A REFUGE FOR PREDATORS After Etosha, Kaudom is Namibia's most important reserve for large carnivores. One of only two protected populations of **lions** occurs here and it is the only place in Namibia where **African wild dogs** can be spotted. They regularly visit Sikereti Camp in the south, but these nomads range widely and frequently wander over the border into Botswana. Tsoana waterhole and waterholes along the eastern side of the reserve (such as Baikiaea, Leeupan and Tari Kora) are good places to look for wild dogs as well as **spotted hyenas**, **leopards** and **cheetahs**. In the drier winter months, many species of herbivore concentrate at the waterholes, including large herds of **elephants**, **buffalo**, **giraffes**, **Burchell's zebras**, **blue wildebeests**, **greater kudus** and **tsessebes**. The extensive floodplains around Kaudom Camp in the north attract large herds of grazers and hold very good prospects for spotting **roan antelopes**.

In contrast to the other wildlife which disperses during the wet summer, a flush of migratory birdlife is attracted to Kaudom in the rainy season. Woodland residents such as **Meyer's parrots**, **Bradfield's hornbills**, and **Senegal** and **coppery-tailed coucals** are joined by over 70 migrants including **open-billed storks**, **African crakes**, **dwarf bitterns** and **African golden orioles**. Migratory raptors such as **lesser spotted eagles**, **western red-footed falcons** and **Montagu's** and **pallid harriers** can be seen in the summer, while year-round residents include **pygmy falcons**, **red-necked falcons**, **Dickinson's kestrels** and rare **western banded snake eagles**.

WILDLIFE HIGHLIGHTS

» Outside Etosha, the only Namibian reserve where you can easily see lions » Packs of African wild dogs share the park with spotted hyenas, cheetahs and leopards » 320 species of birds, including unusual residents and migrants » Roan antelopes, elephants, buffalo and blue wildebeests are abundant » Giraffes congregate at waterholes in winter

LOCATION 796km north of Windhoek. Only accessible by 4WD and vehicles must travel in pairs.

FACILITIES 300km wildlife drive network.

ACCOMMODATION Cape Cross Lodge has luxury rooms. Basic camps at Sikereti and Kaudom.

WILDLIFE RHYTHMS Large mammals congregate at waterholes year-round but June to October is the best viewing time.

CONTACT Ministry of Environment and Tourism (☎ 061-236975; reservations@iwwn.com.na).

NAMIBIA

●● WATCHING TIPS

Unlike most big wildlife reserves, you can leave your car at any point. Use this privilege judiciously to check the muddy edges of waterholes: fresh tracks of lions, African wild dogs and other predators indicate areas in which to invest some time. Exercise extreme care when searching around waterholes and never alight from a vehicle alone.

LOCATION 155km southeast of Katima Mulilo, access only by 4WD.

FACILITIES Very little.

ACCOMMODATION Undeveloped camp sites throughout the park, visitors must be entirely self-sufficient. A good supply of drinking water is a must. Huts at nearby Mudumu National Park.

WILDLIFE RHYTHMS Wildlife-watching on the two islands is best in winter (June to August). Rains render much of the park inaccessible during prime birding months (December to March).

CONTACT Ministry of Environment and Tourism (☎ 061-236975; reservations@iwwn.com.na).

NAMIBIA

MAMILI NATIONAL PARK

A protracted history of cross-border conflict, resettlement and heavy poaching has severely effected the wildlife of the Caprivi Strip, Namibia's 500km-long fingerlike extension in its extreme northeast. Sitting in the massive Linyanti Swamp and the site of Namibia's largest protected wetland, Mamili has escaped the worst and although antelope numbers were devastated during the 1980s, the wildlife is recovering and approaching the richness of the nearby Okavango Delta. It's seldom visited due to its isolation and difficult roads, but the birdlife alone warrants a trip.

Year-round water creates fertile habitat for birds and nearly 70% of Namibia's total have been recorded from this region. **Wattled cranes** breed on the expansive floodplains, while the waterways are home to **slaty egrets**, **rufous-bellied herons**, **African** and **lesser jacanas**, **pygmy geese** and **swamp boubous**. Seven species of cisticola occur including the papyrus-dwelling **chirping cisticola** and the very similar **black-backed cisticola** (the alarm call of the latter, which sounds like a machine-gun, is the easiest way to differentiate them). **Greater** and **lesser blue-eared starlings**, **western banded snake eagles**, **brown firefinches**, **collared palm thrushes** and **eastern bearded robins** are among the many other species you might see, while **Bradfield's hornbills**, **three-banded coursers** and **white-crowned plovers** are common. Both **yellow-billed** and **red-billed oxpeckers** occur.

Despite heavy poaching in the past, Mamili's rich habitats have remained essentially undiminished and mammal populations are beginning to flourish again. **Red lechwes**, **sitatungas** and **waterbucks** were formerly the poachers' main targets but, except for the shy sitatungas, they are easily seen in the park today. Hundreds of **hippos** and **Nile crocodiles** inhabit the permanent channels, while **elephants**, **buffaloes** and **lions** are common on the two main islands, Lupala and Nkasa. Other predators include **leopards**, **spotted hyenas** and **African wild dogs**. The Mashi River is home to **spotted-necked otters**.

◑◑ WATCHING TIPS

Nearby Mudumu National Park is the only location in Namibia where the coppery sunbird has been recorded, though there is no reason why it should not occur in Mamili – keep a lookout, particularly on the edges of riverine forest.

WILDLIFE HIGHLIGHTS
» Namibia's richest birding region » Sightings of rare bird species include western banded snake eagles, wattled cranes, white-crowned plovers and brown firefinches » Elephant and buffalo are common on the main islands » Occasional lion sightings » Home to a growing population of water-loving antelopes and semiaquatic creatures, including spotted-necked otters

WATERBERG PLATEAU PARK

WATERBERG
PLATEAU
PARK

NAMIBIA

Rising 200m above the surrounding flat terrain, the Waterberg Plateau is a natural geological sanctuary. The steep cliffs of the plateau create a barrier to migration, and wildlife-watching is best in the plateau's open woodlands. Visitors cannot take up their own vehicles, but guided wildlife drives usually produce a wide variety of species including some rare species, particularly **roan** and **sable antelopes**. However, seats are limited (book ahead or as soon as you arrive), wildlife is generally shy here and the tours tend to be rather rushed. By far the best way to experience Waterberg is by its numerous walking trails.

Two extended walks – one accompanied by an armed ranger, the other self-guided – allow the adventurous to explore. There is always the chance of encounters with some dangerous species including **black** and **white rhinos**, **buffaloes** and **leopards** so only experienced bushwalkers should attempt the four-day self-guided trail. Wildlife is generally less approachable by foot than in vehicles, but **giraffes**, **tsessebes**, **greater kudus**, **warthogs** and **chacma baboons** are common sights on the walks. The top predator, the leopard, apparently numbers 70 which, if accurate, makes it one of the highest densities in Southern Africa, but the rangers count themselves lucky if they see two a year.

Birding during the walks really is excellent. The foothills are the preferred habitat of four Namibian endemics: **Hartlaub's francolins**, **Monteiro's hornbills**, **rockrunners** and **short-toed rock thrushes**. Namibia's sole breeding colony of **Cape vultures** roosts in the cliffs of Waterberg's Karakuwisa Mountain; the vulture hide at the foot of the mountain offers excellent viewing of these and other birds of prey including **booted** and **black eagles**, **peregrine** and **lanner falcons** and **augur buzzards**. Carcasses are replenished every Wednesday to attract raptors. Even the short walks around the rest camp can be rewarding and **Rüppell's parrots**, **Carp's tits** and **Bennett's woodpeckers** are specialities that can be seen on the Kambazembi Walk.

LOCATION 300km northeast of Windhoek, 97km east of Otjiwarongo. Final 25km on gravel/sand – check ahead during rains.

FACILITIES Guided walks and wildlife drives, self-guided trails, hides, vulture hide.

ACCOMMODATION Lodges, huts and camping grounds.

WILDLIFE RHYTHMS Viewing is most productive during the dry season (April to October).

CONTACT Ministry of Environment and Tourism (☎ 061-236975; reservations@iwwn.com.na).

NAMIBIA

WILDLIFE HIGHLIGHTS
» Refuge for rare species including black and white rhinos, roan and sable antelopes » Seven endemic species of birds » Namibia's only breeding colony of Cape vultures » Excellent for Damara dik-dik sightings » Frequent sightings of giraffes and tsessebes

👀 WATCHING TIPS

Take time to explore the short tracks around Bernabé de la Bat Rest Camp – early mornings are excellent for viewing pairs of Damara dik-diks close to camp, and this is the only place in Southern Africa aside from Etosha where they are likely to be seen.

OTHER SITES

BRANDBERG Namibia's highest peak, Brandberg Mountain rises abruptly from the Namib Desert and at its highest point towers 2.5km above the gravel plains. Wildlife is very sparse but you will see some painted on the walls: Brandberg preserves an extraordinary gallery of San paintings that are an estimated 15,000 to 16,000 years old, including the famously enigmatic White Lady. Endemic birds such as Rüppell's korhaans, Herero chats and Monteiro's hornbills occur here as well as small numbers of chacma baboons, klipspringers and steenboks.
☎ 061-236975; reservations@iwwn.com.na; 140km west of Omaruru

BWABWATA NATIONAL PARK Combining the former Caprivi Game Reserve with the Mahango Game Reserve and the Kwando Triangle near Kongola, Bwabwata aims to rehabilitate a wilderness that has been heavily affected by poaching. Mahango and Kwando are core conservation areas and also the only spots with any sort of facilities but you'll need a 4WD regardless. Wildlife in Mahango and Kwando is similar to that found in the Okavango Delta and is good in winter when waterholes and rivers are low.
☎ 061-236975; reservations@iwwn.com.na; 220km east of Rundu

CHEETAH CONSERVATION FUND To the east of Otjiwarongo and with almost identical aims of big-cat conservation as Okonjima (p115), the Cheetah Conservation Fund has a research centre and an excellent Cheetah Museum. Displays and interactive exhibits illustrate the ecology of the cheetah in Namibia as well as the conservation problems it faces. Visitors are shown cheetahs rescued from conflict situation on farms, many of which are destined for relocation into safe conservation areas, and Chewbaaka, CCF's tame 'ambassador' cheetah, might also make a thrilling appearance. The centre does not have overnight accommodation, but it's in the middle of the Waterberg Conservancy – a unique alliance of 10 privately owned farms promoting cheetah conservation. A number of the farmers operate beautiful and very hospitable guest houses – by staying with them, you directly support their efforts to conserve the cheetah. CCF doesn't charge for visits to the cheetah museum but donations are their lifeblood.
☎ 067-306225; www.cheetah.org; 50km east of Otjiwarongo

DAAN VILJOEN GAME PARK Just outside of Windhoek and on the road to Swakopmund, the camp site and bungalows at this beautiful little park make a rewarding overnight alternative to the capital. There's only a handful of big game species here but one of them is the endemic Hartmann's mountain zebra, far more visible here than in the rest of their scattered range throughout the Namib. Springboks, red hartebeests, greater kudus, elands, gemsboks and over 200 bird species occur at Daan Viljoen Fame Park. It gets very busy on weekends and holidays.
☎ 061-236975; reservations@iwwn.com.na; 25km west of Windhoek

FISH RIVER CANYON PARK For absolute quiet and otherworldly views, the 2600-million-year-old Fish River Canyon is hard to surpass. It is widely cited as the world's second-largest canyon, after the Grand Canyon, but it depends on your criteria (length, depth or width); Ethiopia's Blue Nile Gorge is far deeper. Regardless, the scenery is quite spectacular and is the main attraction. Wildlife is difficult to see here but during winter when the Orange River dwindles to a few waterholes is the best time. It's also when the outstanding five-day Fish River Hiking Trail is open (May to September). Natural 60°C hot mineral springs soothe aching muscles at the end of the trail at Ai-Ais, which is set up as a spa resort. There's another upwelling of hot springs at the Palm Springs camp site at the start of the trail, accessible also to day walkers.

If you spot enterprising locals along the roadside with handwritten signs showing the park's name, by all means pay their small fee but they'll show you a miniature tributary at the edge of the real thing.
☎ 061-236975; reservations@iwwn.com.na; 94km west of Grünau

HOBATERE LODGE A privately run concession on the western boundary of Etosha NP; the wildlife is similar but the experience and expense is typical of luxury lodges across Southern Africa. Guided wildlife drives ensure you'll see pretty much everything you might encounter on your own in Etosha; they also operate after dark with chances of nocturnal sightings of leopards, small carnivores and owls. The lions and leopards here are part of a fascinating study to determine how big cats live in extremely arid areas – ask owner-manager Steve Brain about it. Steve is also an excellent birder and there are few people in Southern Africa who can match his butterfly knowledge. Hobatere also has access to the tourist-restricted western half of Etosha.
☎ 067-687066; 65km northeast of Kamanjab

MUDUMU NATIONAL PARK Similar to nearby Mamili National Park (see p112), Mudumu was once a hunting concession. It's been protected now for nearly two decades now; wildlife is recolonising this park and is as diverse as in the nearby Okavango Delta, albeit in much smaller numbers. The birdlife is more rewarding, with western banded snake eagles, rufous-bellied herons, wattled cranes and coppery and purple-banded sunbirds among the locals.
☎ 061-236975; reservations@iwwn.com.na; 50km south of Kongola

OKONJIMA Owned by farmers-turned-conservationists the Hanssen family, Okonjima – as much refuge as reserve – is famous for its cats, rescuing cheetahs and leopards which would otherwise end up shot by stockmen. Orphaned cubs are hand-raised, which means a few tame big cats wander around – exhilarating but extremely dangerous, and children under 12 are forbidden. However, wild-caught adults are relocated to safe reserves elsewhere and the Hanssens are doing much to reduce the conflict between farmers and predators – their work is well worth supporting. They also virtually guarantee wild leopard sightings on a backdrop of Namibian red rocks. The photographic opportunities are unique, so long as you don't mind bait-style feeds to attract these normally extremely elusive cats.
☎ 067-687032/3/4, 81 142 1195 (cell); info@okonjima.com; 55km south of Otjiwarango

SPERRGEBIET In an area off-limits to the public for most of the last century, the Namibian government opened the Sperrgebiet ('forbidden zone' in German) in early 2009. The former diamond-mining area is one of the world's most spectacular arid biodiversity hotspots, spanning 26,000 sq km of spectacular dunes, desert tundra and stark, desolate wilderness. About 40% of the park is desert and 30% is grassland; the rest is rocks, granite mountains and moonscape. Though the area has yet to be fully explored, initial scientific assessments have discovered 776 plant species, 230 of which are thought to be unique to the park. There are also populations of gemsbok, hyenas and rare, threatened reptile species including the desert rain frog. Birds include the dune lark, black-headed canary and the African oystercatcher.
☎ 061-236975; reservations@iwwn.com.na; 45km north of Lüderitz

TSAOBIS LEOPARD NATURE PARK This is the only park in Namibia set aside specifically to protect leopards, but you'll need considerable luck to see one here. They're very shy and cross the reserve's fence as they please, but the resident Hartmann's mountain zebras, greater kudus, gemsboks and springboks ensure that there's usually a few around. Best places to look are along the Tsaobis and Swakop riverbeds. You're free to explore on foot here and although you probably won't find any big cats, the rugged scenery and herbivore sightings are rewarding.
☎ 061-236975; reservations@iwwn.com.na; 35km west of Otjimbingwe

BOTSWANA

CAPITAL GABORONE **AREA** 582,000 SQ KM **NATIONAL PARKS** 9 **MAMMAL SPECIES** 162

Land-locked Botswana seems to stretch for millions of miles. Blessed with endless vistas and vast open spaces ideal for Big Five spotting, Botswana has a political landscape that is almost as lush as its scenery.

THE LAND Botswana has a human population of 1.6 million, most of it concentrated along the far eastern border, and vast tracts of the land-locked country are occupied by wildlife alone. Because the Okavango Delta and the Chobe River provide a year-round water supply, nearly all Southern African mammal species are present, meaning superb wildlife-viewing is almost guaranteed.

With few fences and major roads, Botswana's ancient migratory routes continue to span vast distances. Romantic and unspoiled it may be, but you'll need plenty of time and roomy pockets to fully enjoy it. You'll be rewarded with some of the most spectacular wildlife-viewing this life has to offer. That's not to say those short of time or cash shouldn't visit; the town of Maun is

a good base for exploring some of Botswana's most impressive areas.

With an excellent conservation record and an official policy of minimal development in parks, Botswana's protected areas constitute more than 17% of the country – one of the world's highest percentages of land devoted to conservation. Furthermore, parks are linked by largely uninhabited habitat corridors (which allow wildlife to move freely between reserves) and 'wildlife management areas' (where tourism, some hunting and other human activity is permitted), which effectively more than double the amount of land available to wildlife.

With such a large percentage of land area dedicated to conservation, Botswana protects critically important

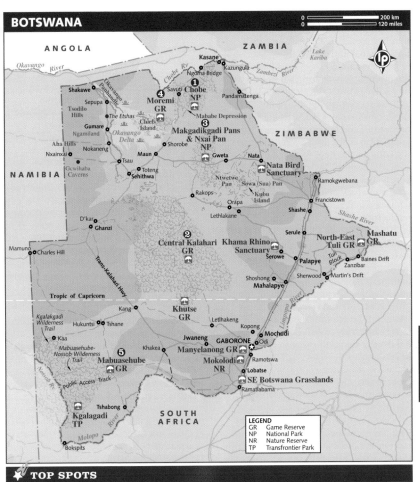

BOTSWANA

⭐ TOP SPOTS

1. CHOBE NATIONAL PARK
(p100) A veritable elephants'
playground, Chobe is home to
Africa's largest concentration. In
rainy seasons, herds migrate to
the park's southern half.

**2. CENTRAL KALAHARI GAME
RESERVE** (p68) The world's
second-largest wildlife reserve
blends vast open plains with
sweeping dunes, inhabited

by giraffes, lions and packs of
howling African wild dogs.

3. NXAI PAN NATIONAL PARK
(p128) Dotted with umbrella
acacia trees and imposing
baobabs, Nxai Pan has a huge
springbok population, plus
leopards, jaguars and cheetahs.

4. MOREMI GAME RESERVE
(p132) A waterbirds' paradise

teeming with feathered
creatures, Moremi offers safaris
by dugout canoe or 4WD. There
are also significant elephant
and big-cat populations.

**5. MABUASEHUBE GAME
RESERVE** (p136) Kalahari red
earth gives way to scrub and
salt pans inhabited by noisy
African bullfrogs, aardwolves
and giraffes.

populations of many large animals. The elephant population is booming, now numbering 120,000 (one for every 14 Botswanans) and talk of an elephant cull to prevent damage to villages has – for the moment – been brushed aside. Other mega-herbivores, like giraffes, hippos and buffaloes, occur in the thousands. Lions, spotted hyenas and leopards are very numerous, and Southern Africa's largest population of the endangered African wild dog occurs here. Huge seasonal congregations of Burchell's zebras and blue wildebeests follow pathways between Nxai Pan and Chobe National Parks, while resident aquatic antelopes such as red lechwes, pukus and sitatungas remain in the well-watered Okavango and Chobe riverfront year-round. In the Makgadik-gadi Pans and Nxai Pan National Parks, herds of wildebeests, zebras and other mammals migrate annually in search of permanent water and stable food supplies.

Most of Botswana consists of a vast and nearly level sand-filled basin charac-terised by scrub-covered savannah. The Kalahari, a semiarid expanse of sandy valleys, covers nearly 85% of the country, including the entire central and south-western regions.

Botswana's successes don't only lie in wildlife protection. Residents of many sub-Saharan countries eye the country with envy and it enjoys a high standard of economic stability, education and health-care. But don't be mistaken – outside of the modern veneer of Botswana's cities, this is a land very much ruled by nature.

WHEN TO GO With 80% of the country covered in dry Kalahari sands, water is the critical resource for wildlife. The wet season between October and April sees the arrival of migratory birds and is when the herds congregate on the fertile marshes and plains. The desert also blooms then, and huge herds of springboks, gemsboks and red hartebeests coalesce in the Central Kalahari Game Reserve and Mabuasehube Game Reserve – followed by their predators. The dry season is less spectacular but limited waterpoints in the Kalahari and Nxai Pan areas produce excellent opportunities for witnessing ambushes by carnivores. Along the Chobe River, the dry-season aggregations of elephants are among the largest anywhere in Africa.

WILDLIFE HIGHLIGHTS

» Witnessing African wild dogs break vehicle speed limits as they race through woodlands in Moremi Game Reserve (p132) » Joining lions in wait at the only water in Nxai Pan (p128), knowing a kill is inevitable » Spotting the shy and mysterious Pel's fishing owl in the Okavango (p132) » Finding cheetah tracks at Nxai Pan (p128) » The sight of Meyer's parrots turning sausage trees blue and red at Third Bridge (p132)

OSTRICHES, NXAI PAN NATIONAL PARK

BOTSWANA ITINERARIES

1. IN THE FOOTPRINTS OF ELEPHANTS Botswana's biggest drawcard is **Chobe National Park** (p120), and it's endowed with wildlife and teeming with thousands of

elephants – you'll want a good few days to explore the park's trails, 4WD routes and waterholes. Even before you catch your first glimpse of the great grey mammals, you'll see the trail of destruction – ripped leaves, crater-like footprints and torn tree bark – that they often leave behind. You'll never tire of Chobe, but when you're ready to move on, get back on the road to Maun, stopping at **Moremi Game Reserve** (p132), another excellent elephant hotspot offering canoe safaris. This route is equally possible beginning at Kasane rather than Maun.

2. BIRDLIFE With 577 species, Botswana is a birdwatcher's paradise. Set off from Maun and head to **Moremi Game Reserve** (p132), where water is abundant and wading birds

populous. There, you can hop into a dugout canoe, sit back and stare up at the big blue sky, raptors and birds of prey circling above you. Then take a side trip to Nata Bird Sanctuary and Sowa Pan – with a combined total of 165 bird species, including flamingos, it's well worth the diversion. Finally, take in **Makgadikgadi Pans and Nxai Pan** (p128) where kestrels, red-necked falcons, martial eagles and bateleurs are frequently seen.

3. DUST AND DESERT Let the dark red sand of the **Kalahari** (p68) coat your boots, and keep an eye out for mongooses, meerkats and small predators such as honey

badgers. After a few days in the wilderness, you'll be ready to hit the South African border and **Mabuasehube Game Reserve** (Kgalagadi Transfrontier Park; p68), which straddles both countries. When you've had your share of maroon earth and bullfrog croaking, head back to Gaborone. Alternatively you could go south, eventually winding up in Cape Town.

BOTSWANA

LOCATION Chobe Gate is 6km west of Kasane (80km west of Victoria Falls); access is by sealed road but internal roads are 4WD. Mababe Gate is 143km north of Maun on sand roads requiring 4WD.

FACILITIES A wildlife-watching road network and lookout points. River cruises and motorboat hire is available from numerous operators in Kasane. San (Bushman) paintings on Tsonxhwaa Hill at Savute, south of Savute Gate.

ACCOMMODATION Good selection of basic and luxury camps and lodges within and around the park.

WILDLIFE RHYTHMS The dry season (August to October) is best along the riverfront and around waterholes at Savute and Ngwezumba. The summer rains (December to February) attract massive Burchell's zebra migrations to Savute Marsh, moving to Linyanti from April onwards. For photographers, winter along the river is thick with dust, making conditions hazy but sunsets extraordinary.

CONTACT Parks and Reserves reservations office (☎ 686 1265; fax 686 1264; Maun). Prior bookings are necessary.

CHOBE NATIONAL PARK

Known largely for enormous congregations of **elephants** and **buffaloes** along the Chobe River, Chobe is actually one of Botswana's most diverse reserves. Encompassing wildlife-rich riverine woodlands, the Okavango-like Linyanti Swamp and the dry savanna-forest mosaic of Savute and Ngwezumba, wildlife here is both varied and abundant. Each area holds distinct attractions which fluctuate according to the cycles of rain and regrowth. Chobe's diversity and abundance ensure first-class viewing but the seasonal differences from one area to the next mean timing can make all the difference.

ALONG THE RIVER OF MANY NAMES Forming the reserve's northern boundary as well as the international border between Botswana and Namibia, the Chobe River (also called the Kwando, Linyanti and Itenge) is undeniably the most popular part of the park. Even before you see **elephants** here, it's clear they are abundant. Depending on seasonal movements, between 35,000 and 55,000 live inside the park and the damage to vegetation is severe. In the winter, the destruction looks stark but this is unquestionably the best time to see the herds as thousands line up along the river each morning and evening. They are exceptionally tolerant of vehicles (but be sure you maintain a reasonable distance) and close-up viewing of elephants interacting, swimming across the river and feeding on the riverine woodland is unsurpassed.

Other land leviathans are here in numbers. Herds of up to 1500 **buffaloes** occupy the riverfront, preferring the tall grass growing on the various 'flats' (where the river spreads out in summer flood). Leave camp early to catch them moving off into the woodlands where they spend the day ruminating. The **lions** here know the pattern and the riverfront offers fine chances to witness a kill. Buffaloes have the advantage in the open but once they reach the wooded bushline, the dense cover allows the lions to isolate a target. Frequently they pick out a youngster (born between January and April) but adults are not

WILDLIFE HIGHLIGHTS

» Clouds of dust and flashes of grey, as elephant herds lumber through the park » Prolific birdlife along the Chobe River includes rare raptors and unusual waterbirds » Watching Chobe bushbucks, sables and pukus kick up a duststorm » Easy sightings of predators such as spotted hyenas and lions » The sight of hundreds of Burchell's zebras invulnerable and the protracted struggle between a bull buffalo and a lion pride is absolutely compelling to witness.

HIPPO PODS & PUKU POCKETS

Large pods of **hippos** are common in the river (one is invariably found near Sedudu Island) and the various boat cruises available are an exhilarating way to view them. This is the only place in Botswana where you can see the **puku**; common in Zambia and the Democratic Republic of Congo, a small enclave of this semi-aquatic antelope occurs here in isolation. The richly marked Chobe subspecies of the **bushbuck** is another riverfront speciality and **red lechwes**, **greater kudus** and **impalas** are common.

Aside from **elephants** and **buffaloes**, there is another major mammal species you will see in abundance here – people. The superb wildlife-viewing and proximity to Victoria Falls (90km away) attracts high numbers of visitors, most of them concentrated between the entrance gate and Serondela Camp. Venture further

west towards Ngoma Gate to avoid the traffic. During the winter, you can drive all day and animals will still be found. This is the best time to look for **Burchell's zebras**, **sables** and **roan antelopes**, which generally drink from mid-morning onwards when the elephants have moved off. For birdwatchers, the quieter areas along the riverfront and surrounding

GROUP OF HIPPOPOTAMUSES BATHING

BOTSWANA

ELEPHANT DAMAGE

As you drive along the Chobe River, the destructive power of elephants is starkly apparent. Tree destruction is actually normal behaviour and not restricted to periods of food shortage. Elephants fell trees for leaves otherwise out of reach and to avoid unappetising foliage. Many trees mobilise unpalatable compounds such as tannins where browsing is greatest – usually lower down the tree where most species feed – and this is the reason elephants and many other species feed briefly before moving on. Knocking over the entire tree makes more palatable leaves accessible, though even uprooted trees produce more toxins when browsed (at least until they die). Although apparently wasteful, uprooting trees opens up dense habitat and promotes soil turnover. However, in enclosed conservation areas where elephant densities can be very high, they can completely destroy woodland with serious consequences for diversity. Woodland-dwelling birds and mammals may eventually be driven to extinction – and this is still the core of the ongoing cull debate.

woodlands are the park's richest areas for birdlife and include numerous species at their southernmost limit such as **African skimmers** and **Souza's shrikes**. Some unusual raptors occur in the woodlands, among them **red-necked falcons** and **African hobbies**, while unexpected pockets of **Knysna louries** and **Natal nightjars** are also found here. Woolly caper bushes at the edge of the floodplains attract **common waxbills**, **swamp boubous** plus **yellow-bellied** and **black-eyed bulbuls**. **Pink-throated longclaws**, **giant kingfishers**, **slaty egrets** and **white-fronted bee-eaters** are often seen on boat trips, and **half-collared kingfishers** and **white-crowned** and **long-toed plovers** are other notable specials among the 450 species that have been recorded.

SAVUTE: LIFE & DEATH ON THE DRY MARSH Almost a day's drive from the Chobe River, Savute is the other major centre of wildlife activity in the park. Frequently likened to the Serengeti Plains for its similar scenery and cycles of migration, the experience here is very different from the riverfront. Once a rich marsh fed by the Savute Channel (which hasn't flowed since the 1980s), the Savute Marsh is now dry for much of the year and wildlife congregates around the waterholes. Late in the dry season (August to October), the larger natural pans, particularly Harvey's Pans and the artificial waterholes near the camp sites, offer superb viewing. The huge

herds of **elephants** are gathered further north along the Chobe at this time but bulls remain here year-round, constantly jostling for dominance at the water and chasing **lions** away. This is one of the few regions in Africa where lions regularly prey upon young elephants, and their intolerance for the big cats is unequivocal.

Although winter viewing of carnivores at the waterholes can be excellent, summer viewing offers even more opportunities as their numbers increase following the arrival of the migratory herds. When the rains arrive (usually November to December), thousands of **Burchell's zebras** move into the area from the north, seeking the new growth out on the marsh. Since the Savute Channel dried out, the numbers have dwindled but they're still impressive. **Lion** and **spotted hyena** numbers swell on the zebra feast, and most foals are born during this period, providing a glut of suitable prey for other predators that can't tackle the adults. **Cheetahs** and **African wild dogs** are most common during this period – the open areas of the marsh are the best places to look for them. Smaller hunters, particularly **black-backed** and **side-striped jackals**, contest kill remains and afterbirth with four **vulture** species (**hooded, white-backed**, **lappet-faced** and **white-headed**) and numerous other **raptors**. Although Savute's drier habitat does not support the diversity of birds seen along the river, an additional summer bonus is the arrival of many migratory species including **Abdim's storks**, **carmine bee-eaters**, **Caspian** and **ringed plovers**, various **sandpipers** and **black-winged pratincoles**. Take note: although the sand roads around Savute are compacted and easy to traverse in the summer, the marsh roads become extremely boggy, sometimes necessitating road closures between December and March, so check ahead.

FAR FROM THE MADDING CROWD

Although the Chobe River is the only part of the reserve that can be called crowded, for those looking for really quiet spots there are two other regions in the park worth exploring. The Ngwezumba region between Savute and Chobe has very little development and is largely ignored by most of the commercial tours. Clay-bottomed pans hold water well into the winter and the two camp sites (Nogatsaa and Tchinga) sit on the edge of pans, allowing some excellent viewing of **elephants**, **buffaloes**, **lions** and numerous species of **antelope** literally from your tent. Nogatsaa Camp acts as a Botswana Defence Force post and can be noisy sometimes, but Tchinga is totally undeveloped (except for an unreliable water pump: carry your own supply).

A very different habitat occurs in the northwest corner of the park at Linyanti, the name given to this stretch of the Chobe River which forms part of the Linyanti Swamp in summer. Like a pocket of the Okavango, a mosaic of savanna, papyrus reeds and mature forest creates an environment particularly rich in birdlife. **Pel's fishing owls**, **slaty egrets**, **rufous-bellied herons**, **white-backed herons** and **African skimmers** are among the species recorded along the river while the forests are home to **Meyer's parrots**, **black-headed orioles** and **green-capped eremomelas**, to name just a few.

Wildlife-watching peaks from April onwards when huge **Burchell's zebra** herds return from Savute to congregate at Linyanti, and while only 7km of the river is accessible to self-drive tourists, the various lookouts over the river produce some excellent viewing. More animals arrive as the winter progresses so it's better to arrive late in the dry season (September to October). Aside from **lions** and reasonable chances for **leopards** and **African wild dogs**, this area is rich in small carnivores, which are very difficult to see elsewhere, including **servals**, **zorillas** and **Selous' mongooses**. However, most of them are active after dark. Private concessions along the river conduct excellent night-drives, but you need to be an overnight guest.

SAFARI GROUP FINDING ELEPHANTS, CHOBE NATIONAL PARK

LOCATION 170km south of Maun or 215km northwest from Gaborone to Khutse. Only accessible by 4WD.

FACILITIES None. Visitors must be entirely self-sufficient here. Water can be obtained at the game scout camps but also take plenty.

ACCOMMODATION Numerous undeveloped camp sites, mostly with pit latrines.

WILDLIFE RHYTHMS Summer rains (usually around December to March) make animals concentrate in the pans systems and this is also the period when many herbivores give birth. Roads during the wet season can get boggy.

CONTACT Parks and Reserves reservations office (☎ 318 0774; fax 318 0775, 391 2354; dwnp@gov.bw). Prior bookings are necessary.

WATCHING TIPS

Possibly because people are so scarce here, the birds in some of the camps show little fear and are quite tame. At Owen's Camp in Deception Valley, Kalahari robins, titbabblers, southern masked weavers and scaly-feathered finches will approach visitors closely. Providing slivers of fruit for birds is probably not too serious, but bear in mind that every action that alters an animal's behaviour, however slight, should be viewed with a critical eye.

CENTRAL KALAHARI GAME RESERVE

There's a reason the Kalahari has become synonymous with self-sufficiency. Located in the most extensive expanse of sand found anywhere in the world lies Botswana's largest wildlife reserve, a vast tract of arid wilderness in the centre of the country three times the size of Swaziland. Originally established to enable the Khwe people to maintain their traditional way of life, it has been opened to tourism only in the last decade and is still largely undeveloped. The Central Kalahari is one of the most remote destinations in Southern Africa – some of its tracks don't see a vehicle for months – and it requires self-sufficiency and experience to explore. Located in Botswana's centre, this immense expanse is home to huge populations of large herbivores and the predators that subsist on them, but for most of the year wildlife is widely dispersed and can be difficult to see. To experience the Kalahari at its most productive requires that a visit is well-timed to coincide with the summer rains, when thousands of animals congregate in the richest parts of the park.

VALLEY OF THE HYENAS Made famous by Mark and Delia Owens, who studied brown hyenas here for seven years, Deception Valley in the northern part of the park is a fossil riverbed that hasn't flowed for 16,000 years. However, the valley is peppered with open pans which become the wildlife focus of the park following the rains. Columns of herbivores move in from the surrounding woodland and scrub, seeking the flush of young, sweet-grass growing on the pans. Driving the length of the valley, it is possible to see thousands of herbivores in a single day – **blue wildebeests**, **springboks** and **gemsboks** dominate but **red hartebeests**, **greater kudus** and **elands** are also common.

The profusion of meat-on-the-hoof means that predators will be nearby and chances are very high for seeing Kalahari **lions**. This is also a fairly reliable time for **cheetahs** and the open terrain offers superb scope for viewing

WILDLIFE HIGHLIGHTS

» Prolific hoofed mammals include springboks, gemsboks and blue wildebeests » A vast array of large predators, notably lions, cheetahs and spotted hyenas » Sightings of smaller animals such as shy bat-eared foxes and iron-jawed honey badgers » Fabulous birdlife, despite such arid land and swathes of sand » Watching eager meerkats dig for scorpions a 100km/h hunt. During December and January, their quarry will almost invariably be the springboks' newborn young. If you are fortunate enough to encounter a mother cheetah with cubs, she may release the young alive for the cubs to practice their hunting skills – sometimes distressing to watch, but crucial experience for the young cheetahs and fascinating to witness. **Spotted hyenas** are often seen in the early mornings and **brown hyenas** (on which Deception's reputation was founded) are common. However, as they're largely nocturnal and shy, you may only catch a glimpse of a brown hyena on your way back to camp at dusk.

The burst of green also brings hordes of insects and other invertebrates, a rich food source for aerial and terrestrial hunters alike. **Honey badgers**, **bat-eared foxes**, **yellow mongooses** and **meerkats** dig relentlessly in the sandy soil, often for **scorpions**, which are prolific in summer. The most forbidding-looking ones with oversized pincers are actually relatively harmless, but beware of the smaller species with thick tails and small pincers (family Buthidae): their poison is extremely dangerous. **Kori bustards**, **red-crested** and **black korhaans** and **secretary birds** stride through the short grass, snapping up insects as well as lizards and the occasional rodent, while bug-and-seed specialists such as **Marico flycatchers**, **chat flycatchers** and 10 species of **lark** and **finchlark** are abundant. Raptors

PAIR OF SPRINGBOK RAMS DUELLING, CENTRAL KALAHARI GAME RESERVE

BOTSWANA

include **martial eagles, bateleurs, black-breasted snake eagles, pale chanting goshawks**, numerous **falcons** and **black-shouldered kites**.

In the winter, wildlife in Deception Valley can be as thin on the ground as in the rest of the park but if you do visit in the dry, drive the length of the valley to Piper's Pan where there are two camp grounds. With its solar-powered pump, it is far more reliable than the erratic water supplies at other artificial waterholes (Sunday, Letiahau and Passarge) and offers the best chances for wildlife-viewing. **Springboks**, **gemsboks** and **ostriches** are assured, though in much smaller numbers than the summer herds, and other species such as **blue wildebeests**, **giraffes** and **greater kudus** have usually dispersed.

KHUTSE: GAME-VIEWING BY CAMP CHAIR The maps show the Khutse region as a separate game reserve but this applies on paper only. Forming the southernmost extension of the Central Kalahari, it was once part of an ancient river system that held enough surface water to give rise to its name, which means 'where one kneels down to drink'. Nowadays, as in the north, it is dry for most of the year but during the wet summer its scattering of about 60 pans are focal points for wildlife activity. The concentrations rarely reach the densities found in Deception but the same species are present. Predators tend not to be as commonly viewed as in the north (perhaps because the number of people is greater around Khutse), but it is well known for its **lions**, which make regular visits to the permanent waterhole at Molose.

Almost all the camp sites in Khutse are situated close to pans; many of them are right on the pan's edge which means you don't have to travel far to see animals. Some of the sites are ideally placed to sit in camp and wait for animals to arrive. If you're reasonably quiet and avoid standing or moving around (animals are very wary of the human shape but don't appear to recognise it if you stay seated) you can see just about everything from the comfort of your camp chair. If you do decide to drive around, it's possible to cover Khutse's entire network (about 160km) in a day but it's generally far more rewarding to focus activity in one area. Overlapping the border of Khutse and the Central Kalahari is a series of closely clustered pans (most with camp sites) where, if there's nothing at one pan, there'll probably be something at the next. Khutse is easily reached from the south providing you have a 4WD, but if you're planning on driving through the reserve don't expect to see much wildlife on the 290km arid stretch between Xade and Khanke Pan on the Central Kalahari–Khutse border.

VETERINARY FENCES

If you approach the Central Kalahari from the north or east, you'll have to pass through the Kuke veterinary fence to enter the park. In fact, veterinary fences (intended to isolate supposed disease-carrying wildlife from cattle) criss-cross the entire country, carving up Botswana into livestock and non-livestock areas. Fences are nothing new to Botswana's cattle ranchers but during a severe drought in the 1980s, their effects on wildlife reached catastrophic levels. When the Central Kalahari's blue wildebeests attempted to migrate from the park to better grazing in the north, an estimated 65,000 to 70,000 died against the Kuke fence. Similar fences prevent migrations between Nxai Pan and the Okavango, between northern Botswana and Namibia's Caprivi Strip and elsewhere around the country, including the arid northwest where three new fences have been erected since 1995.

Even so, despite the indisputable costs to wildlife (an estimated 1.5 million head of large ungulates have been killed since 1960), the fences also have benefits. They exclude cattle from core wildlife areas, often the only barrier to wilderness being converted to farmland by relentless encroachment. In a country where cattle numbers only continue to escalate, fences may be the ultimate hope for maintaining wildlife areas.

PEOPLE OF THE KALAHARI

Unique among African reserves, the Central Kalahari was originally proclaimed to protect the hunter-gatherer existence of the indigenous Khwe ('Bushmen') who have lived here for at least 30,000 years. You can still encounter their villages and those of more recent arrivals, the Bkagalagadi people, in the park. Until 1997, almost 2000 people lived here, but against their wishes the government has begun resettling them outside the reserve, ostensibly to improve their access to amenities, though cynics believe the move clears the way for large-scale mining of extensive diamond deposits. In three big clearances, in 1997, 2002 and 2005, virtually all the Bushmen were forced out and although they won the right in court to go back to their lands in 2006, many Bushmen still feel unable to return.

KHWE (KALAHARI BUSHMEN)

MAKGADIKGADI
PANS &
NXAI PAN
NATIONAL PARKS

BOTSWANA

LOCATION 162km east of Maun. Accessible only by 4WD.

FACILITIES Wildlife-watching hide at Nxai Pan National Park.

ACCOMMODATION Four basic camp sites. Nxai Pan sites and Khumaga have shower blocks with water; Njuca Hills has pit latrines and no water.

WILDLIFE RHYTHMS
Summer rains (usually around December to March) concentrate animals at Nxai Pan and is also the period many herbivores give birth. Wildlife-watching is best at Makgadikgadi late in the dry season (October). Massive flamingo flocks arrive at the salt pans following the rain, but roads during the wet can be very boggy and driving on the pans is extremely dangerous.

CONTACT Parks and Reserves reservations office (☎ 686 1265; fax 318 0775, 391 2354; dwnp@gov.bw; Gaborone).

MAKGADIKGADI PANS & NXAI PAN NATIONAL PARKS

Deep Kalahari sands surrounding endless salt pans hardly seem a likely habitat for abundant wildlife, and perhaps for this reason these parks experience moderate tourist traffic. However, while it lacks the richness of the Okavango Delta or Chobe National Park, its open scenery and perfect visibility offer rare chances to view seldom-seen wildlife events such as predators making kills and the birth of herbivores. Makgadikgadi Pans and Nxai Pan are divided only by the tarred Maun-Nata highway – be alert driving this stretch as there are no fences, and animals move freely between the two reserves. Never predictable, wildlife movements may cover huge distances; the key to enjoying these reserves is knowing where to be when the rain comes and where to be when it doesn't.

MAKGADIKGADI PANS: MIGRATIONS & CONGREGATIONS Dominated by the massive Ntwetwe and Sowa (or Sua) salt pans, Makgadikgadi can be rather lifeless during the dry winter. The pans themselves are too salty to support any vegetation or much wildlife, but for unparalleled, moonscape-like vistas they are best visited in the dry season (May to November) when it is safe to drive on them. Most wildlife action occurs in the west where the national park actually begins, with its western boundary (the Boteti River) forming the main focus for much of the year. Here, the pans and dry grasslands give way to riverine woodlands where animals congregate looking for pools in the riverbed. The build-up takes place gradually from about May. By October, the congregations of **Burchell's zebras**, **blue wildebeests**, **giraffes** and **greater kudus** can be massive, and **lions**, **spotted hyenas** and **leopards** are regularly sighted. Khumaga Camp overlooks the Boteti, and the river road offers numerous lookout points to spot wildlife.

As soon as the rains arrive, the herds are no longer tied

WILDLIFE HIGHLIGHTS
» Year-round giraffe populations » Summer visits from migratory Burchell's zebras and blue wildebeests »Huge flocks of flamingos grace salt pans in the wet season
» One of the best places in Botswana to see cheetahs
» Red hartebeests and impalas are hunted by lions and leopards

BOTSWANA

to the river and begin to disperse. Usually from December onwards, they begin the search for new growth carpeting the plains and you need to travel further afield to find them. Njuca Hills Camp makes a good base to explore the grasslands. The drives are very long unless you double back but are well worth the effort to catch the migration as it heads south. By about March, the herds are concentrated in the southeast of the reserve or have moved out of the park altogether, moving back towards the Boteti in May.

Highly variable, it's easy to miss the throng of herbivores, but equally breathtaking congregations take place on the flooded pans themselves. Tens of thousands of **greater** and **lesser flamingos** arrive, drawn to millions of tiny crustaceans (which remained dormant in eggs

WATCHING TIPS

Hollows in the isolated baobabs scattered throughout Nxai Pan and Makgadikgadi make perfect roosts for various birds. Barn owls nest in one such hollow of Baines' baobabs (the famous trees painted by explorer Thomas Baines during his 1862 expedition) and southern yellow-billed hornbills, lilac-breasted and purple rollers nest in the baobabs on Kubu Island. The deep folds in their massive trunks attract bees which nest in the crevices, such as in the single baobab on Baobab Loop at Nxai Pan. When this nest is active, people have experienced the terrific privilege of being guided to the nest by a greater honeyguide.

during the winter) and the algae, which flourishes in the warm, shallow water. The location of the huge flocks varies, but probably the most reliable place to see them is actually outside the national park at the Nata Bird Sanctuary on the north-

BOTSWANA

SAFARI GROUP WATHING CHEETAHS DEVOURING PREY

BOTSWANA

WHY DO ZEBRAS HAVE STRIPES?

Watching the huge zebra herds at Makgadikgadi and Nxai, it's difficult not to ponder the most obvious question: why do they have stripes? There are many theories and no single answer is entirely satisfactory. The most enduring suggests that stripes break up the zebra's outline, disorienting predators during the hunt. However, given that many carnivores easily capture zebras, the effect, if any, must be minimal. Rather than confusing predators, the stripes' function may be directed towards other zebras. Highly attracted to stripes (even painted on safari trucks), zebras might rely on them to maintain contact. Contrasting bands are a clear visual signal in dark, dusty conditions (such as during a nocturnal hunt), possibly assisting zebras to avoid being separated and becoming an easy kill. Stripes are also thought to be a mechanism for foals and mothers to recognise one another but, like most of the theories, this has never been verified.

eastern side of Sowa Pan. Other summer migrants include **African fish eagles**, **saddle-billed storks**, **wattled cranes** and many species of **wader** and **plover**.

ABANDON HOPE, YE WHO DRINK HERE Unlike the bare, salt-encrusted pans of Makgadikgadi, Nxai Pan itself supports a layer of sweet grass and is surrounded by mopane woodland, providing a mixture of habitats for grazers and browsers. During the long dry winter, many herbivores leave the park but arid-adapted **springboks** usually remain, becoming the main food source for Nxai's carnivores. In particularly dry winters, the artificial waterhole just north of South Camp holds exceptional opportunities to watch interactions between predators and prey. Despite virtually no cover, **lions** position themselves around the pan, knowing that the **springboks** will inevitably attempt to drink. Equally aware of the lions' presence, the springboks are extremely cautious but invariably, one lingers a fraction too long at the water when the lions unleash their rush. In the course of a single winter's day at the waterhole, it is quite possible to witness three or four kills.

Cheetahs enjoy the habitat at Nxai: the savanna-woodland mosaic is ideal hunting terrain and also offers refuges for raising cubs. The resident springbok herds provide a year-round larder but cheetahs don't wait at waterholes like lions. Drive the roads that criss-cross the pan and make frequent stops to scan for them with binoculars. Be out searching at dawn when, in addition, you are almost certain to see numerous smaller predators, including **bat-eared foxes** huddled together in the winter sun, or **honey badgers**, sometimes accompanied by **pale chanting goshawks** hoping for a mouse or lizard escaping the badger's attention. Other raptors such as **kestrels**, **red-necked falcons**, **martial eagles** and **bateleurs** are common. **Kori bustards**, **black korhaans**, **red-billed francolins** and four different **coursers** (**Burchell's**, **Temminck's**, **double-banded** and **bronze-winged**) are just a few of the other birds commonly seen. At South Camp there are very visible **blue**, **violet-eared** and **black-cheeked waxbills**.

SUMMER'S FLOOD OF LIFE For all the rewards of winter at Nxai, it's during the wet summer that the park erupts with life. Beginning around December, the rains bring a green flush to the heavily grazed vegetation and thousands of herbivores move to the pan. It's probably the closest thing in Southern Africa to the Serengeti migrations; huge herds of **Burchell's zebras** and **blue wildebeests** accompanied by smaller numbers of **elands**, **red hartebeests**, **impalas** and **giraffes** join the **springboks**, many of them to drop their young.

Plentiful water means that predators have to wander further to hunt but the sheer abundance of animals, particularly young vulnerable ones, means that success is virtually assured – though of course, it might occur anywhere and seeing the action is less predictable than during winter.

Summer also sees the return of **elephant** herds. While small groups of bulls can be seen year-round, breeding herds with calves require the flush of summer growth. They're hard to miss, but if you don't see them drive the roads through the mopane woodlands near North Camp and to Kgama-Kgama Pan. Other summer visitors include **Abdim's storks**, **European bee-eaters** and **dusky larks**.

BOTSWANA

BAINE'S BAOBABS AT DAWN, MAKGADIKGADI PANS GAMES RESERVE

LOCATION 97km north of Maun (to South Gate) – all roads in Moremi require 4WD.

FACILITIES Extensive wildlife drive network, hide at Dombo Hippo Pool. Mokoro rides and boat trips available at many lodges and camps.

ACCOMMODATION Four public camp sites in Moremi and two on the periphery (Gunn's Camp and Oddball's, both private concessions), also three camp sites in the Panhandle (Drostsky's Cabins, Shakawe Fishing Camp and Makwena). Five lodges operate inside the park but there are many on the periphery and throughout the Okavango.

WILDLIFE RHYTHMS The dry season is generally the most productive because summer rains make many areas inaccessible and dense vegetation impedes viewing. Additionally, while less pronounced than elsewhere, animals congregate at permanent water during winter. Late in the dry season (September to October) is best but temperatures can be high.

CONTACT Parks and Reserves reservations office (☎ 686 1265; Maun). Prior bookings are required.

MOREMI GAME RESERVE

The only part of Botswana with abundant, year-round water, the Okavango Delta is a massive oasis where the density of many wildlife species reaches its peak for the entire country. Protecting almost one-third of the Okavango, Moremi Game Reserve encompasses some of the most productive areas of an inherently bountiful region. Except for rhinos, the **Big Five** are abundant, and Africa's largest and most southern population of the semiaquatic **red lechwe** occurs here. Their abundance (there are over 30,000 in the delta) as well as extremely high densities of **impalas** contribute to making this ideal habitat for Southern Africa's most endangered large carnivore, the **African wild dog**. Aside from the multitude of other wildlife species that can be seen here, most people visit Moremi because it is the best place in Southern Africa to see them.

THE PAINTED WOLVES OF WINTER The Okavango contains one of the largest remaining populations of **African wild dogs** in Africa, many with permanent home ranges inside Moremi (there are no fences in the reserve and they are free to roam throughout the delta). They have become inured to the constant presence of vehicles and their indifference permits rare encounters, including witnessing hunts and watching young pups at den sites. You're unlikely to stumble upon an active den without some local knowledge, but even if you don't see puppies, the packs make morning and evening forays onto the wildlife-rich floodplains and woodland edges in the Xakanaxa area, on Mboma Island (particularly the Northern Loop) and along the Khwai River.

Midwinter, when the pups are born, coincides with peak prey concentrations along the permanent water sources. Abundant water in Moremi means cyclical wildlife movements are less pronounced than elsewhere in Botswana, but as the smaller pools dwindle, large herds of **red lechwes**, **impalas**, **waterbucks** and **blue wildebeests** congregate near the deeper channels and pools. The dry winter also experiences an influx of **elephants**, **buffaloes** and **Burchell's zebras** from drier regions outside the delta, augmenting the resident herds that remain

WILDLIFE HIGHLIGHTS
» Excellent for Big Five (except rhinos) » Breeding colonies of waterbirds number in the thousands » Prime site for African wild dogs » More sightings of Pel's fishing owl than anywhere in Africa » Watching raptors soar over the Khwai River from a dugout mokoro canoe

year-round. Although wildlife exists in profusion all year, it is generally best viewed in winter.

STREAMS & EXTREMES Although much of Moremi is permanently underwater, the main land mass in the east and extensive sandy islands provide far more diverse habitats than the constantly flooded central delta. Forests of mature mopane trees (characterised by small butterfly-shaped leaves) are dominated by the constant presence of two mammalian extremes: **elephants** and **tree squirrels**. Virtually everything in between also occurs in the forests, but for better viewing, head towards the floodplains where the mopane gives way to open woodlands of knobthorns (with very distinctive knob-ridden trunks) and rain trees, named for the mistlike droplets exuded by frog-hoppers (spittle bugs), which siphon off the sap and excrete the excess fluid – the 'rain'. These edge woodlands are the richest wildlife habitat and apart from being favoured by **African**

wild dogs, hold excellent chances for **lions** and **leopards** as well as most of Moremi's large herbivores. Birdlife is prolific and includes very common **Arnot's chats**, **black-collared barbets** and **arrow-marked babblers** and some rarer species such as **Bradfield's hornbills**. As these woodlands open further onto the floodplains, check the reedbeds and woodlands lining the channels for three species of **coucal**

AFRICAN WILD DOGS AT THE KILL, MOREMI GAME RESERVE

(**black**, **coppery-tailed** and **Senegal**).

With water in such abundance, it's no surprise that wading birds are prolific. Eighteen different members of the heron family occur here, including **goliath herons**, **slaty egrets**, **black egrets**, **white-backed night herons**, **rufous-bellied herons** and all three Southern African **bittern** species. While the more secretive species are largely solitary, communally roosting species such as **grey herons**, **black-headed herons** and **little egrets** as well as various **storks** and **cormorants** form large breeding colonies. During the breeding season from August to November (peaking September to October), over a thousand birds of various species can be seen in a few hours at one of these 'heronries'. The best sites are Xakanaxa Lediba, Gcodikwe Lediba and Xobega Lediba (lediba means 'lagoon' in Setswana), all of them along the Moanachira River – you'll need to boat or mokoro to reach them. Along the permanent pools and waterways, viewing of **wattled cranes**, **saddle-billed storks**, **pygmy geese**, **fulvous ducks**, **darters** and dozens more species is excellent – the hide at Dombo Hippo Pool and the interconnected Gau, Mokutshumu and Mmalwswana Pans near Xakanaxa are prime spots.

RAPTORS OVER THE RIVER KHWAI
In addition to ever-present waterbirds, the Khwai River is also well known for congregations of raptors. During the dry season (July to November), the northern reaches of the river are particularly rewarding: take the Zambwaya Rd to see large numbers of **bateleurs**, **African fish eagles**, **tawny eagles**, **black-breasted snake eagles**, **martial eagles** and many smaller species. Ten species of **owl** occur in the reserve: four species (**giant eagle**, **spotted eagle**, **white-faced** and **pearl-spotted**) are often seen in daylight if you look carefully in the woodland trees. The Okavango is also arguably the best place in Africa to view the rare and secretive **Pel's fishing owl**: at sunset, they perch on the poles marking the various river crossings but for the best chances, take a boat or mokoro very early in the morning or at dusk – also your best chance to catch a glimpse of the very elusive **sitatunga** (best seen in the Jao area).

Besides aerial predators, the Khwai region produces excellent viewing of terrestrial hunters. **Lions** and **spotted hyenas** are common and the floodplains here are probably the best place in Moremi to look for **cheetahs**. **Leopards** and **African wild dogs** are regularly seen and the well-watered grasslands are optimum habitat for **servals**. Long-legged rodent specialists, servals are more crepuscular (active at dawn and dusk) than most small cats, so keep a careful lookout when departing and returning to camp. Moremi is also excellent for **side-striped jackals**. Less common and less studied than the abundant black-backed species, they look very similar from a distance but their white-tipped tail is a giveaway (black-backed jackals have a black tail tip).

THE MOKORO

Appearing on every tourist brochure ever produced on the Okavango and suffering slightly from a 'must-do' tag, the dugout mokoro (plural: mekoro) has actually been used by delta fishermen since the mid-1700s. Fashioned by hand using small axes, their manufacture can take as long as five months, a back-breaking task because rot-resistant hardwoods such as kiaat and jackalberry trees are preferred. Even so, mekoro only last for a few years and with the increase of tourism in the Okavango, mokoro-making is threatening the hardwood trees and placing demands on many other species which, traditionally, were never used. Many lodges and operations now offer trips in fibreglass mekoro or conventional-style canoes. Don't be disappointed; regardless of the material used, the trips are a silent, intimate way to explore the Okavango's waterways, and the fibreglass option is doing much to conserve the delta's large trees.

THE CARNIVORE CHAIN OF COMMAND

With such an abundance of large carnivores, Moremi is one of the finest reserves for witnessing interactions between the superpredators. As competitors for the same resources, they share no affinity and encounters between them are typically hostile. By far the largest African carnivore, the lion sits largely unchallenged at the top of the pecking order. Lions usually kill anything they can and that includes all other large predators if they get hold of one. Adult lions mostly only worry about other lions, but large spotted hyena clans occasionally kill injured or subadult lions and are certainly able to drive small prides off their kills. Spotted hyenas also dominate the other hunters, and Moremi is excellent for observing them trailing African wild dogs on the hunt, hoping for a free meal. Again, weight of numbers is a factor: a few spotted hyenas can lord over an entire African wild dog pack but a single spotted hyena is easily harassed into retreat. Both spotted-hyena clans and wild dog packs also dominate leopards, but individuals do so at their peril: leopards sometimes kill lone spotted hyenas and wild dogs. At the very bottom of the hierarchy sits the cheetah. They've sacrificed brute force for speed and can't physically overpower the other superpredators. Further, they simply cannot afford the risk of injury and invariably give way to other large predators, regardless of numbers.

BOTSWANA

FEMALE LEOPARD LOUGING IN A LEADWOOD TREE, MOREMI GAME RESERVE

LOCATION 82km north of Tshabong, 4WD access only.

FACILITIES None; water for cooking available at the game scout camp.

ACCOMMODATION
Undeveloped camp sites at Khiding, Lesholoago, Mabuasehube and Mpaathutlwa Pans.

WILDLIFE RHYTHMS
December to March is the rainy season when newly sprouted grass and flowing water give rise to congregations of herbivores and their hunters around the pans.

CONTACT OFFICE Parks and Reserves Reservations Office (☎ 686 1265; fax 318 0775, 391 2354; dwnp@gov.bw; Gaborone).

MABUASEHUBE GAME RESERVE (KGALAGADI TRANSFRONTIER PARK)

Adjoining the Kgalagadi Transfrontier Park (KTP), most maps show Mabuasehube as a separate entity, but it's now officially part of the KTP. But except for the extremely sandy and remote track along the KTP's southern boundary, there is no link for vehicles between the two and most people visit Mabuasehube as its own destination. With seven large pans and a legion of smaller ones clustered into an area only 5% the size of the KTP, Mabuasehube is a hotspot for wildlife activity.

Encircling the pan system, Mabuasehube's road network is all on Kalahari red sand (the name means 'the place of red earth'). Strictly 4WD, the circuit is best during the rainy season when the sand is compacted. This is also the best time for wildlife-watching, when water-filled pans and the new grass around them attract large herds of **gemsboks**, **springboks**, **elands** and **red hartebeests**. **Big cats**, **spotted hyenas** and occasionally **African wild dogs** follow. Bosobogolo and Mpaathutlwa Pans have excellent grass cover in summer. The white clay pan at Mabuasehube is mostly bare of vegetation year-round but the mineral-rich soil attracts the herds for another reason: they lick the surface for supplementary salts or drink them in solution after a downpour. Thousands of **African bullfrogs** emerge to breed following the first rain. At up to 2kg, the adult males are extremely aggressive and even attack **lions** in defence of their tadpole brood.

With basic camp sites overlooking four of the pans, sometimes you needn't even leave camp for some excellent viewing. It's illegal to drive after dark here, but armed with a fold-out chair and a decent torch (spotlights are prohibited), you can illuminate a few nocturnal sights from the comfort of camp. **Brown hyenas** and **black-backed jackals** usually won't be far away if you've been cooking meat, and at both the Mabuasehube and Lesholoago camp sites **honey badgers** and **Cape foxes** will sometimes wander in. And although they won't be interested in your cooking, insectivorous **aardwolves** are another possibility, especially when the rain brings a breeding flush of **termites** to the surface.

WILDLIFE HIGHLIGHTS
» Watching big cats roam the sands, red dust on their paws » Listening to the low-pitched tones of thousands of amorous African bullfrogs » Witnessing aggressive honey badgers catch prey with a ferocity rivalled only by big cats » Large summer concentrations of hoofed animals including blue wildebeests and elands » Southern Kalahari fauna draws a variety of herbivores

OTHER SITES

GCWIHABA CAVERNS (DROTSKY'S CAVE) Remote and challenging, Gcwihaba ('hyena's hole') Caverns have had only a few hundred visitors. There are no guides or reliably mapped routes, so don't try unless you're an experienced caver. One of the least tricky routes (from the lower entrance) is a boon for bat-lovers: thousands of Commerson's leaf-nosed bats, Egyptian slit-faced bats and Dent's horseshoe bats roost beside stalactites. Stay at Drotsky's Cabins on the Okavango Delta.
289km east of Maun

KHAMA RHINO SANCTUARY This sanctuary was established to protect Botswana's few remaining rhinos (fewer than a dozen), and it offers the best chances in Botswana of spotting one, along with Kalahari wildlife like red hartebeests, elands, brown hyenas, bat-eared foxes and ostriches. The minimal gate fee contributes directly to rhino conservation. The ridiculously affordable camp site, Mekonwa, makes an excellent overnight stop en route to the Central Kalahari Game Reserve or Makgadikgadi Pans National Park.
☎ 463 0713/460 0204; www.khama rhinosanctuary.com; 20km northwest of Serowe, 180km south of Orapa

KWANDO WILDLIFE EXPERIENCES Kwando offers fabulous wildlife-viewing and luxury accommodation in one of Southern Africa's most remote areas. Kwando's swamp habitat ensures high numbers of resident animals; viewing is superb year-round. Everything on the lists for Moremi Game Reserve and Chobe National Park is here, and guided wildlife drives virtually guarantee you'll see them. African wild dogs den here annually and Kwando delivers views of the rare Selous' mongoose without fail.
☎ 880 6138

MANYELANONG GAME RESERVE This reserve protects Botswana's largest Cape vulture colony, once numbering in the thousands but now with only a few hundred. The species has been in decline for years, due to decreasing wildlife numbers and the erection of electricity pylons. It's worth a stop, especially between April and July when they nest. Bring a folding chair and binoculars.
45km south of Gaborone, 15km from Lobatse (just south of the village of Otse)

MOKOLODI NATURE RESERVE Mokolodi is a combination of game reserve, environmental education centre and animal rehabilitation facility. Antelopes, hippos, Burchell's zebras, giraffes and a few white rhinos can be seen; guided night drives may let you glimpse a brown hyena or honey badger. A small herd of semi-tame young elephants roams free during the day; visitors can walk with them for a fee. The reserve is a small but definitive slice of Botswana, so much so that some of the television series *Number One Ladies' Detective Agency* was shot here.
☎ 316 1955, 316 1956; www.mokolodi.com; 12km south of Gaborone

MASHATU GAME RESERVE This collection of private reserves shares its boundaries with South Africa and Zimbabwe and includes the Tuli Game Reserve. The landscape has riverine forests, sandstone and hills; large predators are elusive, but lions and leopards are fairly common. Bird sightings are excellent (over 375 species). There is talk of a 'bio fence' of wild-dog droppings, intended to boost populations in the game reserve.
335km southeast of Francistown

SOUTHEAST BOTSWANA GRASSLANDS An easy trip from Gaborone or Lobatse, the grasslands combine farmland, undulating hills and dry savannah, stretching from Ramatlabama at the South African border to Moshawong Valley. The area is home to half of the world's population of short-clawed lark, a threatened species. Also worth hanging around for is the grasslands' dizzying array of raptors, including kestrels, falcons and bustards.
32km south of Lobatse

ZIMBABWE

CAPITAL HARARE **AREA** 390,580 SQ KM **NATIONAL PARKS** 11 **MAMMAL SPECIES** 270

Zimbabwe makes headlines for all the wrong reasons, but behind the grim statistics lies one of Southern Africa's most beautiful and, today, untouristed countries, blessed with a temperate climate, beautiful wilderness areas and fine national parks.

THE LAND Most of Zimbabwe spreads across a series of plateaus, affording it clement weather conditions although it lies entirely within the tropics. Zimbabwe's highveld (1200m to 1700m) extends from the southwest across to the Eastern Highlands, separating the Zambezi and Limpopo–Sabi Basins. Its middleveld (900m to 1200m) comprises 40% of the country and is dominated by miombo woodlands, interspersed with koppies, settlements and cultivation. However, it's Zimbabwe's low-lying regions that attract most wildlife-watchers. The Zambezi Valley's mopane woodlands, riverine forests and grasslands support high numbers of mammals, and this is where most of the national parks are located. The Zambezi flows over Victoria Falls (a World Heritage Site), winds through deep gorges then enters Lake Kariba before continuing east – providing year-round water for the region's wildlife. In the south, Zimbabwe's arid lowveld slopes down to the Limpopo and Save Rivers, an area of mopane woodlands, savanna and the gateway to the Great Limpopo Transfrontier Park (boxed text, p148; also known as the Gaza-Gonarezhou-Kruger Transfrontier Park).

Around 13% of Zimbabwe consists of national parks and safari areas. The 11 national parks, run by the Department of National Parks and Wildlife, are home to a large proportion of the country's almost 100,000 elephants as well as populations of lions, leopards, buffaloes, antelopes,

ZIMBABWE

Legend: ZAMBIA · MOZAMBIQUE · BOTSWANA · SOUTH AFRICA · MOZAMBIQUE

Labels on map: Luangwa, Zambezi River, Chirundu, Mana Pools NP ②, Muzerabani, Kariba, Mount Darwin, Karoi, Mvurwi, Nyamapanda, Matusadona NP ⑤, Chinhoyi, Bindura, Shamva, Mutoko, Sengwa, Slabuwa, Chegutu, HARARE, Chitungwiza, Nyanga NP, Nyangani (2592m), Zambezi NP, Kazungula, Livingstone, Binga, Gokwe, Kadoma, Marondera, Nyanga, Victoria Falls, Mlibizi, Manjolo, Rusape, Batoka Gorge, Hwange, Gwaai River, Victoria Falls NP, Pandamatenga, Dete, Kwe Kwe, Chivhu, Mutare, Lupane, Shangani River, Mvuma, Bvumba Botanic Gardens & Reserve, Haroni-Rusitu Reserves, Hwange NP ①, Daisyfield Siding, Gweru, Wengezi, Chimanimani, Shangani, Shurugwi, Masvingo, Birchenough Bridge, Chimanimani NP, Bulawayo, Zvishavane, Chipinge, Plumtree, Matobo NP, Gwanda, Lake Mutirikwe, Mt Selinda, Rutenga, Chiredzi, Thuli, Gonarezhou NP ④, Beitbridge, Limpopo River, Lake Kariba, Lake Chivero, Mvurwi Range, Eastern Highlands, Sanyati River, Sengwa River, Save River, Bubi River, Shashe River

Scale: 0 — 200 km / 0 — 120 miles

LEGEND
BR Botanical Reserve
GS Game Sanctuary
NP National Park
RP Recreational Park

⭐ TOP SPOTS

1. HWANGE NATIONAL PARK (p142) The country's main and most accessible wildlife park, with a major elephant population, a number of black rhinos and great herds of buffalo in dry season.

2. MANA POOLS NATIONAL PARK (p150) Hugging the Zambezi river, this is the place to view wildlife by boat with plenty of Nile crocs, hippos, elephants

and buffalo. Waterbirds are much in evidence and it is one of the country's few places to see nyalas.

3. VICTORIA FALLS & ZAMBEZI NATIONAL PARK (p156) It's not just about plummeting waters; here you'll also find hippos and crocs wallowing in the Zambezi river and vibrant, bird-filled rainforest around the falls.

4. GONAREZHOU NATIONAL PARK (p146) The spectacular landscape may be low on mammals but makes up for it with some of the best birdwatching opportunities in the country.

5. MATUSADONA NATIONAL PARK (p154) Home to Zimbabwe's highest concentration of lions; it's also boasts black rhinos, both wild and protected.

ZIMBABWE

hippos and endangered African wild dogs. Zimbabwe's premier park, Hwange National Park, houses one of the world's highest concentrations of elephants and its battered mopane woodlands bear testament to their ability to transform habitats. At least 20% of its woodlands have already been destroyed and the park's at more than twice its elephant-carrying capacity. Elephants devour over 70% of all plant matter consumed in Zimbabwe's parks and managing their activity is a constant source of controversy.

The Eastern Highlands, which form the spine of southeast Africa, house endemic subspecies of Cape buntings and bokmakieries. Highland forests feature Afro-tropical flora and fauna, and near-endemics such as Swynnerton's robins and red-faced crimsonwings. Montane grasslands spotted with ericas, aloes and proteas (typical of Cape fynbos) attract Gurney's sugarbirds and sunbirds, while waterside sward provides breeding sites for endangered blue swallows. In November and December pockets of evergreen forest in the Eastern Highlands and Gonarezhou National Park attract migrants such as Angola pittas and African broadbills. This is the best time to search for Zimbabwe's 666 bird species.

Over the past few years the country's parks and reserves have faced major problems. Foreign visitors are at an all-time low, artificially pumped waterholes are running dry, facilities are shabby, and the main source of revenue is now hunting. What's more, reserves have come under threat from land seizures, and poachers are running wild.

WHEN TO GO Zimbabwe stretches over a high plateau and enjoys a pleasantly temperate climate during the dry season. The cooler, drier months (May to October) are similar to the Mediterranean summer, with warm, sunny days and cold, clear nights. Most of Zimbabwe's rain falls in brief afternoon deluges and electrical storms in the relatively humid and warmer months from November to April.

In winter night-time temperatures can fall below freezing, while in summer daytime temperatures can climb to 35°C. Winter is the best time for wildlife-viewing because animals tend to congregate around a diminishing number of waterholes, and are therefore easier to glimpse.

WILDLIFE HIGHLIGHTS

» **Stalking rhinos on an adrenalin-charged walking safari at Matusadona** (p154)
» **Weaving past Nile crocodiles as you canoe along the Zambezi River** (p156)
» **Watching herds of buffalo amble in to drink, bathe and dust-bathe at a Hwange waterhole** (p142) » **Listening to the thunder of Victoria Falls while searching for birds such as Taita falcons, trumpeter hornbills and Schalow's louries** (p156)
» **Scanning Mahenye Forest in Gonarezhou National Park for narina trogons** (p146)
» **Seeing an elephant stand on its hind legs to strip a winter-thorn acacia of its pods at Mana Pools** (p150) » **Following an African wild dog pack as it courses through the woodlands of Hwange** (p142)

CROCODILE BASKING IN THE SUN, LAKE KARIBA

ZIMBABWE

ZIMBABWE ITINERARIES

1. TRACKING THE BIG FIVE If your passion is for big game, then head for **Hwange National Park** (p142), Zimbabwe's premier attraction and the country's most easily

reached Big Five destination. Elephants are easy to spot, with over 30,000 in the park. Great herds of buffalo roam the plains in the dry season, and this is one of the few places in Zimbabwe to see black rhino. Big-cat fans won't be disappointed either – there are good numbers of lion here, though the chance of seeing a leopard is remote. For that pleasure spend some time in **Matobo National Park** (p160), to the southeast, where sightings are more common.

2. WALKING WILDLIFE One of Zimbabwe's best spots for safaris on foot is **Mana Pools National Park** (p150). If you're keen, spend a couple of days near the park's

southern boundaries, by the Chitake River, where the best walking safaris take place, and try to visit in November, when wildlife viewing is at its best. Private lodges in other areas of the park also organise walking safaris and, for the very brave (or foolhardy), unescorted wanderings are sometimes allowed. Continue your walking odyssey at **Matusadona National Park** (p154), where early-morning tracking expeditions in search of wild black rhinos and lions are a real highlight.

ZIMBABWE

3. FEATHERED FRIENDS To get plentiful viewings of raptors, **Gonarezhou National Park** (p146) is the place to be. Martial and tawny eagles are common, as are lappet-faced vultures (Africa's largest), and red sandstone cliffs hide peregrine and lanner falcons. For more of the same, head on up to **Victoria Falls** (p156). Though it's famous for the smoke that thunders, the gorges below are where the rare Taita falcon makes its home. In fact, there are 36 species of raptor in total here, including black eagles. Finish your bird-watching journey at **Mana Pools National Park** (p150), where herons and storks feature among the many waterbirds.

LOCATION Main Camp is 288km northwest of Bulawayo, 199km from Victoria Falls (sealed road). Robins is 93km south of Victoria Falls. Sinamatella turn-off near Hwange town, then 45km of dirt (4WD best).

FACILITIES Stores, fuel, viewing platforms, Main Camp museum, night drives on full moon, walking safaris and hides.

ACCOMMODATION Camping grounds, caravan sites, self-catering chalets and lodges (book in advance). Private luxury lodges on the edge of park.

WILDLIFE RHYTHMS Best April to October (dry season); very cold May to August. Game-viewing roads around Robins closed November to April; others may close during rainy season. Excellent birding November to February.

CONTACT National Parks and Wildlife (☎ 04-706077/8; www.zimparks.com; Harare).

HWANGE NATIONAL PARK

The size of Northern Ireland, Hwange is the largest and best known of Zimbabwe's national parks. The construction of 60 artificial waterholes in Hwange – an area that has few permanent sources of water and a low rainfall of 620mm per year – has helped create a wildlife-rich park that boasts the greatest diversity and abundance of animals in Zimbabwe. It is also an important breeding area for the endangered **African wild dog** and **black rhino**. The park is regionally and administratively divided into three parts – Main Camp, Robins and Sinamatella.

You are likely to encounter animals before you get into Hwange. The 20km stretch of road into the park is flanked by msasa, mnondo, false mopane and Zimbabwe teaks – the teak's big mauve flowers that bloom in the late rainy season are popular with **giraffes**, **chacma baboons** and birds. The classic plains animals – **blue wildebeests**, **Burchell's zebras** and **impalas** – are likely to be seen grazing side by side in the patches of open ground. Even **lions** might be observed before entering the park.

HWANGE'S BIRDLIFE Around Main Camp, semi-tame birds await you near the cafe tables; they include friendly **white-browed sparrow-weavers** and **glossy starlings**. There are seven hornbill species in the park, including a Hwange speciality, **Bradfield's hornbill**, which reaches the eastern edge of its range here. The largest hornbill is the turkey-sized **ground hornbill**, which is typically seen feeding in open areas in groups of five to six. The **southern yellow-billed hornbill** ('the flying banana') is found in thornveld, the **red-billed** and **crowned hornbill** are associated with the mopane woodlands in the northwest of the park, and **grey hornbills** can be found throughout. Hornbills have a lolloping, 'drunken' flight pattern so are easy to identify on the wing. In the leaf litter **kurrichane thrushes** peck for worms, while flocks of **southern pied babblers** chatter incessantly. Mammals aren't abundant in Main Camp, except for chirrupy groups of **banded mongooses**. However, long-term staff witnessed a few **lion** kills inside the camp before an electric fence was constructed around it.

WILDLIFE HIGHLIGHTS
» 107 species of mammal, 435 birds, 104 reptiles and more than 116 butterflies » 30,000-strong elephant population » Blue wildebeests, Burchell's zebras, and great herds of buffalo in the dry season » Good numbers of lions and major stronghold for African wild dogs » One of the few places to see giraffes and black rhinos in Zimbabwe

Only the northern third of Hwange is open to the public and few visitors see more than a fraction of this: most vehicles concentrate on the 'Ten-Mile Drive'. There are many other dirt-road loops, each taking several hours, perhaps a day, to negotiate. On average, waterholes tend to be about 10km apart, and the terrain is mostly flat and carpeted by deep, pale Kalahari sands. Teak woodlands dominate much of the Main Camp section, and it is in the denser vegetation that stately **greater kudus** will often be seen browsing.

Areas of acacia savanna are favoured by **giraffes,** and the trimmed bases of the camelthorn trees are the work of their handy 45cm tongues. Very little habitat in Zimbabwe is suitable for giraffes, and this is one of the few places in the country that they can be seen. While watching them also keep an eye out for **red-billed** and **yellow-billed oxpeckers**. Although yellow-billed oxpeckers also perch on buffaloes, warthogs and hippos, giraffes are the red-billed oxpecker's favourite host.

TOO MANY ELEPHANTS? Further south, the trees give way to patches of leadwoods; tall trees with tangled, dendritic branches. The solitary dead leadwood standing in the middle of the Makwa Pan supports a large **red-billed buffalo weavers'** nest. In the pan lurk **terrapins**; there are five species of **tortoise** and terrapin in Hwange. In the rainy season (November to April) two types of terrapin can be seen moving between waterpoints as they disperse to colonise new areas.

ZEBRA AND WILDEBEEST, HWANGE NATIONAL PARK

ZIMBABWE

This open area is good for seeing plains animals as well as **lions** and **elephants**. The feeding pressure of too many elephants is immediately apparent around Sinanga Pan (and other waterholes). Their destructive foraging has killed trees, and the woodland has been broken off to a uniform head-height for half a kilometre in every direction. The elephant problem in Hwange is vexing. The provision of artificial water supplies has resulted in a population of well over 30,000 – twice the number that the park's food supply can support. The elephants are not only eating themselves out of food, they are eating out the food supply of other animals. Control of elephant numbers seems imperative for the long-term survival of the park and its flora and fauna.

Although the chance of seeing the elusive and nocturnal **leopard** is remote (night drives are not routinely permitted), listen for its distinctive sawing cough if staying over at the Ngweshla picnic site. In the height of the dry season, when elephants monopolise the waterholes, one leopard regularly climbed under the fence to drink out of the camp's birdbath. Leopards have also been to known to park their dead prey in the branches of the tall trees around this camp. Up high their food is safe from theft by lions and hyenas. The vlei and waterhole here are also especially good for seeing **waterbucks**.

The **roan** is a species not often encountered in Zimbabwe. The best places in the Main Camp region to see them are on the southern loop around Ngweshla, and towards the three Manga Pans and Jambile Pan. Further north, the camelthorn-dominated area around Dopi Pan is a quiet spot to see herds of **elephants** during the dry season. The Guvalala Platform, located at a vlei surrounded by *Terminalia,* is a good place to see a diverse array of species; large groups of bull elephants often gather here. From there, heading west, the road soon deteriorates into potholes and the landscape turns from scrub into mopane woodland as you venture towards Robins and Sinamatella (this is good habitat for **Arnot's chats**).

GRANITE LOOKOUTS & RHINO-TRACKING Escape busy Main Camp and journey to the northwestern border to see **black rhinos** and take in the view from Sinamatella Camp. Sinamatella sits 55m above a waterhole so you actually look down on the birds and mammals coming in to drink and bathe: at the height of summer, great clouds of dust tumbling across the floodplain herald the arrival of 1000-strong **buffalo** herds to the waterhole. A tail thrashing under a shady bush may reveal **lions** (lions and **spotted hyenas** are plentiful). **African wild dogs** are in good number, but sightings are unpredictable because of their large home ranges. Visitors can go on guided walking safaris of several days' duration – this provides the best chance of seeing **black rhinos**. Also, there are several picnic spots, viewing platforms and dams; Mandavu and Masuma Dams are favourite viewing spots among many (Mandavu, the largest, is home to **Nile crocodiles** and Masuma has **hippos**).

NECKING GIRAFFES

Hwange is Zimbabwe's premier park for giraffe-watching and you might get to observe giraffes 'necking'. This is not necessarily affection. Males gently neck with females during courtship, but males also get into a rough version with each other as a way of sorting out dominance. The males twist their necks around each other and arch their necks to sledge the other on the body with their horns. It seems like a gentle dance because the giraffes take a while to swing their neck and build up momentum. But the thump likely packs a punch because it can be heard 100m away and a struck giraffe usually jumps on impact. These bruising displays can go on for half an hour. You may notice that the ends of the horns of male giraffes lack the tufts of hair visible on the females' horns – this is rubbed off during fighting.

In contrast to the Kalahari sands that cover two-thirds of Hwange, the Robins and Sinamatella areas are rockier. Granite outcrops around Sinamatella are good places for spotting **tawny** and **martial eagles**. At nightfall Sinamatella becomes a hunting ground for **honey badgers**.

Most visitors come to Hwange during the dry winter season. During the rains, the vleis fill and the Deka and Lukosi Rivers flow, the animals disperse and the long grass make viewing difficult. Even the **elephants** seem to vanish, probably migrating south into the wild and inaccessible part of Hwange. Yet for birders and **butterfly** enthusiasts this is one of the best times to visit the north of the park. The top time for birding is from November to February; Salt Pan Dam near Robins is a favourite spot for viewing **waders** and **waterbirds**.

ELEPHANT RECYCLING

A glance at any Hwange waterhole is enough to convince most visitors that there are too many elephants in the park. While elephant overpopulation is a concern, the park's vegetation is being recycled, not trashed. At Hwange elephants eat woody vegetation faster than it can regenerate, bulldozing woodland into savanna. However, about 80% of what is consumed is returned to the soil in the form of dung.

Many species actually benefit from the elephants' activity. Ilala palmnuts germinate after passing through an elephant's digestive tract and being deposited in a pile of fertiliser. Battered mopanes burst into leaf after the rains, sprouting new branches out of wounds; and the felling of trees (and branches) provides small ungulates, like impalas and bushbucks, with access to browse. So elephant feeding need not be viewed as purely destructive. Whether Hwange's elephants are decreasing the number of other browsers is a matter of contention, but if resources are short, are they really the species to blame?

ZIMBABWE

ELEPHANTS AT A WATERHOLE, HWANGE NATIONAL PARK

ZIMBABWE

GONAREZHOU
NATIONAL
PARK

LOCATION Chipinda HQ
550km south of Harare,
Mabalauta HQ 667km south
of Harare.

FACILITIES Viewing platforms,
birdwatching, walking safaris.

ACCOMMODATION
Camping grounds; luxury
accommodation available
outside park.

WILDLIFE RHYTHMS Best
for mammals September to
January, as rivers dry up to
form pools. Narina trogons
and Angola pittas breed
January to February.

CONTACT National Parks and
Wildlife (☎ 04-706077/8;
www.zimparks.com; Harare).

ZIMBABWE

GONAREZHOU NATIONAL PARK

Gonarezhou is harsh and untamed – fiercely hot in
summer, with a low and erratic rainfall, this park is part
of the parched, harsh lowveld, and contains rugged,
spectacular gorges. While mammal diversity is high and
elephants occur in large numbers, animal numbers are
low – this is not a place to rush about and tick off big animals. But birding here is some of the finest in Zimbabwe
and you often have much of the park to yourself.

Some 40 years ago, the park was devastated by ill-
conceived management practices (the shooting of thousands of animals in an attempt to control tsetse flies), by
poaching during war, and by the worst drought in Zimbabwe's history in 1992. Gonarezhou reopened in 1994
and began to recover but, as with the country's other
parks, has been hit by Zimbabwe's political troubles,
leading to a loss of habitat and an increase in poaching.

Gonarezhou is divided into two areas, which are
named after rivers – the Save–Runde subregion in the
north and the Mwenezi subregion in the south. The Save
River holds a **Nile crocodile** density second only to the
Zambezi. The rivers contain **hippos** and large numbers
of freshwater fish including the **tiger fish** and endemic
black bream. Marine fish sometimes venture up the Save
from the Indian Ocean and even **Zambezi sharks** have
been recorded. **African fish eagles** are ever-present near
the rivers and **Pel's fishing owls** occur at Runde and
Mwenezi, best seen during the rains when pools form.

CONVERGENCE OF WATERS & WILDLIFE The
highest concentrations of animals are found in the
north, especially near the pans and rivers and around
the junction of the Save and Runde Rivers – a tangle of
ilala palms, fever trees and nyala berries. **Green coucals**
skulk through thickets and the descending *du-du-du-
du* call of blue-spotted doves continues throughout
the day. Between mid-November and late January at
Mahenye Forest, migrant **narina trogons** are vocal
in the early morning and evening before breeding in

WILDLIFE HIGHLIGHTS
» Elephants, crocs, hippos, buffaloes and fabulous birds
(400 species) » Outstanding for raptors, such as bateleurs,
lanner and peregrine falcons, and lappet-faced vultures
» Two endemics among 108 reptile species – Warren's
girdled lizard and the marbled tree snake » Wild dogs
and black rhinos at Save Valley Conservancy » Occasional
sightings of roans and nyalas

February. **Angola pittas** arrive between late December and early January and have even noisier courtships. Both species disappear by late March. Tembwahata and Machaniwa Pans contain numerous **ducks, storks, geese, herons, ibises** and **pipits**, plus an occasional **hippo**.

Away from the rivers and pans, the bush turns into endless *Combretum* and mopane woodlands. The congregation of **elephants** in this area is evident by the broken-off, stunted mopane trees. The park has some 5000 elephants, which is around carrying capacity. However, part of the hunting legacy remains: many of Gonarezhou's elephants still associate vehicles and people with trouble, and elephants here have a reputation for being extremely dangerous.

Impalas are found throughout the park, and herds of up to 150 **buffaloes** can be encountered. Of the smaller animals, the quivering tails of **tree squirrels** will readily catch your eye. Check the trees that they dash up and you will often find their grass nests (dreys) sticking out of trunk hollows. **Southern yellow-billed hornbills, long-tailed starlings, lilac-breasted rollers, hoopoes** and **red-billed woodhoopoes** are common in this area. On the ground, **Natal francolins** wander across the road, and camouflaged **double-banded sandgrouse** break with a flurry of wing beats if you get close. Clouds of tiny **queleas** and **waxbills** fly up from feeding on seeds, and the deep *oomph, oomph-oomph* signals that **ground hornbills** are nearby.

ZIMBABWE

LILAC-BREASTED ROLLER

OUTSTANDING RAPTORS Raptors are common in Gonarezhou, especially at Tembwahata Pan. **Martial eagles**, **tawny eagles** and **bateleurs** are common and the park contains a substantial breeding population of **lappet-faced vultures**. This is the largest African vulture and is less frequently seen than most others – its size and red face are distinctive. The most common vultures are **white-backed vultures** and their nests – an untidy mass of sticks – are commonly seen in baobab trees. Also in baobabs are the large thorny nests of **buffalo weavers**. Throughout the park you will see an enormous number of baobabs, including a 'forest' just east of Tembwahata Pan. With their hollows, limbs, flesh, fruit and flowers, some baobabs have provided animals with refuge and food for hundreds of years. It is one of the few trees that is able to withstand ringbarking by elephants – although some botanists argue that they are succulents, not trees. **Squirrels**, **parrots (Cape, Meyer's** and **brown-headed)** and **hornbills** all use the baobabs' hollows. Rare swiftlike **mottled spinetails** nest at Shadreck's Office, an open baobab that used to house a poacher.

The famous Chilojo Cliffs, layered red and ochre sandstone rock faces, stretch for about 30km along the Runde River. **Lanner** and **peregrine falcons** breed in the cliffs, and holes in the exposed river bank house noisy **white-fronted bee-eaters**. **Sables** are often seen below the cliffs, and waterholes on the plateau above the cliffs are excellent places to look for **roan antelopes**.

Nyalas reach the major northern edge of their African range here (they also occur in Mana Pools, and Lengwe in Malawi). Herds of up to 20 might be seen around the Chipinda Pools and the Benji area – the shaggy manes and greyer colour of males distinguishes them from **greater kudus**. **African wild dogs** are a highlight in the park, though their numbers have dwindled recently. However, the Nyavasikana River area can be a good spot to check. Early-morning drives to the cliffs from Chipinda can be rewarding, as **cheetahs** sometimes sun themselves on the main track. Everywhere, **hyena** numbers are good.

MWENEZI REGION The southern section of Gonarezhou is dominated by the meandering Mwenezi River, which snakes through dry woodland and ridges topped by baobabs and ironwoods. In winter wildlife focuses on the tiny pools that dot the region. Buffalo Bend on the Mwenezi River is particularly good during dry season; Swimuwini Camp overlooks the Bend and **elephants** and **nyalas** visit its small pond. **Cheetahs** are uncommon at Gonarezhou – the best place to see them is around the Mabalauta area, where **lion** numbers are low.

GREAT LIMPOPO TRANSFRONTIER PARK

In November 2000 Mozambique, South Africa and Zimbabwe agreed to remove the barriers between Kruger, Limpopo and Gonarezhou National Parks to form one giant superpark, and in December 2002 they signed an international treaty to establish the Great Limpopo Transfrontier Park (GLTP; also known as Gaza-Gonarezhou-Kruger Transfrontier Park). The park has a total area of 35,000 sq km and tourists will be able to drive freely between international borders. Animals – particularly elephants, buffaloes and antelopes – traditionally moved across these political boundaries with the changing seasons, but these migratory pathways had been blocked by fences and animal numbers controlled by controversial culling and translocation programs. With ecotourism being a major earner, the project has the potential not only to re-establish traditional animal migration routes but to aid local communities in and around these areas. Kilometres of fence have already come down between Kruger and Limpopo and an access facility between Limpopo and Kruger opened in 2006, though the park has yet to be officially opened. However, some conservationists claim that this will create a poachers' paradise, while other critics have expressed concern about the flow-on effects of land appropriation in Zimbabwe's lowveld. Only time will tell.

SAVE VALLEY

Try to visit the Save Valley Conservancy, 60km north of Gonarezhou. In the early 1990s poor farming returns and drought convinced 23 ranchers to invest in photographic tourism and sustainable hunting. Fences were pulled down, stock removed and wildlife reintroduced. Animal numbers are greater than in Gonarezhou, with black rhinos and African wild dogs the highlights. Under the care of so many landholders their movements are known, so early-morning tracking can lead to seeing either species; the best time to visit is from June to August when the dogs are denning. The staff at Senuko Lodge (www .senuko.com) are expert birders. Malilangwe is another private conservancy bordering Gonarezhou, and Nduna Lodge (www.ndunasafarilodge.com) has excellent birding guides. In recent years the conservancy has felt the full force of Zimbabwe's political woes. The resettlement of subsistence farmers (taking over a quarter of the land) has led to a loss of habitat and a rise in poaching, with black rhino in particular being hit – up to 100 were shot in 2008. Revenue from tourists is low, and as in many of the country's wildlife conservancies, allowing hunting of non-endangered species is the only way to bring money in.

YELLOW-BILLED HORNBILL

ZIMBABWE

MANA POOLS NATIONAL PARK

With the Zambezi River as its northern boundary, the terraced floodplains of Mana Pools rise behind pods of **hippos** and basking **Nile crocodiles**. Marshy areas support a profusion of **birds**, and **elephants** and **buffaloes** graze along the river banks. This World Heritage Site is usually explored by canoe safaris.

PADDLING AMONG HIPPOS Canoe safaris range from a short paddle to a safari that lasts for days – starting in Kariba and ending on the Mozambique border. One of the first things you are told is to avoid Mana's abundant **hippos** at all cost. This entails zigzagging along the river to stay out of their fiercely defended territories. Pods of up to 60 stay submerged during the day to protect their delicate skin from the sun – often only eyes, ears and nostrils show above the water. Most snort, grunt and submerge as you pass, but if they feel threatened they may attack – canoeing is not for the faint-hearted! The Zambezi also teems with **Nile crocodiles**, which bask on sand bars, especially during winter (June to August).

On shore, **elephants** and **buffaloes** drink, wallow and rub parasites off their hides. High banks often house colonies of **white-fronted bee-eaters**, which are joined by **blue-cheeked bee-eaters** between October and April. The striking **carmine bee-eaters** arrive in August, departing in December. Tern-like **African skimmers** rest on sandbanks, and fish by trailing their lower bill through the water. Among 90 waterbird species are **woolly-necked storks**, **rufous-bellied herons**, **pygmy geese** and **white-crowned plovers**. **Long-toed plovers** wade through weedy channels. Fifty-two of the area's 400 bird species are raptors and owls, with the most conspicuous being the **African fish eagle**. **Pel's fishing owl** might be seen perched cryptically in dense overhanging foliage. In the riverine scrub the 'big twitch' is **Shelley's sunbird** – previously unknown south of Zambia, during summer it has been found here.

LOCATION Nyamepi HQ is 388km from Harare (4WD is best). Mostly off-limits to vehicles November to April, otherwise travel in by boat, plane or canoe.

FACILITIES No fuel or stores. Nyamepi HQ sells a bird list and map; canoes and scouts for hire.

ACCOMMODATION Camping sites, self-catering lodges and all-inclusive luxury lodges.

WILDLIFE RHYTHMS Good wildlife-watching May to September, but best in October (although hot). Migrant birds present August to April.

CONTACT National Parks and Wildlife (☎ 04-706077/8; www.zimparks.com; Harare).

ZIMBABWE

●● WATCHING TIPS

A crack-of-dawn drive between Vundu and Nkupe camps may reward you with lion sightings. Zebra Vlei, below Mucheni Camp, is the place to search for African wild dogs, especially between August and October.

WILDLIFE HIGHLIGHTS
» Zambezi abounds with hippos and Nile crocs, and is great to explore by canoe » Abundant elephants and buffaloes » African wild dogs occur in the park
» Hyenas, baboons and vervet monkeys are common; impalas, elands and greater kudus are widespread; and Burchell's zebras occur near the pools » High concentration of lions and leopards in the south

WHEELS & WALKING 'Mana' means four and refers to four pools close together at the northern end of the park. These pools, especially Long Pool and Chine Pools, are the prime animal-viewing spots during the height of dry season (July to November). Long Pool is usually occupied by **hippos** and **Nile crocodiles**, and **Burchell's zebras** and **impalas** graze in the surrounding open areas.

The flat 'floodplain' here is actually river terracing, caused by the Zambezi receding as its course changes over time. Effectively, the pools are remnant oxbow lakes. Tall Natal mahoganies and winter-thorns grow on the alluvial soils of these flats. The foliage of the broad-leafed mahogany is trimmed at head-height by **impalas**, **greater kudus**, **elands** and **nyalas**; the winter-thorn's browse line is up high, courtesy of elephants. Between August and October, when few trees fruit and most are losing their leaves, the pods and leaves of the winter-thorn (or apple-ring acacia – its pods are coiled like

HIKERS WATCHING BUFFALO, MANA POOLS NATIONAL PARK

ZIMBABWE

apple peelings) provide a vital winter food source. Elephants ringbark these trees but leave the evergreen mahogany alone. Its scientific name, *Trichilia emetica,* refers to the protective emetic (nausea-inducing substance) contained in the bark. Away from the river, sandy areas are dominated by jesse bush – a tangle of shrubby *Combretum* and *Terminalia*.

From the lodges and camping grounds near the river you can observe the goings-on along the Zambezi. **Elephants** spied on the Zambian side may cross and wander past during dinner. During the night **hippos** come ashore and munch on grass only 20m away from campers. At the popular Nyamepi Camp anything left out at night will be pinched by fearless **honey badgers** or **spotted hyenas**. During the day the **baboons** and **vervet monkeys** fill that role. In the morning you may wake up to find your tent being used as a trampoline by young vervets.

Elephants abound at Mana; while you're here look closely at the females. Many of them have no tusks – probably a genetic anomaly that has been exacerbated by the selective hunting of elephants with tusks. Mana's cows have a reputation for being aggressive – little wonder when they are without the protection of tusks. Here too are some very relaxed **buffaloes** – old 'dagha boys' (males in bachelor herds) often used to snooze in the road, refusing to budge even when nudged by a Land Rover.

SOUTHWARDS The park's southern reaches are much drier. The area's clay soils are dominated by mopane, and giant baobabs dot the horizon. **White-browed sparrow-weaver** nests dangling from the mopanes are clustered on the western side where they are protected from the weather. During summer, male **broad-tailed paradise whydahs**, with their dramatically long tail, display for their mates. **Lilian's lovebirds** mass in large flocks in the mopane – Mana is one of the few places this lovebird occurs south of the Zambezi.

The southern boundary of the park cuts through the mountainous Zambezi Escarpment. This is the watershed of the Chitake River, where the adventurous can embark on walking safaris. It's hot, dusty and uncomfortable during November, but this is the best time for walking safaris. By August, the small water pans have dried up and in the south the only water source is the Chitake, a tapering, 1km-long stream where everything comes to drink – large herds of **elephants**, **antelopes** and **buffaloes** are readily seen. For predators the riverside is easy pickings: Chitake is the place to see **lions** in action and they are regularly found within 200m of the river during the height of the dry season. Guided walks in other areas of the park can also be undertaken from private lodges. Incomprehensibly, visitors are allowed to walk unescorted in Mana. Given the numbers of elephants and buffaloes in the park, this is only for those with a death wish.

BUTTERFLY LEAVES & MOPANE WORMS

Mana is covered in endless mopane woodland. This hardy tree is easily recognised by its butterfly-shaped leaves, which fold together and hang vertically during the heat of the day to reduce water loss. The leaves are packed with protein and phosphorus – even after they have turned russet and fallen, they retain some nutrients and ensure a winter source of food for many animals. At times the leaves become covered in waxy psyllids, which baboons and monkeys carefully pick off. But the invertebrate most associated with this tree is the 'mopane worm' – these large hairless caterpillars occur in the thousands in the rainy season. Parcels of fatty protein, they are great pickings for birds, monkeys, baboons and even people. Mopane wood hollows easily, often due to elephant damage, and provides nest sites for hornbills, woodpeckers, barbets and tree (Smith's bush) squirrels, which cache food over winter in them.

THE DIRT ON MANA POOLS

The history of Mana Pools is etched on its soils: shaped by water, wind and humans. The valley is marked by wide floodplain terraces, dry channels and pools – all remnants of the Zambezi River's gradual movement northwards. Sandy soils adjacent to channels support winter-thorns, while older 'islands' are covered in woodlands of sausage trees, rain trees and Natal mahoganies. Mana's low-lying floodplains have not been subject to major flooding since 1958, when the Kariba Dam was completed upstream. As a result, the floodplain soils are not seasonally replenished with alluvium, leading to gradual soil degradation.

Soils differ across the valley, giving rise to various layers of vegetation. Browsers such as greater kudus and nyalas feed on mopane woodlands, which dominate clay soils, and spiky jesse. During drier months, grazers such as buffaloes and zebras concentrate on the floodplains, also utilising grassed miombo woodlands. In wet season, most grazers disappear from the floodplains, exploiting fresh graze further afield. With such diverse 'layers' of grasslands and browse, it's no surprise that elephants – quintessential mixed feeders – are abundant here.

ELEPHANTS, MANA POOLS NATIONAL PARK

ZIMBABWE

MATUSADONA
NATIONAL
PARK

ZIMBABWE

LOCATION 468km northwest of Harare. Boat or fly in from Kariba (18km away). The drive in is back-breaking, 4WD only. Inaccessible by road in wet season.

FACILITIES No fuel or stores. Maps, guides (if available) and canoes from Tashinga.

ACCOMMODATION A couple of camp sites and lodges; houseboats.

WILDLIFE RHYTHMS Best wildlife-watching June to November.

CONTACT National Parks and Wildlife (☎ 04-706 077/8; www.zimparks.com; Harare).

MATUSADONA NATIONAL PARK

Matusadona stretches up from the shores of Lake Kariba and over the rugged Zambezi Escarpment. Two-thirds of the park is largely unexplored jesse-tangled hills and most visitors confine their activities to the lake's inlets and mopane-fringed plains near the shore. The foreshore is rich in **waterbirds** (around 200 species recorded), and there are plenty of **hippos**, **Nile crocodiles**, **elephants** and **buffaloes**. Matusadona has the highest density of **lions** in Zimbabwe and is also one of the few reserves containing **black rhinos**.

PROTECTED ZONES Matusadona is bounded by the Ume River to the west and the deep Sanyati Gorge to the east; many visitors travel along these and the lake in boats or view wildlife from moored houseboats. Craggy dead mopane trees, drowned when the Zambezi River was dammed to create Lake Kariba, dominate the lake's edge (as the water level rose, 5000 marooned animals were rescued and resettled in Matusadona National Park). Perched on these are **cormorants**, **darters** and an enormous population of **African fish eagles**. The lake teems with **vundu**, **barbel**, **bream** and **tiger fish**, which attract anglers from far and wide.

Torpedo grass dominates the shoreline, attracting **buffaloes**, **elephants** and **antelopes** throughout the dry season (June to December). **Waterbucks** and **impalas** are common, while **roans**, **sables** and **elands** occur in inaccessible miombo woodlands and ridges, coming to water in the drier months. **Saddle-billed storks** and **plovers** are abundant along the shore, and **malachite kingfishers** perch on stumps and reeds. **Pied kingfishers**, which normally feed along shorelines, fly well out over the lake to catch the introduced kapenta (sardine), and **grey-headed gulls** and **white-winged terns** whisk over the water. A journey through the dramatic Sanyati Gorge is a way to see **African fish eagles** and their nests, and **bee-eaters** nest in the banks. The shy, darterlike

👀 WATCHING TIPS

If travelling independently, consider hiring a wildlife scout from the park HQ at Tashinga so you can get out on foot. There are sometimes cheetah sightings here; a small population was released into the park in the mid-1990s.

WILDLIFE HIGHLIGHTS
» At the lakeshore hippos, Nile crocs, elephants and buffaloes are abundant » Highest lion concentration in Zimbabwe » Black rhinos are present both in a protection zone and roaming free – safaris on foot to track rhinos and lions are a highlight » Kudus, impalas and waterbucks are common and Burchell's zebras occur in small numbers » Around 400 bird species recorded, including finfoots and abundant fish eagles

African finfoot also inhabits this area.

Matusadona is one of the few Zimbabwean IPZs (Intensive Protection Zones) and has a population of **black rhinos**. Monitoring teams watch the rhino's progress, and from 1996 to 2003 Matusadona undertook an intensive hand-rearing program for young rhinos, starting with a single orphan. By the program's end, nine rhinos had graduated and ongoing monitoring of the park's rhino population has seen three of the rhinos from the hand-rearing program give birth.

Wild black rhinos in Matusadona are rarely seen and are usually found only on walking safaris – the ultimate African adventure. The 'Daily News', as guides call the sandy tracks and riverbeds, tells a new story each morning and broadcasts the night's events. In sand, signs may be as obvious as firm hoof prints but on stony ground they can be as subtle as a stone polished by the brush of a hoof. Signs such as bent grass or freshly broken branches also lead the way. Tracking is done at first light when the rhinos are still active. The alarm hiss of **oxpeckers**, frequent companions of rhinos, may be the first clue that you are near. The sound of the rhinos' big molars chewing may the next – in the still of the morning this sound can carry 50m or more. A rhino's senses of smell and hearing are acute, so from here it is a downwind, stealthy approach to get close. Exciting stuff! Short walking safaris (conducted by lodges and camps) often get you close to **elephants**, and tracking **lions** is a major draw of the park. Alternatively, wildlife drives will get you even closer to **lions** and **buffaloes**, while keeping you within your comfort zone.

FLOPPY TRUNK SYNDROME

Floppy trunk syndrome (FTS) is a condition of progressive paralysis of the elephant's trunk, principally affecting older males. First observed in East Africa, FTS appeared among Matusadona's elephants in 1989. Since then a handful of cases have been reported. In the worst situations loss of trunk function interferes with the elephant's ability to feed and drink and they eventually die. But others can be minimally affected and survive; some even recover. Scientists examine vegetation, soil and water for likely culprits such as pesticides, heavy metals and toxins. The exact cause is uncertain but it appears to be a toxin. FTS appeared in Kruger National Park in 1993 (also affecting elephant's limbs) and researchers pinpointed the cause as long-term exposure to a neurotoxin – elephants recover once removed from the area but the exact nature of the neurotoxin remains unknown.

ZIMBABWE

MATUZVIADONHA HILLS, MATUSADONA NATIONAL PARK

VICTORIA FALLS &
ZAMBEZI NATIONAL PARKS

ZIMBABWE

LOCATION 875km west
of Harare, 448km from
Bulawayo.

FACILITIES Tourist office,
organised tours at Victoria
Falls. Night drives, horse
trails and walking safaris in
and around Zambezi
National Park.

ACCOMMODATION Camp
sites, lodges and hotels at
Victoria Falls. Camp sites,
lodges in Zambezi National
Park.

WILDLIFE RHYTHMS Best
viewing in dry season (July to
September) although good
any time.

CONTACT Victoria Falls and
Zambezi National Parks
(☎ 013-42294), National
Parks and Wildlife (☎ 04-706
077/8; www.zimparks.com;
Harare).

ZIMBABWE

●● WATCHING TIPS

Birders should consider
staying at Imbabala Safari
Lodge about 70km west
of town, near the intersec-
tion of Namibia, Zimbabwe,
Botswana and Zambia, and
home to several 'Okavango
specials'. Slaty egrets are
resident, rufous-bellied
herons are regular visitors,
coppery-tailed coucals occur
among the reeds and white-
rumped babblers are found in
woodlands. Other specialities
include chirping cisticola, red-
shouldered widow and long-
toed plover. Ruddy turnstones
and grey plovers are common
migratory visitors.

VICTORIA FALLS & ZAMBEZI NATIONAL PARKS

Centre stage are the falls – a World Heritage Site
and one of the natural wonders of the world – where
550,000 cu metres of water hurtle over each minute,
plummeting more than 100m and sending up a plume
of spray that can rise 500m above. Victoria Falls comprises five separate falls and there are pathways that
provide a view of each. The spray nurtures a rainforest
area surrounding the falls, replete with figs, twisted
vines, ferns and orchids. Mammals are scarce but you
may encounter **baboons**, **vervet monkeys**, **banded
mongooses** and **Chobe bushbucks**. Small birds such
as **waxbills**, **firefinches**, **mannikins** and **whydahs** (distinguished by their long tails in the wet season) inhabit
open grassy areas. Viewpoint Number IV is a reliable
spot to look for large **trumpeter** and **crowned hornbills**, but the species to watch for is **Schalow's lourie**;
in Zimbabwe it is restricted to this area. Despite its
conspicuous size and brilliant green coloration it's not
readily seen – a walk upstream is your best bet.

Away from the falls, most people head upstream and
explore the palm islands and channels by canoe, motorboat or barge. Although it's busy on the water this is a
good way to see **hippos**, **Nile crocodiles**, **white-crowned
plovers**, **African finfoots** and **rock pratincoles**. The
rare **Taita falcon** has breeding sites in the Batoka Gorge
below the falls. Indeed the whole 120km stretch of gorge
is a dream for raptor-lovers – 36 species include **African
hawkeagle**, and **black** and **crowned eagles**.

Victoria Falls town has a surprising number of animals venturing through. **Elephants** wander about and
buffaloes are occasionally encountered. During a walk
on the Elephant Hills golf course you should encounter **impalas**, **waterbucks** and **greater kudus**. It's also
good **birding** territory and **warthogs** dig up the putting
greens with their snout. A journey around Zambezi
Dr will typically reveal **greater kudus**, **elephants**, **buffaloes** and **impalas**. The 'Big Tree' is a good place for
elephants and buffaloes in the dry season (as is the wa-

WILDLIFE HIGHLIGHTS
» Elephants, lions, sables, buffaloes and African wild dogs
in Zambezi National Park » Zambezi River good for hippos
and Nile crocs » Birding highlights include African finfoot,
collared palm thrush, rock pratincole and Schalow's lourie
» Taita falcon at Batoka Gorge, trumpeter hornbills at
Victoria Falls

terhole at Victoria Falls Safari Lodge). A walk along the river (at your own risk) usually reveals **collared palm thrushes** and **tropical boubous** flittering amid the wild date palms.

Just 4km from town, the Zambezi River forms Zambezi National Park's northern boundary, and numerous picnic spots and fishing camps are located along the river's edge. This northern section is dominated by mopane woodland and riverine vegetation (apple-ring acacia, figs and ebony). This is a good place to find **elephants**, **buffaloes**, **waterbucks**, **impalas** and **greater kudus**. Over 400 bird species have been recorded, and the river has throngs of **herons**, **egrets**, **storks** and **ibises**. **Pel's fishing owl** is a sought-after treat and **African skimmers** are present between August and December. A road follows the river and there are a couple of loops (inaccessible in wet season). The Liunga Loop is a good area for **giraffes** and occasionally **lions** are seen. **Hippos** wallow near Picnic Site 23, especially during dry season. For **elephants** visit Chundu I and II. You can take guided walks near Hippo Creek and along its spring lines. **African wild dogs** occur in the park and the best opportunity to see them is between May and August when they den.

A single road crosses the centre of the southern part of the park through the Chamabonda Vlei to the Njoko Pan and its wildlife-viewing platform. The south is dominated by teak, but the road follows a stretch of grassland and this is the place to see **Burchell's zebras** and the regal **sable**. **Elephants** frequent waterholes, there are reasonable **buffalo** herds and you are more likely to see **lions** here than in the riverine area. **Stanley's bustard**, a rarity in Zimbabwe, has been seen here occasionally.

TAITA FALCON

The gorges below Victoria Falls are home to the rare Taita falcon. This small peregrine-like falcon has a discontinuous distribution stretching from Ethiopia to South Africa, but it doesn't appear to breed in East Africa and is incredibly rare throughout its range. The falcon's stronghold is the gorges and mountains of Zimbabwe, where it is estimated to have about 50 breeding sites (breeding between July and October). A good lookout for this species is near the Victoria Falls Hotel; but you'll need a falcon's eye to distinguish it from male peregrines. Why this falcon is so rare is uncertain – it's been suggested that their breeding sites are so inaccessible that the birds aren't being recorded. This seems unlikely and a more common view is that they suffer competition for nest sites from the larger lanner and peregrine falcons.

ZIMBABWE

RAINBOW AND MIST AT VICTORIA FALLS

ZIMBABWE

CHIMANIMANI
NATIONAL PARK &
VUMBA MOUNTAINS

LOCATION Vumba is 28km southeast of Mutare. Chimanimani National Park is 157km southeast of Mutare.

FACILITIES Vumba is good for birdwatching. Information board at the Chimanimani Hotel, no facilities in park.

ACCOMMODATION Vumba has camp site, self-catering lodge. Chimanimani has a hut, camp site, camping permissible anywhere.

WILDLIFE RHYTHMS At Vumba, blue swallows and cuckoos return August. Chimanimani is best June to September.

CONTACT Curator, Vumba Botanical Gardens (☎ 020-67592), National Parks and Wildlife (☎ 04-706077/8; www.zimparks.com; Harare).

ZIMBABWE

●● WATCHING TIPS

One of the rarest highland birds is found at Chimanimani. This area is the only known location of a recently described subspecies of bokmakierie. It is quite commonly seen and the *Philippia*-covered rocky hillsides are a good place look.

CHIMANIMANI NATIONAL PARK & VUMBA MOUNTAINS

Mountain mists, evergreen forests and elements of West, East and Southern African montane flora and fauna characterise the Eastern Highlands. Vumba is a trove of birdlife, Chimanimani a mountain wilderness.

The Vumba Mountains contain the whole range of Zimbabwe's Afro-tropical highland bird species. In addition to birds, **samango monkeys** forage in trees at Bvumba Botanical Gardens & Reserve. There are birdfeeders at Tony's Coffee Shop while White Horse Inn and Eden Lodge are favoured places to search for samangos, birdwatch in gardens and take walks to local forests. Birding can also be done by horseback at Fern Gully New Forest Stud. Proteas are farmed in the region and these attract **sunbirds** and **Gurney's sugarbird**, which breeds here in winter.

For specialist birding everyone heads to Seldomseen Bird Study Station at the reserve for guided birding with world-renowned Peter Mwadziwana. Near-endemics include **Swynnerton's robin**, which hop along the forest floor, and **Roberts' prinia**, which is usually located by its loud *cha-cha-cha-cha* call. The **Chirinda apalis**, another near-endemic, forages high up in the canopy, which is also home to the **stripe-cheeked bulbul**. Other specialities include **forest weavers**, **white-tailed fly-catchers**, **orange ground thrushes** and **black-fronted bush shrikes**. The finchlike **red-faced crimsonwing** can be spied feeding on seeds on the ground.

Between March and May, noisy flocks of **silvery-cheeked hornbills** fly in through the mountains at dawn and dusk. After feeding during the day, they return to their roosts in the nearby mountains, and after May they return to Mozambique. With them go the **red-chested**, **Jacobin**, **Klaas'** and **emerald cuckoos**, which breed here during summer. They return in August, at the same time as the endangered **blue swallow** – its metallic dark-blue plumage and streaming paired tail feathers are distinctive as it hawks for insects low over open montane scrub. About four to six pairs are known

WILDLIFE HIGHLIGHTS
» Only area in Zimbabwe to see samango monkeys
» 249 bird species including 48 specials and four near-endemics at Vumba » Chirinda apalis, red-faced crimsonwing, blue swallow, Gurney's sugarbird, Taita falcon and a new bokmakierie subspecies

to visit Vumba and it remains a mystery where this swallow goes when it departs in autumn. Vumba also has a variety of **butterflies** – many of Zimbabwe's 500 species occur here, including several rarities.

This rugged wilderness, with it peaks, gorges, and plateau grasslands, is the spot for serious hikers. Chimanimani is a village and nearby is the Bridal Veil Falls. Around the village you'll readily see **samango monkeys** and the **white-necked raven**, a high-altitude species. Its massive bill distinguishes it from the common pied crow.

About 17km from the village is the base camp for hikes into the park. From there it is a three-hour hike to the mountain hut, from where hikers take various routes over the mountains. Mammals are not readily visible although **elands**, **sables**, **roans**, **blue duikers** and **bushbucks** are present. While there is plenty of evidence of **leopards**, they are rarely seen. Of the 186 recorded bird species on the mountain, nearly 30 have a restricted range or assemblage; two are East African coastal specialities and seven are Zambezian. The **blue swallow** visits during the rainy season and the most reliable place to see this rarity is around Sawerombi (although this area is being consumed by timber plantations).

The Bundi Valley's meadows are interspersed with heathers and ericas; **Shelley's francolins** flutter up from rocky scrub. **Gurney's sugarbirds** can often be seen feeding on proteas, and the wooded streambeds are the place to look for **malachite sunbirds**. Haroni River Gorge is a well-known site for **kingfishers**, **wagtails** and **louries**. Among a variety of birds of prey in these mountains is one of the rarest, the **Taita falcon**. They turn up with some regularity on the telephone lines that run right along Roy Bennet's tobacco field, which is easily seen on the road to base camp. About 60 plant species are restricted to this mountain range, as well as over 300 **orchids** and several **amphibians**.

HARONI–RUSITU JUNCTION

Keen birders should visit the Haroni and Rusitu reserves, near to Chimanimani but hard to get to and lower lying. This is one of the most biologically complex areas in Zimbabwe because its forest has affiliations with Mozambique coastal forests and Congo forests. Haroni Forest Botanical Reserve is mostly cleared so Rusitu Reserve is the better area to visit. This is the only Zimbabwe locality for several tree, fern and orchid species and is home to special reptiles, amphibians and mammals – including a rare East African fruit-bat (the collared fruit-bat), Grant's bushbaby and the tree civet. Among 233 bird species are nine East African coastal species, 10 Afro-tropical highland species and seven Zambezian species. These include barred cuckoo, silvery-cheeked hornbill, little spotted woodpecker, African broadbill, slender bulbul, Vanga flycatcher, Mozambique and Woodward's batises, black-headed apalis, Delegorgue's pigeon, chestnut-fronted helmet-shrike, Nyasa seedcracker and the prized Angola pitta, which breeds here in December.

ROCK FORMATIONS, CHIMANIMANI NATIONAL PARK

ZIMBABWE

MATOBO
NATIONAL
PARK

LOCATION 53km south of Bulawayo; year-round access, some roads 4WD only.

FACILITIES Guided walks in Whovi (book ahead), interpretation centres, horse-riding safaris, walking trails in wilderness areas.

ACCOMMODATION Camping, caravan sites, self-catering chalets, lodges nearby.

WILDLIFE RHYTHMS Best April to October.

CONTACT National Parks and Wildlife (Bulawayo ☎ 09-63646, Harare ☎ 04-706 077/8; www.zimparks.com).

ZIMBABWE

MATOBO NATIONAL PARK

Domes of weathered granite balancing on top of each other form giant koppies that rise above the msasa and munondo mosaic to give Matobo its unusual beauty. Streaks of yellow lichen stain the rock faces, and pairs of **klipspringer** stand stock still on boulders. Above, **black (Verreaux's) eagles** spiral in the thermals as the day heats up, hunting for their favoured prey, rabbit-sized **dassies** that live among the rocks.

One of the most scenic and significant cultural areas in Zimbabwe, Matobo is also home to elusive **leopards** and **rhinos**, and the world's highest concentration of **black eagles**. Driving at dawn and dusk to spot a leopard is worthwhile here (night drives are not permitted). To the west, inside the Whovi Game Park, is Zimbabwe's greatest number of **white rhinos** and some **black rhinos**. Relaxed in the safety of this Intensive Protection Zone, the sociable whites often graze or snooze under the trees around the water trough just past the entrance. Whovi's boundaries are no barrier to **purple-crested louries**, but **giraffes**, **elands**, most of the **Burchell's zebras** and all **hippos** are restricted to the wildlife park. Hippos are found only in Mpopoma and Chintampa Dams, and at all the dams the cry of the **African fish eagle** can be heard.

Whovi is open only to vehicles, but in the rest of Matobo you can walk to caves and Bushman paintings. Walk carefully: Matobo boasts a large population of **black mambas**, growing up to 3.5m and with a reputation for aggression. **Greater kudus**, **sables**, **blue wildebeests**, **impalas** and **waterbucks** can be seen when walking or driving, and **baboons**, **vervet monkeys** and **warthogs** keep campers company – warthogs at Maleme Dam camp site are outrageously tame. The park is topped off by the panoramic Malindidzimu or 'View of the World' lookout.

WATCHING TIPS

From 'View of the World' scan for crowned eagles, and lanner and peregrine falcons.

WILDLIFE HIGHLIGHTS
» More than 300 birds recorded – 32 raptor species breed here » White rhinos, elands, giraffes and hippos at Whovi
» Dassies and klipspringers common in rocky areas
» Waterbirds excellent at Toghwana and Mjelele Dams
» Black eagles and leopards fairly common

NYANGA NATIONAL PARK

The section of the Eastern Highlands closest to Harare, Nyanga is a popular retreat with fabulous views, gorges and waterfalls. Home to Zimbabwe's highest mountain (Mt Nyangani, 2592m) and Africa's second-highest waterfall (Mtarazi Falls, 762m), the park has relatively few mammals.

The park's three main dams are good places for birding. The Rhodes Nyanga Hotel's gardens attract lots of birds, some of which breed in the surrounds. **Waterbucks** are sometimes seen around the hotel and park HQ. Antelopes, including **greater kudus**, visit nearby Udu Dam at dusk. This dam is a good spot to observe noisy **Natal francolins** and **little bee-eaters**; **red bishops** and **orange-breasted waxbills** breed among the reeds.

The rare **blue swallow** might be seen in the grasslands during the rainy season – when insects are hatching up to eight have been observed in the evening on some dams (such as Troutbeck). **Black-collared** and **crested barbets**, and the flashy **purple-crested lourie** can be seen in woodlands.

Mtarazi Falls is a good place to look for bird species such as the **orange ground thrush**, **starred robin**, **Chirinda apalis**, **red-faced crimsonwing** and **striped-cheeked bulbul**. If you hike up Mt Nyangani, watch for **Gurney's sugarbird** on the lower reaches. This bird is attracted to aloes (flowering between June and July), heather and proteas.

Nyanga seems an odd environment to encounter **secretary birds** but you may see them stalking through the mountain grasslands. **Blue wildebeests** seem out of place here, but they were introduced to Nyanga and are regularly seen around the Troutbeck Rd.

Next to Nyanga National Park is the Nyazengu National Reserve, a popular birding area. East of Mt Nyangani, the Honde Valley is another excellent birding area, famous for the presence of the **marsh tchagra**. The rare **palmnut vulture** is often seen in the *Raffia* palms near the Aberfoyle Country Club; ask at the club for a bird guide who can show you the birds of the nearby Gleneagles Estates.

LOCATION 100km southeast of Harare.

FACILITIES Park HQ, museum at Ziwa site, museum at Rhodes Nyanga Hotel, horse riding. Signposted walks at Nyazenga National Reserve.

ACCOMMODATION Camping, caravan sites, upmarket lodges.

WILDLIFE RHYTHMS Best November to May.

CONTACT Nyanga Tourist Association (☎ 04-298435)

WILDLIFE HIGHLIGHTS
» Great for birding, with at least 276 species recorded
» Specialities include blue swallow, red-faced crimsonwing, orange ground thrush, starred robin, Chirinda apalis and Gurney's sugarbird » Three Protea species are endemic to the Eastern Highlands

●●● WATCHING TIPS

November is the height of breeding activity for birds in evergreen forests. Forest-edge and woodland birds breed a little later. A visit during early summer (November to December) could be the most rewarding to hear the birds calling, in breeding plumage and displaying. Migrants are also present at that time. Birds seasonally cross borders and change altitudes, so walks in different habitats and altitudes should yield the greatest variety.

ZIMBABWE

MALAWI

CAPITAL LILONGWE **AREA** 118,484 SQ KM **NATIONAL PARKS** 9 **MAMMAL SPECIES** 645

Though not known for its big animals, Malawi has wildlife aplenty. Head for its glittering lake to swim with some 1000 species of fish, or explore its many nature and forest reserves to see elephants, hippos, and varied and unique bird species.

THE LAND Malawi stretches 900km along a trench formed by the Rift Valley system. Dominating this long, thin country is sea-like Lake Malawi, which covers 20% of the country's total area. In the northwest, a narrow strip of shoreline gives way to steep escarpments which rise to the Nyika and Viphaya Plateaus. South of these highlands is a series of plateaus undulating between 760m and 1370m. Lake Malawi (Africa's third-largest lake) has only one outlet – the Shire River, which courses south to the Zambezi in Mozambique. East of the Shire is the Zomba Plateau and Malawi's highest point, Mt Mulanje (3001m).

Lake Malawi is famous for its cichlids, a tropical freshwater fish family number-ing over 1000 species here. Lake Malawi National Park (a World Heritage Site) is one of several places where you can snorkel and scuba dive among these colourful fish – visibility is best between August and October.

Malawi's dramatic variation in altitude has given rise to diverse soils, vegetation and climatic zones. Rich plateau soils are mostly cultivated; poor escarpment soils are covered in miombo woodlands, giving way to evergreen forests at higher altitudes. One exception is the Nyika Plateau, which Malawi shares with Zambia. Here, above 2000m, rolling montane grasslands support roans, elands and other mammals, 435 bird species (including four endemic subspecies) and a rich montane

TOP SPOTS

1. LAKE MALAWI NATIONAL PARK (p166)
Dominating the landscape is Lake Malawi, home to over 1000 species of colourful fish and prime snorkelling and scuba-diving territory.

2. NYIKA NATIONAL PARK (p170) Malawi's sweeping, misty grasslands are home to zebras, antelopes, hyenas and leopards, and are excellent for hiking and horse riding.

3. LIWONDE NATIONAL PARK (p168) Hugging the Shire River, Liwonde offers safaris by boat, vehicle or on foot and has fabulous birdlife and a healthy elephant population.

4. VWAZA MARSH WILDLIFE RESERVE (p173)
This birdwatchers' paradise is home to over 300 species of feathered friends, including plenty of waterbirds and rare white-winged starlings.

5. LENGWE NATIONAL PARK (p172) Ignore the thick undergrowth and head for Lengwe's watering holes for a chance to see nyalas, warthogs and Malawi's largest herd of buffalo. For bird-lovers, the park's thickets are good for spotting flycatchers and warblers.

flora including 200 orchid species (12 endemics), proteas, lobelias and juniper forests.

Less than 40% of Malawi is woodlands and some 50,000 hectares of this is cleared each year for human exploitation, while many parks suffer from poaching and population encroachment. Malawi's premier 'island' of wildlife is Liwonde National Park, located on the Shire River. Surrounded by a density of over 130 people per square kilometre, Liwonde's riverine vegetation and mopane woodlands support elephants, Nile crocodiles, hippos, sables and a few reintroduced, but seldom seen, black rhinos.

Light on mammals, Malawi's big drawcard is its 645 bird species: around one-tenth occur nowhere else in Southern Africa, including 30 specialities (with limited distributions elsewhere). Liwonde specialities include Pel's fishing owls, brown-breasted barbets and Lilian's lovebirds. Vwaza Marsh Wildlife Reserve is good for waterbirds and miombo specials, and another twitching

MALAWI

site is thicket-filled Lengwe National Park.

Malawi's five national parks and four wildlife reserves are administered by the Ministry of Tourism, Parks and Wildlife. In major parks, accommodation is provided by private operators. While facilities and roads have improved, some parks are inaccessible in the wet season.

WHEN TO GO

Malawi has a single wet season, from November to April, when daytime temperatures are warm and conditions humid. The best time to visit Malawi is during the dry season from April/May to October. The months of October and November, at the end of the dry season, are the best time for wildlife-viewing. Average daytime maximums in the lower areas are about 21°C in July and 26°C in January. In highland areas, average daytime temperatures in July are between 10°C and 15°C, while in September they reach 20°C and above.

WILDLIFE HIGHLIGHTS

» Taking a boat trip in Liwonde (p168) and getting scarily close to the Shire River's many hippos » Hiking or horse riding across the sweeping Nyika Plateau (p170) and looking out for Burchell's zebras in the grasslands » Scuba-diving the depths of Lake Malawi (p166) and swimming through schools of cichlids » Sitting back and relaxing at Mvuu Camp in Liwonde National Park (p168) as brown-breasted barbets fossick in the undergrowth » Exploring Lake Malawi (p166) by kayak, listening to the cry of African fish eagles ('Malawi sparrows') as you paddle » Enjoying the solitude of Vwaza Marsh Wildlife Reserve (p113) and having a herd of elephants all to yourself » Waiting and watching at Lengwe National Park's Main Hide (p172) to catch a glimpse of one of the park's nyalas » Looking out for endangered wattled cranes strutting across the grassy Nyika Plateau (p170)

MALAWI

HIPPOPOTAMUSES, LIWONDE NATIONAL PARK

MALAWI ITINERARIES

1. BIRDING Your first stop should be Malawi's big hitter, **Liwonde National Park** (p168) – the birdlife here is as diverse as the landscape. It's the only place in the country

where Lilian's lovebirds are regularly seen, and night drives reveal owls and nightjars. Then head north to **Vwaza Marsh Wildlife Reserve** (p173), where lakes and waterways hide a plethora of bird species including herons and southern crowned cranes. Scoot up a bit to visit **Nyika National Park** (p170), a must for bird-lovers with its 435 species. Follow highland and forest trails to glimpse the endemic red-winged francolins as well as the endangered wattled crane and Denham's bustard.

2. WATER-BASED ADVENTURES Base yourself at Cape Maclear, home to **Lake Malawi National Park** (p166). Spend a few days learning to scuba dive or just snorkel

among schools of brightly coloured cichlids. You could also kayak around nearby Mumbo Island to see cormorants and otters. Then head north to Nkhata Bay for a few more days of underwater fun. You'll see crabs and catfish this time and night-time dives can reveal eels and dolphin fish. For adventures above the water, head to **Liwonde National Park** (p168). Take a canoe safari and watch hippos, Nile crocodiles and waterbirds go by and search for elephants near the water's edge.

3. WALKING SAFARIS **Nyika National Park** (p170) is the best place for hiking close to wildlife. There are plenty of walking trails in the area, taking from a few hours to a

few days. Walking through the grasslands is a great way to get up close to antelopes, zebras and bushpigs; and camping at night you might hear the sound of foraging hyenas. Way down south, **Liwonde National Park** (p168) is the place for guided walking safaris, especially if you want to get a taste of big game. The park's camps and lodges offer excellent walks, which are a good way to get near the park's many elephants.

MALAWI

LOCATION Cape Maclear is 250km southeast of Lilongwe, Senga Bay is 123km east of Lilongwe, Nkhata Bay is 430km north of Lilongwe.

FACILITIES Scuba schools, diving equipment, boats and guides for hire at all three areas. Visitor centre at the Lake Malawi National Park HQ in Cape Maclear.

ACCOMMODATION Camping, simple to upmarket accommodation available at all areas.

WILDLIFE RHYTHMS Best diving is between August and September; poor visibility in wet season; June and July are windy months.

CONTACT Ministry of Tourism, Parks and Wildlife (☎ 771295; fax 770650), Parks and Wildlife officer, Lake Malawi National Park (☎ 587456).

LAKE MALAWI

Pre-metric Lake Malawi was described as 365 miles long by 52 miles wide – hence the nickname 'the calendar lake'. The third-largest lake in Africa and third-deepest in the world, it fills a trench formed by the eastern Great Rift Valley. For tourists, Lake Malawi is synonymous with sun, snorkelling and diving; and it's the lifeblood of most Malawians. But for nature buffs it means **cichlids**. These brilliant freshwater fish occur in their thousands and some dives here are like swimming in an overstocked aquarium. Conservatively there are at least 1000 different species of cichlids in the lake, perhaps 1500 – only around 400 species have been scientifically described. The main diving areas are Cape Maclear (which contains Lake Malawi) and Nkhata Bay and Senga Bay.

Lake Malawi National Park, a World Heritage Site, is comprised of 13 islands, part of the lake and the Nankumba Peninsula. Over 300 birds are recorded in the region, and a hike to Mt Nkunguni may yield a few. Near the park HQ and visitor centre is Otter Point, which has a popular snorkelling trail. From Cape Maclear you have access to two islands: Thumbi (2km offshore) and Domwe (4km). 'The Aquarium' in front of Thumbi is a busy snorkelling site with a variety of **cichlids** – night dives here reveal schools of **Cornish jacks**, eel-like predatory fish.

Among Domwe Island's granite rocks are **agama lizards**, **skinks** and **snakes**. **Vervet monkeys** and **yellow baboons** are common. There are two walks here – a short one to a lookout point, or a two-hour climb to the summit. Alternatively, bound along the boulders on the shore. You'll see **Nile monitors**, **dassies**, maybe **Cape clawless otters**, lots of **pied kingfishers**, **white-breasted cormorants** and loads of **lizards**. **Scarlet-chested sunbirds** hang around camp and **trumpeter hornbills** regularly fly over in the early evening.

Access is restricted to use by clients of Kayak Africa (p313), but the waters near Mumbo Island (10km from

WILDLIFE HIGHLIGHTS
» Diving and snorkelling to see cichlids » Fantastic fish-watching sites at 'The Aquarium' at Thumbi, Namanje Island, Meliere's Islands and Nkhata Bay » Otters, Nile monitors and a cormorant colony at Mumbo Island » Namanje Island for another look at monitors and cormorant colonies

shore) offer the best visibility in the area. The island itself has plenty of **monitors** and harmless **snakes**, and ever-watchful **African fish eagles**. This is easier to walk around than Domwe and birds recorded include **paradise flycatchers**, **little bee-eaters**, **red bishops** and **red-billed firefinches**. **White-breasted cormorants** nest on the northern side between March and October. Rather relaxed **otters** sometimes swim alongside snorkellers. Over 10km from shore are the rarely dived Zimbabwe Rocks (Lighthouse Rock). Deep dives here feature lots of big **catfish** and **kampango**.

DIVING FOR DOLPHIN FISH North of Cape Maclear is Senga Bay – those who do their scuba training here will usually be taken to Namanje Island (Bird or Lizard Island) which lies just offshore. This island has large **monitors**, and breeding colonies of **white-breasted** and **reed cormorants**. **African fish eagles** are fed here to provide tourists with photo opportunities (although this activity may foster dependence). Other regular dive sites include an area 15km offshore near Nankanlenga Island, one of the three Meliere's Islands – this area reputedly has more **cichlids** than 'The Aquarium' at Cape Maclear. Around 30km north of Senga Bay is Mbenjii Island, which is a target for hard-core divers. Diving here is best between August and September; from February to March silt reduces visibility.

Far north on the lake is Nkhata Bay. The bay here has a stepped shoreline that rapidly drops off to 150m just 500m from the shore, so dives here are shore-hugging. In addition to **cichlids** are **catfish** and **crabs**, and night dives reveal schools of **dolphins fish** and occasionally **eels**. Best visibility here (average 12m to 15m) is from September to December. South of Nkhata, the Chintheche Strip has superb birding – **green coucals**, **Gunning's robins**, **narina trogons** and **palm-nut vultures** are all seen at camps here.

CICHLIDS BY THE MOUTHFUL

The huge array of cichlids that inhabit the Rift Valley lakes evolved from a few river-dwelling species to fill every feeding niche and form the largest freshwater family in Africa. To attract mates, males build sandy courtship sites or establish rocky territories; rival suitors are grappled, tossed and chased away. Females are attracted by the males' brilliant coloration and shepherded in. Females lay their eggs one at a time (up to 200), grasping each in their mouth and nuzzling the genitalia and anal fin (which look uncannily like fish eggs) of several males. Sperm is released, which she sucks into her mouth where the eggs are fertilised and develop. When hatchlings leave the mouth they stay close to their mother, darting back into the mouth of the nearest female if danger arises – fingerlings of several broods and even different species can end up in the same mouth. But one predatory species has overcome even this defence by knocking eggs out of the mouth of other cichlids.

MALAWI

SHORES OF LAKE MALAWI

LOCATION Entrance 6km from Liwonde town, Mvuu Camp 33km from town and accessible by boat and light aircraft. Endangered Species of Malawi project 1km east of Mvuu Camp.

FACILITIES Mvuu offers wildlife drives (day and night), boating and walks. Hiking in hills is the main activity at Chiunguni.

ACCOMMODATION Camping, self-catering chalets, camps and tented lodge.

WILDLIFE RHYTHMS Best birding and wildlife between September and December.

CONTACT Central African Wilderness Safaris (☎ 771153; www .wilderness-safaris.com), Chinguni Lodge (☎ 284772; www.chinguni.com).

MALAWI

👀 WATCHING TIPS

Chiunguni Hill is good for klipspringers and oribis, and the caves on its side house porcupines and civets. For Pel's fishing owls, ask staff whether these are roosting at the end of the lagoon at Mvuu Lodge. A pair of brown-breasted barbets nests near there and also in the fever tree between tents 2 and 3 of this lodge.

LIWONDE NATIONAL PARK

Hugging the banks of the Shire River, the waterway that drains Lake Malawi and courses down to the Zambezi River, Malawi's premier park has terrific birdlife. Boat trips along the Shire get very close to large numbers of **waterbirds** and in dry season (June to December) **elephants** are common along the water's edge. The elephants disperse with the rains but the river remains thick with **hippos** and **Nile crocodiles** all year. Self-drive visitors can explore the roads during the day or join guided wildlife drives, walks and night drives.

Yellow baboons and **vervet monkeys** are common throughout the park and with a little effort you should be able to find **sable antelopes**; 300 are resident and in dry season they often mill on the floodplain north of Mvuu. A herd of about 150 occurs near the Likuzu River and a small herd frequents the southern Chiunguni area. Down here near the Likwenu River – the park's southern boundary – is the best place to see **greater kudus** and **waterbucks**. Greater kudus can also be found in and near Liwonde's Endangered Species of Malawi project and sanctuary. Liwonde is the only park in Malawi where there is a chance to see **black rhinos**, and nine are kept in the safety of the sanctuary's fences. Thick vegetation and high grass reduce the chance of seeing rhinos, but concentrations of some animals are higher inside the sanctuary than outside, and **impalas**, **warthogs** and **sables** are often spotted. After reintroduction in 1997, there are now over 300 **buffalos** in the park.

LOOKING FOR LOVEBIRDS Liwonde's bird variety reflects the diversity of vegetation in the park. There are grasslands, thickets, mopane woodlands thick with python vine, open areas dotted with baobabs, riverine forest fringed by fever trees and palms, and the Shire River itself. Boat trips drift past an array of **kingfishers**, **herons**, **egrets**, **ducks** and **storks**, while **African fish eagles** are ever present. Hyphaene palms on the river's edge are whitewashed with the guano of vast numbers of **white-breasted cormorants**. The main breeding colony is located at the boat launch for Mvuu Camp –

WILDLIFE HIGHLIGHTS

» **407 bird species including Lilian's lovebirds, brown-breasted barbets, Böhm's bee-eaters and Pel's fishing owls** » **Boat safaris past waterbirds, hippos, Nile crocodiles and elephants in dry season** » **Malawi's largest sable population** » **A black rhino sanctuary** » **Excellent guides at Liwonde are a boon to birdwatchers**

it's risky to be hatless in this area. On the river's sand bars **African skimmers** are present from September to January and **Pel's fishing owls** roost in shady trees close to the river – the best time to see them is between October and December. **Swallow-tailed bee-eaters** appear in September and breed in the river banks, and **white-backed night herons** roost in thickets overhanging the water.

On dry land a guided walk will usually find **Böhm's bee-eaters** (this is the best place in Malawi to see this species). Keep a lookout for **mosque swallows** and **mottled spinetails** around the baobabs in which they nest. Around the open area of towering cathedral mopane north of Mvuu, watch out for **racket-tailed rollers** and **Arnot's chats**. The speciality of this habitat type is **Lilian's lovebirds** and Liwonde is the only place in Malawi where they are regularly seen. They are particularly fond of the flowers and fruits of the enormous candelabra-like euphorbias so look around these when they are in flower (August to September). At Mvuu Camp **collared palm thrushes** flit through the dining room while normally retiring **green coucals** scamper outside.

Night drives routinely reveal the eyeshine of **genets**, **white-tailed mongooses**, **four-toed elephant shrews**, **bushpigs**, **bushbucks** and **bushbabies**.

The artificial waterhole 300m from Mvuu Camp is a favourite dusk spot for **scrub hares** and **impalas**. **Dikkops**, **coursers** and **nightjars** are commonly seen at night, and **African barred owlets** and **white-faced owls** might be seen in mopane areas. One of Liwonde's guides is renowned for spotting chameleons at night so you may even see **flap-necked chameleons**.

FIRST THERE WERE TWO

In an ocean of dusty mango tree savanna, Liwonde is a defiant island of wilderness. Years of hunting, 'pest control' and poaching decimated its wildlife and nine species of large mammal disappeared. Yet Liwonde has recovered, mainly thanks to the Frankfurt Zoological Society and the J&B 'Care for the Rare' program. It began with a breeding pair of black rhinos in 1993 then another pair in 1998 and 2000, which have produced offspring. In 1999 buffaloes, Burchell's zebras, elands, hartebeests and roans were reintroduced, and all have bred successfully. Cookson's wildebeests were introduced in 2001. The park is also now home to lions that have migrated into Malawi from eastern Mozambique. Improved relations with villagers bordering the park and increased vigilance against poaching have also paid off.

CROCODILE ON THE BANKS OF THE SHIRE RIVER, LIWONDE NATIONAL PARK

LOCATION Chelinda 189km north of Mzuzu, 507km north of Lilongwe.

FACILITIES Walking trails.

ACCOMMODATION Camping, lodge.

WILDLIFE RHYTHMS October best for wildflowers and mammals. Best for birds October to April, orchids January to March.

CONTACT Ministry of Tourism, Parks and Wildlife (☎ 771295; fax 770650).

NYIKA NATIONAL PARK

Malawi's largest park is located some 2600m high on a plateau of rolling montane grasslands interspersed with granite hills, streams and soggy dambos. Small remnant patches of montane forest are tucked down near the heads of valleys. In the north the escarpment drops sharply, and below 2000m grasslands change into woodland. Nyika is home to several mammal species but birds, a wealth of orchids and walking trails are the highlights.

Chelinda Camp was once the centre of activity in the park. It had been closed for several months at the time of writing but was likely to re-open in the future. The greatest concentration of animals is within about a 10km radius of here. The Chosi Loop area is a good place to begin exploring as it contains two dams which attract wildlife, especially herds of **roan antelopes**. In the grasslands roans are readily seen and often associate with **Crawshay's zebras** – this subspecies has thin, tight stripes and lacks shadow-stripes. There are old salt licks around Chelinda in which the zebras like to roll – perhaps to remove parasites. **Southern reedbucks** muster in small groups on the grasslands and if you think you've spotted a **puku** among them you are not mistaken – this is not puku country but one seems to have taken up residence here. **Elands** graze and browse the plateau but they, zebras and roans move off the grasslands in dry season. Meander around the forested areas near Chelinda to look for **bushbucks** – normally shy, here they are more approachable. Predators on the plateau include **side-striped jackals**, which can be seen during the day and on night drives – which may also yield **bushpigs**. **Spotted hyenas** are also common – in the absence of carcasses left by other predators (although in some years **leopards** appear abundant) they rely on their hunting skills and regularly dispatch reedbucks at the dams.

The best way to get close to Nyika's wildlife is on horseback – you can often get within 50m of **roans** or **reedbucks**. Horse-riding safaris used to be offered from Chelinda and hopefully these will resume in the near future. Within walking distance of Chelinda, Lake Kaulime is a good bird and mammal spot. For keen hikers (come self-sufficient), hire a scout and head for the wilderness trails

👀 WATCHING TIPS

Despite the hilly terrain, the reedbuck species at Nyika is not the mountain reedbuck (which does not occur in Malawi): this is a southern reedbuck. For birds, try neighbouring Chowo and Manyenjere forests in Zambia (access is no problem); around 30 pairs of Sharpe's akalats occur in Manyenjere. Zovo-Chipolo Forest (Malawi side) has trails through forest, bogs and grasslands – look here for bar-tailed trogons and moustached green tinker barbets.

WILDLIFE HIGHLIGHTS
» A must for serious birdwatchers: there are some 435 species » Roan antelopes, Crawshay's zebras, reedbucks, elands, bushbucks, spotted hyenas and jackals are common » One of the richest orchid areas in south-central Africa, with 200 species identified – twelve endemic to Nyika » Two frogs and two skinks are also endemic

within the park or the Nyika Highlands, or the popular trail to Livingstonia.

Some 50 species of birds recorded at Nyika don't appear in South African bird books. In addition, four subspecies are entirely restricted to Nyika and four species have their only Malawi presence here. Nyika is also the Malawi stronghold of two threatened species – **wattled crane** and **Denham's bustard**. Although only eight pairs of wattled cranes occur here, they are readily visible and often feed around the dambos. Giant lobelias in the dambos attract **scarlet-tufted malachite sunbirds** (one of Nyika's 14 sunbirds). Large **Denham's bustards** strut through the grasslands – usually seen singly or in pairs, up to 50 have been recorded following a burn (burning is a common management practice in the grasslands). **Red-winged francolins** (a subspecies endemic to Nyika) are typically spotted darting along the road. Of the more common species, **red-breasted sparrowhawks** hunt with their wingtips almost touching the ground, often skimming along the road in front of vehicles. **Cisticolas** and **larks** are commonly flushed from the grasses beside the road, while **white-necked ravens** fly above. From October to April the dambos and grasslands are great for seeing **pallid**, **Montagu's** and other **harriers**. **Yellow-billed ducks** and **little grebes** frequent the dams, and **black-headed herons** might be spotted at the dam below Chelinda Camp.

UNIQUE MONTANE FLORA

Isolated by steep escarpments and populated by East, West and Southern African montane flora, many of Nyika's plants have evolved into separate subspecies and even new species. Below 1800m, proteas abut bracken and msuku woodland. In the zone above are relatively poor grasses in soil that has been leached of its nutrients by rains – this is why some antelopes leave the plateau in dry season in search of fertile sward. Lobelias sprout in bogs, as do yellow lilies, irises and insectivorous sundews. In grasslands and evergreen forests are epiphytic and ground-dwelling orchids. Highland woodlands are stocked with rosewoods and Nyika is Malawi's southernmost point for junipers. After grassland fires, Nyika's legume (pea family) species come into flower then produce pods. Legumes convert nitrogen in the air into plant proteins stored in the pods, which are consumed by antelopes, particularly reedbucks. With the plateau's poor graze, legumes play a vital role in the ecosystem.

ROAN ANTELOPES, NYIKA NATIONAL PARK

LOCATION 83km southwest of Blantyre; closed in wet season.

FACILITIES Waterholes, hides, 2.5km self-guided walking trail. Facilities generally poor.

ACCOMMODATION Camping, chalets at Nyala Lodge.

WILDLIFE RHYTHMS Dry season good (July to November), best birding December to January.

CONTACT Ministry of Tourism, Parks and Wildlife (☎ 771295; fax 770650).

MALAWI

●● WATCHING TIPS

Southeast of Lengwe, Elephant Marsh is renowned for its waterbirds including colourful malachite kingfishers, goliath herons, pygmy geese, and African and lesser jacanas. Boat trips can be organised at Mchaba James village, at the southern end of the wetlands.

LENGWE NATIONAL PARK

Unlike other areas in Malawi, Lengwe is choked with thickets, which makes animal-spotting difficult when driving around the park's road network. But there are no permanent waterways here and in dry season animals congregate at Lengwe's four artificial waterholes. Waiting at waterholes, such as Main Hide, and watching what comes in is a far more productive way of seeing animals here. Thickets are ideal **suni** habitat and in a morning you may see a few hundred **nyalas** drinking at the waterholes. Around 1200 formerly occurred in the park and although poaching has severely reduced their number, you should see nyala herds along the tracks. Early morning is the best time to wait for sunis (they are usually found in pairs); Lengwe's southeast has a high density of sunis – around 15 per square kilometre. **Impalas**, **bushbucks**, **greater kudus**, **warthogs**, **vervet monkeys** and **yellow baboons** are fairly common. Lengwe boasts Malawi's largest herd of **buffaloes** (although they are generally hard to see). There are well over 1000 in the park and they make up a third of Malawi's buffalo population. **Bushpigs**, normally nocturnal, are sometimes seen drinking during the day and there are always big **Nile monitors** at the waterholes. This is one of the few places where you can find **samango monkeys** in lowland forest – these are usually seen around camp in the mornings.

For birders the park's thickets (especially around Main and North Hides) are good for skulking species, flycatchers and warblers. Lengwe is an excellent place in which to see **raptors**, **bush shrikes**, **Böhm's bee-eaters**, **Livingstone's flycatchers**, **crested guineafowl**, **eastern bearded robins** and **grey sunbirds** (try North Thicket Dr). Greenish **yellow-spotted nicators** move slowly through bushes, flashing their yellow-tipped tail in flight. Open patches in the park's south are good for **black-bellied korhaans**.

WILDLIFE HIGHLIGHTS
» Africa's most northerly location for nyalas » One of Malawi's best places to see shy sunis » Samango monkeys and a large buffalo population are present » 334 bird species and the only place in Malawi to see crested guineafowl » One of two locations for Woodward's batises

VWAZA MARSH WILDLIFE RESERVE

The reserve's southeastern corner is easy to get to and most visitors confine activities to the area around Lake Kazuni (Vwaza Marsh, to the north, is inaccessible). On and around Lake Kazuni are some of Vwaza's many bird species – **wattled** and **blacksmith plovers**, **storks** (**open-billed**, **yellow-billed** and **saddle-billed**), **ibises** (**hadeda**, **sacred** and **glossy**), **herons**, **teals**, **ducks**, **sandpipers** and **geese**. On an early-morning walk around the lake (you must take a guide) **yellow baboons** may be seen digging for grass bulbs, and **open-billed storks** probe the clay for aquatic snails. Approximately 200 **hippos** inhabit the lake area, **buffaloes** are present and you'll often see **impalas**, **reedbucks** and **greater kudus**. Solitary **slender mongooses** and groups of **banded mongooses** are both common residents. Around the camp on the lake's edge, **arrow-marked babblers**, 'bubbling' **tropical boubous** and **collared palm thrushes** fossick among the bushes. During the night **elephants** may forage through camp, littering the paths with broken branches – they are typically present between January and September, before moving west into Zambia's Luangwa Valley.

If you have wheels Zaro Pools is worth a visit. In addition to **waterbirds** this is the best place in Malawi to see **southern crowned cranes**, which are almost guaranteed. Much of Vwaza is dominated by miombo woodland, which provides camouflage for **greater kudus**, **bushbucks** and **duikers**, and has many woodland birds – **doves**, **drongos**, **lilac-breasted** and **racket-tailed rollers**, **blue-eared starlings** and **widows**. Patience is needed for birdwatching here because birds often amass in 'bird waves' – you'll see nothing for ages, then spot a large, mixed-species flock feeding together. Some species to look out for are **white-winged starlings** (restricted to the north), **chestnut-mantled sparrow-weavers** and **miombo pied barbets**. If entering or exiting the reserve via Kawiya, the woodland at the gate is one of the world's best places to find **white-winged starlings**. Other species here include **spotted creepers**, **Böhm's flycatchers** and **streaky-headed canaries**.

LOCATION Approximately 100km northwest of Mzuzu.

FACILITIES Bird list, guides for hire on walks, and day and night drives.

ACCOMMODATION Camping, basic bush huts.

WILDLIFE RHYTHMS Mammals concentrate from June to November. Birdlife good year-round.

CONTACT Ministry of Tourism, Parks and Wildlife (☎ 771295; fax 770650).

MALAWI

WILDLIFE HIGHLIGHTS

» A quiet but accessible reserve home to 300 recorded species » Elephants, hippos, kudus and waterbirds are all plentiful » Woodlands house numerous special bird species, including white-winged starlings » Best site in Malawi for southern crowned cranes

ZAMBIA

CAPITAL LUSAKA **AREA** 752 614 SQ KM **NATIONAL PARKS** 19 **MAMMAL SPECIES** 237

Though it's home to some of the continent's best wildlife parks, Zambia sees surprisingly few tourists. Those who make it here find vast open spaces ripe for Big Five spotting, and rivers and marshland dense with spectacular birdlife – and all this with plenty of space to breathe.

THE LAND Zambia is wedged like a jigsaw piece between Central, East and Southern Africa, and its flora and fauna have affinities with all three regions. Most of the country undulates across a plateau between 1000m and 1600m that is fissured by several rift valleys, dipping at the Bangweulu Basin and at Lakes Kariba, Mweru and Tanganyika. In Zambia's west are the Mafinga Hills, while to the east rise the Muchinga Mountains, which divide the Luangwa and Congo watersheds. Miombo woodlands cover 70% of the country, while river valleys are characterised by mopane and acacia woodlands, riverine forests, grasslands and wetlands – habitats typical of most of its 19 national parks. The southwest is

dominated by Kalahari sands while the tropical north has higher rainfall (over 1500mm) and moist evergreen forests.

With a moderate climate, Zambia's top wildlife-viewing period is during winter (May to August) and the dry, hot months from September to November. During wet season (December to April) floodplains such as Busanga and Bangweulu often become inaccessible.

Zambia's geography has created isolated pockets of wildlife and this has resulted in several unique subspecies of mammals. The Luangwa Valley shelters Cookson's wildebeests and Thornicroft's giraffes, while the Kafue region has endemic subspecies of lechwes and waterbucks. Black lechwes are endemic and are

ZAMBIA

200 km
120 miles

TANZANIA

DEMOCRATIC
REPUBLIC
OF CONGO

Lake
Tanganyika   Kalumbo Falls
Mpulungu   Mbala
Lake
Mweru
Kashikishi   Nakonde
Chitipa
Kasenga   Kasama   Isoka

Mansa   Lake
Bangweulu   Shiwa
Ng'andu
Samfya   **4 Bangweulu
Swamps**

Kasumbalesa   Chikuni   Lake
Waka-   **North Luangwa**
Waka   **National
1850m   Park 1**

ANGOLA

Mwinilunga   Mufulira   **Kasanka**   1788m   **Lukusuzi**
Kalulushi   Kitwe   **National Park**   **South**   **National**
Luanshya   Ndola   **5**   **Luangwa**   **Park**
Lake   Mpongwe   Mkushi   **National Park**

Zambezi   Kabompo   **Kafue**   Kapiri   Katete   **MALAWI**
2 National   Kabwe   Mposhi   Petauke   Miolo
Kaoma   **Park**   Chipata
Kalabo   Limulunga   Mumbwa   **Lower Zambezi**   Great East Road
Lealui   Mongu   **3**   **National Park**   Luangwa
Kafue Flats   **LUSAKA**   Bridge   Luangwa
Lochinvar   Kafue River   Chilanga
Shangombo   Senanga   **National**   Kafue   **MOZAMBIQUE**
Kalongola   **Park**   Nteme
Sioma   Monze   Siavonga   Lago de Cahora Bassa
Ngonye Falls   Batoka   Chipepo
Choma   Lake
Kalomo   Kariba
Sinazongwe   Chete
Kazungula   Island
Livingstone   **ZIMBABWE**

NAMIBIA

BOTSWANA

⭐ TOP SPOTS

**1. SOUTH LUANGWA
NATIONAL PARK** (p178) The
best park in the country,
accessible all year round
and home to endemic
species of giraffe and
wildebeest as well as big
wildlife.

2. KAFUE NATIONAL PARK
(p182) Wild, huge and
little-visited, Kafue is famed
for its red lechwes and is a

good place to spot leopards
and other big cats.

**3. LOWER ZAMBEZI NATIONAL
PARK** (p184) This riverside
park hides a barrage of
water-loving creatures,
including crocodiles, hippos
and elephants – the perfect
place for a safari by boat.

4. BANGWEULU SWAMPS
(p186) Zambia's wetlands

and floodplains are home
to a menagerie of birdlife as
well as the rare semi-aquatic
black lechwe.

**5. KASANKA NATIONAL
PARK** (p187) A swampy
paradise for bird-lovers
and your best chance to
see the elusive situtanga.
Elephants and antelopes
also make their home here.

best seen at the Bangweulu Swamps. Aside from endemics, Zambia has two of Africa's prime leopard spots – South Luangwa and Kafue National Parks. An astonishing 750 bird species occur in Zambia but only one is endemic: Chaplin's barbet of southern Kafue. Zambia's 'big tick' is the shoebill, which breeds at Lake Bangweulu. Its many migrants start arriving in September and October, most departing by April.

Zambia still has vast tracts of wilderness untouched by pastoralism, but poaching is widespread and animals remain difficult to approach in some areas. In recent years Kafue and Lower Zambezi National Parks have staged impressive recoveries, while community-based ecotourism initiatives are showing promise at South Luangwa and Kasanka National Parks.

Surrounding many parks are Zambia's 35 Game Management Areas, effectively buffer zones where hunting is permitted. Hunting by Zambian citizens is poorly monitored, but hunting safaris bring in revenue for communities and the government. However, possibly the biggest hurdle to tourism is Zambia's poor roads. Many lesser-known parks are difficult to visit, while most parks are inaccessible in the wet season. In contrast, Zambia's premier park, South Luangwa, is accessible year-round.

WHEN TO GO Zambia's altitude creates a temperate climate. There are three distinct seasons: the dry season (mid-April to August), when temperatures drop at night and the landscape is green and lush; the hot season (September to mid-November), which is the best time to see wildlife as flora is sparse; and the wet season (mid-November to mid-April), which is ideal for birdwatching, though some camps and lodges in the national parks close due to flooded roads. Rainfall is higher in the north of the country.

WILDLIFE HIGHLIGHTS

» **Watching the solitary, whale-like head of a shoebill rise above the reeds at Lake Bangweulu** (p186) » **Tracking lions on a hike through Nsefu, South Luangwa** (p178) » **Sitting in a tree hide in Kasanka's swamp forest** (p187), **waiting for sitatungas** » **Watching the sun go down by the Luangwa River** (p178), **then setting off to spotlight leopards** » **Canoeing the Zambezi** (p1184) **past bathing elephants** » **The sound of lechwe hooves as they crash through the water at Bangweulu Swamps** (p186) » **Scouring Kafue's vast Bu-sanga Plains** (p182) **for big cats such as cheetahs** » **Massive fishing parties of birds such as pelicans, gathering around lagoons in the Luangwa Valley** (p178)

ZAMBIA

LION AND LIONESS AT REST, KAFUE NATIONAL PARK

ZAMBIA ITINERARIES

1. BIG WILDLIFE HUNTING Start at **South Luangwa National Park** (p178) for a few days of traditional guided safari, tracking lions and elephants. Make sure to go on a

night drive to see the park's famous leopards and to track animals on foot – African walking safaris were born in this park. For large herds of buffalo, make the long journey to neighbouring **North Luangwa National Park** (boxed text, p181), spending several days at one of the park's three small wilderness lodges. Walking safaris are a speciality here. With more time on your hands head west to the wild expanses of **Kafue National Park** (p182) – a great place to spot leopards and other big wildlife.

2. WATCHING FROM WATER Water-loving animals throng to **Lower Zambezi National Park** (p184). Base yourself at a luxury lodge along the river and take a boat or

canoe safari. Glide past crocodiles, hippos and elephants, and soak up the sounds of the resident birdlife, including African fish eagles. Then make the journey north to **Bangweulu Swamps** (p186), where the flooding and receding of the wetlands determine wildlife-viewing. Come between March and July and you'll see thousands of semiaquatic black lechwe.

3. BIRDING Northern Zambia is excellent for birdwatching and it's fairly untouristed so you'll have many of the best sites to yourself. The **Bangweulu Swamps** (p186) attract

all kinds of waterbirds from marabou storks to pelicans and are perhaps the best place in Africa to see the shoebill. Spend a few days exploring the waterways here before heading south to **Kasanka National Park** (p187) where you'll find species more typical of Central Africa, including the brightly coloured Ross' lourie. Arrange a river trip and spot kingfishers, bee-eaters and Pel's fishing owl from the comfort of your canoe.

ZAMBIA

LOCATION Mfuwe 704km northeast of Lusaka.

FACILITIES Map at park entrance, lodges conduct wildlife drives. Last fuel Chipata. International airport.

ACCOMMODATION Camping ground and lodges outside park. Bush camps and lodges inside park.

WILDLIFE RHYTHMS Animals concentrate around water from June to October. Migrant birds are present from November to April.

CONTACT Zambian Wildlife Authority (www.zawa .org.zm).

SOUTH LUANGWA NATIONAL PARK

About 700km long and 100km wide, the Luangwa Valley is the western part of the Great Rift Valley and an isolated haven for unique races of **giraffe** and **wildebeest**. A mosaic of mopane, miombo woodlands, acacia and grasslands carpets the valley, through which the Luangwa River carves a tortuous and ever-changing course south to the Zambezi River. Each wet season the river floods and slices new shortcuts, leaving behind bends that eventually form oxbow lakes. Most of the park's roads lead to these oxbows, around lagoons and along the shore of the river. Only a small section of South Luangwa is accessible: Mfuwe sector is much visited while use of the Nsefu sector is largely restricted to specific tour operators. Mfuwe's loamy sandy soil and all-weather roads ensure year-round access when other areas are waterlogged.

UNIQUE ZEBRAS & DARK-NECKED GIRAFFES As you approach the park, the 1km stretch before Luangwa Bridge is where **bushbucks** are often seen. Once inside the park, **impalas** and **pukus** are common and the stretch between Mfuwe Lagoon and Luangwa Wafwa is especially good for seeing **waterbucks**. Cryptically striped **greater kudus** meld with woodlands, but most other antelopes are rarely seen; **roans** and **sables** live in the Muchinga Mountains west of the park, and **duikers** are nocturnal and shy.

Chacma baboons, **vervet monkeys** and **warthogs** are common everywhere, and this is great **elephant** country. In the late afternoon, elephants wade or 'snorkel' across the river (watch this near Flatdogs Camp). The river is filled with **hippos**, and numerous 3m-long **Nile crocodiles** bask on the banks of Luangwa Wafwa. Just north of here, between Wafwa and the main river, is an area where **antelopes**, **Crawshay's zebras**, **giraffes** and **greater kudus** are regularly seen.

Look carefully at the **zebras** here – their stripes are thin, numerous and extend down to the hooves, under the

ZAMBIA

WILDLIFE HIGHLIGHTS
» Thornicroft's giraffes and Cookson's wildebeests are endemic » A limited-range subspecies of zebra lives in the park » Lions, leopards, elephants, crocs, hippos, pukus, waterbucks, impalas, bushbucks and kudus are plentiful and used to vehicles » Night drives and walking safaris are a speciality with high-quality guides » Lagoons attract spectacular bird 'fishing parties' in the dry season

belly and have no shadow stripe. These zebras are an intermediate form between the extra-stripy subspecies in Mozambique and the subspecies in East Africa. **Thornicroft's giraffes** are restricted to Luangwa Valley and are distinguished from other giraffes by their dark-brown neck blotches (most apparent in older males) and lack of blotches below the knees. More than half of all Thornicroft's giraffes reside in South Luangwa – it was partly their presence that created the impetus for Luangwa to be made a national park. On the river's western bank, giraffes range from Manze in the south to Chibembe. Between November and April, when other areas are sodden, they concentrate around Mfuwe.

The defined banks of oxbow lakes house colonies of **sand martins** and migratory **carmine bee-eaters**. One large accessible colony forms between August and September near the western end of Luangwa Wafwa; this is also an excellent place for **waders** from August onwards. As small lagoons dry out in winter, fish writhe about in isolated mud pools and birds mass together to form 'fishing parties'. **Pelicans** and **yellow-billed storks** stuff themselves to the point that they can't fly. **Herons, spoonbills** and **marabou storks** join the party and up to 40 **saddle-billed storks** have gathered. Often at this time, the grasses and seeds around the lagoon attract a moving

ZAMBIA

YELLOW-BILLED STORK, SOUTH LUANGWA NATIONAL PARK

carpet of colour as **Lilian's lovebirds** and **queleas** mass in their thousands to feed. Anywhere grassland abuts watercourses, **southern crowned cranes** can be found probing. These can congregate in flocks of up to 300 during winter.

UNUSUAL WILDEBEESTS & OTHER INTERESTING CREATURES The Nsefu region is on the eastern side of the Luangwa River and large, skittish herds of **elands** are often seen. **Cookson's (Nyassa) wildebeests** (a subspecies confined to the valley) and **Lichtenstein's hartebeests** are found in wooded grasslands. Cookson's are smaller and have a browner pelt than other wildebeests; they are most abundant in the northern reaches of the park. The east bank has more **giraffes** than the west, and these are mainly south of Nsefu. Populations may mix when the river is low, communicating by sight the rest of the year. During winter animals regularly ford the shallow streams and **Nile crocs** lie in wait. Chipela Lagoon, 10km north of Nsefu Camp, has the largest colony of **yellow-billed storks** in Africa – it contains over 1000 nests, perched in massive trees.

NOCTURNAL HUNTERS
Night drives (organised through lodges) are a major drawcard of the park. **El-ephant shrews** are plentiful in thickets and dash across the roads; **genets**, **civets**, **scrub hares** and **white-tailed mongooses** are all readily seen. **Lions** are often found and Luangwa is well known for its high density of **leopards**. **Giant eagle-owls** and **nightjars** are common night birds, and **pennant-winged nightjars** arrive in the wet season, their streamerlike flight feathers unmistakable. Animals are not subjected to endless scrutiny and vehicles must leave the park at 8.30pm.

If you're staying in a bush camp the activity never stops. Harmless **spotted (variegated) bush snakes** move across rafters and you may share your shower with **square-marked toads** or **grey tree frogs** – the largest arboreal frogs in Southern Africa. At night, **geckos** cling to the walls. Dinner may be accompanied by the rumble of **buffalo** hooves (in dry season herds of up to 1000 form) and the cacophony of **hyenas** trashing the kitchen stores. No matter where you stay, expect at sometime to open a tent flap and find an **elephant** munching on greenery out-side your abode. Even in upmarket lodges elephants amble through camp and take a drink out of the pool. **Hippos** have been known to take a dip in Mfuwe Lodge's pool!

Although mammals disperse dur-ing the rains, this is a fantastic time for birding because of the migrants. Also, **butterflies** come out – **monarchs**, **pan-sies**, **swallowtails**, **common leopards** and **common jokers** to mention a few. **Scorpions** and **spiders** become active, including palm-sized **baboon spiders** (so named for their coarse hair) and frenetic 'hunting spiders' – these are **solifuges**, not spiders.

FOOT POWER

Luangwa is the birthplace of African walking safaris. They were conceived by Norman Carr, a champion of conservation, and today's options range from mobile safaris to casual strolls. All the small things missed from a vehicle become apparent and even poo becomes fascinating – you compare size, shape, spread and texture. A freshly renewed impala dung midden signals the active territory of an impala (leopards roll in these to disguise their smell); dispersed, thinly spread pellets are giraffe dung; elephant dung often contains buffalo-thorn fruit, its red seed coat digested. Baboons, squirrels and birds spread this out in search of insects, especially dung beetles. Then there are the tracks – of porcupines, giraffes, buffaloes and lions. The chance of encountering lions is high so instructions are given beforehand – stand still, stay in single file behind the scout and back off slowly while facing the lions. And no panicking.

NORTH LUANGWA NATIONAL PARK

South Luangwa's sister park, North Luangwa, is open between May and October. The southern end of the park is accessible only through three private operators – Shiwa Safaris (☎ 229261; www.shiwasafaris.com), Remote Africa Safaris (www.remoteafrica.com) and Kutandala Camp (www.kutandala.com), which have semipermanent camps along the Mwaleshi River and specialise in walking safaris. Visitors with their own vehicles can self-drive in the park's northern sections, but this is only recommended for the very experienced.

The park's habitats and fauna are similar to South Luangwa, but North Luangwa's appeal lies in its isolation and the lack of other visitors. Mammal specials include elands, Cookson's wildebeests and Lichtenstein's hartebeests – all scarcer further south. Lions and spotted hyenas are regularly seen, as are large buffalo herds, particularly between August and September when smaller streams dry up. Owing to years of poaching, elephants here remain difficult to approach.

ELEPHANTS IN RIVERBED

ZAMBIA

LOCATION Chunga HQ is 360km from Lusaka, 4WD only. Flying in is recommended.

FACILITIES Lodges provide day and night drives, walking and boating safaris, horse-riding safaris.

ACCOMMODATION Camping, self-catering chalets, fully inclusive lodges.

WILDLIFE RHYTHMS Animals concentrate about water sources between July and October. Busanga best between August and October.

CONTACT Zambian Wildlife Authority (www.zawa .org.zm).

KAFUE NATIONAL PARK

At 22,480 sq km, around the size of Israel, Kafue is the second-largest national park in Africa. It is part of the Kavango-Zambezi Transfrontier Conservation Area, or Kaza Park. This initiative involves Botswana, Angola, Namibia, Zambia and Zimbabwe, and besides Kafue it incorporates some of Africa's greatest national parks, including Chobe, the Okavango Delta, Hwange and Victoria Falls. Vast and wild, the park boasts 482 bird species and a diverse array of antelopes including **red lechwes** in thousand-strong herds. Predators occur in good numbers including packs of endangered **African wild dogs**.

Administratively Kafue is divided into the south and north. In the north is the Kafue River, and its main tributaries – the Lufupa and Lunga – are the places to head out on boat safaris to see **hippos** and **Nile crocodiles** and to do a little birding. Riparian forest along the water's edge conceals **Pel's fishing owls**, **African green pigeons** and **purple-crested** and **Knysna louries**. **African finfoots** lurk cryptically around tangled root systems while **African fish eagles** are conspicuous atop exposed limbs. **Nile monitors** forage for crocodile eggs and bask on riverbanks.

Away from the rivers is a mixture of miombo woodland and open grassy areas – **waterbucks**, **pukus** and **impalas** inhabit the dambos. A variety of **storks**, **egrets**, **herons** and **cranes** – which includes **wattled** and **southern crowned cranes** – are regular sights. In wet season (November to April) the floodplains become an impenetrable quagmire.

To the far north is the star attraction of the park – the vast Busanga Plain, which is home to thousands of **red lechwes**. Inaccessible during and following the rains, it can only be reached between July and November. On approaching the plains the first species likely to be encountered are **roan antelopes** and **oribis**, at the drier fringes of the floodplains. Lechwes become visible from Shumba Camp onwards. **Lions** and **spotted hyenas** are plentiful and this is the region to look for **cheetahs**. During the dry season **buffaloes**, **Burchell's zebras** and

⬤⬤ WATCHING TIPS

To be assured of access to Busanga Plain, plan to visit after August; in some years heavy or long rains can keep the area off-limits longer than anticipated. Once there, scan the wild date palm clusters that litter the plains – they often shade predators.

WILDLIFE HIGHLIGHTS
» Kafue is renowned for its diversity of antelopes
» The plains are home to thousands of red lechwes
» One of the best places to see leopards » Good numbers of lions and cheetahs and African wild dogs present
» Bird specials include black-cheeked lovebirds (southern sector)

blue wildebeests move onto the plain from the surrounding areas. **Sitatungas** occur here but are rarely seen as they reside in inaccessible wetlands. **Servals** and **secretary birds** stalk small prey across the grasslands. In July **eastern white pelicans** and **wattled cranes** congregate in large flocks.

Night drives can be undertaken if staying at a lodge. A speciality of the Lufupa Camp is leopard-spotting: habituated to spotlights, **leopards** are an almost guaranteed sighting on night drives and this is one of the best places in Africa to see them. Other night-drive regulars are **African civets**, **genets**, **bushbabies** and **African wild cats**. **Dikkops** stand in the middle of the road and **white-faced owls** might be seen atop termite mounds. After the first rains keep a look out for snakes – **rock pythons** become a regular sight on night drives.

As in the north, a main feature of south Kafue is the river. This has been dammed to form the Itezhi-Tezhi Dam where you can go out by boat to view **hippos**, **Nile crocs** and **waterbirds**. The Nanzhila Plains support an abundance of **red lechwes** and among them you can find **oribis**, **roans**, **sables**, **Lichtenstein's hartebeests**, **blue wildebeests** and **pukus**. Herds of 400 **buffaloes** occur in the area, and **lions** and **cheetahs** are present. Zambia's only endemic bird, **Chaplin's barbet**, is seldom seen but occurs in woodlands stretching east from the dam.

South Kafue is by far the best area to visit if you want to see **elephants** (found at Ngoma in tracts of Zambezi teak forest). The south is also the stronghold for **black-cheeked lovebirds** – keep a look out for them around Kalenje Post.

LOCHINVAR NATIONAL PARK

En route to Kafue's eastern entrance, Lochinvar National Park is a stop-off birders shouldn't miss. Sitting on the Kafue Flats, the park is dominated by a vast clay-bottomed floodplain where the Kafue River spills into the Chunga Lagoon. On the species list here are 428 birds, including huge flocks of wetland residents, summer Palaearctic migrants (December onwards) and more than 50 different raptors. Lochinvar is low on mammal sightings, with the spectacular exception of more than 50,000 Kafue lechwes (a distinctive subspecies). In summer, males defend tiny territories, called leks, crammed around the lagoon; females visit them for a brief weeklong period to mate during December and January. You'll need a 4WD for most of the roads but walking is encouraged (and recommended); WWF operates a nice camp site near the southern gate and Lechwe Plains Tented Camp provides luxury accommodation.

RED LECHWE, KAFUE NATIONAL PARK

LOCATION Chongwe entrance is 216km southeast of Lusaka. Alternatively canoe, powerboat or fly in.

FACILITIES Lodges provide bird lists, wildlife drives, canoes, boats, walking safaris.

ACCOMMODATION Camping and self-catering camps (park edge) or all-inclusive lodges. Kingfisher and Kayila open year-round. Most camps close during wet season.

WILDLIFE RHYTHMS Good between May and November. Top wildlife-viewing between August and October. Migrant birds present between October and April.

CONTACT Private operators are the best source of information. Zambian Wildlife Authority (www.zawa.org.zm).

WATCHING TIPS

The best wildlife is seen in the area that extends between the Chongwe and Mushika rivers. Chifungulu Channel (between Sausage Tree and Mwambashi camps) is nicknamed 'Hippo City' and in addition to hippos, often has lions and large herds of buffaloes in dry season. Chongwe Falls is a pretty spot to spy rock-dwelling species such as klipspringers and dassies.

ZAMBIA

LOWER ZAMBEZI NATIONAL PARK

Once devastated by poaching, Lower Zambezi National Park has recovered over the past 10 years and is now in excellent shape with good numbers of **elephants** and **lions**. It sits opposite Zimbabwe's Mana Pools National Park, but it is not a mirror image. The Muchinga Escarpment drops dramatically from nearly 1500m down to 600m, forming a backdrop covered in miombo woodlands – the inaccessible northern region of the park. Most visitors explore the Zambezi River and the western section of the valley – sandy flats fringed by acacia and mopane woodland. There are no maps, so many visitors opt to stay at the park's camps and join guided walks, wildlife drives (day and night), boat trips and canoe safaris.

CANOEING WITH CROCODILES From a canoe or boat you'll see countless **Nile crocodiles** and **hippos** along the park's 120km river frontage. The density of crocodiles is estimated at 100 per kilometre of river; the hippo density stands at 70 per kilometre. Although they're mostly nocturnal feeders, hippos often graze the grassy flats during the day. If disturbed they trundle back to the safety of the river – both in and out of water they must be given a wide berth. **Buffaloes** and **elephants** feed along the shoreline and in the marshy grasses on exposed shallows, while **waterbucks** crop grassy islands. Elephants casually wander through camps, so being escorted to and from tents is a good precaution.

The Zambezi's birdlife creates a constant background din – from the alarm calls of **blacksmith** and **white-crowned plovers** and the ringing duets of **African fish eagles** to **trumpeter hornbills** wailing atop ebony trees. **Storks**, **egrets** and **herons** probe the shallows, **spur-winged geese** honk and **African jacanas** tiptoe across water shields. Vertical riverbanks are dotted with the holes of bee-eaters with **white-fronted bee-eaters**

WILDLIFE HIGHLIGHTS

» Water-loving animals include crocs, hippos, elephants and buffaloes » Waterbucks, impalas and bushbucks are common » The park has good numbers of lions and leopards » Approximately 400 bird species, including palmnut vultures and Angola pittas » Ideal for boat and canoe safaris resident, and **blue-cheeked** and **carmine** appearing in October and August, respectively. **African skimmers** gather on sandbars but their numbers, and those of **white-fronted plovers**, are falling because vegetation is encroaching on the sandbanks they require for breeding sites (Kariba Dam now prevents the annual flooding which used to keep the sandbanks free of growth).

Kingfisher Lodge is close to the steep, forested Mpata Gorge – a fabulous place for seeing **raptors. Palmnut vultures** – also called vulturine fish eagles because they feed on fish and crabs, in addition to palm nuts – are often seen perched here. The hilly area around the lodge is the place to look for **roan antelopes**.

ON DRY LAND Away from the water, the shore is flat and sandy, and it is in this poor soil that winter-thorn acacias grow. Their protein-rich seeds are relished by animals and **elephants** sometimes stand on their hind legs, grasping at the topmost pods with their trunk. Patches of open plains studded with baobabs occur throughout the valley floor and these areas are ideal for searching the horizon for evidence of kills. A swirl of descending **vultures** and **marabou storks** often marks the spot. **Ground hornbills** wander in open areas and if staying at Chiawa Camp you may meet 'Momba', an outrageously behaved, tame ground hornbill (she even has her own website).

Vervet monkeys, **chacma baboons** and **Meyer's parrots** forage through fig and nyala-berry trees and tangled riverine gullies that lead onto floodplains. The baboons here are slighter and more yellow than the chacma baboons south of the Zambezi and appear more like yellow baboons. Search the leaf litter of thickets for brilliant **Angola pittas**; once disturbed they may perch and sit still. These intra-African migrants arrive with the rains and breed here. The **narina trogon** is another colourful migrant that favours thick forest. Listen for its hoarse hoot and look for its bobbing tail among foliage.

A THORNY LARDER

Exiting the flats and entering acacia woodland, the limbs of winter-thorns arch overhead, almost touching each other's spindly branches and creating a ceiling of thorns, tiny leaves and spiralling pods. Aside from their majesty, winter-thorns are larders during cool dry months. The average *Acacia albida* produces 300kg of pods each year and sprouts leaves during the dry season, which provide shade and protein. Elephants shake their limbs for pods, then pick them up with their trunk as impalas vainly try to snare a few. At other times, bushbucks pick through seedpod litter discarded by baboons. The pods are resilient, and even after passing through an elephant's digestive system they are mostly intact, enabling seed dispersion.

BUFFALO, LOWER ZAMBEZI NATIONAL PARK

ZAMBIA

LOCATION 700km north of Lusaka. In wet season prearrange boat transfers.

FACILITIES Shoebill Camp conducts drives, walks and canoe trips. Scouts for hire at Chikuni.

ACCOMMODATION Permanent tents at Shoebill Island, chalets at Nsobe Camp (open May to December).

WILDLIFE RHYTHMS March to July is good for seeing shoebills and lechwes.

CONTACT Best information from Kasanka Trust (☎ satellite 00 873 762 067 957; www.kasanka.com), Zambian Wildlife Authority (www.zawa.org.zm).

BANGWEULU SWAMPS

Emerging out of woodlands onto Bangweulu's expansive floodplain, you are immediately among thousands of **black lechwes**. Bangweulu is the only place where these semiaquatic antelopes occur, and nights at Shoebill Island feature the sound of splashing hooves as lechwes retreat into the reeds. At the edge of the plains are herds of **tsessebes**, and tiny **oribis** can be found singly or in pairs in adjacent dry grasslands.

Wildlife-watching at Bangweulu is determined by the seasonal flooding and receding of the wetlands. Seventeen rivers feed the Bangweulu Basin, which supports extensive reedbeds dissected by hundreds of streams. Its plains are dotted with termite mounds from which waterberry and sausage trees grow. These become islands once the floodwaters arrive.

From December to March floodwaters spill across the plains, providing feeding grounds for **migratory birds**. As floodwaters recede exposing fresh graze, herds of **lechwes** and **tsessebes** congregate, and **waterbirds** concentrate around isolated pools. Hundreds of **sacred ibises** probe the grassland, and mix with flocks of **wattled cranes** and **ground hornbills**. **Denham's bustards** are common, and **Abdim's** and **white storks** seasonally drop in. Pools teem with **eastern white pelicans**, and **yellow-billed** and **marabou storks**.

Bangweulu is one of the few places to see the rare **shoebill**. Often called the shoebill stork, its closest relative is in fact thought to be the pelican. Standing up to 1.5m high with a huge cloglike bill, shoebills ambush prey by lunging both beak and feet forward. Typically found deep in wetlands, shoebills sometimes wander around Shoebill Camp during wet season. Even in June several are often spotted not far from camp. Once the floods recede you can walk or take a canoe into the marshy areas – look among floating mats of papyrus. If you're very lucky, you may flush a **sitatunga**. Bangweulu is sometimes referred to as a national park, but it isn't – there is intense fishing throughout. Tourist interest in Bangweulu's wildlife seems imperative to protect it.

WILDLIFE HIGHLIGHTS
» The only place to see black lechwes, which mass in their thousands » Possibly Africa's best site for shoebills » Tsessebes and oribis occur in large number » Oodles of waterbirds and floodplain-associated birds

KASANKA NATIONAL PARK

Anyone who has searched fruitlessly through mosquito-infested swamps for a glimpse of the elusive **sitatunga** will appreciate Kasanka. From Fibwe Tree Hide **sitatungas** can be seen most mornings and evenings grazing below in the Kapabi Swamp amid reeds and papyrus. Their long, splayed hooves are adapted to wading through floating vegetation and bogs.

Tiny Kasanka is Zambia's only privately managed park. It lies in a high-rainfall area close to the Democratic Republic of Congon border, and many birds found here are more typical of species you would expect in Central Africa. Top of the list is **Ross' lourie** – big, noisy and brightly coloured, it is easy to find around Fibwe Hide and other streams and lakes. This species is not found south of the Zambezi and is one of Kasanka's two-dozen 'Zambian specials'; others include **red-and-blue sunbirds, Anchieta's** and **black-backed barbets,** and **Böhm's flycatchers.** Also watch out for **Schalow's louries.**

The park's flat terrain accumulates water during the summer rains and maintains a permanent wetland that attracts a diverse array of **waterbirds. African marsh harriers, spur-winged geese, African fish eagles** and **wattled cranes** are common sights around the main camp at Lake Wasa. Guided walks through miombo woodland and patches of evergreen forest are a must for birders.

During November and December, visit Fibwe at dusk – millions of **straw-coloured fruit-bats** flap out of the canopy of this red mahogany swamp forest. Other mammals at Kasanka include **pukus**, which are common near water sources. The airstrip is a favourite place to look for **sable antelopes** and **Lichtenstein's hartebeests**, while an early-morning drive out to Mpuelwe Hill may reward you with sightings of **roan antelopes**. Other mammals include **elephants, bushbucks, grey duikers, reedbucks, baboons, vervet monkeys** and **warthogs.** Night drives regularly reveal **genets, African civets, bushbabies, elephant shrews, mongooses** and **side-striped jackals.**

LOCATION Approximately 520km northwest of Lusaka.

FACILITIES Tree hide, canoes, guided game drives, boat trips and walks. Bird list at Wasa Camp. Child-friendly.

ACCOMMODATION Two camps with self-catering or fully inclusive bungalows. Camping by prior arrangement.

WILDLIFE RHYTHMS Wildlife-viewing best between July and November. Fruit-bats between November and December.

CONTACT Best information from Kasanka Trust (☎ satellite 00 873 762 067 957; www.kasanka.com), Zambian Wildlife Authority (www.zawa.org.zm)

WILDLIFE HIGHLIGHTS

» One of the best places in Southern Africa to see sitatungas and Ross' louries » Hippos, crocodiles, pukus, hartebeests and sables are all readily visible » Fruit-bats occur in their millions in season » No fewer than 24 of Kasanka's 400 bird species are so-called 'Zambian specials' » Kasanka is accessible in the wet season

◉◉ WATCHING TIPS

Boat and canoe trips can be arranged at Luwombwa Camp. Drifting down the river, you pass kingfishers, bee-eaters, slender-snouted and Nile crocodiles, Nile monitors and, if lucky, Cape clawless otters. Scan trees for blue monkeys.

ZAMBIA

WILDLIFE GUIDE
FINDING, RECOGNISING AND UNDERSTANDING WILDLIFE

MAMMALS

SOUTHERN AFRICAN MAMMALS

With a complement of more than 350 mammal species, Southern Africa is a must for wildlifers who like their fauna furred. About two-thirds of these mammals are tiny, nocturnal and secretive, so unless you're a rodent or bat specialist, you're not likely to find most of them. But of course, it's the other third that most people come here to see.

Southern Africa is, as the ecologists would have it, a haven for charismatic mega-vertebrates (big game). In a few weeks' worth of dedicated viewing, you could easily clock up 50 species including some of the most sought-after creatures on earth.

Elephants are abundant, big cats are remarkably tolerant of human observers, and there are more rhinos here than on the rest of the planet combined. At least four of the Big Five are virtually guaranteed, and, with a bit of luck, even chances of sighting leopards are high. Nowhere else on earth will you feel such a sense of what it must have been like for our hominid ancestors. The distant roar of a lion or the frenzied whoops

CHEETAH WITH HER CUBS

of a hyena clan evoke memories from a past when humankind regularly formed a part of the food web. Even today, there are more mammalian species in Africa known to kill humans than on any other continent. But rest assured, most of them prefer to avoid our kind, and it's usually only those people who do the wrong thing that become lion food. For everyone who sticks to the rules, Southern Africa has the potential to be the most rewarding – and entirely safe – mammal-watching destination they'll ever visit.

This section highlights the species most likely to be seen, and aims to provide a little insight into what makes them tick. Some people come on safari hoping simply to notch up a long list of species spotted: Southern Africa certainly won't disappoint there, but take some time to actually observe the wildlife. There are few places on earth where so many different species allow us so closely into their world and reveal their behaviour. Whether it's the lone territorial defence of male antelopes, the love-hate relationship among Cape fur-seals, or the prodigious reproductive capacity of lions, Southern Africa is an extraordinary arena where every possible facet of animal behaviour is on show.

CHACMA BABOON

RECOGNITION Chacmas have uniform grey-brown fur, large dog-faced head and distinctive kinked tail. A yellowish subspecies known as the yellow baboon occurs in Malawi and northern Zambia.

HABITAT All habitats where refuges (tall trees or cliffs) and water occur.

BEHAVIOUR Highly social and strictly diurnal; sleeps in trees or on the sides of cliffs at night. Most active early morning and evening.

BREEDING Breeds year-round. Single young born after 140-day gestation approximately every two years.

FEEDING Mostly fruits, seeds, bulbs and insects, occasionally catches small mammals and birds.

VOICE Very vocal, most distinctive call is the two-toned *wa-hoo!* alarm bark.

COMPLEX SOCIALITES The largest primate in the region (aside from humans), and also one of the most common, is easily overlooked once you've crossed it off your list. However, their intensely complex social behaviour ensures constant action and spending a little longer with them reveals alliances, cliques, cooperation and deceit. Continual social tension within the troop fuels the drama. Living in a troop helps to avoid predation because many pairs of eyes increase the chances of spotting carnivores. But it also heightens competition for food, so individual baboons are torn between the benefits of foraging alone and the need to stay with companions to avoid winding up as a leopard's next meal.

To ensure antagonistic competitors don't steal every morsel, baboons make friends. Grooming strengthens the bonds between potential allies that might assist in a dispute over food, and every baboon spends a large percentage of its day cultivating and maintaining friendships. Such alliances also help during clashes over dominance, particularly for females, where allies often assist in clashes with rivals. Interestingly, male baboons elsewhere in Africa also form alliances, but not in the southern subregion.

With such complex relationships, the potential for deception is rife, and baboons exploit this using their considerable intelligence. Subordinates give false predator alarm calls to distract attacking rivals, and young males may form enduring associations with babies, which are used as a kind of peace offering to inhibit attacks by dominant males. The deception starts young. Juvenile baboons scream as though being attacked to incite their mother to set upon a troop member who has food the youngster wants.

Although life within the troop may seem like a Machiavellian struggle, group members unite against a common threat. Adult males form the front line of defence and cooperate to drive off rival troops and predators. Males are formidable combatants, and alone are easily able to kill dogs; together, they can occasionally kill leopards.

MAMMALS

VERVET MONKEY

BUSHVELD LINGUISTS Africa's most common monkey is also one of the most terrestrial, and like baboons, vervets spend much of their time foraging on the ground. However, combined with their smaller size, being abundant and ground-dwelling means they attract a greater range of predators than their larger relative, and have evolved a complex vocabulary in response. Six different calls are used to indicate different predators and vervets respond accordingly. When a leopard is spotted, a sharp staccato bark tells the troop to race for the treetops where big cats can't follow. If the danger is a raptor, the 'eagle' call sends them into dense thickets or the inner branches of trees, while the 'snake chutter' causes vervets to stand on their hind legs and search the surrounding grass. Other calls indicate minor threats such as small cats or African wild dogs, and where vervets are persecuted by people they have yet another call to say 'run for it!'

Dominant males do most of the sentry duty, and troop members are more likely to heed their calls than those of unreliable sentinels, such as youngsters. Juvenile vervets have to learn the appropriate calls for different threats, and are prone to false alarms. Falling leaves or harmless birds can provoke the 'eagle' cry, while distant antelopes may be mistaken for leopards.

In total, at least 36 different calls are used for communication, but complex visual signals have an equally important role in vervet language. Raising the eyebrows exposes bright white eyelids to indicate aggression, a gesture stereotyped enough that young vervets will respond to clumsy human imitations. Increasing aggression is shown by displaying canine teeth; subordinate monkeys indicate compliance by looking away and grimacing, or else risk attack. The dominant male signals his status by showing his powder-blue scrotum and vivid scarlet penis.

RECOGNITION Grizzled grey coat with white underparts, dark feet and hands. Black face is fringed by white.

HABITAT All wooded habitats except for dense forest. Common in open savanna, but never far from trees.

BEHAVIOUR Highly social, occurs in troops of about 20 with a single dominant male and complex dominance relationships within the troop. Strictly diurnal, sleeps in trees or cliffs.

BREEDING Mate March to May. Single infant born after 140-day gestation.

FEEDING Omnivorous: fruits, seeds, flowers, leaves, sap, grass, invertebrates and occasionally lizards, eggs and nestlings.

VOICE At least 36 calls known. Loudest and most obvious are alarm signals.

MAMMALS

⭐ HOTSPOTS

- Kruger NP (p60)
- Hwange NP (p142)
- Moremi GR (p132)
- South Luangwa NP (p178)

SAMANGO MONKEY

RECOGNITION Vervetlike but darker; blue-grey to dark-grey above and creamy-white underparts. Back is grizzled olive to rusty.

HABITAT Various evergreen forests including montane and coastal. Deciduous sand-forest.

BEHAVIOUR Multi-female troops up to 35-strong with a single alpha male. Diurnal, with foraging peaks in the morning and mid-afternoon.

BREEDING Mates to time births with the onset of the rainy season. Single young born after 140-day gestation.

FEEDING Very herbivorous, concentrating on fruit, leaves and flowers. Occasionally insects.

VOICE A relatively quiet monkey with seven known calls. Males give the only loud calls, including a low-frequency 'boom' to keep troop members in touch.

THE GENTLE MONKEY Also known as blue monkeys, samangos are larger and much darker than related vervet monkeys. They're also the sole southern forest-dwelling representative of a family which, in the rich equatorial forests of East and Central Africa, numbers almost 20 species. Southern Africa's relatively poor forest cover doesn't support multiple species, freeing up samango monkeys from intense competition. Combined with a stable social structure centred on a matriline (a group of closely related females), this is thought to contribute to the samango's unusually placid nature. Conflict among troop members is rare, and dominance relationships are weak, giving rise to yet another name, the gentle monkey.

Troops are territorial, but even among strangers, clashes are low-key and injuries are rare. The troop's females band together and make unified charges at the enemy until one family decides to move off. Unusually for primates, adult males show little interest in defending the family's turf. However, of all troop members they are the most vigilant and usually the first to spot the opposition, as well as their main predator, crowned eagles.

Dominant males may be indifferent to turf wars, but they defend their harem fiercely from other males, the only extreme aggression usually observed in samangos. Young males are violently evicted from the troop before sexual maturity, and live as loners or form small bachelor groups of two to three. During the mating season, these 'floaters' attach themselves to a troop, and attempt to sneak copulations with females out of sight of the alpha male. The dense vegetation of the canopy, and the samangos' tendency to spread out while they forage, facilitate matings by these satellite males, which almost certainly father some of the troop's infants. If caught in the act, the ensuing battle can leave them with severe wounds, which the attacking males inflict on the head and shoulders. Such encounters are occasionally fatal and are not always one-sided. Challengers regularly oust the troop's leader, and males are replaced every one to three years.

★ HOTSPOTS

- Nyanga MP (p161)
- Nyika NP (p170)
- iSimangaliso Wetland Park (p80)

MAMMALS

GREATER BUSHBABY

Named after their childlike wailing cry used to demarcate territory and communicate with family members, bushbabies (galagos) are primitive primates related to Madagascar's lemurs. The largest and most social species, the greater (or thick-tailed) bushbaby occupies individual home ranges, but tolerates considerable overlap. Although they forage alone, fruit clusters and gum seeps attract up to 10 individuals, which feed amicably, and indulge in occasional grooming sessions. Such interactions are most common during summer, which is outside the mating season, and when food is more abundant.

With the onset of dry season, clashes between adult females increase, and dominant males become intolerant of other males as they prepare for the breeding season. Females attempt to stake out productive territories to ensure that they can provide for their offspring, while males fight for the right to control up to five females' ranges. Their rewards are considerable. Females in a given population synchronise their oestrous periods to within a two-week period, during which dominant males attempt to insemi-nate all females in their area. However, competition for females during this period is intense from neighbouring males and transient subordinates. Perhaps in an effort to guard receptive females, matings last almost an hour.

RECOGNITION Cat-sized, woolly grey-brown fur, bushy tail, large eyes and rounded ears.

HABITAT Woodland and forest.

BEHAVIOUR Nocturnal.

BREEDING One to three young at start of rainy season.

FEEDING Insects, fruit and gum.

VOICE 18 different calls; most common is 'baby crying' wail.

✸ HOT SPOTS

- Mana Pools NP (p150)
- South Luangwa NP (p178)
- Hluhluwe-iMfolozi GR (p64)

LESSER BUSHBABY

Heightened night vision, extremely sensitive hearing and unparalleled agility make these tiny primates formidable nocturnal hunters. Insects are their staple, plucked from foliage or in midflight with a snakelike strike anchored by the hind feet holding a branch. Even more acrobatically, they sometimes launch themselves into the air at aerial prey. However, their real agility is displayed in 5m-long leaps between trees as they commute between known food sources or flee predators such as genets and owls.

Like the much larger greater (thick-tailed) bushbaby, related females often share home ranges. Along with their young, and sometimes the resident male, familiar females occupy daytime nests in a tight, furry cluster of up to seven animals. Dominant males avoid contact with one another, and maintain territories with prodigious urine marking and a high-pitched barking call. Proclaiming ownership of turf is only one function of their complex vocal repertoire of at least 25 different calls. All family members use calls to maintain contact and warn of danger. Unlike greater bushbabies, lesser bushbabies can call when inhaling as well as exhaling, and the distinctive two-toned result is easily mistaken for a calling pair.

RECOGNITION Tiny, silvery-grey to grey-brown with bushy tail, huge ears and eyes.

HABITAT Savanna, wood-lands, mopane forests.

BEHAVIOUR Nocturnal.

BREEDING Usually twins.

FEEDING Insects and gum.

VOICE Alarm 'chipping'.

✸ HOTSPOTS

- Mana Pools NP (p150)
- Kafue NP (p182)
- Pilanesberg NP (p72)

MAMMALS

CAPE PANGOLIN

RECOGNITION Up to 1m long, covered in brown scales.

HABITAT Savanna, woodland, grasslands and semidesert.

BEHAVIOUR Solitary; largely nocturnal. Adults rest in underground dens during the day.

BREEDING Single young born July to August.

FEEDING Ants and termites.

VOICE Usually silent.

★ HOT SPOTS

- Hwange NP (p142)
- Kafue NP (p182)
- Kruger NP (p60)
- Moremi GR (p132)

Belonging to a unique order comprising seven species worldwide, there are two pangolins in the region and both are rare, special sightings. Diminutive tree pangolins of the Central African rainforest just make it into the extreme northwest of Zambia and their nocturnal, arboreal habits mean they're rarely seen. However the terrestrial and relatively widespread Cape pangolin is a much better prospect, often sighted crossing roads at night in search of their prey. Entirely insectivorous, these large pangolins eat ants and termites which they lap up with a 25cm-long tongue and then (as they completely lack teeth) grind up using ingested sand in their muscular stomach.

Even more remarkable is the pangolin's unique defence – modified hair in the form of hard, overlapping platelike scales. When threatened, pangolins roll into a tight ball, protecting the vulnerable face and belly, and presenting their attacker with layers of impenetrable, sharp-edged scales; it looks like an enormous pinecone. This defensive tactic also protects the vulnerable young: females carry their single offspring on their backs, but pull the baby onto the stomach and roll around it when threatened. The scales are highly valued for traditional medicine, and human collectors are their primary predator.

AARDVARK

RECOGNITION Pinkish-grey colour; 1.4m to 1.7m long.

HABITAT Grasslands, open woodland and farmlands.

BEHAVIOUR Primarily nocturnal, spends the day in a burrow.

BREEDING Single young born after seven-month gestation.

FEEDING Ants, termites and aardvark cucumbers.

VOICE Mostly silent.

★ HOTSPOTS

- Gonarezhou NP (p146)
- Chobe NP (p120)
- Karoo NP (p84)

Resembling pangolins only in diet, aardvarks have no close relatives, and are the only living member of a once widespread group of mammals. And even though their Afrikaans name means earth-pig, they're only superficially porcine, with an appearance as unique as their ancestry. With a sparse covering of coarse hair over pink-grey skin, an elongated movable snout, tubular ears and a heavy kangaroo-like tail, there is no other mammal like it. Powerful front legs end in massive claws suited to excavating insect prey or digging itself out of danger. Indeed, aardvarks are the most prolific diggers of all African mammals.

Widely distributed throughout Southern Africa, aardvarks are rarely seen because they usually emerge from their deep burrows very late at night. When foraging, they walk at a leisurely pace, sniffing the ground for ant and termite nests, which are speedily excavated and then tackled with the long ribbonlike tongue and its coat of sticky saliva. Aardvarks are extremely resistant to the noxious chemical defences of their prey, and a feeding bout may carry on until their entire body is submerged in the cavity.

MAMMALS

HARES & RABBITS

LONG-EARED LAGOMORPHS Often mistakenly classified as rodents, hares and rabbits actually belong in their own order called lagomorphs. There are six of them in Southern Africa (not including the introduced European rabbit): two hares and four rabbits. All of them prefer fresh sprouting grass, but readily browse shrubs, and also practise coprophagy, the reingestion of soft faecal pellets for a second round of digestion. In the field, the two groups are usually distinguished by their ears: hares have very prominent ones, rabbits less so. It's a useful rule of thumb, but the differences are blurred among Southern African representatives. Both the lanky scrub hare and the smaller Cape hare have elongated ears, but the latter are overall more rabbitlike with a small, 'rabbity' face and body. Riverine rabbits have extremely prominent ears, enough for them to be once considered hares.

Hares and rabbits are very similar in appearance, but they differ in one fundamental way. Hares give birth to precocial young – fully furred with open eyes and ears, and mobile within 48 hours. In contrast, rabbits have young that are altricial – blind, naked and helpless, with closed eyes and ears. Whereas young hares move about and seek the nearest available cover when the mother leaves to forage, female rabbits construct a nest in which to raise their kittens.

Their distribution overlaps, but another useful way to distinguish hares and rabbits is by habitat. The two hare species prefer open savanna terrain: semiarid

SCRUB HARE

scrublands for Cape hares, but any scrub, grasslands and open woodlands for the ubiquitous scrub hare. Southern Africa's rabbits, however, are either rock or riverine dwellers. Between them, the three rock-rabbit species (Natal red, Smith's red and Jameson's red) inhabit the rocky hillsides of the Drakensberg Mountains, the fold mountains of the Cape, Namibia's Naukluft Massif and Zimbabwe's Matobo Hills. In contrast, as its name suggests, the endemic riverine rabbit is confined to the dense scrub alongside rivers. Except for the common and occasionally diurnal scrub hare, all the lagomorphs are nocturnal and fairly difficult to see; night drives usually turn up at least one species.

MAMMALS

HOTSPOTS

- Karoo NP (p84) One of the few places where riverine rabbits occur, as well as Smith's rock rabbits and both hares
- Makgadikgadi Pans & Nxai Pan NPs (p128) Excellent for both hare species, often flushed by diurnal hunters on winter mornings
- Pilanesberg NP (p72) Abundant Jameson's rock rabbits and scrub hares

SQUIRRELS

GROUND SQUIRREL

CAMP-SITE COMPANIONS Most of Southern Africa's 80-plus rodents are tiny, timid and nocturnal, but although they may not always be visible, rodents occupy every available land habitat in the region. Five species of mole-rats live underground, cane rats infest sugar-cane fields, and the Drakensberg Mountains are home to little ice rats. Most people see few of these, but there are a few species that are far more conspicuous.

Heading the list, Cape ground squirrels are restricted to the region's semiarid southwest. Diurnal and highly gregarious, they form groups based around a core of related females, while the males roam between colonies looking for mating opportunities. Colonies number up to 30, and sometimes share their burrows with meerkats and yellow mongooses. Although mongooses occasionally eat young squirrels, the two species respond to one another's alarm calls, and young of both play with one another. Like all rodents, ground squirrels are mainly herbivorous, and forage during the heat of the day for grass, leaves, roots and bulbs. Their distinctive bushy tail is held over the body like an umbrella, but in midsummer, they invariably head below ground for a noon siesta. Around camp sites they become extremely tame, and will beg for food; biscuits are a favourite but sweet handouts can result in serious nutritional problems.

Well above ground, there are a further four squirrel species. Resembling the squirrels of the northern hemisphere (but not closely related to them), they're all tree-dwellers, and mostly inhabit dense forest. Northern Namibia's striped tree squirrel and the sun squirrel of northern Mozambique and Zimbabwe's Eastern Highlands are both extremely elusive. Far more common, the vividly coloured red squirrel and the tree squirrel are closely related to each other, and share many similarities. Both are diurnal, and form small groups comprising a number of females and their pups, with a single male heading the hierarchy. The red squirrel is restricted to the coastal and montane forests of the eastern seaboard, but the tree squirrel is widespread throughout savannas where it is probably the region's most visible rodent.

✦ HOTSPOTS

- Etosha NP (p100) Camp sites have extremely tame ground squirrels
- iSimangaliso Wetland Park (p80) Tree squirrels very tame here, and red squirrels can also be spotted
- Victoria Falls & Zambezi NPs (p156) Tree squirrels are very common

SPRINGHARE

Resembling a miniature, rabbit-faced kangaroo, the nocturnal springhare is the only truly bipedal mammal in Southern Africa aside from humans. They prefer the nutritious, short grasses growing on dry pan beds and floodplains, so they're fairly easy to spot on night drives. Nocturnal predators have the same idea, and everything from owls and mongooses to hyenas and lions prey on them. Springhares always have a bolthole close by, and rarely forage further than 400m from a burrow; on bright moonlit nights they stick to cover.

Springhares spend days below ground, generally on their own. Their burrows are usually no deeper than a metre but can be almost 50m long, with up to a dozen entrances; some are plugged with soil to keep out smaller carnivores and snakes. Although springhares are not particularly gregarious, their day burrows are often clustered together, and small groups of up to a dozen congregate amicably to share feeding patches.

With no close relatives and no evidence of their ancestry (they've been classified in their own family), they're a unique species well worth searching for. The characteristic bobbing motion of their eyeshine – due to their kangaroo-like locomotion – when spotlit is a giveaway.

RECOGNITION Rufous cinnamon with black-tipped tail. Eyeshine usually blue-green.

HABITAT Savanna grasslands.

BEHAVIOUR Strictly nocturnal.

BREEDING Usually one young.

FEEDING Grass, roots, stems, leaves and seeds.

VOICE Usually quiet. Bleats and screams in distress.

★ HOT SPOTS

- Central Kalahari GR **(p124)**
- Pilanesberg NP **(p72)**
- Gonarezhou NP **(p146)**

CAPE PORCUPINE

Africa's largest rodent, the Cape porcupine occurs in virtually all habitats, but are largely nocturnal – another reason to book a night drive. Typical small family groups comprise a single adult breeding pair and their young, but they mostly forage alone. Juveniles younger than six months are accompanied by an adult, usually the male, to help deter predators. Rodents are fair game to a legion of predators, but porcupines are one of the very few species with any advanced defence mechanism. Modified hairs in the form of quills discourage many a threat, but contrary to legend, the quills are not poisonous or barbed, and cannot be fired at their foes. And they're not foolproof: lions, leopards and caracals will harry a porcupine until it's too exhausted to defend itself. In the Kalahari, about a quarter of all lion kills are porcupines. Although inexperienced cats sometimes wind up with a face full of quills, debilitating injuries are actually quite rare.

Porcupines are monogamous and remain in close physical contact for much of the time; females do not come into oestrus unless the male is present. The young of past years often share the territory, and families share extended burrow systems where up to a dozen may shelter.

RECOGNITION Covered in glossy black fur and quills.

HABITAT All in the region.

BEHAVIOUR Sociable in small family groups. Teeth chattering and quill rattling are used to warn predators.

BREEDING One to three young.

FEEDING Bulbs, roots, fruit and bark.

VOICE Largely silent.

★ HOTSPOTS

- Hluhluwe-iMfolozi GR **(p64)**
- Chobe NP **(p120)**

MAMMALS

AARDWOLF

RECOGNITION Miniature yellow-grey hyena.

HABITAT Grasslands and open woodlands.

BEHAVIOUR Monogamous pairs defend a small territory.

BREEDING Two to four cubs born in October. Both sexes care for the cubs.

FEEDING Termites; ignores meat.

VOICE Largely silent.

✦ HOT SPOTS

- Karoo NP (p84)
- Kgalagadi Transfrontier Park (p68)
- Pilanesberg NP (p72)

The smallest of the hyena family (which comprises only four species), the aardwolf is also its least predatory member. Unlike their carnivorous relatives, aardwolves subsist almost entirely on termites. Nocturnal harvester termites give away their position by feeding sounds – the whisper of thousands of tiny jaws cutting grass – and aardwolves home in with their acute hearing. Sound carries best on still, dry nights: the best time for aardwolves to hunt and also the best time to look for them. With their long pink tongue coated in glue-like saliva, aardwolves may spend 10 hours of the night foraging, and can lap up 250,000 termites.

While its diet is unique among the family, the aardwolf's hyena ancestry remains apparent. A caustic digestive system enables them to cope with noxious terpenes secreted by defensive termites. Although their cheek teeth are mere stumps, they retain a carnivore's prominent canine teeth, used in territorial clashes and to defend their cubs from their main predator, black-backed jackals. And like all hyenas, they also have well-developed scent glands and assiduously scent-mark their turf with a pungent paste-like secretion. Perhaps also because of their predatory heritage, they are widely persecuted in the entirely erroneous belief that they kill livestock.

BROWN HYENA

RECOGNITION Dark, shaggy hyena. Pale neck and striped legs.

HABITAT Arid savanna, woodland and desert.

BEHAVIOUR Nocturnal.

BREEDING One to five cubs.

FEEDING Scavenges. Eats insects and small mammals.

VOICE Mostly silent. Growls during territorial clashes.

✦ HOTSPOTS

- Central Kalahari GR (p124)
- Kgalagadi Transfrontier Park (p68)
- Pilanesberg NP (p72)

With their massive head, sloping back and shaggy dark cape, it's easy to think brown hyenas the inspiration for the werewolves of European mythology. But these medium-sized hyenas are not nearly as rapacious as they look, and live almost entirely off scavenging. Their mainstay is the remains of kills left by other predators; in the arid southwest region, they're virtually guaranteed visitors to large carcasses.

The large cats provide brown hyenas with most of their spoils, but it's an uneasy relationship. Brown hyenas may drive cheetahs and occasionally even leopards from their kills, but lions kill hyenas when they can; brown hyenas linger at a safe distance, usually more than 50m away, until the lions leave.

Though mostly seen alone, brown hyenas live in loose clans of up to a dozen. They forage solo but come together at large kills, and all may carry food back to the den to feed cubs. Interestingly, the clan males are usually not the cubs' fathers. Typically, all clan members are related, so the females avoid inbreeding by finding nomadic males who visit only for a brief mating period and then move on.

MAMMALS

SPOTTED HYENA

MALIGNED MAMMALS Probably the most maligned mammal in Africa, the spotted hyena is also one of the continent's most fascinating. Unusually among mammals, females dominate hyena society. Averaging 10kg heavier than their male counterparts, females have also assumed other, more extreme male attributes. High levels of male hormones (androgens) have led to an extraordinary masculinisation in which females have a fully erectile pseudo-penis and false scrotum. It's important during their greeting display, when clan members erect their genitals for mutual inspection, and it takes an expert to differentiate the sexes. At a distance, the most reliable way is to look for the female's prominent nipples (only apparent if she's had a litter).

Females are terrifically aggressive on kills; it's probably the evolutionary drive that led to their 'maleness'. Being able to compete for meat is crucial for mothers with the huge energetic burden of suckling cubs, and the fastest step to aggression (as well as increased size and strength) is via elevated androgen levels. This also means that females are the clan's warriors, and tend to take the initiative in the sometimes violent clashes against rival groups.

Females are dominant to males, and live in a strict hierarchy led by a single matriarch. Female cubs inherit their mother's rank, and fight furiously for it from birth. Born with eyes open and fully developed teeth, they emerge from the womb awash with androgens, and siblings (particularly female twins) sometimes kill one another in the resulting fights. Called siblicide, this ehaviour is common among birds, but spotted hyenas are the only mammals in which it regularly occurs.

Spotted hyena society may seem harsh, but the clan functions to make them one of the most efficient and versatile of all carnivores. Together, they are able to kill buffaloes, and may even drive lions from their kills. Long considered a cowardly scavenger, the spotted hyena is in fact the most successful large predator in Africa.

RECOGNITION Heavily built and doglike. Off-white to reddish brown with dark spots that fade with age.

HABITAT Open woodland, savannas and semidesert.

BEHAVIOUR Largely nocturnal. Clans may be as large as 80 but are fluid, with individuals and small groups breaking off constantly and rejoining later.

BREEDING Nonseasonal. One to three cubs born after a three-month gestation. Females den communally with up to 20 litters together. Typically, females only suckle their own cubs.

FEEDING Scavengers but also very efficient cooperative hunters.

VOICE Very vocal; long-distance *whoop*. Also whine, moan, giggle and cackle, especially when they congregate on kills.

MAMMALS

HOTSPOTS

- Kruger NP (p60)
- Etosha NP (p100)
- Chobe NP (p120)
- Kgalagadi Transfrontier Park (p68)

LION

RECOGNITION Africa's largest cat; males up to 240kg.

HABITAT Wide habitat tolerance including open plains, woodlands, thick bush and semidesert.

BEHAVIOUR Prides number up to 50. Related females form the core of the pride. Male coalitions hold tenure for two to four years. Young males expelled around three years old.

BREEDING Nonseasonal. one to five cubs. Related lionesses suckle each other's cubs.

FEEDING Kills virtually everything, even elephants in extreme cases, though usually large herbivores like wildebeests and zebras. Scavenges up to 25% of its diet.

VOICE Roar proclaims territory and maintains contact between pride members. Low grunts for close-range contact.

KING OF THE JUNGLE Probably the single greatest wildlife drawcard in Africa, lions are actually easy to find. Abundant in large reserves, and with few natural enemies, lions lie in the open and mostly tolerate vehicles. However, the challenge with lions is seeing them in action. It's true they spend most of the day asleep, but to a lion, this makes perfect sense. It's too hot to hunt during the day, and sunlight foils efforts to sneak up on prey. To see lions at their best, go on a guided night drive; darkness provides cover for over 90% of their hunts.

Lionesses usually lead the hunt, but contrary to popular belief, males are active and competent hunters. They tend to let the females initiate the work, but their presence is crucial for dispatching large prey such as buffaloes and giraffes. Separated from the females, they are successful hunters in their own right. Male coalitions spend much of their time away from the pride on territorial patrols, during which they make up to 85% of their own kills.

If nocturnal viewing is impossible, early morning and late afternoon are worthwhile. Lions snoozing during the day usually stay at the same spot until nightfall, so head back there in the afternoon, particularly if there are cubs, which inevitably start playing as the temperature drops. A male and female away from the pride are probably mating, which guarantees constant action. Lions may mate hundreds of times during the female's three- to four-day oestrous, sometimes as often as every 15 minutes. This prodigious frequency probably stems from the high failure rate of matings: only about one in three copulations results in cubs. By being difficult to inseminate, females are probably ensuring that they conceive to a healthy male and to a good father. Males play a critical role in protecting cubs from intruding males, so for a female, the more persistent a male is, the greater likelihood he'll be around until her cubs are grown.

MAMMALS

⭐ **HOTSPOTS**

LEOPARD

SILENT STALKER Ironically, Africa's most common large cat is also the most difficult to spot. Leopards are more abundant and widespread than both lions and cheetahs, but you're far less likely to see one. They are the quintessential cat: stealthy, secretive and adaptable. Tolerant of great environmental extremes, they occur in the desolate riverbeds of the Namib Desert, the swamps of the Okavango, and occasionally in the mountains above Cape Town.

A remarkably catholic diet is one reason behind their success. Eating everything from dung beetles to baby elephants, leopards can persist in areas long devoid of other large predators. They prefer medium-sized antelopes like impalas, but if those are lacking, they turn to dassies, porcupines and francolins. At waterholes in the Kalahari, leopards may spend hours making repeated catches of doves as they come in to drink. Leopards can drink water from hot thermal springs, and survive on domestic dogs near cities.

However, it's in the protection of parks and reserves where leopards really thrive. Where antelope prey is abundant, individual leopards can occupy very small home ranges, allowing them to reach high densities. Furthermore, although leopards are territorial, they tolerate some overlap with neighbours, allowing even greater numbers. Rivals appear to avoid one another in the shared areas in a sort of timeshare system: if a resident is active in a particular portion of overlapping turf, his neighbour avoids the area. However, a week or a month later, the situation may be reversed. Neighbours show mutual respect for this arrangement, reducing the likelihood of conflict.

Some of the finest reserves in which to view leopards are found in Southern Africa. Largely free of persecution and poaching, they have enjoyed decades of protection, and have grown completely accustomed to vehicles, permitting some unparalleled viewing. Of course, don't expect a leopard to just stroll across the road or lie lazing about in the sun. You're going to need to break out the binoculars and scan the treetops, though your reward will be a glimpse of this silent stalker.

RECOGNITION Muscular, lithe cat up to 2.3m long. Orange-yellow fur with black rosettes.

HABITAT Wide habitat tolerance, but most easily seen in open woodland-savanna mosaics.

BEHAVIOUR Largely solitary. Mostly nocturnal, but often active in early morning and evening. Seeks out large trees in which to sleep and to store kills.

BREEDING Nonseasonal. One to four cubs born and hidden in dens until about eight weeks old. Females raise cubs.

FEEDING Very broad tastes with at least 92 prey species on record. Usually small to medium-sized antelopes.

VOICE Rasping cough, which sounds like a wood saw, proclaims territory (both sexes) or advertises sexual readiness (females).

MAMMALS

HOTSPOTS

- Kruger NP **(p60)**
- Kgalagadi Transfrontier Park **(p68)**
- Moremi GR **(p132)**
- South Luangwa NP **(p178)**

CHEETAH

RECOGNITION Tall, slender cat with black coin-like spots on yellow fur. Face has 'tear streaks'.

HABITAT Prefers open savanna-woodland mosaics.

BEHAVIOUR Most active in the early morning and late afternoon. Mothers may hunt during the heat of the day.

BREEDING Nonseasonal. As many as nine (but usually three to six) cubs born after a 95-day gestation.

FEEDING Mainly small and medium-sized antelopes. Also hares, large birds (including ostriches), and the young of large herbivores. Male coalitions can tackle prey up to the size of near-adult wildebeests.

VOICE High yelps used to maintain contact; in cubs, this call sounds like a bird. Growls, barks and 'chutters' during courtship.

KALAHARI FERRARI To see a cheetah at top speed is for many the pinnacle of African wildlife-viewing. Reliably clocked at 105km/h (but probably able to hit 115 km/h to 120km/h), there is no animal faster on land, and cheetahs are probably the fastest land mammals ever to have existed. Nonetheless, nature's arms race has equipped the cheetah's favourite prey with almost comparable fleetness, and some gazelle species can clock almost 100km/h. Antelopes also easily outperform cheetahs in endurance, so like all cats, cheetahs stalk close to their prey before unleashing their phenomenal acceleration. Most sprints begin within 60m of the quarry, and if they haven't succeeded after around 500m, the crushing physiological stresses imposed by the chase force them to give up.

Although widely considered solitary, cheetah social life actually falls somewhere between the lone existence of most felids and the extended family structure of lions. Females are loners, but males form lifelong alliances known as coalitions. Males defend their turf from interlopers, and teamwork makes all the difference in a fight. Usually, coalitions consist of brothers born in the same litter, but lone males will often team up with other, unrelated singletons. On their own, male cheetahs have little hope of a carving out a territory, but by recruiting a 'friend' they have a chance at securing turf and, of course, the females that go with it.

The process is complicated by the females' tendency to wander. Female cheetahs are nonterritorial, covering huge ranges that they don't defend. So males have to look for those areas where females are likely to spend much of their time. Prey concentration and the availability of cover in which to hide cubs are the critical factors, but both vary with the seasons. So some males never form territories and adopt an alternative tactic, roaming over vast distances in search of the wide-ranging females.

MAMMALS

CARACAL

With its tufted ears and shortened tail, it's little wonder that the caracal is often called the African lynx. However, caracals are only distantly related to the lynxes; in fact, they're more closely allied to the African golden cat of Central Africa's rainforests. But unlike that rare and little-known felid, the caracal can exist just about everywhere. Highly adaptable, their range includes most of Africa and Southwest Asia, but nowhere are they more abundant than in Southern Africa. Inhabiting every conservation area in the region except for a narrow coastal band of the Namib, caracals tolerate high levels of human activity, and are also widespread on farmlands. Much of its success is due to its explosive hunting prowess. They tackle antelopes three times their weight, and execute 4m-high leaps to take birds in flight – ancient Asian nobility hunted birds with tame caracals. Today however, their relationship with people is largely adversarial, and farmers persecute caracals relentlessly for occasionally taking young sheep and goats. They are extremely shy, and tend to avoid people, which makes spotting one a rare event. Mountain habitats offer the best chances where klipspringer, dassie and black eagle alarm calls often give them away.

RECOGNITION Medium-sized muscular cat. Sandy to rust red. Black ear tufts.

HABITAT All habitats except true desert and rainforest.

BEHAVIOUR Largely nocturnal and solitary.

BREEDING One to four cubs.

FEEDING Birds, rodents and up to medium-sized antelopes.

VOICE Spits, hisses and growls when threatened.

★ HOT SPOTS

- Mountain Zebra NP **(p90)**
- Matobo NP **(p160)**

SERVAL

Raised on stiltlike legs, and with its huge oval ears, the serval is uniquely equipped as a specialist rodent-killer. Preferring wetland grasses and reeds where small mammals are abundant, servals hunt primarily by sound. Extremely keen hearing pinpoints rodent rustles, which the cat homes in on until it's close enough to launch a characteristic arching pounce, up to 4m long and 1m high. Sometimes they land directly on the unseen target, but if that fails, the attack often flushes the prey, and about half of all hunts are successful.

Servals are essentially solitary, occupying home ranges as large as 30 sq km. However, overlap between ranges may be extensive, and unusually among cats, they seem not to defend a territory. Instead they avoid one another by very frequent urine-marking and defecation, which indicate areas in use; neighbours avoid areas with fresh marks and conflict is rare. This system of land-sharing means that they can be quite common in optimum habitat, but are shy and difficult to spot. Fortunately, they are most active at dawn and dusk, probably to exploit the peak activity periods of certain diurnal rodent species – be out looking at sunrise and late afternoon for a chance to find one.

RECOGNITION Tall, medium-sized cat. Fur pale yellow; long blotches and spots.

HABITAT Well-watered long grass.

BEHAVIOUR Crepuscular. Nocturnal near human activity.

BREEDING One to five kittens.

FEEDING Mostly rodents.

VOICE Largely silent.

★ HOTSPOTS

- Moremi GR **(p132)**
- iSimangaliso Wetland Park **(p80)**
- Maloti-Drakensberg Transfrontier Area **(p89)**

MAMMALS

RECOGNITION Similar to domestic tabby. Red-backed ears and long, striped legs.

HABITAT All including desert watercourses.

BEHAVIOUR Primarily nocturnal. Active at dawn and dusk in protected areas.

BREEDING Two to five kittens.

FEEDING Primarily rodents.

VOICE Similar to domestic cat.

⚡ HOT SPOTS

- Kgalagadi Transfrontier Park **(p68)**
- Central Kalahari GR **(p124)**
- South Luangwa NP **(p178)**

AFRICAN WILD CAT

At first glance, these little cats barely differ from domestic kitties. Indeed, tamed African wild cats actually gave rise to our pets at least 6000 years ago, probably in the Middle East and Egypt where wild cats were kept to hunt mice in grain stores. Although the similarity is unmistakable, African wild cats have longer, striped legs, a leaner build and, most distinctive of all, russet-red backs to the ears. Ironically, their link to the past is probably their greatest threat. Wild cats freely interbreed with domestic cats (most specialists classify them as the same species), and their genetic purity has been eroded wherever people and their cats have settled. Pure African wild cats now exist in only the most remote places; their red ears distinguish them from hybrids in which the colour is lost.

Despite being Africa's most common and widespread cat, there is surprisingly little known of the species in the wild. They appear to follow the typical felid pattern of being largely solitary, and are probably territorial. Unlike feral domestic cats, they are not inclined to form colonies; domestication has almost certainly selected individuals tolerant of one another, and has gradually given rise to heightened sociality in pet cats. Except for females with kittens, wild cats are nearly always spotted alone.

BLACK-FOOTED CAT

RECOGNITION Tiny squat cat. Dark spots, blotches on buff to tawny fur.

HABITAT Arid, short-medium grass savanna.

BEHAVIOUR Nocturnal, solitary.

BREEDING 1–4 kittens.

FEEDING Rodents, shrews, birds and reptiles.

VOICE Loud rough during mating period.

⚡ HOTSPOTS

- Kgalagadi Transfrontier Park **(p68)**
- Central Kalahari GR **(p124)**
- Makgadikgadi Pans NP **(p128)**
- Nxai Pan NP **(p128)**

The region's only endemic cat, the black-footed cat is also one of the world's smallest. The largest males weigh in at only 2.4kg and stand about 25cm high. But its miniature stature conceals a predatory Goliath. An accelerated metabolism and the low prey density of their arid habitat means that black-footed cats have to hunt continually to satisfy their energetic needs. Covering up to 15 to 20km a night, these little powerhouses average a kill every 50 minutes. Mice, shrews and small birds constitute most of their diet, but they are capable of attacking prey much larger than themselves including hares and korhaans.

Flexible hunting methods contribute to their predatory success, and black-footed cats use at least three different strategies. Like all cats, they stalk inexorably closer to prey before the final, explosive rush. But like jackals, they also employ a fast zigzagging trot through high grass to flush prey from hiding. Particularly effective with ground-roosting birds, success depends on their ability to take birds on the wing in acrobatic leaps six times their height. Finally, they also use ambush tactics, waiting outside rodent burrows for up to an hour in the hope that the occupant emerges.

MAMMALS

CIVETS & GENETS

MUSKY TREE-DWELLERS Nocturnal and quick to duck for cover, these distant relatives of the cat family are usually seen as fleeting glimpses in headlights. But except for the rare and little known tree civet of northwest Malawi and eastern Zimbabwe, the viverrids are common and widespread. Largest of all African species, the solitary African civet sports a dark facial mask, vivid white throat-stripes and dark blotches on a light grey–coloured body. Equipped with a robust capacity to digest toxins, civets are able to deal with noxious species like millipedes, scorpions, toads and even highly venomous snakes. Civets produce their own pungent defence, a greasy powerful-smelling paste secreted from perineal glands (a pair of glands situated near the anus of certain mammals). Named after its animal source, musky 'civet' has been collected from captive individuals for centuries as the basis of perfume manufacture. In some parts of Africa, the practice still continues.

Whereas the civet's squat, doglike build confines it to a terrestrial existence, other members of the family are equally at home in trees or on the ground. The region's two genet species – the large-spotted and small-spotted – have fully retractile claws and long, counter-balancing tails for treetop agility, but actually do most of their hunting on ground. It takes experience to tell them apart though the tail tip

SPOTTED GENET

is usually a giveaway – white in small-spotted genets and black in large-spotteds. Genets are also almost identical in lifestyle. Like all viverrids, they are largely solitary, and adults only pair up to mate. After a gestation of 10 to 11 weeks, between two and four kittens are born, usually during the summer, though a second litter can be produced later in the same year. The male has little to do with raising the young. The female teaches them how to hunt (rodents mostly, their main prey) so that by around the age of six months, they leave her to become independent.

Though secretive and nocturnal, civets and genets are occasional night-time visitors to camp barbecues; to see them in their element, try spotlighting along trails and roads – genets can be called in close on night drives by kissing the back of your hand.

MAMMALS

HOTSPOTS

- Kruger NP (p60) Night drives and camp-site barbeques hold good chances for African civets and both genets
- Nyika NP (p170) Tree civets in forested areas, but spotting one is a real challenge
- Chimanimani NP (p158)
- Moremi GR (p132)

MONGOOSES

LOYAL COMRADES A symphony of birdlike peeps, chirps and twitters announces the presence of some of the most gregarious animals on earth. While most mongooses are solitary, a few African species display a level of cooperation rarely equalled in the animal world. From diminutive dwarf mongooses weighing only 400g, to slightly larger 1.5kg banded mongooses, these little social carnivores are surrounded by potential predators, and tightknit family groups have the advantage over loners in spotting danger.

Among desert-dwelling meerkats (suricates), keeping a lookout is refined to a dedicated art. While the troop forages for scorpions, insects and lizards, a lone sentinel occupies a high point, and braves temperatures topping 50°C to watch for eagles and jackals. One shrill alarm shriek from the guard and the band rushes for cover. When escape is impossible, mongoose troops show extraordinary tenacity. Faced with predators many times their size, the entire family bunches together to form a bristling, chattering collective to intimidate the enemy. Troops of banded mongooses – inhabitants of more wooded and grassland regions – will even mob predators that have taken a family member, and adults will climb trees to harass eagles that have snatched an unwary youngster.

DWARF MONGOOSES, MOREMI WILDLIFE RESERVE

MAMMALS

Raising the young is also a communal effort. All adults in the band provide for youngsters, and relinquish even the most prized prey to their begging cries. They even leave a babysitter behind at the den to tend kittens too young to join foraging expeditions. Most adult meerkats and banded mongooses breed and collectively care for each kitten as their own, but reproduction in dwarf mongooses is largely restricted to the dominant pair; other troop members act as 'helpers' in raising the young. Even so, these tiny mongooses are highly vulnerable to predation, and only 30% of kittens survive to adulthood.

There is a legion of less social species, likely to be spotted as a fleeting blur dashing across the road. Driving through the semiarid southwest, you'll almost certainly spot a yellow mongoose. Varying from light grey to russet-yellow with a white-tipped tail, this little mongoose lives in colonies usually three to 12 strong, but forages alone. They probably represent an intermediate stage of sociality, somewhere between the gregarious species and true loners. Similarly, the ubiquitous slender mongoose has a halfway social system, in which males sometimes form coalitions, probably to defend multiple ranges of the solitary females. They carry their tail aloft when running, the flaglike black tip giving rise to their other name, black-tipped mongoose.

Among the true loners, the largest mongoose in the region, the white-tailed mongoose, weighs up to 4.5kg. Spending most of the night foraging

SNAKE KILLERS

Famed for their snake-killing prowess, most mongooses actually avoid dangerous snakes. African rock pythons are one of their most feared predators, active at night and able to slide into the subterranean mongoose burrows as they sleep. Encountered during the day, pythons are less threatening, and mongoose families gang up to drive them away. Lightning reflexes keep the mongooses out of danger, and severe nips to the tail force the snake to seek cover. The same tactic is used on highly venomous species including cobras, mambas and puff adders.

So how did the reputation for snake-killing arise? African mongooses do kill snakes, usually juveniles or harmless species. However, some Asian mongooses are true snake specialists: all loners, what they lack in numbers they make up for with unique immunity. One species, the common Indian mongoose, can withstand a dose of cobra venom that would kill a child.

for insects, frogs and rodents, it is the most common nocturnal mongoose and readily seen while spotlighting.

Finally, two similar species, the large grey and small grey mongoose, are best distinguished by size; around 3kg in the former and rarely above 1kg in the latter. Both are common around camping grounds of the southwest Cape, and while the large grey's distribution heads north around the coast into Mozambique, the small grey's range extends the other way into Namibia.

MAMMALS

★ HOTSPOTS

- Kruger NP (p60) Excellent for slender, dwarf and, on night drives, white-tailed mongooses
- Kgalagadi Transfrontier Park (p68) Virtually guaranteed meerkats, yellow mongooses and Kalahari slender mongooses (red phase)
- Chobe NP (p120) Bandeds, dwarves and (rare) Selous' mongooses in the northwest

AFRICAN WILD DOG

RECOGNITION Collie-sized dog with mottled yellow, black, brown and white markings and prominent rounded ears.

HABITAT Savanna, woodlands, plains and semiarid bushland.

BEHAVIOUR Diurnally active with hunting peaks at dawn and dusk. Pack members are highly social and rarely apart. Small same-sex groups sporadically emigrate in search of opposite-sex groups to form a new pack.

BREEDING Up to 21 pups in midwinter. Denning period about 13 weeks.

FEEDING Probably the most efficient hunters in Africa. Concentrate on medium-sized herbivores, especially impalas, but can tackle larger prey.

VOICE High-pitched twittering when excited, owl-like *hoo* contact call and deep, inquiring growl-bark when alarmed.

MAMMALS

PAINTED WOLVES Science named the African wild dog *Lycaon pictus*, the painted wolf, accurately capturing its mottled, multicoloured appearance and lifestyle, if not ancestry. Wild dogs are not closely related to wolves, but in behaviour and ecological niche, they are very wolflike. Highly social, their packs may number as many as 50 (but average 12 to 20), and are usually centred around a dominant male and female. Known as the alpha pair, these individuals are responsible for most of the breeding in the group, and all other pack members help raise their pups. If a subordinate female breeds, the alpha female may kidnap the pups and raise them, or, in extreme cases, kill them. This is probably dependent on prey availability, and functions to protect the pack from starvation by attempting to raise too many puppies; her tolerance increases in good times. When prey is abundant, as many as three females may breed, and share the suckling duties of the combined litters.

Wild dogs are great wanderers, and a pack's home range may be as large as 2000 sq km. This probably arose in response to the migratory movements of prey, but even where herbivores are resident, wild dogs move over vast areas. Only when the pups are very young is the pack tied to a small area for about three months until the youngsters can accompany the adults. Their need for huge areas is just one factor that has made them one of Africa's most endangered large mammals. Diseases, particularly from domestic dogs, and human persecution have also taken a heavy toll. They kill by eating their prey alive, as quick and probably as 'humane' as any method, but they have been widely condemned as cruel and wasteful, and were once shot even in reserves. Although now considered a special sighting in parks, they are still killed on farms and rangelands. Even protected areas are an imperfect refuge; lions kill many wild dogs, and they avoid otherwise ideal habitat if there are lions about.

BLACK-BACKED JACKAL

Probably the region's most common carnivores, black-backed jackals are ubiquitous around the kills of other hunters. But, although they're superbly opportunistic scavengers, they're also much underrated hunters. Usually foraging alone or in pairs, jackals easily take duiker-sized prey, and larger groups cooperate to kill impalas and springboks. Individuals take turns to harry large victims to the point of exhaustion, and then the group jointly pulls down the prey. Often, a single jackal administers a suffocating throat hold, a typically feline technique rarely used by members of the dog family.

Jackal social life is equally versatile. They form monogamous pairs, probably for life – an unusual social pattern in mammals. Grown pups from the previous season often stay on to help raise new pups before leaving to find mates of their own. Helpers gain valuable knowledge about raising young, and also delay leaving the area they know intimately for the dangers of unknown turf. Jackal families are territorial, but away from the den, they behave as members of a larger society. Unrelated groups share large carcasses, and may function as a cohesive pack to tackle large prey. Widely dismissed as 'lowly', their social and predatory adaptability has led to them being the most successful small carnivore of the region.

RECOGNITION Small, foxlike dog. Reddish-buff; silvery-grey saddle. Black-tipped tail.

HABITAT All bar dense forest.

BEHAVIOUR Nocturnal and diurnal. Highly ritualised at carcasses.

BREEDING One to six pups.

FEEDING Scavenges. Fruit, insects, reptiles, rodents and medium-sized mammals.

VOICE Wailing contact call.

HOT SPOTS

- Hwange NP (p142)
- Etosha NP (p100)
- Kgalagadi Transfrontier Park (p68)

SIDE-STRIPED JACKAL

Least predatory of all jackal species, side-striped jackals are true omnivores, subsisting on wild fruit, rodents, insects, reptiles, birds, nuts, maize and eggs, enabling them to persist where there is very little mammalian prey. But where large mammals and the inevitable carcasses occur, like the black-backed jackals they turn to scavenging. Unlike others, however, they rarely hunt prey much larger than mice, though they are capable of taking unguarded antelope fawns. Presumably, they have ample opportunity to do so during the birth season as they often follow herbivore herds to clean up afterbirth, but the final word on their predatory abilities is still disputed.

Like all jackals, side-striped jackals form long-lasting pairs, which maintain a small territory. Their offspring of the previous year remain with them to help raise pups and defend their range. But whereas other jackal species often congregate to hunt or share carcasses, side-striped jackals of different families rarely interact. They tend to take turns at kill remains, and have not been observed hunting cooperatively for large prey. As a result, they do not reach the densities of black-backed jackals in the region, and although fairly common, are less likely to be seen.

RECOGNITION Lacks the black-backed's grey saddle. White rib stripe. White-tipped tail.

HABITAT Woodland savannas.

BEHAVIOUR Usually seen alone or in pairs.

BREEDING Three to six pups.

FEEDING Highly omnivorous.

VOICE Yapping *raou* for contact and when mobbing predators.

HOTSPOTS

- Mana Pools NP (p150)
- Moremi GR (p132)
- Kafue NP (p182)

MAMMALS

BAT-EARED FOX

RECOGNITION Dark grey fox. Huge ears and bushy tail.

HABITAT Semiarid woodland and open savanna.

BEHAVIOUR Forms family groups.

BREEDING Two to five pups.

FEEDING Mainly insects, also rodents, reptiles and scorpions.

VOICE Alarm bark and soft whining contact call.

✸ HOT SPOTS

- Etosha NP (p100)
- Central Kalahari GR (p124)
- Kgalagadi Transfrontier Park (p68)

The enormous ears of these little foxes are their livelihood. Concentrating mostly on the rustle of surface feeders like harvester termites, they also listen for subterranean prey when topside pickings are slim. Swivelling like two radar dishes, their ears rotate independently a few inches above the ground to pinpoint beetle larvae, millipedes and other invertebrates below the surface. With a burst of frantic digging, they unearth their prize, and pulverise it almost instantaneously using a unique jaw musculature that allows them to chew five times a second.

Like jackals (to which they're not closely related), bat-eared foxes usually live as monogamous pairs with attendant helpers. However, unlike jackals, males often take a second mate, and the two females communally suckle and care for their combined litters. These groups are not territorial, and different families often intermingle when foraging is good (for example, after rains when large patches of insects abound). Although the pair bond may persist for many years, they are not loyal to the same range, and they establish dens wherever food is abundant. Highly social, these diminutive foxes will fiercely harass predators, such as jackals and caracals, to rescue a captured relative.

CAPE FOX

RECOGNITION Small, slender silvery-grey fox. Bushy tail.

HABITAT Arid grassland, dry woodlands and semidesert scrub.

BEHAVIOUR Nocturnal.

BREEDING One to five pups.

FEEDING Primarily insects and mice. Occasionally scavenges. Eats wild fruit.

VOICE High-pitched *wow* repeated several times.

✸ HOTSPOTS

- Etosha NP (p100)
- Central Kalahari GR (p124)
- Kgalagadi Transfrontier Park (p68)

Found only in Southern Africa, Cape foxes are restricted to the region's arid southwest. A limited range is no reflection of their abundance however: they thrive wherever there are insects and rodents. Farmlands offer rich pickings for Cape foxes; though they probably help farmers by keeping pest numbers down, thousands are killed each year in the mistaken belief that they kill lambs. Fortunately, human persecution is probably balanced by the removal of their enemies, such as brown hyenas, jackals, leopards, caracals and honey badgers, all of which hunt them. Diminutive and essentially defenceless, they have a remarkably agile zigzagging escape pattern in which the bushy tail apparently acts as a decoy.

Despite being widespread, Cape foxes are poorly studied. They are thought to be less social than other canids, and are usually observed alone. However, monogamous pairs are probably the norm, at least during the breeding season if not year-round. Larger groups are known, suggesting that more than one female may den together and, like other small canids, helpers probably assist in raising the pups. Cape foxes are shy, but in protected areas viewing young pups at dens can be enormously rewarding.

MAMMALS

HONEY BADGER

TINY TERROR Armed with potent secretions produced by their perineal glands, a pugnacious nature and astonishing strength, honey badgers (ratels) deserve a wide berth. They attack fearlessly when threatened, and, like a bantam bull terrier, have a massively constructed skull in which the jaw can 'lock'; incensed honey badgers will clamp on until their opponent is dead or sometimes until the honey badger itself is killed. Much larger predators usually leave them alone.

But while their reputation for ferocity is well earned, honey badgers are not the indomitable warmongers so often portrayed. Like all animals, they prefer to avoid conflict, and only unleash their formidable defences if provoked. And while they're mostly solitary, occasional gatherings of up to eight adults show them to be tolerant and playful with their own kind. Stories of them dispatching large herbivores by mauling the testicles are probably folklore, and while they occasionally scavenge from lion kills with the owners still feeding, lions do kill them.

But of all the campfire stories told about honey badgers, the most enduring is the one about honeyguides. Greater honeyguides supposedly direct honey badgers to beehives; honey badgers use their bearlike ability to plunder hives for honey, and the bird's reward is access to beeswax, a favourite food. But the honey badger's mostly nocturnal behaviour means that it was probably never a very reliable partner for the diurnal honeyguide. So how did the tale arise? Surprisingly, the bird does form a hive-hunting partnership, but not with honey badgers. As abundant, diurnal lovers of honey, human hunter-gatherers were (and in some areas, still are) perfect partners. Honeyguides might show hives to honey badgers, but until irrefutable evidence presents itself, we are their only confirmed accomplices.

While their relationship with honeyguides is dubious, foraging honey badgers are often accompanied by an entourage of pale chanting goshawks, hoping to catch small birds and rodents making their escape. Small clusters of these raptors, particularly on stumps and low bushes are an effective beacon for spotting honey badgers.

RECOGNITION Low-slung, robust build, up to 1m long and 15kg. Silvery-grey cape over black underparts.

HABITAT Most habitats; common in semiarid areas.

BEHAVIOUR Usually nocturnal, active around dawn and dusk, especially in winter. Very little is known about their social system; they seem to be nonterritorial and home ranges probably overlap considerably. They may congregate where food is readily available.

BREEDING Poorly known. Apparently breeds year-round. One to four (typically two) young.

FEEDING Mostly rodents, scorpions and snakes; readily scavenges carrion; honey is probably a rare treat.

VOICE Usually quiet. Rattling growl given in threat.

MAMMALS

✦ HOTSPOTS

- Hwange NP **(p142)**
- Kgalagadi Transfrontier Park **(p68)**
- Central Kalahari GR **(p124)**

WEASELS & ZORILLA

Like their larger relative the honey badger, both the zorilla (or striped polecat) and African weasel have evolved pungent perineal secretions and aposematism (warning coloration). However, weighing 1kg in the largest zorillas and 350g for African weasels, they lack the honey badger's brute force, and rely chiefly on nocturnal, secretive behaviour to elude predators; if they do encounter trouble, they're quick to air their acrid, chemical punch.

Both zorillas and African weasels are rodent killers. The weasel kills little else, and, contrary to many field guides, rarely takes insects, snakes or eggs. Zorillas have wider tastes, supplementing their rodent kills with reptiles, scorpions, spiders and insects. Their generalist diet lets them occupy a broad range of habitats, and zorillas occur throughout the region. Weasels, however, require prolific rodent populations to sustain them, which makes farmland ideal habitat – at least in theory. Overgrazing reduces rodent numbers, and weasels are easy targets for farm dogs. Persecuted by farmers merely for being a predator, weasels are now rare. Zorillas are spotted more often, especially on guided night drives.

★ HOT SPOTS

- Maloti-Drakensberg Transfrontier Area **(p89)**
- Kruger NP **(p60)**
- Kgalagadi Transfrontier Park **(p68)**

OTTERS

Amphibious members of the weasel family, both otter species take watery refuge at the slightest disturbance. Size is a useful clue for distinguishing them: with an average top weight around 18kg, Cape clawless otters are the largest of Africa's four otter species; the much smaller spotted-necked otter has a top weight around 6kg. Otter paws provide a further lead. If the tracks lack obvious claws and webbing, the owner is a Cape clawless; claws and webs mean spotted-necks. Finally, while their ranges overlap, spotted-necks are restricted to freshwater.

Cape clawless otters' dexterous 'fingers' allow them to manipulate fish, crabs, reptiles, frogs, birds, insects and small mammals, and they hunt 'by hand'. In contrast, spotted-necks make all their catches by mouth and concentrate on fish, crabs or frogs. Both species are mainly solitary, though breeding adults are playful and young male spotted-necks sometimes form small groups.

★ HOT SPOTS

- Lake Malawi NP **(p166)**
- Maloti-Drakensberg Transfrontier Area **(p89)**
- Tsitsikamma NP **(p95)**

MAMMALS

CAPE FUR-SEAL

ANTI-SOCIAL SOCIALITES There are seven seal species in Southern African waters, but except for very occasional vagrants from the Antarctic and sub-Antarctic islands, the only mainland species is the Cape fur-seal. It's also a Southern African endemic, but this limited range is no indication of numbers; there are an estimated two million scattered along the Southern African coastline. Communal to the extreme, this massive population is divided between only about 25 different colonies; a few of them, like Kleinsee on South Africa's west coast, number up to 400,000.

Despite their gregariousness, Cape fur-seals are not especially sociable; colony living makes sense for breeding opportunities, and to reduce the chance of predators sneaking up, but individual seals are essentially loners on land, and constantly quarrel over their own little patch. Except for pups playing with each other in crèche-like 'playgrounds', virtually every other interaction in the colony is hostile, creating extraordinary opportunities for watching behaviour.

Seals are far more playful with each other in the water, where staying close together also has survival value. The massive congregations attract their main predator, the great white shark, in droves. Between Cape Town's False Bay and Mossel Bay, the sharks have developed a unique predatory breaching tactic for seals, launching themselves vertically from deep water with astonishing power. The seals' main defence is to cluster together as they enter the water, benefiting from the 'many-eyes effect' in spotting sharks. If they do see one, a frantic scramble for landfall results, but if caught in open water, seals occasionally mob the massive fish, speeding along behind it in the shark's slipstream. Being far more agile in the water, it's the safest place for them until they can reach land, and the shark hasn't a chance of a kill with the element of surprise lost. Only when sharks are absent do seals disperse to forage – but often the predator is merely lurking in deeper waters.

RECOGNITION Large, grey-brown seal. Pups born black. Adult males are usually dark. Top weight 350kg (males), 80kg (females).

HABITAT Rocky or sandy beaches and small rocky islands.

BEHAVIOUR Highly communal but generally forages alone, usually during the day. Dives to 400m and can submerge for 10 minutes.

BREEDING Highly seasonal, from November to December. Single pup. Female mates within six days of giving birth and the embryo goes into 'hibernation' for four months.

FEEDING Mainly fish, also squid, cuttlefish, lobsters and occasionally smaller crustaceans.

VOICE Highly vocal. All growl and bellow over territories. Females *maaaa* for their pups. Pups have a lamb-like bleat.

MAMMALS

⚡ HOTSPOTS

- Cape Cross Seal Reserve **(p110)**
- Skeleton Coast NP **(p108)**

AFRICAN ELEPHANT

RECOGNITION Unmistakable. Colour varies from dark slate grey, reddish-brown to light grey. Both sexes carry tusks or may be tuskless.

HABITAT Primarily savanna and woodland habitats. Semidesert at very low densities.

BEHAVIOUR Small family groups are the basic social unit, congregating into larger herds around water or food. Active around the clock; rest during the heat of the day. Entirely nocturnal where persecuted.

BREEDING Nonseasonal. Gestation is 22 months. Single calf suckled for up to two years.

FEEDING Leaves, bark, wood, bulbs, grass, fruit, flowers, shrubs and roots.

VOICE Trumpets, growls, rumbles and snorts. Infrasound for long-distance communication, largely inaudible to humans except in upper range (sounds like a rumbling belly).

INTELLIGENT TERRESTRIALS The largest mammal on earth is also one of the most social. Leading a core group of closely related females, one of the older females makes most of the decisions about where and when the herd forages, drinks and rests. Younger members of the herd act as nannies to the calves, and all family members are protective of the calves. Males live alone or in small bachelor groups, often comprising an old male accompanied by two or three 'apprentices', known as askaris, and only join herds when females are in heat. The askaris are prevented from coming into musth – the heightened state of a bull's sexual readiness – by the presence of mature bulls, a system which probably prevents young males from attempting to breed until they are fully mature. Elephants live for about 65 years, during which they maintain enduring relationships with the same individuals; the death of a family member provokes grieving behaviour very similar to our own.

Reaching seven tons and 4m in height, an elephant's daily requirements are prodigious. They eat up to 170kg of vegetation each day, and drink 60L to 70L of water (though a thirsty elephant can guzzle twice that volume). Massive resource demands translate to unrivalled destructive potential, and the damage wrought by feeding elephants can transform entire habitats, converting dense woodlands into plains. The process opens up overgrown habitat , returns nutrients to the ground, and promotes soil turnover, but it may also drive woodland species toward extinction. A natural factor in the functioning of savanna ecosystems, elephant engineering may be extreme where populations are confined to reserves, true for almost all of Southern Africa's population. Having enjoyed far greater protection than their counterparts elsewhere in Africa, elephants are now one of the most intensively managed species on the continent. Capture, culling, contraception, translocation and trading their precious ivory are among the arsenal of controversial strategies employed in the effort to establish a balance.

MAMMALS

★ HOTSPOTS

- Chobe NP (p120)
- Addo Elephant NP (p76)
- Hwange NP (p142)

DASSIES

LITTLE BADGERS Known throughout Southern Africa by their Afrikaans name dassie, which means 'little badger' (elsewhere they are called hyraxes), and looking like a portly guinea pig, these unusual creatures are neither badger nor rodent. In fact, as improbable as it may seem, their closest relatives are elephants, dugongs and manatees. Padded hooves and open-rooted tusks are the only outward similarities, but DNA and anatomical analyses reveal a far deeper resemblance. Even so, dassies have probably been separate and distinct from the elephant's ancestors for perhaps 75 million years, and they should be thought of as distant branches of the one evolutionary tree rather than close relatives.

Southern Africa has three species, of which rock dassies are the most obvious. Widely spread throughout the region except in dense forest or where rocky outcrops are lacking, these dassies live in colonies that may number in the hundreds. Within the colony, family groups are territorial, and adult males acquire a harem of up to a dozen females by fighting other males using their extremely sharp tusks. Despite their aggression, rock dassies are entirely vegetarian, and utilise a wide variety of plant matter; they graze when grass is abundant, and browse on leaves, buds and twigs when it's not. When foraging, a sentinel (usually an older female) keeps a lookout for danger, and

ROCK DASSIE

sends the colony racing for a cover with a shrill warning bark.

In Zimbabwe, western Botswana and northern South Africa, they share their rock habitat with very similar yellow-spotted dassies. Distinguishable by the yellow-pigmented gland on their back, and generally lighter colouring, the two species have very similar behaviour, and often occur in close association. In fact, they respond to one another's alarm calls, groom one another and even share nurseries.

The rarest dassie in the region occurs along the KwaZulu-Natal and Eastern Cape coast, and in much of Zambia and Malawi. As their name suggests, tree dassies normally eschew rocks and live in forests. They're skilful climbers, solitary and nocturnal; the closest most people come to them is hearing their tremulous, screaming call.

MAMMALS

★ HOTSPOTS

- Augrabies Falls NP (p78) Very obvious and tame rock dassies
- Nyanga NP (p161) Good chances for seeing mixed colonies of rock and yellow-spotted dassies
- Kasanka NP (p187) Tree dassies occur, but are elusive

WHITE RHINOCEROS

RECOGNITION Males weigh up to 2000kg, females 1800kg. Larger size, square-shaped lip and massive neck hump distinguishes them from black rhinos.

HABITAT Well-watered savanna and open woodland. Feeds on open grasslands but never far from cover.

BEHAVIOUR Mostly diurnal, though often feeds at night. Forms groups of up to 10 comprising a few females, their calves and subadults. Adult males maintain exclusive territories and attempt to herd oestrous females into their patch.

BREEDING Nonseasonal. Most calves are born March to July after a 16-month gestation.

FEEDING Exclusively grazes, favouring short young grass.

VOICE Pant, snort and huff when startled. Bellow in threat, calves squeal when alarmed.

MAMMALS

SQUARE-LIPPED GIANTS Despite their armoured appearance and formidable bulk, white rhinos are actually fairly placid. In fact, although Southern Africa has the best rhino-viewing on the continent, exciting moments are rare because they spend most of their lives doing one thing – eating. Rhinos need to process up to 100kg of food each day, and spend about 50% of daylight hours cropping grass with their distinctive broad snout (hence their alternative name, the square-lipped rhino). Their preference for short, young grass means they are easily spotted on plains and in open woodland, but early morning is the best time to go looking; as the day warms up, white rhinos do even less than normal, and seek shade to rest and ferment their gargantuan breakfast.

Although often seen alone, white rhinos are the most gregarious of the world's five rhino species and social interactions flesh out their behavioural repertoire beyond the basics. Friendly rhinos nuzzle and rub against one another, and always rest with close body contact. Waterholes can provide rewarding viewing, especially in the early morning as the small family groups come to drink and wallow. A mud coating provides a cooling layer, and helps to rid their hide of parasites like ticks. The ritual is almost always followed by a bout of obviously pleasurable rubbing against trees, termite mounds or rocks. Favourite sites become polished with use, and are well worth noting for excellent chances of seeing rhinos at their best.

Water also attracts rivals, in which the interactions may be less amenable. Bulls are territorial, but will allow intruding males to commute to water so long as they perform the oddly menacing but actually submissive ritual of roaring and squealing with the tail raised and ears laid back. Failure to do so can lead to titanic jousts that are sometimes fatal. Perhaps even more dangerous, mothers are extremely protective of calves; maintain a healthy distance, but do spend some time watching the young – baby rhinos can be hysterically playful.

★ HOTSPOTS

- Hluhluwe-iMfolozi GR **(p64)**
- Pilanesberg NP **(p72)**

BLACK RHINOCEROS

THE HEDGE-CLIPPER More solitary, less relaxed and far more endangered than their white counterparts (which are, in fact, essentially the same colour), black rhinos present more of a challenge for wildlife-watchers. They mostly avoid open areas, and a sighting is usually the result of some time invested looking in the right places. Black rhinos prefer thick vegetation, and gravitate towards thorn-tree thickets and the denser bush in valleys or lining rivers. As well as providing cover, thick bush reflects their feeding specialisation as a browser of small trees and shrubs. The triangular-shaped upper lip is highly mobile, and acts like a giraffe's tongue, grasping branches and pulling them into the mouth. Black rhinos literally prune trees, neatly slicing off the branch tips at a precise 45-degree angle. The clipped tips are extremely distinctive, both on the trees themselves, and strewn in middens, large mounds of accumulated dung used as a territorial signpost. The presence of uniformly clipped twigs with 45-degree edges is a sure way to determine the midden belongs to a black rhino rather than to its grass-eating cousin. However, don't be surprised if you find one containing both grass and twigs; occasionally, both species use the same mound.

If you do see black rhinos, chances are they won't hang around for long. Despite their size and weaponry, they're nervous animals, and inclined to flee when disturbed. However, if they feel threatened, they are far more likely than white rhinos to confront the danger. An adult black rhino huffing curiously a few metres away is a wildlife experience without parallel.

RECOGNITION Smaller than white rhinos, males reach a maximum of 1200kg, females 800kg. Lip is triangular rather than square. Lacks the neck hump of white rhino.

HABITAT From semidesert to dense woodland. Avoids open spaces (except at night).

BEHAVIOUR Largely solitary. Bulls set up exclusive territories and may kill intruding young males. Females nonterritorial, but remain in the same home range accompanied by successive calves.

BREEDING Nonseasonal. Single calf is born after a 15-month gestation.

FEEDING Trees, bushes and leaves. They occasionally eat grass if nutritionally stressed.

VOICE Repeated explosive snorts when charging and loud grunts, growls and screams when fighting. Calves mew as a contact call.

MAMMALS

★ **HOTSPOTS**

- Etosha NP (p100)
- Mkhuze GR (p86)
- Pilanesberg NP (p72)

RECOGNITION Small, stocky Cape subspecies is around 1.2m tall at the shoulder and weighs up to 260kg. Hartmann's is about 1.5m tall and weighs 320kg to 350kg.

HABITAT Mountain grasslands.

BEHAVIOUR Nonterritorial and shares home ranges but at much lower densities than Burchell's. Mostly diurnal.

BREEDING Year-round with a peak over summer. Gestation is 12 months and a single foal is born.

FEEDING Largely a grazer, using both high- and low-quality grasses. Browses only when nutritionally stressed. Requires water daily.

VOICE Quieter than Burchell's. Stallions utter an alarm snort and high-pitched alarm call. Subordinate males use a prolonged squeal to signal submission.

MAMMALS

MOUNTAIN ZEBRA

STRIPED STALLIONS Found only in Southern Africa, mountain zebras are a distinct species from the savanna-dwelling Burchell's zebras. Their natural distributions probably never overlapped, but Burchell's zebras have been widely introduced across South Africa. They're very similar, but a minute's careful observation reveals a suite of distinctive characteristics unique to mountain zebras: a dewlap under the throat, a gridlike pattern of close-set stripes over the rump and a lack of shadow stripes. Their legs are richly striped all the way to the hooves (Burchell's usually aren't), and the stripes on the face fade into a rich rusty colour. Finally, whereas Burchell's stripes extend all the way across their belly, mountain zebras' underparts are unstriped white.

Once you've mastered these differences, the challenge is in identifying different mountain zebra races – there are actually two distinct subspecies. Fortunately though, their ranges don't overlap, so discrimination by geography is easy. Anywhere along Namibia's central rocky escarpment, they're Hartmann's mountain zebras, while Cape mountain zebras only occur in South Africa's Cape region.

Mountain-zebra society is based on the same building blocks that make up the large herds of Burchell's: small family groups and bachelor herds. But their arid habitat generally prohibits large congregations, and small discrete units are the norm. Interactions between families are less frequent, but within the small groups, it's easier to discern the subtle dominance behaviour common to all zebra species. The stallion heads the hierarchy, herding his harem with head held low and ears laid back. A strict pecking order also exists among his mares, who use the same signals to display dominance; a submissive mare lowers her head, and makes open-mouthed chewing movements exposing the teeth. Very frequent friendly contact among family members balances out the little power plays, and all zebras in the group groom and nuzzle one another regularly.

BURCHELL'S ZEBRA

WATER-DEPENDANT EQUINES Probably the most recognisably African herbivore after the elephant, zebras are a guaranteed sighting. In fact, in certain parts of the region they form the largest herds of any ungulate in Southern Africa. At first glance a haphazard horde without order, a zebra congregation actually comprises many small groups with very defined relationships. Adult stallions each command a harem of between four and 10 mares, which they defend vigorously from other males. Rivals will attempt to abduct one another's females so stallions maintain strenuous control over their charges, herding wanderers back to the fold and racing ahead to engage challengers. Established herd males largely leave one another alone, but small clusters of young bachelors constantly attempt to acquire individual females to kick-start their own harem. The bachelors form the main target of the herd stallions' aggression, so in large herds, bachelor males keep a low profile by sticking to the fringes. This makes them more vulnerable to predation, so as well as watching for irate stallions and unattended females, bachelors must keep a constant watch for lions.

Zebras are dependent on water, and rarely occur more than 15km from a source – an easy day's walk for them. Family groups and bachelors intermingle at waterholes, an excellent spot to observe skirmishing stallions. Like a fingerprint, every zebra's stripes are unique, a useful way to identify individuals, though it takes terrific powers of observation to keep track in the melee. Zebras' main enemy – lions – also converge on waterholes to lay ambushes. Even single lions are able to take down a zebra, but it's a dangerous task; zebras defend themselves with lethal kicks that easily break a jaw or leg. Except for lions and large hyena groups, adult zebras are beyond the grasp of most predators, but their foals are easy pickings. However, stallions are formidable guardians, and, so long as the attacker isn't a lion (in which case it's every zebra for itself), they have been known to kick a predator to death.

RECOGNITION Large horse covered in black-and-white stripes, often with brown 'shadow stripes' on the rump.

HABITAT Grasslands and savanna woodlands. Avoids dense vegetation and requires water daily.

BEHAVIOUR Nonterritorial. Fairly stable home ranges, which are shared with other family groups and bachelors. In some areas, they migrate between separate summer and winter ranges.

BREEDING Single foal born after gestation of 360 to 390 days. Foals born year-round, with a peak over summer.

FEEDING Primarily a grazer, attracted to short fresh growth.

VOICE Very vocal; the alarm, contact and territorial calls are variations of a braying *kwa-ha*. Snorts when uncertain of danger.

MAMMALS

★ HOTSPOTS

- Makgadikgadi Pans & Nxai Pan NPs **(p128)**
- Chobe NP **(p120)**
- Etosha NP **(p100)**

RECOGNITION Reddish-brown pig with white facial blazes. Averages 60kg.

HABITAT Forests and riverine vegetation.

BEHAVIOUR Largely nocturnal.

BREEDING Three to four piglets.

FEEDING Roots and fruits.

VOICE Grunts.

⚡ HOT SPOTS

- Hluhluwe-iMfolozi GR (p64)
- Liwonde NP (p168)
- Kruger NP (p60)

BUSHPIG

Far less conspicuous than warthogs, bushpigs are nocturnal residents of dense forest or riverine thickets. Resembling the European boar, they're covered in a shaggy coat of coarse reddish-brown hair with a white mane of bristles fringing the face and along the spine. Like warthogs, bushpigs live in 'sounders', small family groups numbering about six to eight animals. But unlike the warthog's matrilineal clans, bushpig groups are usually headed by an alpha pair dominant to their family of younger sows and piglets. The boar actually assumes the protection of the piglets and is the frontline of defence against predators. Lions occasionally take bushpigs, but their main predator is the arboreal leopard; snatching a bush-piglet from the family, leopards retreat treewards to escape the wrath of the group. Adult bushpigs use their elongated lower incisors to fight back, and inexperienced big cats risk serious injury.

Bushpigs remember favourite feeding areas and habitually return to them from their daytime rest sites in dense cover. This habit creates narrow well-worn trails, a good sign of bushpig activity, particularly where they lead to waterholes – bushpigs require water daily, and a night's foraging is usually prefaced with a drink and a mud bath.

RECOGNITION Stocky grey, sparsely haired pig. Males up to 70cm high and 80kg.

HABITAT Mostly savannas and grasslands.

BEHAVIOUR Diurnal.

BREEDING One to eight piglets.

FEEDING Mainly grass, also bulbs, roots, fruit, occasionally carrion.

VOICE Grunts when feeding, screams in distress.

⚡ HOTSPOTS

- Kruger NP (p60)
- Pilanesberg NP (p72)
- Chobe NP (p120)
- Hwange NP (p142)

WARTHOG

The ubiquitous warthog is a diurnal, savanna-woodland dweller, and the butt of endless ridicule about its appearance. But each of its homely features has important survival value. Protruding high-set eyes and large flaplike ears maintain constant vigilance for predators while warthogs feed head-down. The massive, oversized head acts as a powerful lever for shovelling up bulbs and roots, as well as during clashes, when the 'warts' – densely packed connective tissue – protect the skull during head-hammering contests between males. Males' warts are much larger than the females', and they have two pairs rather than females' single set. Even their spindly, stringy tail has a function; raised like a flag when the warthog is alarmed, it probably helps fleeing warthogs stay together in long grass.

Warthog society revolves around matriarchal groups of related females and their offspring. Lone males or bachelor groups visit them only to mate. Despite the male's more formidable arsenal (both sexes have tusks but the males' are generally much larger), it's the females who defend youngsters from predators. A mother warthog will bravely engage cheetahs, African wild dogs and even leopards or lone hyenas, but they're essentially helpless against lions.

MAMMALS

HIPPOPOTAMUS

RIVER PIGS Distantly related to pigs, hippos are the only large amphibious mammal in the region. They spend the day resting in water or close to it, and at first glance their small social groups are easily mistaken for clusters of water-polished boulders. Family groups numbering around 15 are the norm, lorded over by a dominant bull that controls a small stretch of the river or lake shore. Bulls are extremely aggressive to challengers, but subordinate males are tolerated so long as they avoid sexual behaviour. Sociable by day in water, they emerge at sunset to graze alone on nearby grasslands. Except for calves, who remain near their mothers, hippos have few predators on land, and can afford to forage on their own. Floodplain grasses near the water are preferred, but they may commute up to 10km a night in search of good grazing; regardless, they always return to the water before dawn.

For such a recognisable and widely distributed mammal, hippos are difficult to study. Their nocturnal habits, huge mass and aquatic behaviour makes them difficult to capture for marking or radio-collaring, without which individual hippos are very difficult to tell apart. This may be why such a rich mythology surrounds the species. One of the most dramatic falsehoods is that heat-stressed hippos sweat blood. In fact, hippos lack sweat glands entirely, and mucous glands in the skin exude a gluey, bright-red fluid that hardens into a lacquered, natural sunscreen.

Another tall story claims that hippo mothers transport their calves on their backs. You may witness this for yourself, but calves are good swimmers and don't actually hitch a ride to get around; they climb onto adults' backs merely to sunbathe and snooze. And finally, among mammals, hippos are universally held to be the number-one people-killers in Africa. Though they're undeniably dangerous (extremely so, in some circumstances), accurate figures have never been compiled. Simply by virtue of their greater abundance and habit of raiding villages and crops, the top-killer title probably belongs to the elephants.

RECOGNITION Unmistakable. Adults average around 1500kg. Males are usually larger and covered in scars from territorial battles.

HABITAT Deep freshwater bodies with nearby grasslands.

BEHAVIOUR Remains close to water during the day and can submerge for up to six minutes. Grazes on land and always by night.

BREEDING Nonseasonal. Single calf is usually born in shallow water. Females are extremely protective of their young. They hide the calf in reeds for up to a week before rejoining the pod.

FEEDING Crops grasses with the broad lips. Very occasionally eats carrion.

VOICE Very vocal. Grunts, squeals and growls used in social interactions. Prolonged honking grunt used to proclaim territory.

MAMMALS

⚜ HOTSPOTS

- Vwaza Marsh WR **(p173)**
- iSimangaliso Wetland Park **(p80)**
- Chobe NP **(p120)**
- Victoria Falls & Zambezi NPs **(p156)**

GIRAFFE

RECOGNITION Unmistakable. Males grow to 5.5m tall and weigh 900kg to 1800kg. Females 4, to 4.4m and 600kg to 1000kg.

HABITAT Mainly open acacia savannas, also woodlands and scrub.

BEHAVIOUR Active day and night. They sleep standing or resting on their haunches. Nonterritorial and move over large home ranges, intermixing with other giraffes they encounter.

BREEDING Nonseasonal. Single calf suckled for up to a year.

FEEDING Leaves, flowers and pods, primarily of acacia trees. Very occasionally grazes and chews bones (osteophagia) for trace elements.

VOICE Most communication is by infrasound, which is too low for human hearing. Grunt and bellow under stress, prolonged huff in alarm.

LONG-NECKED BROWSERS As the world's tallest mammal, giraffes are able to exploit a feeding niche that is shared only with elephants. And even among giraffes, 'niche differentiation' occurs. Males can reach a metre higher than females, and browse the tops of trees up to 6m high, whereas females tend to bend down and feed from smaller trees: at a distance, this is one way to distinguish the sexes. Apart from their elongated neck (which, contrary to most sources, has eight vertebrae, one more than most mammals) and a 45cm-long tongue, other adaptations assist feeding. An extremely convoluted stomach gives giraffes the most efficient digestive system of any ruminant, and they can survive on less than half the browse that would be otherwise predicted by their massive size. This means giraffes can afford to be terrifically selective, and they use their horny lips and tongue to choose the most nutritious leaves. Even so, thorns slow the process down, and they can spend as many as 20 hours a day feeding to fulfil their 25kg to 35kg daily quota of browse.

Beyond modifications for feeding, their unique form carries further adaptations. When giraffes move or lower their heads, sudden changes in blood pressure are buffered by muscular valves in the blood vessels of the neck, an intricate filigree of vessels (called a rete) at the base of the brain, and a 7cm-thick heart. Being so large also requires prodigious heat dissipation, and the giraffe's markings function to channel heat build-up out through the skin. Markings are unique to individuals, and although one theory suggests they may also be important for individual recognition, their very loose social system hardly requires it. Giraffes are gregarious, but float among groups without any enduring bonds except for those between mother and calf. Group composition changes constantly, and at any one time, there can be any combination of age and sex categories in a herd. A day later, it could be entirely different.

MAMMALS

★ **HOTSPOTS**

○ Kruger NP (p60)
○ Etosha NP (p100)
○ Hwange NP (p142)
○ South Luangwa NP (p178)

BLUE & BLACK WILDEBEESTS

GREGARIOUS HERDERS Often described as looking like a cross between a horse and a goat, wildebeests actually belong to the same family as all African antelopes, the Bovidae. Southern Africa is home to two species, the widespread blue wildebeest, and a South African endemic, the black wildebeest. Having similar coloration, their common names can be confusing; their alternate names make better sense (though they're not widely used). The brindled gnu (blue wildebeest) arises from the characteristic dark bands on its neck and shoulders, while the black wildebeest's other appellation, the white-tailed gnu, highlights its most distinctive feature, one which cannot be confused with its dark-tailed cousin.

Minor cosmetic differences aside, the two species have much in common. Wildebeests are gregarious, with small groups of females and their calves forming the most common unit. The female herds wander widely in order to maximise their reproductive chances, and lone males carve out small territories where the females are likely to congregate. In the case of blue wildebeests, good sites are those with the best grazing, such as riverbeds in the Kalahari, which are more productive than the surrounding dunes and bound to attract females. For highveld-dwelling black wildebeests, visibility rather than grazing is the key, and the best territories are those with an expansive view of their surroundings. In both species, young males or those that fail to defend a territory form floating bachelor herds.

In productive habitats like the moist bushveld of South Africa's KwaZulu-Natal, localised female herds and territorial bulls can be the norm year-round, but where conditions fluctuate, wildebeests become nomadic or migratory. Female herds aggregate, and males abandon turf to move together in huge herds in search of better grazing. A biannual event in East Africa, wildebeest migrations in Southern Africa are now rare due to human-made obstacles.

RECOGNITION Blue: Males stand up to 1.5m at the shoulder and weigh 250kg. Black: Males are 1.2m and 160kg. Both sexes (in both species) have horns.

HABITAT Blue: Occurs throughout savanna grasslands. Black: Restricted to the Karoo and highveld grasslands.

BEHAVIOUR Diurnal and gregarious. Blue: Form herds between 10 and many thousand. Black: Herds rarely larger than 30.

BREEDING Seasonal breeders, mating March to April, calving in summer.

FEEDING Primarily short grasses, also some herbs and shrubs.

VOICE A metallic-sounding low is made by wildebeests in herds. Territorial males *gnu* (blue) or *oink* (black). Both species snort in alarm and bleat in distress.

MAMMALS

★ HOTSPOTS

- Mountain Zebra NP (p90)
- Kruger NP (p60)
- South Luangwa NP (p178)
- Etosha NP (p100)

RECOGNITION Large, reddish, heavy-bodied antelope, with elongated head, humped shoulders and sloping back. Both sexes have angular, curving Z-shaped horns.

HABITAT Open grassland, sparsely treed woodlands and the ecotone between them.

BEHAVIOUR Mostly active early morning and late afternoon, moving to water later in the morning. Territorial males mark with dung piles and stand prominently on mounds.

BREEDING Rut occurs March to April. Peak birth period is October to November. Single calf born.

FEEDING Medium-length grasses and new grass growth. Occasionally browses to increase water intake.

VOICE Horse-like, sneezing alarm snort.

RED HARTEBEEST

ARID DWELLERS Hartebeests once had a distribution that encompassed virtually all of Africa with the exception of the equatorial forests and the Sahara. Now extinct in northern Africa, and much reduced over the rest of their range, they still occur fairly widely in grassland-savanna habitat s across the continent, but in mostly disjunct populations. The differences between them can be considerable, and at least 50 different forms have been described, but today most authorities distinguish between eight and 12 subspecies. There are two forms in Southern Africa, although this is still a source of disagreement between experts. The widespread red hartebeests are universally recognised as the most southern subspecies of the Africa-wide hartebeest group, making them the same species as Coke's hartebeest (kongoni) of Kenya and Tanzania. But whereas Lichtenstein's hartebeests are occasionally included as yet another race in this huge species-complex, they probably should be treated as a separate species entirely. Taxonomy aside, Lichtenstein's are one of the rarest antelopes in the region, but red hartebeests are easily seen.

Red hartebeests are dwellers of open, arid country where resources are thinly spread. They need to cover large distances for water and grazing, so herds roam in home ranges of around 1000 sq km. However, solitary adult bulls seek out higher-quality patches as territories, defending an area that may be only one-eighth the size. The payoff for them comes when female herds, numbering up to 30, seek out the productive patches. Territorial males are particularly aggressive defending their harem, and fatal fights are not uncommon.

Territory maintenance becomes untenable, particularly during dry seasons, and (like many arid-adapted antelopes) males abandon their turf and join the female herds. The resulting congregations can number in the thousands as they amass in the search for grazing and water. They're most dramatic in Botswana, where veterinary fences now largely curtail the migrations, and many thousands of hartebeests die against the barriers.

HOTSPOTS

- Mountain Zebra NP **(p90)**
- Kgalagadi Transfrontier Park **(p68)**
- Central Kalahari GR **(p124)**
- Hwange NP **(p142)**

MAMMALS

BONTEBOKS, BLESBOKS & TSESSEBES

SHORT GRASS GRAZERS These three antelopes are closely related, and all occupy a very similar ecological niche – that of a medium-bodied grazer preferring short grasses. Competition for the same resources is probably why they have clearly distinct distributions, meaning you have to travel around a little to see all three.

Generally accepted as two races of the one species, bonteboks and blesboks are both South African endemics, and very similar in appearance, but easily separated by geography. Bonteboks only occur on fynbos grasslands in the south-west Cape, whereas blesboks have a wide distribution throughout central South Africa (and elsewhere from artificial introductions). The bontebok was driven to near extinction in the 1830s, but today both are fairly easily found.

Like many gregarious antelopes, their social system is driven by clusters of females, which solitary, territorial bulls attempt to 'acquire'. Bontebok males compete for herds of two to eight females but in blesboks, the harems can be as large as 25. In both subspecies, young bulls and subordinate males form bachelor herds and are excluded from the territorial patches but will attempt to mate unguarded females. The rut is the most exciting time to watch as males chase the bachelors and engage in highly ritualised stand-offs with neighbours.

Like their relatives, hartebeests and

BONTEBOK

wildebeests, tsessebes have elongated forelegs, and high shoulders, producing a characteristic sloping back. The resulting appearance is ungainly, but it enables tsessebes to adopt an energetically economical canter. Tsessebe social structure is similar to that of its relatives, with female herds, territorial males and bachelor groups. But across their considerable range (including East and Central Africa, where they're a distinct race called topis), they show more social flexibility than virtually any other antelope. In poor habitat , they become nomadic, and males only occupy territories in good seasons, but in better areas, some males remain territorial year-round. Most extremely, they also form leks, huge breeding arenas where males compete for central positions, which females seek out only when ready to mate.

MAMMALS

⭐ HOTSPOTS

- ○ Bontebok NP **Virtually assured bonteboks**
- ○ Mountain Zebra NP **(p90) Good herds of blesboks**
- ○ Waterberg Plateau Park **(p113) Tsessebes**

SMALL ANTELOPES

BUSH DIVERS Easily overshadowed by their larger relatives, there's a legion of miniature antelopes in Southern Africa. Along with their diminutive stature, most are very shy, keep to dense cover, and don't form the obvious herds of large species. Nonetheless, while most mammals of their size are strictly nocturnal, small antelopes are active around the clock; dawn and dusk hold reasonable chances of spotting them.

Named with an Afrikaans word describing their habit of diving into thick bush when alarmed, duikers are found in all the forests and woodlands of Africa,

and four species occur in the southern region. The appropriately named grey (or common) duiker is the most likely to be seen. Unlike the rest of this forest-loving group, they occur throughout open savanna and grasslands, providing there are thickets in which to take cover. They're also the only duiker in the region in which the female lacks horns, but be sure to check closely; as with all duikers, a conspicuous tuft of hair can obscure the horns.

The goliaths of the group, yellow-backed duikers grow to the size of a small calf and weigh up to 80kg, but,

GREY DUIKER, KRUGER NATIONAL PARK

MAMMALS

despite their size, they're difficult to spot. Characteristic of Central Africa's forests, they're at the southern limit of their range here, and are restricted to the very dense forests of northern Zambia.

The other two species, red duikers and blue duikers, inhabit the indigenous forests along the eastern seaboard. Watch for troops of vervet and samango monkeys; they're often accompanied by a duiker retinue mopping up fallen leaves, fruits and flowers (the mainstay of their diet). Whether grey, blue, yellow-backed or red, duikers spend most of their time alone, but deeper bonds exist just under the surface. In the case of tiny blue duikers, this extends to lifelong pairs, but the arrangement is looser for other species, in which pairs jointly occupy a territory but only come together intermittently. Regardless, breeding takes place throughout the year.

Known collectively as the dwarf antelopes, a further seven species make up a separate tribe, but being the stem group which gave rise to duikers, they share many characteristics. Permanent pair bonds are the basis of their social system, most apparent in klipspringers, dik-diks and oribis, which are almost always together. Pairs jointly hold a territory, and while both scent-mark with conspicuous facial glands and dung piles, males readily over-mark their mates to conceal the female's presence from rivals. Steenboks and sunis are usually spotted alone, but like most duikers, pairs share a territory and come together to groom, share a food patch or to breed. Most solitary of them all, the grysboks (two

WHY MONOGAMY?

Very unusual among mammals, the monogamous behaviour of small antelopes (like the Damara dik-dik) is driven by numerous factors, but size is the key. Africa's highly variable rainfall drives large-bodied antelopes to wander in huge home ranges, or else migrate to satisfy their food and water needs. However, antelopes weighing less than 20kg can subsist in far smaller areas, even during the dry season. Occupying the same range means little antelopes grow extremely familiar with the best places to find food and flee predators. By teaming up with a long-term partner, they also eliminate the risk of leaving home to find a mate, and double their chances of spotting danger, all without the conspicuousness of large herds.

species, Sharpe's and Cape) seem to have the loosest bonds. Males are territorial, and may associate with the same female in consecutive years, but only if she remains in the area.

Except for oribis, which feed mostly on grass, dwarf antelopes have a duikerlike diet of leaves, flowers, fruits and herbs. Steenboks and grysboks are also fond of crops and adopt nocturnal behaviour to raid farmlands. This leads to inevitable conflict with people, but while their secrecy baffles reliable population estimates, most dwarf antelopes seem secure. As with duikers, the spread of agriculture and plantations is their greatest threat, not only due to habitat destruction but also because of the inevitable influx of domestic dogs.

MAMMALS

★ HOTSPOTS

- iSimangaliso Wetland Park (p80) Three duikers as well as sunis and steenboks
- Etosha NP (p100) The best place for dik-diks
- Augrabies Falls NP (p78) Excellent for klipspringers
- Kafue NP (p182) Yellow-backed duikers

SPRINGBOK

RECOGNITION Medium-sized antelope with distinctive tan, white and brown coat. Both sexes have ringed lyre-shaped horns.

HABITAT Dry short-grass plains and semidesert.

BEHAVIOUR Diurnal and gregarious, forms mixed-sex herds (up to 50), sometimes much larger herds in high-quality grazing. Males form territories but may accompany the herds. Females with young form separate nursery herds.

BREEDING Year-round but mostly during the rut, which may be associated with rainfall.

FEEDING Primarily grazes, but browses when grass is limited. Eats roots and tubers for moisture.

VOICE Sharp nasal alarm-whistle, short recognition bleat and males make a loud *urrrr* during the rut.

THE SOUTHERN GAZELLE Across the open plains of Africa (and Eurasia's steppes), small-bodied antelopes, which could afford to select the freshest grass and had the narrow muzzles to do so, proliferated in the niches unavailable to larger herbivores. These are the gazelles and their relatives. They reach their greatest diversity in East and North Africa where they number 10 species, but Southern Africa's woodland-dominated habitat held fewer opportunities for them, and there is only a single species here, the springbok.

Restricted to arid zones, this southern endemic is well adapted to dry and unpredictable conditions. They're very selective feeders, always choosing the best-quality food available. Following rainfall, they concentrate on young grass shoots and flowers, but as conditions deteriorate, springboks switch to the leaves and buds of bushes – less nutritious than new grass but the best food in dry season. Like other gazelles, they're highly mobile, and undertake large migrations to track flushes of new growth. In the past, these 'treks' numbered in the tens of thousands, and although springboks are still common, fences and habitat fragmentation means such massive migrations are a thing of the past.

Obstacles notwithstanding, springboks become no-madic where possible, and herds move widely to exploit better feeding patches. In the dry season, herds are usually small and dispersed as they track fleeting cloud-bursts and the temporary flush of growth that follows. For mature males, however, holding a territory that will eventually attract many females is more important, and they tend to stay put. In their arid habitat , that often means securing a stretch of riverbed, which is why lone males can be seen evenly spaced along the Nossob and Auob in the Kgalagadi year-round. When the rains arrive, the influx of females makes the wait worthwhile. But having to endure poor feeding during the dry season and remaining alone makes them particularly vulnerable to predators. Clocked at 88km/h, they rely on their speed and hyper-vigilance to escape danger.

MAMMALS

IMPALA

BUSHVELD SHEEP With more than 100,000 in Kruger alone, impalas are often the first African mammal to be checked off the list, and locals understandably dismiss them as 'bushveld sheep' or 'Zambezi goats'. But their success is due to a suite of adaptations that warrant a second, closer look. Foremost is dietary flexibility. Impalas are mixed feeders, able to alternate between grass and browse as the need arises. Combined with a prodigious capacity to reproduce quickly, this has enabled them to invade the transition zone between open plains and dense woodlands, a habitat which has spread with increased human agriculture. Unlike most species, impalas have spread where people have spread. And they're not fussy about sticking with family. Impalas have very loose inter-relationships, and, except for the bond between mother and lamb, they have no enduring social ties. Although they're highly gregarious and generally remain in the same home range, overlap with other groups means that intermixing and exchange of herd members is routine. It further enhances impalas' ability to colonise; lacking strong social ties, they're uninhibited in their exploitation of new areas.

Despite their social promiscuity, there are distinct rules for the breeding season. As the rut approaches, adult males abandon their bachelor herds and seek out female herds. They furiously set about carving out a territory, frantically herding the harem, chasing challengers and mating with oestrous females. It's an exhausting routine, and males usually hold their patch for only a few weeks then yield to a challenger. Regardless, by the end of the rut, all adult females will be pregnant, and will synchronise their births to within a couple of weeks of each other. Known as 'predator swamping', it's a reproductive strategy that relies on there simply being too many lambs for carnivores to catch them all. Even so, up to 50% will be killed in the first few weeks, but enough will survive to ensure as much as a staggering 35% increase in the population each year.

RECOGNITION Medium-sized antelope with red-brown, fawn and white coat. Only males have horns. Black-faced impalas are slightly darker with a black facial blaze.

HABITAT Woodland savannas, ecotone between open plains and bush. Water-dependent.

BEHAVIOUR Females and young form herds of 30 to 150, which occasionally amass into larger clans. Males form separate bachelor herds (less than 30), which break down during the rut.

BREEDING The rut takes place March to April. Single lambs are dropped mid-November to January.

FEEDING Grass, leaves, acacia pods, fruit.

VOICE Males roar during the rut. A sharp nasal snort is given in alarm and a soft murmuring grunt is given between herd members.

MAMMALS

HOTSPOTS

- Kruger NP (p60)
- Etosha NP (p100)
- Chobe NP (p120)
- Hwange NP (p142)

RECOGNITION Third-largest bovid; weighs up to 300kg. Strawberry-roan colour. Black-and-white facial mask. Both sexes carry horns.

HABITAT Open savanna and tall grasslands.

BEHAVIOUR Small breeding groups and bachelor herds.

BREEDING Single calf.

FEEDING Grass.

VOICE Alarm snort.

HOT SPOTS

- Waterberg Plateau Park (p113)
- Nyika NP (p170)
- Marakele NP (p94)

ROAN ANTELOPE

With a horse-like bulk that defies most predators, and a distribution that encompasses virtually all woodlands south of the Sahara, roan antelopes seem a highly successful species. Yet they're actually a surprisingly specialised antelope, one with such a strict criteria of requirements that they are common nowhere.

Firstly, they're very selective grazers, preferring to crop the tips of medium-length grasses, a diet that makes them vulnerable to drought as well as to competition from less fussy eaters like zebras and wildebeests. And despite their size, roans also actively seek out areas where predators are few. Wherever there are many other herbivores, and the predators which follow them, roans are rare or absent.

This means that roans tend to be pushed into marginal areas where other wildlife is thin on the ground, but they are extremely loyal to their home ranges. breeding herds, numbering up to 15 with a single adult bull, sometimes stick to a few square kilometres for months, especially in the wet season when grazing is good. Their dry-season wanderings inflate the range but if left alone, a herd will stay in the same area for years. A little local knowledge is invaluable for finding them.

SABLE ANTELOPE

RECOGNITION Large horse-like antelope. Both sexes carry backward-curving horns.

HABITAT Open woodlands.

BEHAVIOUR Females and juveniles form herds. Adult males territorial.

BREEDING Most calves born January to March.

FEEDING Mostly grass.

VOICE Territorial males bellow and roar.

HOTSPOTS

- Pilanesberg NP (p72)
- Hwange NP (p142)
- Kafue NP (p182)

With its monochrome mask and ringed half-moon horns, the sable's shared ancestry with the roan is obvious. But while the roan's body colour reflects the subdued colours of the bush, sables exhibit one of the most striking of all antelope coats. Physical presence proclaims rank in sables, and they advertise it by colour – the blacker, the better. Adult males in command of a harem are a glossy raven black, high-ranking females are very dark brown, and low-ranking females are a russet colour. Born pale sepia, sables assume their regalia as they age.

Being obvious helps to intimidate rivals, and males assume very erect poses in prominent places to declare ownership of a herd. Even so, their custody is fleeting. Female herds wander widely, and territorial males can only hope to mate when a group enters their patch. And females are only worth fighting for when they enter oestrous, usually around April to June, so males spend the bulk of their time alone. Nonetheless, they hold their patch year-round, and assume the territorial posturing at any time. It makes them extremely photogenic, but more importantly, very conspicuous to predators. Fortunately for them, sables are alert, and able combatants; males defend themselves against all comers except lions.

MAMMALS

GEMSBOK

DESERT DWELLERS Sometimes called the southern oryx, gemsboks are endemic icons of the arid zone. Much admired by hunters for their rapierlike horns, and by wildlife photographers for their conspicuous, contrasting beauty, gemsboks are desert specialists without equal. A lowered metabolism is the nucleus of their adaptive repertoire. It enables them to survive on far less than equally sized wildebeests, which means they evade the obligatory nomadism that forces other desert inhabitants to wander over huge ranges. It also frees them of the need to regularly trek to water, and they can survive indefinitely without drinking; gemsboks extract all the moisture they need from water-rich tsama melons and subterranean taproots. A slower metabolism also lowers their body temperature to minimise the risk of overheating, further enhanced by their short, reflective coat. Even so, gemsboks can tolerate body temperatures that would kill other mammals. Allowing the body to heat up to 45°C conserves valuable water that would be lost by panting or sweating. All the while, a remarkable network of blood vessels inside the nose called the carotid rete is cooled by inhaled air so that blood going to the brain maintains a comfortable 36°C.

Gemsboks maintain far smaller ranges than species less suited to arid conditions, but resources are thinly spread for all desert species, and gemsboks nonetheless cover large distances. Herds of females and their young average a range of about 1000 sq km, but like most large antelopes, dominant males are faithful to a much smaller territory. Females moving onto a territory are checked by the resident male for sexual readiness, and any in heat are subsequently mated. In prolonged droughts, even males are forced to abandon their home turf, and they accompany the female herds. Clashes between males are common, and they fight one another viciously with a well-honed stabbing technique, but injuries are actually rare. Both sexes also use their horns against predators: there are a few reliable accounts of gemsboks impaling even lions.

RECOGNITION Heavily built antelope; males weigh up to 240kg, females 200kg. Both sexes carry horns, longer and more slender in the females.

HABITAT Arid grasslands, rocky deserts and dune fields.

BEHAVIOUR Gregarious; females, young and subordinate males form herds up to 30. Larger herds assemble during the rains. Dominant males are usually territorial. Restricts activity to morning and evening to avoid overheating and may be active at night.

BREEDING Nonseasonal but births tend to correspond with rains. Single calf is cinnamon-coloured for camouflage.

FEEDING Mostly grazes, resorting to leaves and flowers in dry season.

VOICE Largely silent except for a deep alarm snort.

MAMMALS

★ HOTSPOTS

- Etosha NP (p100)
- Kgalagadi Transfrontier Park (p68)
- Central Kalahari GR (p124)

SPIRAL-HORNED ANTELOPES

HORNED HERBIVORES Ranging in size from 45kg bushbucks to 940kg elands, this small tribe of antelopes (called the Tragelaphini) are instantly recognisable by their horns. As with all antelopes, each horn is a single unbranched structure, but in tragelaphines it undergoes a gentle corkscrew twist as it grows. There are nine species Africa-wide, five of which occur in the subregion; for all of them, if your antelope comes with a twist, it's one of the tragelaphines.

The tragelaphines are exceptional among antelopes not only for their spiral horns, but also for their social organization: males never establish territories. Rather than defend a patch and command those females that come onto it, they go directly to the reason for territory – the females themselves. Males wander between female groups and compete constantly with one another for the right to mate. It's a system that has given rise to elaborate displays by which males establish dominance. In the 'lateral presentation' contest, two rivals walk stiffly opposite each other with manes and crests raised, showing off their potency. A flattened body profile and striking

KUDU STAG, KRUGER NATIONAL PARK

MAMMALS

white markings enhance the show, and although the differences between competing males are typically too subtle for human onlookers to pick, males usually resolve their differences without combat. The most spectacular lateral displays are performed by nyalas, and they're least obvious in bushbucks and sitatungas, in which the females are solitary or form small groups. As opposed to the clustered resource that female greater kudu and nyala herds represent, scattered lone females provoke less male interest, and contests between male sitatungas and bushbucks are rare.

Spiral-horned antelopes are predominantly browsers, but they also have a penchant for fresh grass, a combination which means they inhabit all types of woodlands, from the very open to the very closed. Nyalas and bushbucks rarely venture out of thick bush, but greater kudus and elands inhabit open woodlands and tolerate the dry bush of northern Namibia and Botswana.

The exception among them are sitatungas. They're restricted to permanently inundated swamps and marshes, feeding off fresh reed tips. Capable swimmers, they take refuge by submerging and make their way through reedbeds with extremely elongated hooves that spread their weight like snowshoes. Largely solitary and extremely shy, they are very difficult to spot. Like all the tragelaphines, they have a deep, gruff bark given in alarm. It's a giveaway to their position, but mostly heard at night; nocturnal boat trips make the calls well worth following but sitatungas disappear

FEMALE IMPERSONATORS

Sexual dimorphism among the tragelaphines is very marked. Apart from the females lacking horns (except elands) and being considerably smaller, they lack the accoutrements that males use to judge one another's status: dewlaps, manes, crests, beards and dark pigmentation. So too, of course, do the young. In fact, all tragelaphines at birth look exactly like a miniature female. Young males start out looking like their sisters, and only begin developing their male adornments at about a year old. By mimicking the females, they avoid the aggressive attention of the constantly competing males until they're old enough to fend for themselves. Ultimately, their maturing maleness will give them away, and they'll be evicted from the herd to form small bachelor groups. It usually happens between 12 and 18 months, but adolescent elands stay for an extra year or two; perhaps because females have horns, their sex remains inconspicuous for longer.

beneath the surface when spotlit directly.

The spiral-horns breed year-round, but most of them have a distinct birth peak; winter for sitatungas, early winter and spring for nyalas and bushbucks, early summer for elands and late summer for greater kudus. All give birth to a single calf (very rarely twins), which in all species, bar elands, lies up for one to two months during which the female visits it for suckling. Perhaps because elands are the most nomadic of the group, their calves accompany the female within a few hours of birth.

MAMMALS

HOTSPOTS

- Etosha NP (p100) Excellent for photogenic greater kudus and elands
- Mkhuze GR (p86) Abundant nyalas, greater kudus and bushbucks, as well as a few elands
- Kasanka NP (p187) Best areas for sitatungas

AFRICAN BUFFALO

RECOGNITION Massive dark brown to black cattle-like bovid weighing up to 800kg. Both sexes have heavy curving horns meeting in a central 'boss', which is massive in the male.

HABITAT Open and wooded savanna with suitable grass cover.

BEHAVIOUR Mostly diurnal. Breeding herds, comprising all age and sex categories (except old males), occupy home ranges but are nonterritorial and tolerate overlap with other herds.

BREEDING Single calf born year-round, but birthing peak is during February.

FEEDING Mainly fresh grass but also the leaves of shrubs and trees during drought.

VOICE A variety of cattle-like lows and bellows.

BULLISH BOVIDS Buffaloes belong to the same tribe as domestic cattle, and are Africa's only wild cows. However, despite their basic bovine appearance, their similarity to their docile domestic counterparts is slight, and early trophy hunters included buffaloes as one of the Big Five, the five most dangerous species to hunt. Even so, not all buffaloes are killers. Large herds are fairly relaxed, and unlikely to attack except when confronted by a known threat, particularly their main enemy, the lion. However, older males usually live away from the herd, alone or in small groups, and are more easily provoked into a charge, perhaps because they lack the safety of numbers. They're known as dagha boys, and their 'attack is the best defence' tactic makes them extremely dangerous. Take note of the warnings posted at lodges, especially at night; lone males readily stake out a patch of cultivated lawn at sunset and sleep there.

Dagha boys inhabit the fringes of buffalo society, but only during the dry season. Following the summer rains, they seek out females for breeding and rejoin the small family groups, which are the basic buffalo social unit. Normally, a number of these units congregate to form huge 'breeding herds', creating a concentration of females worth fighting for. The arriving bulls establish a pecking order with head-tossing, soil-gouging, 'tall-walking' and other ritualised threats. Occasionally, colossal duels are required, but a single bone-crunching charge is usually enough to resolve the hierarchy. Best seen during the summer (winter in Moremi) when grazing is rich, breeding herds may be a few thousand strong. The massing persists all year when conditions are good, but splits into individual family groups during particularly dry winters.

Buffalo herds have fairly predictable movements, seeking out good grazing and water during the early morning and again towards dusk – the best times to view them. As the day warms up, they disappear into thick cover to rest and ruminate.

MAMMALS

⭐ **HOTSPOTS**

- South Luangwa NP **(p178)**
- Chobe NP **(p120)**
- Gonarezhou NP **(p146)**
- Moremi GR **(p132)**

SOUTHERN & MOUNTAIN REEDBUCKS

HIGH-QUALITY BROWSERS The two reedbuck species in Southern Africa look similar, but are easily distinguished by habitat . Southern or common reedbucks are found in reeds, floodplains and moist grasslands. In contrast, mountain reedbucks favour grassy mountain slopes, and are quite at home on scree-covered hillsides where southern reedbucks rarely venture. Further aiding identification, mountain reedbucks are much smaller; the average weight for a mountain ram is about 32kg, less than half the average for southern reedbuck males, which can top 75kg. If you're still unsure, geography is often the decider. Southern reedbucks occur throughout Southern Africa, whereas mountain reedbucks are only found in South Africa and just over the border on Botswana's Manyelanong Hills. Even so, there is one final obstacle to a positive identification: mountain reedbucks look very similar to grey rhebucks, another mountain dweller. The easiest way to differentiate them is by their horns – curved and forward-facing in mountain reedbucks, pencil-slim and straight in rhebucks.

Differences aside, the two reedbuck species demonstrate their shared pedigree in numerous ways. Both are primarily grazers, appropriate for the large-bodied southern reedbucks with their productive abitat rich in new grass, but surprising for mountain reedbucks. Smaller antelopes usually target high-quality browse because their small rumens could never accommodate enough grass to satisfy their energetic needs. Mountain reedbucks overcome this by selecting the freshest, youngest grass growth, but during the dry season where there is none, they rely on an oversized, compartmentalised rumen to extract the most from dry, coarse feed. Both reedbucks also employ a common 'language'. They're mostly silent, but their shrill *tzeee* alarm-whistle is very distinctive. Accompanying the call, they raise their tail as they flee, exposing fluffy white underparts like a flag and adopting a stiff-legged 'rocking horse' gait. Both displays signal danger to other reedbucks and might also act to inform a predator that it has been spotted.

RECOGNITION Both medium-sized, tawny-grey antelopes. Only males have horns. Southern: Up to 95cm at the shoulder. Mountain: Up to 75cm.

HABITAT Southern: Moist, usually low-lying, grasslands. Mountain: Grassy mountain slopes.

BEHAVIOUR Territorial males defend small family groups, often pairs in southern reedbucks but up to eight females in mountain reedbucks.

BREEDING Throughout the year, births peaking in summer. Single calf.

FEEDING Primarily grasses, small quantities of herbs.

VOICE Largely silent except for shrill alarm whistle.

MAMMALS

★ HOTSPOTS

- iSimangaliso Wetland Park **(p80)**
- Karoo NP **(p84)**
- Maloti-Drakensberg Transfrontier Area **(p89)**
- Pilanesberg NP **(p72)**

WATERBUCK

RECOGNITION Robust, grey-brown. White rump ring or patch.

HABITAT Woodlands, floodplains and riverine forest.

BEHAVIOUR Herds of six to twelve, occasionally larger.

BREEDING Nonseasonal. Birth peak in mid-summer.

FEEDING Good-quality grasses and browse.

VOICE Snorts in alarm.

★ HOT SPOTS

- Victoria Falls & Zambezi NPs (p156)
- Kafue NP (p182)
- Moremi GR (p132)
- Mamili NP (p112)

Although not nearly as aquatic as sitatungas, red lechwes and pukus, waterbucks are never far from permanent water sources. These large antelopes drink daily, and prefer the high-quality grass that grows along river edges and on floodplains. Their diet brings them out into the open, but waterbucks are always close to dense vegetation. Despite their size, they are vulnerable in the open, and they are often preyed upon at great levels, considering their numbers. The trend may arise from being overly conspicuous. Waterbucks have a very strong musky smell, and a characteristic white ring or patch around the rump, both probably to maintain contact between herd members. But this also means they're easily found by predators (even humans can smell them at a distance), so the beleaguered waterbuck's solution is to take refuge in woodlands.

Small herds and small home ranges are the norm for waterbucks. Females and calves form loosely aggregated groups, which overlap in range with other small herds. They are tolerant of familiar animals in the overlapping areas, and herd composition can change daily. Lording over the female groups, males are territorial, but they tolerate males they know, so long as the trespasser is suitably submissive.

LECHWE

RECOGNITION Medium to large reddish antelope. Males have backward-curving, lyre-shaped horns.

HABITAT Floodplains and grasslands near swamps.

BEHAVIOUR High variation in herd sizes and composition.

BREEDING Single lamb.

FEEDING Wetland grasses.

VOICE Bleats and snorts.

★ HOTSPOTS

- Moremi GR (p132)
- Kafue NP (p182)

The most aquatic antelope after the sitatunga, lechwes are tied to their watery habitat by a number of adaptations. They eat the grasses and sedges that grow in shallow water, which entails lechwes following the seasonally fluctuating water's edge. Tracking good-quality graze can lead to extremely high densities. As well as diet, they rely on water to escape predators. Their dramatically shortened forelegs create a characteristic sloping build – rather slow and awkward on dry land, but swift and powerful in shallow water. Elongated, pliant hooves enhance the advantage (restricting them to soft, water-sodden soils).

There are three races of lechwes, the extremes of which look like entirely different species; the black 'shin-guard' stripes are the key. Red lechwes have the least pigment, with black restricted to the legs. In the Kafue lechwe of the Kafue Flats, the black creeps up onto the body in a distinctive shoulder blaze. And most extreme of all, black lechwes of northern Zambia have black on most of their body, fading to russet along the spine and hindquarters.

MAMMALS

PUKU

Water-loving pukus share with lechwes a preference for grasses and sedges that grow in permanently soaked soils. But they're also able to utilise various other foods, and unlike lechwes, they venture into woodlands to browse young leaves, flowers and even seeds. Pukus usually spend the early morning and late evening grazing in the open and retreat into nearby woodlands as the day warms up, but they are not averse to spending the entire day in the open.

Common to many African antelopes, the basic structure of puku society is small female herds roaming widely over the territories of lone males. When a herd wanders onto a male's patch, he divides his attention between attending oestrous females and chasing young males. Once their horns begin appearing after their first year, young males are viewed as competition by adult males, and are driven out to form nonbreeding bachelor herds. If they survive, all territorial males will also end up in the bachelor herds as the maturing younger males in turn drive them from their patch.

RECOGNITION Impala-sized but stockier and lacks three-coloured coat.

HABITAT Floodplains, riverine woodland.

BEHAVIOUR Crepuscular.

BREEDING Single calf.

FEEDING Wetland grasses, forbs, herbs and some browse.

VOICE Whistles.

★ HOT SPOTS

- South Luangwa NP (p178)
- Kafue NP (p182)
- Chobe NP (p120)

GREY RHEBUCK

With no close relatives, grey rhebucks (or rheboks) are classified in their own unique tribe. Their relationship to other antelopes is hazy, but their appearance and morphology suggests distant affinities to both the kob tribe (reedbucks, lechwes and pukus) as well as to sheep and goats; they most resemble mountain reedbucks with straight horns and a moderately woolly coat. Grey rhebucks are endemic to South Africa and are an extremely graceful species, running in a reedbucklike, rocking-horse motion and leaping fluidly over obstacles. No doubt this why the South African founders of the Reebok sports company considered them suitably athletic inspiration.

Rhebucks live in small family groups of a few females and their young, usually accompanied by a male harem-master. The males are territorial and aggressive to intruders; their fights are sometimes fatal, and they also have a reputation for attacking mountain reedbucks, though this is probably very rare. Their belligerent behaviour extends to protecting the family group, and males occasionally even attack baboon troops, presumably because they sometimes prey on lambs. But rhebucks prefer to flee when danger looms, making most sightings distant and fleeting.

RECOGNITION Slender, medium-sized antelope. Males have narrow, spikelike horns.

HABITAT Mountain slopes, plateau grasslands and fynbos grasslands.

BEHAVIOUR Diurnal. Forms small herds.

BREEDING Single lamb.

FEEDING Mostly browses.

VOICE Snorts in alarm.

★ HOTSPOTS

- Karoo NP (p84)
- Maloti-Drakensberg Transfrontier Area (p89)

MAMMALS

SOUTHERN AFRICAN BIRDS

Even if you're not a birder, it's impossible to ignore the conspicuousness, diversity and sheer abundance of Southern Africa's birdlife. There are around 1075 species here, 938 of which can be spotted if you don't go any further north than the Zambezi River. Zambia and Malawi collectively hold an additional 140-odd species; most are East African inhabitants at the southern limits of their ranges, as well as a few Central and West African specials that just make it into northern Zambia. Regardless of where you go, even without trying, you'll see far more species of bird than mammal.

The key to their ecological success is a covering of feathers, a unique adaptation shared by all birds, but not by any other creature. Birds evolved from reptiles, and feathers from scales; like reptilian scales, feathers overlap to serve as waterproof insulation, but they have further diversified to provide insulation against extreme heat or cold (keeping birds warm enough to maintain a high level of activity), and showy courtship plumes. As organs of flight, feathers are unsurpassed: they adjust subtly to the lightest breeze, and compensate instantly for wind strength, direction and lift. Each group of birds has differently shaped wings to exploit their preferred habitat , and the independence afforded by aerial manoeuvrability has allowed the evolution of diverse hind legs, with feet adapted, for example, to swimming, grasping or running.

Among the bird families with dozens of Southern African members are herons and egrets, thrushes and robins, larks, flycatchers, warblers and birds of prey. There are also 10 uniquely African families on show: sugarbirds, louries, mousebirds, woodhoopoes, guineafowl, whydahs, oxpeckers, helmet shrikes, and two families each with a single member: the secretary bird and hamerkop. Despite their endemism, most are easy to spot. And groups whose familiar urban representatives usually provoke indifference

GREY CROWNED CRANE

take on new life here: starlings come in astonishing iridescent and wattled finery, and the sparrow family includes architecturally gifted weavers, flocks of queleas numbering hundreds of thousands and widows with flamboyant tails almost 10 times their body length.

The other undeniable appeal of birds is that the vast bulk of them are diurnal. Except for owls, nightjars and a few others, every species on the list can be relied upon to make daylight appearances. And although dawn and dusk are as fruitful for spotting birds as other wildlife, birds are less troubled than mammals by high midday temperatures. The small size of most birds translates to efficient heat dissipation, so many species brave the hottest part of the day when mammals

are seeking shady asylum. When you do likewise at lunchtime, rest assured that finches, starlings and hornbills will still be looking for handouts around camp, tinker barbets and emerald-spotted doves will be calling endlessly, and vultures will still be riding thermals in their quest for carrion.

If you're a confirmed bird lover, Southern Africa holds obvious attractions. But even if you've never really taken the time to watch birds, you'll probably surprise yourself here. Whether you're sitting in camp trying to identify feathered scroungers at your feet, or just filling in time at a waterhole between mammal appearances, birdwatching in Southern Africa holds rewards for everyone.

BIRDS

BIRDS

RECOGNITION Huge bird with long, featherless neck and muscular legs. Loose plumage is black and white in male, grey-brown in female.

HABITAT Dry, open savanna, desert and semidesert; not dependent on water.

BEHAVIOUR Alone or in groups. Runs from danger; males aggressive to people and predators. Young follow parents for 12 months. Sexually mature at three to four years; may live 30 to 40 years.

BREEDING Nest a shallow scrape; about 20 eggs incubated for six weeks. Chicks run immediately after hatching and form crèches.

FEEDING Seeds, fruits, leaves, insects and small reptiles. Sand, stones and even coins and nails are swallowed to help digestion.

VOICE Usually silent. Snaps bill and hisses. breeding males utter a deep, descending boom.

★ **HOTSPOTS**

- Hwange NP **(p142)**
- Makgadikgadi Pans & Nxai Pan NP **(p128)**
- Etosha NP **(p100)**

OSTRICH

WORLD'S TALLEST BIRD Ostriches don't bury their heads in the sand, although they sometimes sit on their nests with neck outstretched along the ground to protect their eggs or chicks. The ostrich is a ratite, part of an ancient group of flightless birds distributed across the southern hemisphere. Being the world's tallest living bird (up to 2.75m) with the largest eyes of any land animal (50mm in diameter), they normally detect danger from afar. That includes you, but these huge birds become fairly used to vehicles in protected areas. Except during breeding, when pairs are the rule, they generally seek safety in small flocks. Watch for chicks trotting at the heels of adults; and look among herds of antelopes or zebras, with which they often mingle to lessen the chance of being surprised by predators. If threatened they're off, clocking up sprints of 70km/h in 3.5m-long strides, and outlasting any predator with sustained runs of 50km/h for up to 30 minutes. In a tight spot, an ostrich can kill a hyena by kicking with its massive feet – the inner claw is modified into a 10cm-long spike.

During his mesmerising courtship display, the male crouches while rotating outstretched wings and swaying his neck from side to side, his neck and legs glowing bright pink. Several females – normally two to five, but up to 18 – lay eggs (the world's biggest, weighing 1.5kg) in the same nest, although only the male and major hen (she who lays first) incubate them, he by night and she by day.

An incredible total of 78 eggs was recorded in one nest, but since only 20 can be incubated at a time, the major hen rolls away those that aren't hers – perhaps recognising her own eggs by the size, structure and shape of pores in the shell. The abandoned eggs become a feast for other animals: hyenas and jackals are partial to ostrich eggs. Hatchlings leave the nest within three days and follow the parents; when two families meet a dispute usually ensues and the winning pair adopts the other crèche – groups of 100 to 300 young occasionally result.

JACKASS PENGUIN

ECSTATIC BRAYERS One of four penguin species that occur in African waters, the jackass or African penguin is the only one restricted to the continental shore (the rest are Antarctic and sub-Antarctic species). It's also a Southern African endemic, and breeds only on approximately 18 offshore islands and a handful of mainland locations. It occurs from the Mozambique/South African border, all the way around to northern Namibia, but most birds (and the most visible ones) live on the western coast.

Their common name arises from the male's donkey-like bray, which can be heard continually in the colonies when the penguins are breeding. It forms part of the male's 'ecstatic' courting display, in which he points his bill skywards and holds his flippers out horizontally like a plane's wings. Building to a crescendo, he heaves his breast at an attentive female, and then lets fly with a raucous braying chorus. It's obviously an infectious display as nearby birds readily take up the call, setting off a chain of braying with each bird calling for up to a minute. Jackass penguins breed year-round, but for the best chance of seeing the ritual en masse, try dawn and dusk during early summer (November to December).

Jackass penguins forage close to shore, setting out in small groups to hunt for small fish, like anchovies, crustaceans and squid. They cruise along on the surface, each bird performing constant head-dipping checks for prey, until, with target spotted, the group dives as one. They are superb swimmers and underwater chases sometimes top 20km/h.

Like many small penguin species, jackasses nest in colonies, and lay their eggs (usually two but sometimes one) in burrows or between rocks; where humans have built near colonies, the penguins often nest under buildings or jetties. Egg and guano harvesting (which disturbs the nests; now banned), as well as oil spills and depletion of fish stocks have reduced their numbers, but they are still locally common and a few of the colonies are extremely tame.

RECOGNITION Black upperparts, white underparts with black ring in between. Stout grey-black bill, black face and bare pink skin over eye. Length 60cm.

HABITAT Offshore islands and a few mainland beaches.

BEHAVIOUR Forages mostly by day, usually in groups. Roosts and breeds in large colonies. Elaborate 'ecstatic display' performed by courting male.

BREEDING Mainly in summer. Lays one or two eggs, usually in a burrow.

FEEDING Fish, small crustaceans and squid.

VOICE Donkeylike braying, honks and growls. Chicks hiss when threatened.

BIRDS

★ HOTSPOTS

○ Bird Island NR (p94)

PELICANS, CORMORANTS & DARTERS

GREAT WHITE PELICAN

FISHING ARMADAS At first glance, the varied members of this order of birds don't appear to have much in common with one another. But apart from their water-loving habits, all of them share throat pouches, webbed feet, and nonfunctional nostrils sealed off by bone. Most conspicuous of the group, pelicans have very prominent pouches. Checking the pouch colour is the easiest way of distinguishing the two species: bright yellow in the eastern white pelican, flesh coloured in the pink-backed. In the breeding season, the pouch becomes particularly colourful. In summer, pelicans are often seen pulsating their pouch to cool off.

Cooperative feeding in pelicans is a fascinating sight: up to 40 pelicans form a horseshoe and simultaneously dip their bills in the water to drive fish into the shallows; in a river they form parallel rows and move towards each other with a similar effect. With their prey effectively 'corralled', each pelican scoops fish and up to 13.5L of water into the pouch; the water is then forced out through the closed bill and the fish are swallowed.

Southern Africa's five cormorant species also hunt fish, as well as frogs, crustaceans and octopuses. But unlike pelicans, they mostly feed alone, chasing their prey on prolonged dives, which may last for a minute. The exception to the rule is the Cape cormorant, which targets pelagic baitfish schools, and feeds in flocks that may number in the thousands. The Cape's gregarious behaviour is often an effective method for telling it apart from the endemic bank cormorant, also found along the coasts but a loner; if in doubt, check for naked, yellow skin around the Cape's bill. Another endemic species, the crowned cormorant has a small crest, which it typically holds erect.

BIRDS

★ HOTSPOTS

- iSimangaliso Wetland Park (p80) Breeding colonies of both pelicans, plus darters and white-breasted and reed cormorants
- Bird Island NR (p94) Cape, crowned, white-breasted and bank cormorants
- Namib-Naukluft Park (p104) Both pelicans and four cormorant species (Cape, crowned, white-breasted and bank)

CAPE GANNET

Related to pelicans and their kin, Cape gannets breed in just six colonies scattered around the Cape and Namibian coasts. But they disperse widely from these population hubs to forage, and may be seen in huge flocks anywhere around the Southern African coastline; young birds leave the colonies after fledging, and may stay at sea for up to three years, dispersing as far as Kenya in the east and the Gulf of Guinea on the west coast.

For really extraordinary viewing, the colonies during the breeding peak are hard to beat. A few adults remain year-round, but from about July huge numbers return to find their mates. Cape gannets are monogamous, and renew their ties with long-term partners by elaborate fencing, bowing and mutual preening displays that continue throughout the breeding season. Locating partners is no doubt helped by fidelity to the nest site: Cape gannets return to the same colony each year, and nest in the same small space. Both sexes help build a hollow-topped mound on their little patch, reinforcing guano with seaweed and sticks. One egg is laid (rarely two) from about September through to December, and both adults share incubation, feeding and guarding of the chick.

Their gentle 'devotion' to one another and the chick does not extend to neighbours and they constantly threaten and jab nearby birds. As spectacular as the mayhem of the colonies, Cape gannets feed in flocks that may number in the thousands. Large shoals of baitfish, such as pilchards, anchovies and juvenile mackerel, are attacked by high-speed plunge-dives from as high as 30m. In fact, they are so good at locating the shoals that fishing fleets have used the gannets as a beacon for good fishing: commercial exploitation of the gannet's fish-finding abilities actually resulted in a crash of pilchard numbers in the 1960s. Various gannet colonies were affected by the decline; some of those off Namibia are still decreasing but most other colonies are stable.

RECOGNITION Large white seabird with yellow-orange head and neck, black tail and primary feathers. Sexes are alike but males are larger. Length 85cm.

HABITAT Offshore islands; fishes in coastal and open waters.

BEHAVIOUR Gregarious and monogamous. Many elaborate displays occur in colonies, most to do with breeding, territorial disputes, or as appeasement to hostile neighbours. Usually feed by day.

BREEDING Mainly in summer. One egg laid in guano mound. Both parents care for the chick.

FEEDING Small shoal fish; also offal from fishing boats.

VOICE Rasping *hara-hara-hara* the most common call.

BIRDS

HOTSPOTS

- Bird Island NR (p94)

RECOGNITION Bronze-brown. Crest offset by heavy bill. Length 50cm to 56cm.

HABITAT Lakes and rivers.

BEHAVIOUR Usually solitary, roosting in groups. Associates with large mammals.

BREEDING Lays three to six white eggs year-round.

FEEDING Frogs and fish.

VOICE Strident yelping: *yip-pur, yip-yip-pur-pur-yip.*

⚡ HOT SPOTS

- Lengwe NP (p172)
- Victoria Falls & Zambezi NPs (p156)
- Moremi GR (p132)

HAMERKOP

Related to the herons and storks, and commonly seen in their company, the hamerkop has a distinctive profile; its Afrikaans name means 'hammerhead'. During courtship, and often at other times, hamerkops engage in unique 'false-coupling' behaviour: one bird sits on the back of another (male or female), but mating doesn't always occur, and birds may even face in opposite directions. Feeding is more conventional: they snatch prey from shallow water, and skim fish from the water's surface while flying into a headwind. For unknown reasons they make a huge nest of twigs, sticks and even bones, usually in the fork of a tree, in which is secreted a brood chamber accessible only through a narrow tunnel. These huge constructions can weigh 40kg and be 1.5m deep; not content with one, some pairs have been known to build and abandon several nests in close proximity – giant eagle owls and barn owls readily take over their vacant nests. But perhaps the hamerkop has got it all sorted out: with so many nests to choose from, a would-be predator probably stands more chance of facing a genet, spitting cobra, monitor lizard or bee swarm (all of which use abandoned nests) than the bird itself.

RECOGNITION Large (1.2m high), storklike, blue-grey bird with massive bill.

HABITAT Papyrus swamps and marshy lakes.

BEHAVIOUR Solitary. Walks on floating vegetation.

BREEDING Lays one to three eggs during main rains.

FEEDING Mainly fish.

VOICE Bill-clapping at nest.

⚡ HOTSPOTS

- Kasanka NP (p187)
- Vwaza Marsh Wildlife Reserve (p173)

SHOEBILL

Also known as the whale-headed stork, the shoebill's bulbous, cloglike bill measures some 19cm in length, and is almost as wide. This bird occupies a taxonomic family of its own but shares with herons the habit of flying with neck retracted; has a crest at the back of its head like a pelican; and shows storklike behaviour, such as emptying bills full of water on the nest to cool its young. This solitary and stately bird is avidly sought by birdwatchers, even though most of the time it stands stock-still waiting for prey on floating vegetation or at the water's edge. Lungfish are its favourite meal, and its technique is worth watching. When a likely victim surfaces all hell breaks loose: the massive bill is jerked forward, causing the bird to overbalance, collapse and submerge its entire head. Using wings and bill it then levers itself upright, manipulates vegetation out of its mouth and swallows the victim – usually decapitated by the bill's sharp edges. Accuracy is everything; its bill cannot usually be manoeuvred for a second strike. Incredibly, this unconventional and all-or-nothing fishing method is also practiced in flight on occasion.

BIRDS

HERONS, EGRETS & BITTERNS

WATER-MARGIN FEEDERS Most of the 19 species of heron, egret and bittern in Southern Africa are common and easily recognised, but different enough to make watching them worthwhile. All have long legs, toes and necks, and dagger-shaped bills; differences are chiefly in coloration and size, although the all-white egrets can be difficult to tell apart (bill and leg colour are useful clues). At times the picture of still grace, at others angular and seemingly brittle, all are deadly hunters of fish, frogs, rodents and other small animals. The long neck can be folded in a tight S-shape (and is invariably held thus in flight) and the piercing bill strikes with speed and accuracy to harpoon prey.

GREAT WHITE EGRET

Most species feed at water margins, and at least one is usually present at every waterway, including mudflats and mangroves; several species can feed side by side without competing directly, and their techniques are interesting to watch. All hunt by posing stock-still for long periods before striking, some even from a perch; other techniques include running, stirring mud with their feet or flapping their wings to startle prey. The 1.5m-tall goliath heron, the world's largest member of the group, spears fish farthest from shore; the 30cm-long green-backed heron snaps up tadpoles and insects. The black egret has an amazing 'cloak-and-dagger' technique of spreading its wings in a canopy over the water then spearing fish that shelter beneath it. Night herons are nocturnal; bitterns are solitary, well-camouflaged inhabitants of dense reed beds. Several species of heron and egret attend locust plagues to feed on the insects, and cattle egrets snap up insects disturbed by buffaloes and elephants.

During courtship, several species of heron, egret and bittern grow long, fine plumes, and patches of bare facial skin change to intense colour. Watch for preening behaviour: herons comb their plumage with a special serrated claw on the middle toe. Usually silent, herons often make harsh territorial calls at the nest; most species also nest communally and heronries can be noisy places. Most species also roost communally, sometimes flying great distances in V-shaped flocks at dusk.

BIRDS

HOTSPOTS

- Moremi GR (p132) Excellent for multispecies heronries
- Nylsvlei NR (p95) Good for seeing a wide variety of species

STORKS

MARABOU STORK

STATELY SENTINELS Stately and often colourfully marked, storks are generally found near wetlands, although some species are far less dependent on water for food resources than other waterbirds. Superficially similar to herons, they share with them long legs, toes and neck, although storks generally have thicker necks and an overall bulkier body shape. All storks fly strongly with necks outstretched; they can often be seen soaring high in thermals, where their distinctive bill shapes make identification fairly easy. Marabou and saddle-billed storks are among the largest of flying birds, the latter with a 2.7m wingspan.

All eight species found in Southern Africa are predominantly white, black or black-and-white, and all have large bills adapted to a carnivorous diet consisting of small animals such as frogs, fish and rodents. The more generalised feeders, including white and Abdim's storks, use dagger-shaped bills to snatch insects, small rodents and reptiles; saddle-billed storks jab at fish in the shallows; and yellow-billed storks find aquatic prey in muddy water by the touch of their long, sensitive bill. Marabou storks, the most predatory, have a massive 35cm-long bill used to pick over carrion and slay other animals, including birds as large as flamingos. Most specialised of all is the open-billed stork, an all-black species with a distinctive tweezer-shaped bill, which it uses to remove snails from their shells.

White storks are famous in Europe for arriving en masse in spring and nesting on rooftops; large flocks return to Southern Africa between November and March. The arrival of another migrant, Abdim's stork, is usually associated with rains. Of the resident species, only woolly-necked and saddle-billed storks are solitary nesters; all others nest in colonies, sometimes in association with herons or cormorants. All species construct large, untidy platforms of sticks in trees, often near or over water, in which they lay their eggs. After the chicks have hatched, adults empty bills full of water over them to keep them cool. Marabous have an unusual habit of defecating on their legs to cool off – a habit they share with vultures.

★ HOTSPOTS

- Etosha NP (p100) Flocks of open-billed, white and Abdim's storks arrive between October and April
- Lochinvar NP (p182) Yellow-billed, saddle-billed, woolly necked and marabou storks are widespread and resident

CRANES

REGAL TRUMPETERS The three Southern African cranes hardly need superlatives – suffice to say, they are among the most elegant birds in Africa, and the national birds of numerous African countries for good reason. In the region, South Africa has claimed the blue crane as its own. Like all cranes, this Southern African endemic forms flocks during the nonbreeding season, but pairs off with a long-term partner to mate. In fact, careful observation of nonbreeding flocks usually reveals they are made up of many couples, the members of each pair staying close together.

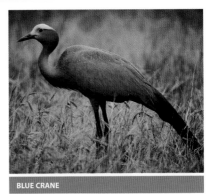

BLUE CRANE

It's no wonder that cultures around the world associate cranes with longevity and fidelity. Pairs of southern crowned cranes stay together until one dies: they preen each other's golden crest, perform loud duets and dance in spontaneous displays of head-bobbing, bowing, stick-tossing and high leaps with wings outstretched. One pair's exuberance will stimulate others in a flock to leap into the air, and up to 60 birds have been seen dancing together for a few minutes before settling down again to feed.

The rarest crane in the region, the wattled crane, rarely forms flocks larger than 40 in Southern Africa, and most observations are of pairs. Common to the crane family, both parents care for the offspring, but wattled cranes only have one chick (other species have two or three) and breed every 14 months, rather than annually; their slow reproductive output is one reason they are declining.

All cranes favour moist grasslands and wetlands, where they forage for rodents, frogs, small reptiles, insects, grass seeds and rhizomes (underground stems). Of all the species, blue cranes are the most tolerant of abitat modification and are able to occupy farmlands. In fact, they are often more common on the agricultural lands surrounding parks than in the parks themselves, something to bear in mind when crane-spotting. Blue cranes often nest on open grassland or in fields but the other species have their chicks in wetlands and marshes. However, blue cranes often commute to nearby plains to feed, sometimes grazing en route or stamping the ground to scare up insects.

HOTSPOTS

- Maloti-Drakensberg Transfrontier Area (p89) One of the few areas where all three species may be seen together
- Lochinvar NP (p182) Very good for crowned and wattled cranes
- Moremi GR (p132) Wattled cranes are relatively common

IBISES & SPOONBILLS

GLOSSY IBIS

SACRED WATERBIRDS Essentially waterbirds, the ibises and spoonbills are biologically akin to herons and storks by dint of their long legs, toes and necks; the differences lie mainly in the shape of their sensitive bills. The most obvious feature of spoonbills – a flattened, spoonlike bill – is swept from side to side as they feed on microscopic water creatures, filtered through fine sieve-like lamellae (bony filters). The bills of ibises are not flattened and curve strongly downwards – adapted for probing the mud for prey. Despite their different bills (and the fact that spoonbills are more tied to wetlands), the two groups are close relatives: occasionally ibises are seen sweeping their bills from side to side and spoonbills poking in soft mud.

The African spoonbill is commonly seen in shallow, slow-moving waterways, often in the company of other waterbirds. Spoonbills and most ibises nest colonially in trees (often in association with herons, storks and cormorants), where they build untidy stick nests.

Ibises use their long, bowed bills to probe for crustaceans, snails and tadpoles. The most widespread species of ibis commonly forages on lawns and grasslands, and adapts readily to agriculture: on occasion it has averted devastation to crops by consuming large numbers of plague locusts. In fact, this common, black-and-white bird was worshipped by ancient Egyptians, who associated its migration with the arrival of the fertile floodwaters of the Nile River every year: it is accurately depicted on wall friezes, mummified specimens have been found in ancient tombs, and to this day it is known as the sacred ibis. While sacred ibises are gregarious waterbirds, nesting in colonies and flying to communal roosts in V-shaped flocks at dusk, pairs of hadeda ibises nest alone and often feed well away from water. The hadeda's brash *ha-haha* call is one of the most distinctive sounds of the savanna, especially at dusk and dawn, and can be heard even in the parks and suburbs of large cities. At the other extreme, the southern bald ibis is the rarest species in the region, restricted to highveld grasslands and mountains. The glossy ibis is similar to both, with predominantly iridescent green plumage, but is rarely seen away from water.

HOTSPOTS

- Mamili NP (p112) Home to all species bar the southern bald ibis
- Maloti-Drakensberg Transfrontier Area (p89) High slopes and cliffs here are the best places to seek southern bald ibises

GREATER & LESSER FLAMINGOS

FLOCKING PINK Masses of pink birds shimmering through the heat haze – audible but inaccessible across fields of treacherous mud – make a tantalising sight, and early Christians considered the flamingo to be the Phoenix, the legendary red bird that rises from the ashes of its own funeral pyre. Flamingos are instantly recognisable by their combination of pink coloration, and long, slender neck and legs. Where the two are found together, the pale-pink greater flamingos tower above the deep rose-pink lessers.

Few large birds are as gregarious as flamingos: great numbers concentrate in shallow lakes too alkaline or saline to support fish (which otherwise compete for the tiny water animals or algae sought by flamingos), and food resources occur in such quantities that competition between individual birds is limited. Flamingos may spend hours standing or floating motionless, but their distinctive and characteristic feeding method makes them unique among birds: typically, flamingos walk through shallow water with head upside-down and submerged, sweeping their angular bill from side to side. Food is caught in lamellae and excess water and mud are forced out by the tongue acting as a piston. Enormous quantities are consumed in this way – 100,000 flamingos account for 18 tons per day – and it is from the algae that flamingos receive their pink coloration.

Courtship rituals are conducted en masse: hundreds or thousands of birds elongate their necks and twist their heads in unison, stretch their wings and legs, and strut through shallow water before abruptly changing direction. These displays synchronise hormone production and ensure a colony takes simultaneous advantage of optimum conditions to raise their young. breeding colonies can be densely packed, and are mostly protected from predators by their location on muddy islands, but breeding sometimes fails catastrophically: rising water levels can wipe out an entire season's efforts, or conversely the lake may dry up leaving young without food or protection.

RECOGNITION Greater: Tall (1.5m) white or pale pink with long pale-pink legs and S-shaped neck. Lesser: Shorter (90cm), deeper pink with darker bill and red legs.

HABITAT Salt lakes, estuaries and coastal lagoons.

BEHAVIOUR Highly nomadic and gregarious. Flock-synchronised courtship. Flies with neck and legs fully extended.

BREEDING Irregular, usually June to July for lesser. Single egg, normally laid on a semiconical nest of mud surrounded by water on inaccessible mudflats.

FEEDING Greater: Aquatic insects, crustaceans and molluscs, some algae. Lesser: Mostly algae. Both filter food by sweeping the beak from side to side underwater.

VOICE Gooselike honking; constant low murmuring while feeding in flocks.

BIRDS

HOTSPOTS

- Etosha NP **(p100)**
- Namib-Naukluft Park **(p104)**
- Makgadikgadi Pans & Nxai Pan NPs **(p128)**
- iSimangaliso Wetland Park **(p80)**

BIRDS OF PREY

RAVENOUS RAPTORS Southern Africa has around 70 species of birds of prey (or raptors) from three distinct families: the falcons; the eagles, hawks, harriers and vultures; and the secretary bird. In open savanna, at least, it is not unusual to see several species in the sky at once, or perched on the same tree. They reach their greatest diversity in the region in semiarid lands, although several species are found in every habitat. Most are fairly plainly coloured in earth tones, although some are adorned with showy crests and contrasting belly plumage.

Raptor-watchers should look for huddled, dark shapes on topmost boughs (larger species take longer to get going, and finish hunting earlier in the day, because they depend on thermals for gaining altitude and soaring). Note large, bulky nests in which an incubating bird may be sitting low with its mate perched nearby; listen for small birds (such as drongos) mobbing; and watch for large hawks drying their outstretched wings on exposed perches after a storm. Other giveaways include antelope legs wedged into branches (eagles' handiwork), piles of feathers where a bird has been plucked, and 'whitewash' below nests on cliffs. Rubbing a piece of styrene foam on glass to imitate a distressed rodent can have spectacular results; and watch for grass fires, from which hawks seize fleeing animals.

BIRDS

BLACK-SHOULDERED KITE WITH THE REMAINS OF A RECENT KILL

Varying in size from pigeon-sized sparrowhawks to mighty eagles with a 2.5m wingspan, nearly all raptors are exclusively carnivorous, with talons to grasp or snatch prey, and a hooked beak for tearing flesh. Raptors have incredible eyesight, spotting a grasshopper at 100m and a hare at 1000m. Woodland hawks are usually on the move with the dawn, and insect-eating raptors start out once the sun makes their prey more active. Sparrowhawks and goshawks feed primarily on birds caught in mad dashes through foliage. Snake eagles sit and wait for hours on a perch then drop onto snakes, which they kill and then swallow whole. The gymnogene or African harrier hawk has long legs with which it reaches into nests, cavities and under bark for prey, even hanging upside down from weavers' nests to extract chicks and eggs. Harriers methodically quarter grasslands, gliding on long, slender wings and dropping onto mammals and birds – their facial feathers, like those of some owls, are arranged in a disc, which heightens their hearing. There are many other hunting strategies: bat hawks swallow bats whole in midair; black eagles haunt cliffs and koppies for dassies; crowned eagles snatch monkeys from the forest canopy; and the martial eagle can bring down a small antelope and carry it back to a perch.

Each species has a different proportion of wing length to breadth, which in turn determines aerobatic manoeuvrability and speed. Thus, the broad wings of forest hawks help them manoeuvre through branches and foliage; and the great eagles

MASTERS OF THE AIR

Falcons are voracious predators that mainly kill birds on the wing, although there are exceptions: kestrels hover and pounce on small animals, and pygmy falcons subsist on insects. Like other raptors, falcons have powerful talons superbly adapted for seizing prey, and a strongly hooked bill. But in flight they show their true mastery, their long, narrow wings scything through the air in quick beats, picking up speed as prey is approached and building to a deadly crescendo in dives known as stoops. Falcons are among the swiftest of birds (although such statistics are rarely measured accurately and doubtless have been exaggerated). The 16 species certainly have few enemies, save larger falcons (such as the lanner falcon), and none normally builds a nest, using instead cliff ledges and the abandoned nests of other birds – the 20cm-long pygmy falcon is smaller than the buffalo weavers whose old nests it uses!

have long, broad wings on which they can glide to great heights and distances. Instead of elaborate plumage, raptors rely on dramatic aerial displays during courtship – such as free falling while grappling talons, and passing prey to one another while one bird flies upside down. Most aerobatic is the bateleur (from the French for 'acrobat'), a consummate glider that in courtship displays performs fast rocking motions on the wing. Hawks often display late in the morning – watching for this behaviour is a good way to detect forest hawks.

BIRDS

★ HOTSPOTS

- Kgalagadi Transfrontier Park (p68) Excellent for raptor watching; dozens of species from sparrowhawks to eagles
- Karoo NP (p84) Cliffs are home to black eagles and several species of falcon
- Moremi GR (p132) Especially Khwai region
- Hwange NP (p142)

SECRETARY BIRD

RECOGNITION Grey with black 'thighs', flight feathers and loose crest. Bare orange facial patch and deep-pink legs and feet. Long central tail feathers and outstretched legs obvious in flight.

HABITAT Short grasslands with scattered thorn trees; common in agricultural land. Avoids hilly or rocky country.

BEHAVIOUR Usually solitary or in pairs, but groups may gather at locust plagues or bushfires. Nests and roosts on flat-topped acacias. Soars high on thermals. Kicks at tufts of grass or dung for prey. Regurgitates large pellets near roosts and nests.

BREEDING Lays one to three-eggs, usually in wet season; only one chick survives and fledges after two to three months.

FEEDING Mainly large insects and spiders, but also reptiles, birds up to small hornbill size, small mammals (such as rodents, hares, mongooses and small cats) and carrion.

VOICE Generally silent; a deep guttural croaking in displays, fights, at nest and in flight.

★ HOTSPOTS

- Central Kalahari GR **(p124)**
- South Luangwa NP **(p178)**
- Matusadona NP **(p154)**
- Pilanesberg NP **(p72)**

A VORACIOUS PEDESTRIAN Stalking across grasslands with jerky precision and standing 1.2m high – tall enough to be seen from hundreds of metres away – this high-stepping bird of prey is unique to Africa. Its body, head and hooked bill resemble those of a large eagle, but it differs from other raptors in a number of ways. For example, its legs are three times as long as those of a 'conventional' raptor, jacking it up to an ideal vantage point from which to look for a meal.

The secretary bird is known to stride up to 20km a day in search of prey, which it kills with a rain of swift kicks from its thick, powerful feet. When a snake is encountered – and dangerous vipers and cobras are attacked with relish – it is stamped to death in a lethal 'flamenco' audible from some distance away. Speed and agility are the keys to handling venomous prey – their legs are heavily scaled, and secretary birds angle their body away from danger until their victim is subdued. Small prey is swallowed whole – that includes snakes, but also eggs, chicks, entire wasps' nests and golf balls (by mistake); larger items are torn apart or cached under a bush for future reference.

The secretary bird's long, black crest flaps in the breeze, and is said to resemble the quill pens worn behind the ears of 19th-century scribes; another theory attributes the name to 'saqur-et-air', French-Arabic for 'hunting bird'. Despite the secretary bird's obvious eaglelike features, aspects of its behaviour point to other possible origins. Its long legs suggest a common ancestry with storks, and other storklike traits include extending its neck in flight, and head-bowing and bill-clapping displays between pairs at the nest. But their courtship flights are very raptorlike, and include 'pendulum displays', where one bird drops in a graceful swoop from a great height with wings folded, and then pulls out of the dive to climb slowly and repeat the show. Pairs also tumble in mid-air with feet outstretched towards each other.

BIRDS

AFRICAN FISH EAGLE

THE VOICE OF AFRICA Whether perched at the top of a *Euphorbia*, head and breast glowing white, or sweeping low on a dive, few birds beg superlatives like this magnificent wetland predator. African fish eagles are common, and in some places live in comparatively high densities: along the Chobe River, pairs can occur every kilometre. At some sites, fish eagles have learned to take fish thrown into the air by boatmen. At first light their loud, ringing calls echo across lakes and river valleys – a sound so distinctive and recognisable that the fish eagle is known as 'the Voice of Africa'. Pairs sometimes duet from perches, throwing their heads back until they are bent almost double.

Closely related to the bald eagle of North America, fish eagles look regal wherever they perch, but these voracious raptors are so effective at fishing they can (and often do) spend as much as 90% of the day resting or preening. A hungry fish eagle stares intently at the water, and when a likely fish is spotted, makes a fast, sweeping dive, at the last second throwing its legs and huge talons forward to seize its slippery catch. Most prey consists of surface-feeding fish taken within 15cm of the top of the water, although if necessary, it will plunge in bodily to a depth of 50cm. The largest catch recorded is 3.7kg, but anything over 2.5kg can't be lifted, and must be dragged or 'rowed' with one foot through the water to shore. Any fish it can carry are consumed at leisure at a favourite perch.

Fish eagles also rob other birds (and each other) of their catch: victims of their piracy can be as large as pelicans, herons and storks, or as small as pied kingfishers. Occasionally, they also prey on waterbirds, killing birds as large as flamingos; more rarely, they take terrestrial prey like monkeys, dassies and monitors.

RECOGNITION Pure-white head, breast, back and tail contrast with rich chestnut belly and 'trousers', and black wings. Bill black with yellow base. Length 75cm.

HABITAT Widespread near lakes, rivers and estuaries (occasionally forest); immature birds may wander far from water.

BEHAVIOUR Adults pairs sedentary and intensely territorial when breeding; may reuse the same nest for 10 years. Groups gather at fish strandings. Immatures may form loose nonbreeding populations. Will cross large arid areas to reach isolated waterways.

BREEDING Usually lays two eggs in large nest of sticks and papyrus near water. Chicks fledge at 65 to 75 days.

FEEDING A large variety of fish and waterbirds (especially young birds); also scavenges dead fish and carrion (immatures may be seen at predators' kills).

VOICE A loud yelping *wee-ah, kyo-kyo-kyo-kyo* from a perch or in flight.

BIRDS

★ HOTSPOTS

- Chobe NP (p120)
- Moremi GR (p132)
- Bangweulu Swamps (p186)
- Mana Pools NP (p150)

VULTURES

CARRION SCAVENGERS Think of the great grasslands, and the nightly carnage left by lions and hyenas, and you'll also probably get an image of squabbling flocks of gore-encrusted vultures eating the stuff few animals will touch. And fair enough: with few exceptions, that is basically what they do. Should they need any introduction, vultures are birds of prey adapted to eat carrion, their chief difference to other raptors being a usually bald head and neck (it's easier to feed and keep clean that way), and feet better suited to walking than grasping. It may not be an appealing way of life to us, but it's an extremely profitable niche to exploit.

Look for these great, bulky birds sitting at the top of acacia trees, and on large, exposed branches – larger species are usually solitary. Although ungainly on the ground, all have long, broad wings superbly adapted for long spells of soaring, and by midmorning these large birds are usually circling high on thermals. Vultures have a poor sense of smell, instead using their keen eyesight to follow other vultures and eagles, or scavenging mammals on the ground that might lead them to a kill. If vultures are circling in the air over a carcass, it's usually a sign that predators are still chewing away at it; if you're on foot, beware.

Early morning is not usually a vulture's best time. After a cold night on the plains, they take a while to get airborne owing to a lack of thermals, especially on an overcast day. Hunched up, most of the eight species are difficult to identify as anything other than vultures, but in flight their various features are more apparent. Larger species usually take precedence at a carcass, although smaller vultures may gang up and chase them away; and each species is specialised to feed differently and thus has different headgear. White-headed vultures and the largest species, the lappet-faced, tear open a carcass, eating the skin as well as bones and sinews. They pave the way for vultures with a long, bare neck

PALM-NUT VULTURE

AFRICAN WHITE-BACKED VULTURE

eggs and smash them on the ground, and have learned to break open ostrich eggs with a rock. The boldly marked palmnut vulture is superficially similar to the African fish eagle (and may in fact be closely related), and like it eats fish and crabs. But, despite its hooked bill, this extraordinary vulture feeds mainly on the protein-rich nuts of *Raphia* palms, a food source sought after by many birds and mammals. All vultures are attentive parents, commuting up to 160km in a day in the search for carcasses before returning to the nest with food.

(Cape and white-backed) to reach right into the guts to eat soft parts without getting their feathers caked in blood; they will even climb inside a rib cage. The comparatively small hooded and Egyptian vultures can't compete with larger species, instead grabbing scraps from the frenzy; crows and marabou storks also loiter for morsels.

Vultures may fast a week between kills, but it's not all gore and blood lust. Hooded vultures pick over human refuse; Egyptian vultures steal birds'

BONE-CRUSHER

Despite its name, which means 'lamb vulture', and great size (having a 2.5m wingspan), the lammergeier probably doesn't kill lambs. In fact, it rarely kills anything in the rugged gorges and alpine areas it frequents. Like all vultures, it is a scavenger, but rather than tearing at flesh (something it could easily do with its hooked bill and curved talons), it eats whole bones and scoops out the marrow with its tongue. It particularly favours large leg bones, and any too large to be swallowed are dropped from a height of about 20m to 80m onto a well-used, flattish area of rock (called an ossuary) until they smash or splinter. Ravens in alpine areas have also been seen trying this trick, although they can't seem to manage it as well as their mentors. Also known as the bearded vulture because of its black, bristly 'beard' of feathers around the beak, the lammergeier is Africa's rarest vulture.

BIRDS

⭐ HOTSPOTS

- Kruger NP (p60) Great spot for vultures because of high concentrations of predators and prey
- Kosi Bay NR (p94) Best chances for palmnut vultures
- Manyelanong GR (p136) Colonies of Cape vultures
- Maloti-Drakensberg Transfrontier Area (p89) Only place in the region for bearded vultures (lammergeiers)

FRANCOLINS

RED-BILLED FRANCOLIN

GAME BIRDS Francolins belong to the great taxonomic grouping of birds loosely known as 'game birds' – the pheasants, quails, partridges and jungle fowl (precursors of the domestic chicken) that have been the focus of hunters' activities for centuries. And it's not just humans – small cats and other predators readily stalk francolins. But these ground-dwelling birds are great survivors: they are abundant and come in many varieties. Francolins nest on the ground (although the retiring habits of some species mean that their nests are as yet unknown), and the downy, precocial chicks are well camouflaged and can run within hours. Walking (and running) are strong francolin traits – all species have stout legs and feet, and run fast to evade predators – and only when push comes to shove will they take to the wing, flying low for a short distance before dropping to the ground again.

The basic francolin design is like a large, upright quail, with heavily streaked upperparts in greys, browns and black for camouflage. Some, such as red-necked and Swainson's francolins, sport naked flesh on the face and neck, which enhances their territorial displays. All have a strong, hooked bill useful for snatching small animals, picking up seeds and fruit, and digging for bulbs. Like domestic hens, many rake the soil and leaf litter with their strong feet, and cocks of most species sport spurs on their legs.

Although a few species occur across Asia, Africa is the centre of diversity for francolins, and the 15 species found in Southern Africa range in size from 28cm to 42cm. Many are common, and a day's birding in any reserve is bound to encounter at least one species. Francolins often feed along roadsides in the early morning and late afternoon, or dart across the road in single file. Two of the most abundant – Swainson's and crested – are decidedly chicken-like, and are commonly seen standing atop termite mounds or roadside banks. Savannas and grasslands with thornbush in particular are their stronghold, although a few (such as grey-wing and red-wing francolins) inhabit the alpine meadows of The Drakensberg; and other species (such as Hartlaub's francolin) are specialised to life in rocky deserts.

HOTSPOTS

- Kruger NP (p60) All the common species
- Etosha NP (p100) Good for the endemic Hartlaub's francolin
- Table Mountain NP (p94) Cape francolins are endemic
- Maloti-Drakensberg Transfrontier Area (p89) Red-wing, grey-wing, Natal and red-necked francolins

BIRDS

GUINEAFOWL

Both Southern African guineafowl species are immediately recognisable by their boxlike shape and black plumage punctuated by tiny white spots. Their bizarre headgear distinguishes them: the crested guineafowl sports a dishevelled mop of black feathers, and the helmeted guineafowl has a bony casque like a top hat.

Guineafowl are opportunistic feeders, consuming a wide variety of small animals such as insects and small vertebrates, and plant matter such as seeds, fruit, berries and bulbs – and they're not averse to raiding crops. They also swallow grit to aid digestion. Helmeted guineafowl gather in flocks to drink, and they associate with mammals, ranging from rhinos to mongooses, whose presence presumably flushes potential prey. Their relationship with baboons is less benevolent, for each tries to steal food from the other, but watch for the forest-dwelling crested guineafowl picking up scraps dropped by troops of monkeys moving through the canopy.

★ HOT SPOTS

- Chobe NP (p120)
- Addo Elephant NP (p76)
- Hwange NP (p142)
- Matusadona NP (p154)

BLACK CRAKE

Crakes and rails almost exclusively exploit the cover and feeding opportunities provided by dense stands of reeds or rushes fringing slow waterways. The downside is that they have a reputation for being difficult to see among the forest of stems. However, the black crake is an exception, and this common bird is readily seen on virtually any Southern African wetland.

Black crakes have a similar shape and size to other crakes and rails, with a rather body, strong legs and feet, and a short bill. Using reeds as cover, crakes typically feed on mud exposed at the water's edge, darting back to cover should danger threaten; the best way to see them is to wait patiently for one to make nervous feeding forays onto the mud. In contrast, black crakes often feed in the open for extended periods, and readily use hippos' backs as stepping stones (although they can fly and swim well). Like most of the family, they feed on a variety of small animals, ranging from worms and snails to insects, tadpoles and frogs. But black crakes also scavenge from carcasses, perch on warthogs' backs to pick off parasites, and climb waterside trees to steal birds' eggs and chicks.

RECOGNITION Slatey black. Pale green bill. Red legs, feet and eyes. Length 20cm.

HABITAT Vegetation beside freshwater lakes and swamps.

BEHAVIOUR Walks on floating vegetation.

BREEDING Lays three eggs.

FEEDING A variety of small animals; some seeds.

VOICE Harsh *krrok*-krraaa.

★ HOTSPOTS

- Moremi GR (p132)
- Vwaza Marsh Wildlife Reserve (p173)
- Lower Zambezi NP (p184)
- Nylsvlei NR (p95)

BIRDS

BUSTARDS & KORHAANS

BLACK-BELLIED KORHAAN

STRUTTING THEIR STUFF Although all bustards and korhaans (an Afrikaans name for the seven smaller members of this family) can fly strongly should the need arise, they are consummate walkers – some would say strutters, because their habit of pointing their bill upwards as they walk away from an intruder gives them a dignified, even aloof, air. Southern Africa is a bustard-watcher's haven with 10 species on show, half of them endemic to the region. Two or three species are common in suitable habitat, but they can be hard to see. Despite their conspicuous size, they are typically decked out in greys and browns that camouflage them among the muted tones of the grasslands, and they don't allow close approaches. Binoculars

are a must, especially to tell apart the females of different species, which are similarly marked. The chicks and eggs are also superbly camouflaged – all species nest on bare open ground or in grass tufts where cryptic colouration is the main defence against predators.

The kori bustard is the biggest species (closely followed by Stanley's) and Africa's heaviest flying bird, weighing up to 18kg and with a wingspan of 2.8m. Despite having long legs, its rather small feet render it incapable of perching in trees; look for it peering over the top of the grass. It's probably also the least shy species, though it certainly cannot be called confiding – no matter how slow and sensitive your approach, koris will always keep a minimum distance of 30m to 40m. Like many bustards, they are especially fond of toasted insects and small animals, and are readily seen gathered at grassfires where pickings are good. Freshly mown wheat fields and other cultivated areas are also rewarding places to look.

The best time to watch bustards is during courtship: the male kori puffs out his white throat feathers in a huge bulging ruff, flips up his startling white undertail feathers and booms loudly. Ludwig's bustard performs a similar routine, the white feathers of his display obvious from great distances. The male black-bellied korhaan stands atop a termite mound and launches himself into the air, falling back to earth as if dead, with wings held high and neck arched back, his black belly standing out.

HOTSPOTS

- Makgadikgadi Pans & Nxai Pan NPs (p128) Red-crested and black korhaans and obvious kori bustards
- Karoo NP (p84) Kori, Stanley's and Ludwig's bustards and Karoo korhaans
- Mountain Zebra NP (p90) White-bellied, blue and black korhaans
- Namib-Naukluft Park (p104) Try here for very elusive Rüppell's korhaans, also kori and Ludwig's bustards

AFRICAN JACANA

Competition for resources is keen at the water's edge, but few birds have adapted to life 'on top' of the water, and none as successfully as the jacanas. Jacanas live virtually their entire life afloat: hugely elongated toes spread their weight so they can run across water lilies, Nile cabbage and other floating masses, as well as soft mud; when walking on submerged vegetation, jacanas can appear to be walking on water. Alternatively, the back of a hippo makes a good vantage point. At a pinch they can dive and fly (clumsily) with legs dangling.

Most bodies of still water with lily pads or other floating vegetation will have a few jacanas (although they can be hard to see if a dropping water level has caused the shadows of drooping lilies to break up the view); watch for the blue headgear, wing stretches and jacanas in flight (they often give their harsh call in flight). The sexes look alike, but jacanas reverse their traditional roles: any aggression is likely to be from a female defending her territory, and all parental care is by the male. The chicks can walk soon after hatching, but the male carries them under his wings for protection, and even moves the eggs in this manner should rising water cause the destruction of the nest.

RECOGNITION Chestnut body, white face and breast. Blue bill and 'shield'. Length 30cm.

HABITAT Swamps and lakes.

BEHAVIOUR Gregarious outside breeding season.

BREEDING Lays two to five eggs on floating vegetation.

FEEDING Insects and small water animals.

VOICE A harsh rattle.

🔥 HOT SPOTS

- Bangweulu Swamps (p186)
- Moremi GR (p132)
- Lake Malawi NP (p166)

SPOTTED DIKKOP

Among the many offshoots from the large shorebirds group is a small family of mainly nocturnal waders known as dikkops. Large for waders, long-legged and equipped with very large eyes, dikkops hunt insects and other small animals at dusk and after dark with rather ploverlike 'walk-pause-peck' behaviour. Spotted dikkops are commonly encountered on tracks at night, but during the day they rest in dry areas under bushes; when accidentally flushed from cover their large size and sudden appearance can be startling. When danger approaches they normally crouch down, lying flat on the ground with neck extended, or else simply walk away and blend in with the countryside. Males and females are thought to mate for life, and both care for the young; their nest is a shallow scrape on the ground sometimes lined with vegetation, stones or animal droppings. As with most waders, spotted dikkop chicks can walk soon after hatching; their down blends superbly with rocky soil when they lie flat to avoid detection. The water dikkop is reputed to lay its eggs near basking crocodiles as a deterrent to predators.

RECOGNITION Fawn upperparts spotted with brown. Long yellow legs.

HABITAT Grasslands, woodland and rocky semiarid country.

BEHAVIOUR Hesitant gait.

BREEDING Lays two eggs.

FEEDING Insects, crustaceans and amphibians

VOICE Musical *pe-pe-pe-peou-PEOU-PEOU-pee*-pi.

🔥 HOTSPOTS

- Kruger NP (p60)
- Hwange NP (p142)

BIRDS

SHOREBIRDS

BLACK-WINGED STILT

MIGRANTS & HOMEBODIES Every spring and summer, thousands of small- to medium-sized shorebirds (commonly known as waders) arrive in Southern Africa to spend the northern winter on coastal mudflats and freshwater swamps. Among them are some long-distance champions – stints, sandpipers, curlew, redshanks and the greenshank – which breed as far away as the Arctic Circle, and make a trip of several thousand kilometres twice annually. All but one (the Ethiopian snipe is resident in Southern African marshes) take advantage of the mild climate to regain condition after the rigours of breeding and migration.

The loose term 'shorebirds' also covers several closely related families, not all of which make these exhausting round trips, and many of which are attractively marked. For example, the black-winged stilt and avocet are black-and-white, and both species are common on shallow inland waterways. The stilt's coral-pink legs are matched only by those of flamingos for length in proportion to body size, while the avocet's distinct upturned bill is used to scythe through shallow water for aquatic insects and crustaceans.

Plovers also commonly fall under the 'wader' umbrella, although many species are found far from water and most are year-round residents. Several large species are often seen on savanna wildlife drives, and act as sentinels of the grasslands, protesting loudly at the approach of any intruder – animal or human. All plovers have a compact body, large head and short, blunt bill. With comparatively long legs, the larger savanna-dwelling species tower above most others, while the smaller species – which tend to stay near the muddy edges of waterways – look decidedly 'dumpy' but run quickly. Savanna specialists eat mainly large insects, but the long-toed plover forages on floating vegetation. Several smaller plovers feed on shorelines and mudflats among other waders; they include some long-distance migrants from the northern hemisphere such as golden and grey plovers, which 'winter' in Southern Africa from October to April.

★ HOTSPOTS

- ○ Namib-Naukluft Park (p104) Sandwich Lagoon attracts a huge summer influx of waders, especially curlew sandpipers, sanderlings and little stints; as well as Arctic, Sandwich and common terns.
- ○ Skeleton Coast NP (p108) Some 20,000 to 30,000 Palaearctic waders arrive here in the summer months, joining resident species such as the white-fronted plover.

PIGEONS & DOVES

COMMON COOERS It would be hard to credit the lives of such ostensibly gentle creatures with any sort of drama, but when it comes to feeding, courting and mating (all of which most pigeons and doves do a lot of), they are as competitive as any other birds. This successful family is represented by 16 species in Southern Africa, although many of the ubiquitous doves and turtle doves look very similar, and pose some tricky identification problems for birders. Several of these mainly ground-feeding birds, including Cape turtle, red-eyed and laughing doves, will commonly be seen walking along tracks at the edge of grasslands. More colourful species, such as the African green and Rameron pigeons, are also common but feed on fruit in trees.

LAUGHING DOVE

All pigeons and doves fly well, the doves and turtle doves often breaking from just under your front wheels. Explosive take-offs are one of the secrets of their survival, along with good camouflage and loose-fitting feathers, which often leave a would-be predator emptymouthed.

They also have a rapid reproductive turnover: most species are prolific breeders (in fact it's all some of them seem to do, and you'll probably see a few bowing and cooing as a preliminary to mating). Their nests are usually just a formality – a loose, untidy platform of twigs, although some nest on rock ledges – but the parents have a legen-

dary propensity to sit tight on the nest, deserting a clutch to a predator only at the last second. And the young grow faster than just about any other birds, developing for the first few days of life on a highly nutritious solution ('pigeon's milk') of digested seeds from the crop of the parent – a trait pigeons and doves share with parrots.

Like the calls of waterfowl and a few other domesticated birds, the calls of pigeons and doves are famous, and many are variations on the familiar cooing. Although similar, once recognised the calls are a useful aid to identification. Forest-dwelling species can be much harder to pin down among dense foliage, but look for them at dawn winging across the canopy or sitting high on exposed snags, something they may do for long spells.

BIRDS

★ HOTSPOTS

- Nyanga NP (p161) A dozen species including blue-spotted wood doves, Delegorgue's and Rameron pigeons
- Mkhuze GR (p86) Good for cinnamon doves and 10 other species
- Nyika NP (p170) Eleven species and the only site in the region with recorded sightings of dusky turtle doves

PARROTS & LOVEBIRDS

The popular conception of parrots screeching across the African sky is a bit misleading: they certainly screech, and all are brightly coloured, but only seven species are found in Southern Africa. Virtually every aspect of parrot biology is related to life in the trees. Strong feet and claws – arranged with two toes pointing back and two forward – grasp food and clamber through foliage. Their distinctive, hooked bills crush nuts and tear bark apart, and act as a 'third leg' when climbing; food is manipulated with the strong, thick tongue while being held in the feet. Their bright colours, so obvious in flight, provide camouflage by disrupting their outline among greenery and blossom. And nests are usually in tree hollows where the eggs are safe from all but monkeys, snakes and a few tree-living mammals. Parrots often alight on exposed perches to take the early sun, and are often noisy when feeding – when a threat appears, the birds fall silent only to explode from the foliage in a burst of colour.

★ HOT SPOTS

- Etosha NP (p100)
- Mamili NP (p112)
- Ndumo GR (p91)
- Lower Zambezi NP (p184)

CUCKOOS & COUCALS

Although the trait of laying eggs in another bird's nest is not unique to cuckoos, few other birds are as adept at shirking the burden of parenthood. And, with around 15 species in Southern Africa alone, their diversity reflects the success of 'nest parasitism'. Although most cuckoos are common and widely-spotted, some aspects of their behaviour are still a mystery. During courtship, males typically call for hours on end and even at night. Females lay their eggs in the nests (usually one per nest) of the 'host' species. Upon hatching, the cuckoo chick evicts the rightful eggs or chicks, and is raised by the unsuspecting parents. Cuckoos typically choose a species much smaller than themselves for this role, but such are the joys of parenting that the adult hosts (often tiny songbirds, such as warblers) don't seem to realise that their pride and joy is many times their own size. Exceptions to the parasitic rule are the six species of coucal, large, mainly ground-dwelling cuckoos that build their own nests and incubate their own eggs.

★ HOT SPOTS

- Kafue NP (p182)
- Liwonde NP (p168)
- Mkhuze GR (p86)

BIRDS

LOURIES

TREE TURKEYS Unique to Africa, louries reach their greatest diversity in the equatorial rainforests further north (where they're known as turacos), but five species occur in Southern Africa. Two of them, the purple-crested and grey, are widespread and easy to see, but the other three species are restricted to dense forest (Knysna and Ross' louries), or can only been seen in a few sites in far northern Zambia (bare-faced go-away bird).

The grey lourie is a guaranteed sighting on safari and, unlike most of the group, inhabits dry woodlands and semi-arid habitat. But like its forest-dwelling relatives, it moves about branches and foliage with agility, running speedily along branches, and hopping nimbly from perch to perch. It's also the most drably marked of all the louries: uniformly smoky grey with olive tinges visible up close. At first glance, the purple-crested lourie may appear similarly drab, if darker, but through binoculars its colourful, metallic violet and green plumage comes to life. In flight, flashes of deep scarlet under the wings are a further surprise as well as an ID giveaway. Most impressive of all, the Knysna or green lourie is decked out in iridescent green with red primary feathers and a helmetlike crest with white tips. In South Africa, the crest is a modest affair, but the further north you go, the longer it becomes. The Knysna louries of Zambia and Malawi (locally called Schalow's louries) have crests rivalling those of cockatoos.

KSYNA LOURIE

All louries are almost exclusively vegetarian, eating fruits (especially figs), leaves, flowers and buds. Grey and Knysna louries are also on record as taking insects, many eaten inadvertently on fruit as well as the occasional intentional catch. Most species leave the trees to drink or bathe, and large parties of grey louries can be seen drinking at pools; despite their tolerance for aridity, they have to drink regularly. Louries are highly vocal birds, and the raucous calls of the forest species may set off a chain of responses throughout the canopy. The grey lourie's nasal *g'way, g'way* is impossible to miss in dry savannas, and gives rise to its other name, the go-away bird. Calls are one of the tricks to locating louries, particularly the forest species, and once recognised, they will be found to be quite common.

BIRDS

★ HOTSPOTS

- South Luangwa NP (p178) Four species, including occasional sightings of bare-faced go-away birds
- Mkhuze GR (p86) Grey, Knysna and very visible purple-crested louries
- Kruger NP (p60) Grey louries and many camp sites excellent for purple-crested louries
- Moremi GR (p132) Abundant grey louries and occasional sightings of Ross' louries

OWLS

GIANT EAGLE OWL

CREATURES OF THE NIGHT Most owls are primarily nocturnal, and no group of birds is more successful at hunting at night. They're armed with grasping talons, hooked bill, and soft plumage for silent flight. But their greatest weapon is a dislike arrangement of facial feathers that funnels sounds to their hypersensitive ears. In some species, like the barn owl, the ears are asymmetrically positioned with one slightly lower and further back on the head than the other: this enhances the ability to pinpoint the source of the softest noises, and owls are able to hunt in absolute darkness.

All owls are carnivorous. Rodents are the preferred prey for most species, but the giants of the group, the eagle owls, take mammals up to the size of a vervet monkey. The largest African owl, the giant eagle owl, has even been observed killing its close relative, the spotted eagle owl. Small owls, like the pearl-spotted and wood owls, concentrate on insects. Specialist feeders include the African scops owl, which takes a high percentage of scorpions in its diet; and Pel's fishing owl, which hunts fish along rivers – even wading to do so.

The owls' nocturnal lifestyle makes seeing them considerably more difficult than hearing them. Fortunately, several of Southern Africa's 12 species are comparatively common. During the day savanna-dwelling eagle owls, such as the pink-lidded giant eagle owl, can sometimes be located by the mobbing behaviour of smaller birds. Not surprisingly, most owls are best seen by spotlighting: blundering about at night with a torch won't produce much, but by driving slowly the eyeshine of one or two species can usually be picked out. Spotted eagle owls are often on the move at dusk, their bulky silhouettes standing out against the sky; and wood owls sometime hawk for insects around lodges. Clusters of pellets at the base of trees or cliffs are usually a sign of owls: four species (barn, grass, African scops and white-faced) regularly regurgitate the undigested remains of prey. Take note of any accumulations, and, if possible, return there at dusk or night for a chance to view the owners.

⭐ HOTSPOTS

- Kruger NP (p60) Night drives hold excellent chances for up to 10 species
- Moremi GR (p132) Abundant Pel's fishing owls, often seen at dusk, and eight other species
- Pilanesberg NP (p72) Night drives see grass, white-faced, and marsh owls as well as all three eagle owls (Cape, spotted and giant)
- Kgalagadi Transfrontier Park (p68) Seven species including abundant white-faced owls, which roost in the rest camps

NIGHTJARS

On a night drive, you're virtually guaranteed to see a few nightjars taking off from the track before you. Like owls, these nocturnal hunters have soft plumage for silent flight, but unlike owls, all are essentially aerial hunters that locate insects with their large eyes and snap them up in flight with their wide gape. Nightjars have weak feet and a small body, but long, usually slender wings; most roost and all nest on the ground, a trait for which the birds are superbly camouflaged. Nightjars cannot hunt effectively in dense forest: watch for them hawking in clearings and over fields or grasslands. The problem with

nightjars is getting one of the seven species to sit still long enough to look at, although if you're very lucky, you may spot one on the ground during the day. Even if you do, identification is extremely difficult for all but a few, and is more reliably made by their distinctive calls. The exception is the pennant-winged nightjar, in which the breeding males have extraordinary 50cm feathers trailing from their wings.

⭐ HOT SPOTS

- Kruger NP (p60)
- Ndumo GR (p91)
- Augrabies Falls NP (p78)
- Pilanesberg NP (p72)

LITTLE SWIFT

Swifts share a similar body plan to swallows (streamlined bodies and long, narrow wings) owing to their similar life-styles – although the wings of swifts are more scythe-like and they are faster fliers. Despite being close lookalikes, the two groups are not closely related. Like swallows, swifts feed in groups, scooping up insects (their sole food) on the wing – look out for them in vast, swirling 'towers' contain-ing thousands of birds moving ahead of storm fronts to hawk insects that hatch with changes in humidity.

There are 13 species of swift in Southern Africa, but one you're sure to see is the widespread little swift. Ironically, it owes its success to humans: it normally nests on cliffside overhangs or caves, but our buildings and bridges provide it with ideal and abundant crannies. From being a fairly uncommon species prior to European colonisation, it is now probably the most common swift in Africa.

Like all the family, little swifts are among the fastest of birds, mobbing their only rivals, falcons, with an insouci-ance that highlights their supreme skills of flight. They are highly gregarious, foraging in large flocks, often with oth-er species of swift. Their colonies may number over 100 nests, but in rafters and eaves, nests are usually solitary.

RECOGNITION Dark plum-age with white rump patch. Length 14cm.

HABITAT Anywhere with cliffs, gorges, hillsides. Also built-up areas.

BEHAVIOUR Gregarious.

BREEDING One to three eggs.

FEEDING Aerial insects.

VOICE Very vocal, high-pitched chitter.

⭐ HOTSPOTS

- Kruger NP (p60)
- Etosha NP (p100)
- Victoria Falls & Zambezi NPs (p156)
- Lower Zambezi NP (p184)

BIRDS

MOUSEBIRDS

MOUSEBIRD

CURIOUS HANGERS Mousebirds are endemic to the African continent, and have an engaging and comical habit of hanging from branches and wires. A mechanism on their toes locks the feet in position, and the articulation of their legs means the feet are held at 'shoulder' height when hanging. Mousebirds are largely vegetarian, and it is thought that hanging in the sun warms their belly, and helps them digest food. But during sleep (something they do for up to 12 hours), their metabolic rate can fall by 90%, and so they also like to warm up in the early morning – pairs even warm each other by hanging breast to breast.

There are three mousebirds species in Southern Africa, and all are highly sociable, living in family groups numbering around eight to 10. They fly with apparent discipline in single file from one bush, only to crash-land in the next. Their flight – whirring wing beats alternating with direct glides – looks fast but actually isn't. Strongly hooked claws help them to clamber about in trees. Large groups may visit a single fruiting tree, a trait that doesn't endear them to gardeners. Garden pests or not, their resemblance to mice is owed to the texture of their soft, hairlike feathers, and to their habit of running fast along branches, up tree trunks and along the ground, long tail trailing behind. When threatened, mousebirds hang in dense vegetation, dropping to the ground to hide if necessary, then climbing back up when danger passes.

Group members cluster together at various times during the day, and even nesting is a social affair: chicks are fed by the parents, and by young birds from previous broods, which act as helpers. Adding to so many unique features is the extraordinary behaviour of the chicks: when about 10 days old they start toying with nest material; once they leave the nest they play games with other young birds (such as running, wrestling and chasing), and also engage in head-shaking, sudden leaps, mutual feeding, building nests and manipulating leaves or twigs.

All three Southern African mousebirds overlap in distribution, but the speckled lives mainly in the well-watered east; the white-backed mousebird replaces it in the arid west; and the red-faced mousebird is distributed over the entire region.

⭐ **HOTSPOTS**

- Karoo NP (p84) All three species, sometimes in association
- Namaqua NP (p95) Visible white-backed and red-faced mousebirds

KINGFISHERS

LONG-BILLED DIVERS Common in most habitats, Southern Africa's 12 species of kingfisher include the world's largest and smallest species, but the basic form doesn't vary: all have a large head with long, pointed bill, compact body and very short legs. During the breeding season, pairs make vocal displays to each other, and to defend their nest – woodland kingfishers are particularly aggressive, chasing away other hole-nesting birds, small hawks and even people. But at other times, and despite their bright coloration, most savanna and forest species are easily overlooked because of their habit of perching motionless for long spells – until a large insect or small lizard walks by, in which case it will be suddenly dived upon, taken back to the perch and bashed repeatedly to remove its legs, wings or pincers before being swallowed whole.

Kingfishers also use the diving approach when bathing and hunting by crash-landing in water. Pied, malachite, giant and a few other kingfishers are usually easier to see because they often dive from exposed perches near water, such as overhanging branches, jetties and boats. The abundant pied kingfisher can also be seen hovering over water up to 3km from land. To catch fish, amphibians and crustaceans, kingfishers have eyes that adjust instantly from daylight to underwater vision, but they must also learn to judge depth, refrac-

STRIPED KINGFISHER, SERENGETI NATIONAL PARK

tion and the likely escape route of their quarry: watch for kingfishers bobbing their head to take aim before diving.

The pied kingfisher is the only species that roosts and nests communally – sometimes alongside colonies of bee-eaters – and one in three pairs has helpers that assist with feeding young and defending the nest. All kingfishers nest in holes, and their short legs are ideal for scuttling along narrow tunnels. Usually they dig a tunnel in a sand bank (a record 8.5m-long tunnel was dug by a pair of giant kingfishers), but smaller species may nest in the sides of aardvark burrows; tree-nesting species always enlarge an existing hole; and woodland-dwelling kingfishers excavate arboreal termite mounds. After the chicks fledge, adults may be seen feeding them outside the nest for a few days.

BIRDS

★ HOTSPOTS

- iSimangaliso Wetland Park (p80) Ten species including pied, giant and mangrove kingfishers
- Moremi GR (p132) Mokoro rides excellent for close-up views of malachite and pygmy species
- Kafue NP (p182) Eleven species including occasional sightings of shining blue and blue-breasted kingfishers in the north

BEE-EATERS & ROLLERS

AERIAL ACROBATS As colourful as kingfishers, and closely related to them, bee-eaters and rollers are bird highlights of any safari. Their glowing range of colours are a delight to the eye, and a relief from the greens and browns of the savanna, especially for travellers from higher northern latitudes where bright colours among birds are comparatively rare.

African bees have a fearsome reputation, but being such an abundant food resource, it was inevitable that at least one group of birds should tackle them. Bee-eaters appear to do so with relish, and have reached their greatest diversity in Africa; 10 species occur in the southern region. All are very similar in size (mostly 20cm to 25cm in length) and

shape: streamlined with pointed, down-curved bills and long, swallowlike wings. But their habit of perching on exposed branches to watch for likely prey makes them easily seen and identified, and their antics and bright colours make them a pleasure to watch.

Many species hunt from perches (such as Böhm's bee-eater), chasing the bees that make up a substantial percentage of their diet, but also tackling dragonflies, cicadas and potentially dangerous wasps and hornets. After a sometimes animated chase, which can include corkscrew turns, they return to their perch and bash the insect against a branch – taking care to rub off the stings of bees and wasps – before swallowing it whole. These thrashings can often be heard from several metres away.

EUROPEAN BEE-EATER

Larger species, such as the European and carmine bee-eaters, spend much time hawking insects on the wing, although the latter follow tractors and bushfires, and readily perch on mobile sites, such as ostriches, bustards, zebras and antelopes, sometimes subduing prey against the bird's back or antelope's horns! Bee-eaters are so specialised at catching insects on the wing that they ignore insects crawling along the ground.

Like their kingfisher cousins, all bee-eaters nest in holes: forest species in trees, others in tunnels excavated in riverbanks or road cuttings. Larger, more aerial feeders often live colonially in cooperative (and competitive) units of related birds. Helpers, usually blood relatives such as the previous year's offspring, assist with incubation and feeding, and in turn gain an apprenticeship in parenthood. But helpers sometimes also lay an egg or two in the nest at which they are helping. In fact, studies of colonies have revealed complicated and shifting alliances: adultery is rife among mated pairs, females lay in the nests of other females (a practice known as 'egg dumping'), and some birds habitually attempt to rob others of food. Pairs will also nest separately, which is the usual practice among smaller species, such as the little and swallow-tailed bee-eaters.

Although hardly musical, bee-eaters have pleasant calls (at least when compared to the kingfishers), described as a liquid, trilling *krreep-krreep*. All species sound more or less the same, and once the basic pattern is learnt, calls are easily recognised and are a good way to detect bee-eaters in the canopy or flying overhead.

ROCKING ROLLERS

The five species of roller are also colourful, and several, such as the lilac-breasted and racket-tailed, sport long tail feathers. The lilac-breasted roller is in places very common, easily seen and photographed, and probably elicits more admiration from visitors than any other bird in Southern Africa. Like most of their relatives, rollers are not known for their song – their typical calls are cackling or croaks – but a male displays by 'rolling' (an aeronautical term): flying slowly upwards with languorous flaps, he coasts down again, rocking from side to side to show off his prominent pale wing patches, and usually cackling as he goes. Rollers also catch prey from a conspicuous perch: savanna species pounce on ground-dwelling invertebrates, while forest species hawk flying insects in the canopy. Lilac-breasted rollers also sometimes follow and catch prey disturbed by dwarf mongooses. You might also be the target of attention from one of these flashy birds – male rollers defend a territory and become pugnacious towards other birds, mammals and even people.

★ HOTSPOTS

- Hwange NP (p142) Has all the rollers and six species of bee-eater (some seasonal)
- Kasanka NP (p187) As above but also with chances for Böhm's and olive bee-eaters
- Kafue NP (p182) Try for blue-breasted and Böhm's bee-eaters
- Moremi GR (p132) Good for blue-cheeked bee-eaters (November to April), carmine bee-eaters (January to March) and numerous rollers

HORNBILLS

YELLOW-BILLED HORNBILL

AFRICAN TOUCANS Omnivorous and voracious, Southern Africa's 10 hornbill species spend much of their day searching for lizards, insects and fruit; and larger species eat virtually any animal they can swallow, including eggs, birds, rodents and snakes. Whatever their preferences, hornbills are among the most conspicuous, noisy and engaging of large birds to be seen in savanna and forest. It's not something you might expect, but hornbills have surprisingly long eyelashes – those of ground hornbills are so long and thick they can be seen easily. And all have a large, sometimes colourful bill, which in some species (such as the trumpeter hornbill) is adorned with a casque – a hollow protuberance thought to resonate when the birds call. Noise plays a big role in a hornbill's life: they call for many reasons (for example, to contact each other or to establish territories), and their nasal honkings are a good way of locating them.

Several species live side by side in most areas, and up to eight may coexist in savanna or forest communities, where different species may even nest in the same tree. Early morning is the time to watch for their complex interactions: calls signal communal roosts waking up and flocks fly across the canopy to fruiting trees with a loud whoosh of wings. They're also often seen in association with other animals, particularly dwarf mongooses. The mongooses' diet of lizards and invertebrates is exactly the same as that of three species of hornbill (grey, southern yellow-billed and red-billed), and a remarkable and possibly unique feeding strategy has evolved: the hornbills walk along with foraging mongooses, snapping up food disturbed or flushed by their companions.

All hornbills nest in cavities, usually in a tree, and pairs spend much time inspecting holes. After mating, females of most species seal themselves into a suitable nest by plastering up the entrance with mud, sticky fruit and droppings, until only a slit remains – an effective barricade against predators. There she raises the chicks, cramped with long tail bent vertically over her back, while the male passes food through the entrance.

★ HOTSPOTS

- Hwange NP (p142) Numerous species, especially good for Bradfield's hornbills at the end of the dry season (especially September to October)
- Kruger NP (p60) Six species including abundant ground-feeders like grey, southern yellow-billed and red-billed on the roads, often with dwarf mongooses
- Nyika NP (p170) Silver-cheeked and crowned hornbills
- Waterberg Plateau Park (p113) Endemic Monteiro's hornbills, plus grey, southern yellow-billed and red-billed

BIRDS

GROUND HORNBILL

GROUND CREW The largest of Africa's hornbills, the ground hornbill is almost entirely terrestrial, and is also the only Southern African bird that walks on the tips of its toes. Like a large turkey (and the ground hornbill is sometimes mistakenly called the turkey buzzard), small groups patrol grasslands and open woodland looking for prey.

The most carnivorous of the hornbills, ground hornbills take insects, snails, frogs, reptiles (including tortoises and snakes) and even mammals up to the size of scrub hares. Sometimes they can be spotted among herds of ungulates, snapping up rodents and insects flushed by the grazers. Their massive black beak is a powerful weapon, and prey is speared to death with a single swift stab before being swallowed whole. In the case of snakes and large prey, the group cooperates: each bird takes turns to make fleeting, violent pecks until the victim is dead, but usually only one bird gets the prize.

The small parties of ground hornbills are usually made up of two to four adults and a few immature birds. Groups are territorial, and conflict sometimes occurs over borders, with neighbouring groups chasing one another in noisy, aerial clashes. It's the only time they make any sort of prolonged flight, though they are powerful flyers, with strong regular wingbeats and – unlike other hornbills – hardly any gliding. They also fly when threatened by predators, usually taking to large trees for refuge; they roost in trees at night.

Like other hornbills, they nest in hollows, usually in trees, but also in cliff-faces and riverbeds. But whereas the females of other species are sealed in, ground hornbill females are not, and they occasionally leave the nest; it's possible the dominant male of the group contributes to incubation duties, but this is still unclear. Of the females in the group, only the dominant female lays eggs, and she may be fed by all the males and some of the younger birds. Despite the group effort, usually only a single chick is raised.

RECOGNITION Very large turkeylike bird, weighing up to 4kg. Mostly black with white primaries visible in flight. Very obvious red wattles around face, with blue throat patch in females. Length 90cm.

HABITAT Open woodlands and grasslands; also agricultural lands.

BEHAVIOUR Gregarious, living in pairs or small related groups. Terrestrial and diurnal. Spends the night in trees, clustered in family groups at the ends of branches.

BREEDING October to November. Lays one or two eggs in a hole in a tree, rock or riverbank.

FEEDING Invertebrates, frogs, tortoises, snakes, rodents and hares.

VOICE Booming territorial call, likened to a distant lion's grunting; performed in group chorus. Harsh squawk in alarm.

BIRDS

★ HOTSPOTS

- Kruger NP **(p60)**
- Chobe NP **(p120)**
- Mana Pools NP **(p150)**

RECOGNITION Metallic green back and breast, red belly (male); female duller.

HABITAT Forest and woodland.

BEHAVIOUR Defends territory against cuckoos, turacos and squirrels.

BREEDING Two or three eggs.

FEEDING Insects and small animals.

VOICE Series of double-hoots.

★ HOT SPOTS

- Ndumo GR **(p91)**
- Lower Zambezi NP **(p184)**

NARINA TROGON

Trogons are a group of colourful, even spectacular, birds vaguely related to kingfishers. Though not uncommon and quite large (about 30cm), narina trogons can be difficult to spot. Almost entirely arboreal, they often perch for long periods with their intense green coloration blending in with the foliage – their kingfisher-like 'sit-and-wait' hunting strategy. If you see one, it's worth watching: sitting hunched and motionless, long tail hanging vertical, the trogon slowly turns its large head as its large eyes watch for movement among the foliage. Seen side on, its stout, wide bill gives the bird a 'smiling' appearance, but a bristled fringe makes the bill an effective insect scoop. Short, rounded wings allow great manoeuvrability among the foliage, and when prey is spotted, trogons become galvanised, darting after insects with acrobatic twists and turns before returning to their perch.

The best way to locate a trogon is by its call (something males often do just before or after rain). Although they can be ventriloqual, males usually call from a conspicuous branch up to 20m above the ground. 'Narina' is a Hottentot word meaning flower.

RECOGNITION Cinnamon with black-and-white wing bars and black tail.

HABITAT Wooded savanna and cultivation.

BEHAVIOUR Pairs territorial.

BREEDING Four to six eggs.

FEEDING Invertebrates and small reptiles.

VOICE Soft hoo-poo-poo.

★ HOTSPOTS

- Waterberg Plateau Park **(p113)**
- Gonarezhou NP **(p146)**
- iSimangaliso WP **(p80)**
- Liwonde NP **(p168)**

HOOPOE

So unique that its image is unmistakable on ancient Egyptian tombs, the hoopoe's name comes from its call; even its scientific name *Upupa epops* evokes the soft *hoo-poo-poo*, which can be heard from several hundred metres away. Their most unusual feature – a large, floppy crest usually held flat along the crown – is held erect when the bird is alarmed. Normally they are ground feeders and often first noticed in flight – a butterfly-like, undulating flap-and-glide showcasing the contrasting black-and-white pattern of their broad wings and banded rump. When feeding, hoopoes walk jerkily on rather short legs (showing an ancestry shared with kingfishers), jabbing at loose soil with their bill or digging vigorously enough to make sods fly. Large prey items may be beaten against a hard surface, another kingfisher trait. When a predator passes overhead, the hoopoe flattens itself against the ground with wings spread, tips almost touching, tail fanned and bill pointing straight up; the pattern on its wings and back makes it almost invisible, especially against rocky ground. Groups of hoopoes sometimes roost one to a tree in copses, using the same perches for weeks on end.

BIRDS

WOODPECKERS

The resonant drumming of woodpeckers is a familiar sound throughout most of the world. Wood is the key to woodpecker ecology – they even drink from small puddles in tree forks – but although some species hammer vigorously to dig out grubs (and all 'drum' to advertise their territories), others pry off flaking bark, glean insects from foliage or extract ants from crevices with a long, barbed tongue. The 10 woodpecker species in Southern Africa exploit many woodland niches (several species can often be found in close proximity), but only one, the olive woodpecker, inhabits

evergreen forests in the region. Wherever they occur, woodpeckers play a pivotal role in wooded ecosystems: not only do other small animals pick over the bark they have removed, woodpeckers are among the only animals that actually create cavities in living wood, and their hole construction benefits many species of bird, mammal, reptile and even insect.

★ HOT SPOTS

- Liwonde NP (p168)
- Tsitsikamma NP (p95)
- Moremi GR (p132)

GREATER HONEYGUIDE

It's not much to look at (and this is the gem among the 14 species), but the greater honeyguide is an amazing bird. Firstly, although its standard fare is insects, it also eats beeswax, which it digests with special stomach bacteria. Secondly, it lays its eggs in other birds' nests. When laying, the female greater honeyguide sometimes punctures or removes the eggs of the host; if she doesn't, her chick has a hooked bill with which it kills its foster siblings (or pushes them out of the nest), so it is raised alone. And finally, and perhaps most astonishingly, greater honeyguides lead people (and possibly also honey badgers) to beehives so they'll break them open.

Conspicuous when 'guiding', it moves from tree to tree with a fluttering flight and a loud, continuous chattering, flicking its white outer tail feathers, and stopping to watch the progress of its follower. After the hive is opened and the honey removed, it feeds on the wax, larvae and eggs – any bee stings are resisted by its thick skin. Greater honeyguides also obtain beeswax without a helper at abandoned hives – if the hive has already been broken – where they become pugnaciously territorial.

RECOGNITION Grey-brown with white ear patch, whitish underparts and black throat. Stubby pink bill, 19cm long.

HABITAT Open woodlands.

BEHAVIOUR Solitary. Perches for hours. Harasses drongos.

BREEDING Lays one white egg.

FEEDING Insects, beeswax, bee larvae and eggs.

VOICE Continuous *bur-witt*.

★ HOTSPOTS

- Makgadikgadi Pans & Nxai Pan NPs (p128)
- Kruger NP (p60)
- Moremi GR (p132)

BIRDS

LARKS

Like many other grassland birds, most of Southern Africa's 23 species of lark are cryptically coloured, their muted upper-parts in shades of brown, tawny and buff often echoing the dominant soil colour wherever they dwell. Superficially, many species resemble pipits, although they are now thought not to be closely related.

Larks are essentially ground dwellers: they feed in open savannas and grass-lands, where they are often encountered along vehicle tracks, and their nests are always well hidden in grass tussocks. Larks have also successfully invaded the rocky deserts of the South West arid zone, and many of these are Southern African endemics.

Larks have strong legs and feet – some species with a long hind claw that facilitates walking over grass tussocks – and their strong, hard bill is adapted to a diet containing a high percentage of seeds. Larks advertise their territories with long display flights that often in-volve complicated and beautiful song sequences.

✦ HOT SPOTS

- Namib-Naukluft Park **(p104)**
- Kgalagadi Transfrontier Park **(p68)**
- Karoo NP **(p84)**

SWALLOWS & MARTINS

Swallows and martins are small, active birds. Their supremely aerial lifestyle has led to a streamlined body with long, nar-row wings for powerful, sustained flight. A short tail adds manoeuvrability, and is taken to extremes by the most agile spe-cies, whose distinctive forked tails with long streamers have lent their names to entirely unrelated butterflies. All feed exclusively on the wing, and tend to be gregarious in flight. Many flash with iridescence, and have contrasting pale underparts or reddish markings on their head and throat. The familiar and cos-mopolitan European swallow is just one of 24 resident and migratory species, in-cluding various martins and saw-wings, that occur in Southern Africa. Swallows and martins sometimes nest in colonies, most building a cup-shaped nest of mud pellets gathered waterside or at drying puddles. Their readiness to attach nests to eaves is well known; a few nest in hole or in cavities.

✦ HOT SPOTS

- Maloti-Drakensberg Transfrontier Area **(p89)**
- Karoo NP **(p84)**
- Moremi GR **(p132)**
- Nyika NP **(p170)**

BIRDS

FORK-TAILED DRONGO

The ubiquitous fork-tailed drongo is an all-black, slightly iridescent bird that can be quite unafraid of people. (The similar square-tailed drongo is found on Southern Africa's eastern coast). They may sit still for long spells, usually conspicuous on a horizontal branch or exposed limb. They fearlessly pursue flying predators such as hawks and crows, sometimes in pairs, and attack with pecks or buffeting. But drongos (the name predates the pejorative Australian slang) are rather voracious predators themselves. They take mainly insects but sometimes rob other birds of their catch, and may even take nestlings. Nonetheless, other small birds readily nest in the same tree as drongos, perhaps comforted by their pugnaciousness towards other predators. Typically, both drongo species chase likely prey from their perch, snatching it in flight or pursuing it to the ground to dispatch or dismember it. Fork-tailed drongos also follow bands of dwarf mongooses, and seize prey disturbed by the mongooses (as do some species of hornbill). They're rather tuneless singers, but enthusiastic: their loud, metallic notes can continue through the day and into the night.

RECOGNITION Black with metallic blue sheen. Forked 'fish tail'. Red eye.

HABITAT Drier, open, grassy areas, and forest edges.

BEHAVIOUR Catches small animals fleeing grassfires.

BREEDING Three eggs.

FEEDING Chiefly insects.

VOICE Metallic 'twanging'.

★ HOT SPOTS

- South Luangwa NP (p178)
- Hwange NP (p142)
- Pilanesberg NP (p72)
- Ndumo GR (p91)

BLACK-HEADED ORIOLE

Usually heard before seen, orioles are medium-sized, rather starling-like birds that live almost their whole lives in woodland and forest canopies. Unlike most starlings, they have no iridescence, but the four species seen in Southern Africa are mainly golden yellow, suffused with olive or with contrasting black on wings and tail. Locate the source of their liquid, fluting calls and you'll see a strongly pointed, bright-red bill and bold, red eyes.

The region's most common oriole species, black-headed orioles live in woodland and wooded savanna; they're also tolerant of human activity, and readily colonise parks, gardens and exotic-tree plantations. Orioles rarely descend to the ground; they fly with deep undulations, sweeping up to a perch like a woodpecker. Watch for them plunge-bathing by dropping into a puddle or pool; during rain, they tip forward on branches with wings outspread.

Generally solitary outside the breeding season, orioles sometimes join mixed feeding flocks. They feed mainly in the canopy, targeting fruiting trees and aloes for the nectar and pollen. They also take insects, either in the treetops or by sweeping close to the ground.

RECOGNITION Mostly yellow with distinctive black head. Length 25cm.

HABITAT Woodlands and forest.

BEHAVIOUR Usually alone or in pairs; often seen flying between thickets.

BREEDING Two or three eggs.

FEEDING Fruit, insects, nectar and pollen.

VOICE Loud bubbling whistle.

★ HOTSPOTS

- Kruger NP (p60)
- Hwange NP (p142)
- Moremi GR (p132)
- Ithala GR (p82)

BIRDS

BABBLERS & ILLADOPSES

RICHARD I'ANSON // LONELY PLANET IMAGES

Throughout their range in Africa and Asia, the large and varied group of birds that includes babblers, illadopses and chatterers are renowned skulkers of forest undergrowth. Fortunately, in Southern Africa, a few species are quite easy to see. Most are thrush-sized birds (20cm to 23cm in length) with strong legs and feet, and they typically forage on the ground, scuffling among the leaf litter for insects and other small animals. The bush blackcap (a South African endemic), once grouped with the bulbuls, is the only non-insectivorous member of the family – it feeds on fruit and berries.

Southern African babblers are mostly not brightly coloured, although some are boldly marked; most are conspicuous by their highly gregarious nature and most are very vocal. The four species of illadopses in the region are real forest skulkers that can pose a challenge to the most ardent birdwatcher.

✤ HOT SPOTS

- Etosha NP (p100)
- Nyika NP (p170)
- Kaudom GR (p111)
- Maloti-Drakensberg Transfrontier Area (p89)

BULBULS

This group of birds is divided among those that are easily discriminated and impossible to miss, and a suite of very similar species that are very difficult to see. Wherever you go in Southern Africa, you'll encounter the three dark-headed bulbul species, but, with largely exclusive distributions, you're only likely to see a single species at any one site. All have smoky grey plumage with black heads and bright yellow vents; you can tell them apart from the eye wattle: white in the Cape bulbul, red in red-eyed and missing in the black-eyed.

The rest of this family (also called greenbuls or brownbuls for their mostly muted colouration) are mostly forest and woodland dwellers. Although their calls are hard to miss, they are particularly elusive. All of them remain under the cover of dense foliage, foraging for fruit, berries, insects and sometimes snails. The exception to the rule, the large yellow-bellied bulbul, often ventures into more open country, foraging in groups.

✤ HOT SPOTS

- Chobe NP (p120)
- iSimangaliso Wetland Park (p80)
- Nyika NP (p170)
- Table Mountain NP (p95)

BIRDS

THRUSHES, CHATS & RELATIVES

BUSH CHORISTERS Apart from the thrushes – famous as songbirds around the world – this large and varied family includes the boldly marked wheatears, which in Africa include both resident and migratory species; a few specialists of cliffs and rocky country (such as the friendly familiar chat and the short-toed rock thrush); and the forest-dwelling alethes, akalats and ground thrushes, which forage among leaf litter for insects, sometimes flushed by columns of driver ants. If the diversity weren't enough, confusion can arise because widely distributed species can go by different names in different countries. For example, Heuglin's robin is also known as the white-browed robin-chat north of the Zambezi River. At least one species is found in nearly every habitat, and several may live in close proximity.

It's hard to generalise about the 56 Southern African members of this enormous family, but all are usually solitary, small- to medium-sized birds with comparatively long legs and a shortish bill; other features, such as body shape, tail length and coloration vary considerably. But among the many variables one feature stands out in a few species at least: vocal ability. Tuneful examples include Heuglin's robin – a common garden bird with a fine repertoire of musical whistling, and a tendency to mimic other birds and frogs – and the widespread

KURRICANE THRUSH

ground scraper thrush, more social than many species and inclined to early-morning group choruses.

The southern olive thrush will probably be the first member of the family you encounter: it has adapted well to human habitation and forages while hopping across lawns. Desert lovers will almost certainly encounter the tractrac chat – a confiding bird at picnic areas throughout the Namib Desert – and possibly also the Karoo chat, another arid-zone species. The drably coloured southern ant-eating chat is a conspicuous species of open country, where it digs nest tunnels in termite mounds (on which it frequently perches) and abandoned aardvark burrows. Wheatears also inhabit open country and migrant species can be abundant en route to their northern breeding grounds.

BIRDS

⚡ HOTSPOTS

- Namib-Naukluft Park (p104) Many arid-zone endemics including tractrac, Karoo and Herero chats and short-toed rock thrushes
- Bangweulu Swamps (p186) Many species including northern wheatears, miombo bearded scrub robins, ground scraper thrushes and Bocage's akalat
- Pilanesberg NP (p72) A mix of arid and bush species, including Kalahari and African white-throated robins, Cape rock thrushes and buff-streaked chats

WAGTAILS, PIPITS & LONGCLAWS

PIED WAGTAIL

GRASSLAND TAIL-PUMPERS
Whether running along safari-lodge rooftops, flitting along streams or snapping up flies from under the hooves of large animals, Southern Africa's six wagtail species are distinctive and common. The African pied wagtail is one of the most easily recognised, and is readily seen foraging in flowerbeds and on lawns, snatching insects off the ground or after a chase. All wagtails pump their tail up and down when standing still (something they don't do very often), and walk, rather than hop, with an exaggerated back-and-forth head movement.

At first sight, pipits bear little resemblance to wagtails, but they are closely related: they too forage on the ground and snap up insects, and typi-cally pump their tail when they stand still. But while many wagtails are boldly marked, most pipits are grassland dwellers, and coloured accordingly in subdued shades of brown and buff. The widespread grassveld pipit is commonly seen running down tracks ahead of a vehicle, pausing often before scooting off again. Several pipits are migratory, and sometimes associate with wagtails outside the breeding season at communal roosts, gathering at dusk in tall trees and reed beds. Many pipits and larks look superficially similar, but they belong to different families, and are generally not regarded as close relatives.

The five species of longclaw (which at 19cm to 21cm in length are the 'giants' of the wagtail, pipit and longclaw family) share the typical pipits' streaky upperparts, but most have colourful underparts with a black 'necklace'. Longclaws – so-called because their hind claw is extremely long, enabling them to walk over grass tussocks – tend to stand more upright than pipits, have longer legs and don't pump their tails. Both pipits and longclaws avoid long grass; longclaws are usually not difficult to spot, and often indulge in melodious territorial songs in flight or from an exposed tussock. Both groups build a grass nest on the ground during and after the rains, when growing grass affords more concealment for nests and young.

HOTSPOTS

- Ndumo GR **(p91)** Three longclaw species (orange-throated, yellow-throated and pink-throated) plus numerous pipits and wagtails
- Liwonde NP **(p168)** Five wagtail species (including grey), yellow-throated longclaws and five pipit species
- Maloti-Drakensberg Transfrontier Area **(p89)** Many pipits including rock, mountain and yellow-breasted; longtailed wagtails and orange-throated longclaws
- Kafue NP **(p182)** Fuelleborn's and pink-throated longclaws plus short-tailed, tree and bushveld pipits

BIRDS

FLYCATCHERS

INSECT EATERS Three families of birds (the 'true' flycatchers, monarch flycatchers, and a family of 'African flycatchers' that includes the batises and wattle-eyes) are broadly lumped as flycatchers, largely as a result of similarities in their foraging behaviour. All are small, sometimes hyperactive birds that catch insects in a variety of ways. Gleaning insects from foliage is a feeding technique common to most, but aerial pursuits launched from a perch are more characteristic of some groups. These insect-catching sallies are also used by other birds, such as drongos and some kingfishers, and are known as 'flycatching' (appropriately enough) regardless of the species. Flycatching is entertaining to watch, and can involve sudden turns and corkscrew movements during which the bill is sometimes heard snapping shut.

One or more flycatchers can be seen in most habitats, and they can be quite tolerant of people. Wattle-eyes are small flycatchers of forest undergrowth, reaching their greatest diversity in equatorial forests and represented in Southern Africa by a single species, the wattle-eyed flycatcher (or black-throated wattle-eye). Wattle-eyes are replaced in drier habitat by batises – small, shrike-like birds boldly marked in grey, black and white – which hunt in pairs or small family groups. Wattle-eyes and batises both 'snap' their wings in flight but are readily distinguished: only wattle-eyes have a coloured fleshy wattle

PARADISE FLYCATCHER

surrounding the eye.

The so-called monarch flycatchers are larger and pugnacious, and some are colourful. They are renowned for their crests and long tails, but without a doubt the most spectacular species is the common, easily recognisable paradise flycatcher. The male's long tail streamers can measure more than twice his body length, and are shown off to perfection in flight. Like many flycatchers, monarchs build a neat, cup-shaped nest decorated with lichen and moss, and bound with spiders' webs. These may be built quite low to the ground, frequently in lodge verandas.

The 'true' flycatchers are rather nondescript grey and brown birds of forest edges, some of which are Eurasian migrants, and an identification challenge to the dedicated birder.

BIRDS

✦ HOTSPOTS

- Nyika NP (p170) Many species including white-tailed, paradise, blue-mantled and wattle-eyed flycatchers
- Mamili NP (p112) Paradise flycatchers (September to March); fan-tailed and Marico flycatchers year-round
- Lower Zambezi NP (p184) Good for Livingstone's and collared flycatchers
- Liwonde NP (p168) Numerous species including Cape batises, and Vanga and wattle-eyed flycatchers

SHRIKES, BUSH SHRIKES & HELMET SHRIKES

FISCAL SHRIKE

LIVING LARDERS With such an abundance of thorns across the savanna, it's not surprising that something has put them to use. Thus lizards, beetles, crickets, small birds and rodents may sometimes be seen impaled on acacia spines (and, since European occupation, barbed wire). This is the work of shrikes, predatory birds boldly marked in black, white, greys and browns.

True shrikes are birds of open country that hunt by waiting on a perch, and dropping onto their victim. Slender and upright, they have short legs, strong feet and hooked claws; at the business end, their large head supports a heavy, thick bill with an obvious hook at the tip. Several species are resident and common; others are migrants, and when passing through can be abundant one week and gone the next.

Glamorous it ain't, but their hunting is effective: small vertebrates are pinned down and killed by repeated strikes to the back of the head before impaling, while insects are usually pinned alive. Spikes steady prey for eating, but immediate needs catered for, shrikes also store food for later – useful on a cool day when insects are few. It's also believed that these larders attract females, who presumably are impressed by the male's hunting skills.

The many species of bush shrike run the gamut of colours from subdued browns and greys to radiant gold and scarlet contrasting with black (the bokmakierie). Most are skulking inhabitants of dense foliage and are difficult to see. Rather than sitting and waiting, they are active hunters and don't impale their prey on spikes. Helmet shrikes are yet another family of shrikes that takes advantage of the abundant insect prey (although some ornithologists don't regard 'true' shrikes, bush shrikes and helmet shrikes to be closely related). Helmet shrikes travel in parties of up to 20 birds (often containing mixed species) searching trunks, branches and leaves for prey.

BIRDS

⭐ HOTSPOTS

- Chobe NP (p120) Good for lesser grey and red-backed shrikes (both October to April), Souza's shrikes and swamp boubous
- Ndumo GR (p91) Chestnut-fronted helmet shrikes, four-coloured and olive bush shrikes
- Addo Elephant NP (p76) Southern boubous, southern tchagras, puffbacks and bokmakieries
- South Luangwa NP (p178) Füelleborn's black and tropical boubous, black-fronted bush shrikes (three colour phases), marsh tchagras and Souza's shrikes

OXPECKERS

The two species of oxpecker are members of the starling family specialised to eat parasites, such as ticks and lice, clinging to the skin of large animals. Red-billed oxpeckers have yellow eye-wattles and red bills; yellow-billed oxpeckers have no eye-wattles, and the base of their bill is yellow with a red tip. Both have stiff tail feathers and particularly sharp claws for clambering up and down their hosts. Flocks of one or both species can usually be seen on or near herds of antelopes and many other herbivores, large and small, including livestock. At first glance, the relationship seems rosy – the oxpeckers perform a service by removing parasites – but

elephants are particularly intolerant of these birds, and pastoralists regard them as a nuisance. Both species certainly eat a significant quantity of parasites (100 adult ticks per day, according to one estimate), but they also keep wounds open to feed on blood, pus and any parasites attracted to the gore – injured animals are particularly susceptible, and often lack the strength to chase the birds off. Oxpeckers also rip mouthfuls of hair from mammals to line their nests.

🔥 HOT SPOTS

- Moremi GR (p132)
- Kaudom GR (p111)
- Kafue NP (p182)
- South Luangwa NP (p178)

PIED CROW

Their large size, black colour and haunting calls see crows and ravens known around the world as harbingers of death (a group of crows is called a 'murder'). Several species commonly associate with humans, and their apparent liking for battlefields has instilled a crow mythology in many cultures. Crows mainly eat small animals, but also carrion when available, and often arrive at a carcass even before vultures and kites. Like many members of the family, pied crows are bold and mischievous, and can be enormously entertaining to observe. They strut around carcasses, harassing birds of prey, even tugging at the tail feathers of much larger vultures. A consummate opportunist, they readily take food scraps discarded by people and are now common scavengers in many settlements, where hundreds may gather at rubbish dumps. In the region they are now found only around people; it is rare to see them in wilderness areas. Many sightings occur along roadsides as they are quick to find roadkill; with larger scavengers such as vultures and eagles mostly gone from inhabited areas, crows usually have the spoils to themselves. In mountainous regions, they give way to the larger white-necked raven, distinguished by its white-tipped bill.

RECOGNITION Glossy black; white saddle and belly.

HABITAT Grassland, cultivation, savanna and towns.

BEHAVIOUR In pairs and small flocks; roosts communally.

BREEDING Four to five eggs.

FEEDING Carrion, small animals, fruit and grain.

VOICE Harsh *aaahnk;* croaks.

BIRDS

🔥 HOTSPOTS

- Virtually any town or village

CAPE SUGARBIRD

RECOGNITION Streaky brown upperparts with rusty breast and white belly. White throat and white stripe below the eye. Very long tail. Bill, legs and feet black. Length up to 44cm.

HABITAT Fynbos in the southwest Cape. Also gardens.

BEHAVIOUR Very active, flying rapidly between protea bushes and then hovering or scrambling over them to feed. Males have a very distinctive territorial display. Solitary, in pairs or groups.

BREEDING April to July. Nest is an untidy cup made with twigs, grass and pine needles, lined with protea 'down'. Lays two eggs (sometimes 1).

FEEDING Nectar, mainly of *Protea* species. Also insects and spiders.

VOICE Male has a grating chirp interspersed with metallic notes. Alarm call like a rusty hinge.

BIRDS

OVERSIZED HUMMINGBIRDS Once considered relatives of Australian honeyeaters, the sugarbirds are a uniquely African group now thought to be distantly related to starlings. There are only two species – both of them Southern African endemics. Gurney's sugarbird has the wider distribution, existing in a string of mountainous pockets beginning in the southern Drakensberg Range and then running north into Zimbabwe's eastern highlands. The other species, the Cape sugarbird, only exists in the southwest Cape's relict fynbos patches, but despite a more limited range, it's a far more conspicuous bird. In the winter when they breed, the males call incessantly, a jangling *churr* interspersed with various metallic notes. Combined with their long tail feathers and territorial display – hovering above a protea bush, jerking his body, beating his wings and flapping his tail – they are hard to miss.

Cape sugarbirds are usually seen alone or in pairs when breeding, but over summer they can be more sociable and form groups numbering up to 12. Despite this, summer actually presents a greater viewing challenge. They rely mainly on the nectar of Cape protea flowers: these all die by midsummer, forcing sugarbirds to disperse to higher altitudes where they can find alternate foods such as aloe nectar. Gardens are also attractive to them, especially where introduced plants such as eucalypts are flowering, and the calling of sugarbird groups is a common feature of Cape Town summers.

Sugarbirds feed similarly to sunbirds, with whom they are often seen feeding on the same bush – though not always amicably. Sugarbirds constantly chase the much smaller sunbirds off 'their' bush, proprietary behaviour that often extends to other sugarbirds. Like an oversized hummingbird, sugarbirds feed by hovering or perching on flowers, and then thrust into the inflorescences with their long beak for nectar. Spiders and insects are also taken this way, and they also hawk insects in flight. Sugarbirds are fast flyers, and the long tail streaming out behind in flight is a giveaway for identification.

★ **HOTSPOTS**

- De Hoop NR (**p88**)
- Table Mountain NP (**p95**)

SUNBIRDS

IRIDESCENT JEWELS They may not be the biggest, but sunbirds are certainly among the most colourful of Africa's birds. They are invariably compared to the hummingbirds (not found in Africa), but the similarity is superficial and they are not closely related. The basic sunbird body plan is small (as small as 8cm, but ranging up to 15cm in some species) with a sharp, down-curved bill. Males of nearly all species have patches of iridescence that can cover most of the body, or be restricted to swatches on the throat, rump or head. Unlike 'normal' feathers, in which colour is caused by pigmentation, iridescence is caused by a modified feather structure that creates a reflective surface. But the rainbow-coloured result comes at the cost of a weakened structure, which means that flight feathers are not iridescent, and are generally drab. Iridescent feathers change colour according to the angle of the viewer. For the wearer, this may have a role in bluff and territorial display: when a male that appears dull side-on suddenly turns to face a rival, the rival is suddenly confronted by an intimidating burst of colour.

The combinations are dazzling, and many species look very similar, providing the type of enticing identification problems so valued by birdwatchers. And it gets harder with females and immature males – these generally have drab plumage with little iridescence. Still, identification isn't everything and

YELLOW-BELLIED SUNBIRD

sunbirds are worth watching as they flit about restlessly – males pugnaciously defend territories against other sunbirds.

Although all sunbirds eat at least some insects, caught in flight or while perched, the main food source for most is nectar sipped with a specialised tongue while beak-deep in a flower, or after the base of the bloom has been pierced with the sharp bill. They lean into flowers while perched next to them, or feed while hanging upside down. Usually solitary or in pairs, larger groups may congregate during seasonal flowerings of favoured plants, such as aloes and mistletoe. Nesting in all species conforms to a pattern: a domed nest woven of grass and fibres of vegetation, usually suspended by several tendrils or fibres from a branch or twig (variations include a 'porch' over the entrance). Most species lay only one or two eggs; both parents raise the young.

BIRDS

★ HOTSPOTS

- Nyika NP (p170) Good for montane and forest species including bronze, miombo double-collared, yellow-bellied and olive sunbirds
- Kasanka NP (p187) Up to 14 species, including green-headed, coppery and Shelley's sunbirds
- Mkhuze GR (p86) Forest/sandforest species such as Neergaard's, purple-banded, olive and grey sunbirds

SPARROWS, WEAVERS, BISHOPS & WIDOWS

EAGER WEAVERS A few finches native to Southern Africa are recognisable as sparrows, even chirping and habitually living near people like their kin across much of the world. But their close relatives have evolved into an extraordinary variety, such as weavers, brightly coloured bishops and widows with elaborate tail plumes. The diversity of these groups is staggering – 141 species worldwide, 43 of which can be spotted in Southern Africa. One, the red-billed quelea, is one of the most abundant birds on the planet, at times so numerous that flocks number in the millions and break branches with their weight when they land.

MALE RED BISHOP

True weavers are decked out mainly in yellow with black, rufous, orange or brown highlights. Confusing enough when nesting, their identification is a birdwatcher's nightmare outside of the breeding season, when many of the colourful males moult into a drab, sparrowlike plumage, and form mixed flocks with females and other species. Still, they are energetic builders of intricate and distinctive woven nests. The majority nest socially, and weaver colonies can become virtual cities of grass apartments smothering entire trees – they can be seen in virtually any town or village, as well as in the wilds, where palms and spreading acacias might be draped with hundreds of nests.

Each weaver species has its own trademark architecture, and the owners of many nests can be identified by the nest's shape alone. Some nests hang from intertwined stems like a pendulum; others are onion-shaped or have a long, narrow entrance like an upside-down flask; some are neat balls holding two papyrus stems together; and red-billed buffalo weavers build large, untidy accumulations of grass with multiple entrances in which several pairs live and roost. Weaver colonies are noisy and constantly busy: birds coming and going with nest material, males courting females, and rivals stealing nest material.

Unlike their savanna counterparts, some forest weavers are solitary or feed in pairs, and don't build colonial nests; they frequently associate with 'bird parties', feeding flocks composed of several unrelated species moving through the forest. Another outstanding species is the cuckoo finch, which lays its eggs in

LESSER MASKED WEAVER

the nests of warblers such as cisticolas.

Outside the breeding season, male bishops and widows are streaked and drab like many other weavers, and sometimes form large, nomadic flocks. But when courting is in full swing, they are eye-catching and colourful birds, moulting into black plumage with flashes of orange, yellow or red; male widows also grow elaborate plumes – those of the long-tailed widow can be three times as long as its body.

Males of most species of bishop and weaver are polygamous, mating with several females if their courtship per-

formances are suitably impressive, and building a nest for each. Male bishops perch conspicuously on stems at regular intervals across swathes of rank grasslands, and perform display flights with feathers fluffed out (some becoming almost spherical in the process). Male widows stake out territories where they display, the most spectacular being the long-tailed widows, which fly slowly over their patch, the down-turned tail perhaps signalling to rivals that the area is occupied.

CUCKOOS UP THE SPOUT

For a weaver, success depends on building a nest secure enough to raise a brood and withstand the attentions of predators. And so successful are many at building such nests that other birds, such as waxbills and pygmy falcons, sometimes find abandoned weavers' nests attractive enough to shelter or nest in themselves. Pygmy falcons are mainly insect hunters, and don't bother the weavers, but there's nothing much the weavers can do about a gymnogene (African harrier hawk) robbing a nest. These specialised raptors hang upside down from the nest, and insert a long, double-jointed leg to extract an egg or chick. And diederik cuckoos commonly parasitise lesser masked weavers, but the weavers are fighting back: certain populations build entrance spouts so tight that the cuckoos can't get into the nest, and have even been found wedged in so tightly they have died in the spout.

BIRDS

⭐ HOTSPOTS

- Etosha NP (p100) Chestnut weavers (January to March) and huge flocks of red-billed queleas at Namutoni and Halali Rest Camps
- Nyika NP (p170) Many species including fire-crowned bishops and forest weavers
- Ndumo GR (p91) Specials include thick-billed, yellow and forest weavers, and red-headed queleas
- Mountain Zebra NP (p90) Red bishops, Cape weavers, and very tame white-browed sparrow weavers

WAXBILLS

VIOLET-EARED WAXBILL

JEWELS IN THE UNDERGROWTH

'Finch' is a term that covers a multitude of forms, from chirpy sparrows to brilliant seedcrackers, and these mainly seed-eating birds are the most diverse bird group in Southern Africa (other finches include the weavers, whydahs and canaries). There's a lot of grass out on the savanna, and a host of finches has evolved ready to pounce on heads of ripe seeds or slide down stalks to pick them off the ground. Many species have a red, waxy-looking bill, and the term 'waxbill' is commonly used to cover some 33 small, mainly colourful species with names such as twinspots, firefinches, crimsonwings, cordon-bleus and mannikins. Many are also popular caged birds and known by other names in captivity (the pet trade has seriously depleted several waxbill species).

Look for waxbills near water, and on roadsides and the edge of savanna and fields, especially where grass is seeding. Many are common and some are confiding (such as the red-billed firefinch), often nesting near human habitation, while a number of brilliantly coloured species, including seedcrackers, crimsonwings and firefinches, inhabit undergrowth of the forest edge. Despite their bright colours, waxbills can easily be overlooked: for example, when flushed, quail finches fly a short distance, then drop vertically to the ground and run like quail; and all twinspot species invariably take refuge in dense thickets when disturbed. Further confounding a good sighting, waxbill calls are often just high-pitched, sibilant whispers that can be mistaken for those of insects; for instance, the locust finch measures only 9cm in length, and looks like a large grasshopper flitting between seed heads. Most waxbills build loose, untidy domed nests of grass. Some simply add material to the gaps under hamerkop or secretary bird nests; others, such as some mannikin species, use old weaver nests; and cordon-bleus and bronze mannikins sometimes build near hornet nests. Chicks have bright spots, usually hardened callosities, on their gape and inside their mouth; these invoke an irresistible feeding response in parents in the darkness of the nest chamber – a feature mimicked by whydah chicks that parasitise waxbill nests.

HOTSPOTS

- Matusadona NP (p154) Many species including red-backed mannikins, red-throated twinspots and golden-backed pytilias
- Matobo NP (p160) Swee, violet-eared and black-cheeked waxbills; and quail and cut-throat finches
- Mkhuze GR (p86) Sixteen species, including green and pink-throated twinspots
- Kafue NP (p182) Many species including fawn-breasted waxbills, black-chinned quail finches and locust finches

CANARIES & SEEDEATERS

If you've ever wondered where those caged songsters come from, Southern Africa has 19 species, some of which go under the name of seedeaters, and one, the oriole finch, looks like a miniature oriole, complete with black head and red bill. Canaries are yet another part of the great assembly of finches, closely related to goldfinches, and quite common in most bush habitats. The streaky seedeater is common near settlements, and a few other species share its reputation as something of a pest. Look at the edge of crops and gardens for canaries, and seedeaters associating in small groups with other canary species and

with other finches. Wild canaries bear little resemblance to their rather pallid captive relatives, although a few are also prodigious songsters – male yellow-eyed canaries gather to sing in treetops and are also caught for the pet trade. Most canaries build cup-shaped nests of grass in trees and bushes, sometimes in loose colonies.

★ HOT SPOTS

- Nyika NP (p170)
- Kasanka NP (p187)

PIN-TAILED WHYDAH

You'll often see birds perched along roadsides, and male pin-tailed whydahs quickly become a familiar sight. These gregarious birds normally travel in small flocks numbering 20 to 30 birds. Males are polygamous; during breeding season, flocks typically comprise one breeding male for every five or six females and nonbreeding males. Outside the breeding season pin-tailed whydahs are conspicuous while feeding: they jump backwards along the ground, scattering soil to expose fallen seeds.

The male attains colouration at the start of the long rains; afterwards he moults through motley stages to finally resemble the females and nonbreeding males. When in the mood, the male pin-tailed whydah is a sight worth seeing: he sings as he flies with gentle undulations around a perched female, his tail bouncing up and down; she responds by shivering her wings. Once the formalities are over, females lay their eggs in the nests of other birds (usually the common waxbill). The female whydah removes one of the host's eggs for each she lays, typically only one or two per nest, but occasionally lays in more than one nest. The parents then abandon their eggs to the unwitting hosts who raise the aliens alongside their own chicks.

RECOGNITION Breeding males black-and-white with long (20cm) tail streamers.

HABITAT Forest edge, savanna and cultivation.

BEHAVIOUR Males sing while perched conspicuously.

BREEDING Lays two eggs.

FEEDING Mostly seeds.

VOICE High-pitched *tseet tseet tsuweet.*

★ HOTSPOTS

- Pilanesberg NP (p72)
- Central Kalahari GR (p124)

BIRDS

OTHER CREATURES

With so many highly visible and world-famous mammals and birds to see, it's hardly surprising that Africa's small, reclusive and cryptic creatures often get overlooked. In fact, the majority of Africa's reptiles, amphibians, fish and invertebrates have never been systematically studied – even though these groups are undoubtedly more diverse than mammals and birds, and some are no less impressive. The showcase includes 6m-long pythons, which can swallow adult antelopes whole, leaping great white sharks, and the world's fastest snake. Less obvious, but everywhere you look – if you do it closely – are literally thousands of smaller creatures that offer an alternative and equally unique experience for the keen wildlife-watcher.

Reptiles are abundant and diverse in Southern Africa, from giant carnivores like the bank-basking Nile crocodile to bold, brightly coloured flat lizards and slow-moving, swivel-eyed chameleons. Snakes are no less varied but, to the relief of thousands, they are mostly retiring; a summer visit will probably notch up a sighting or two, but most encounters are brief and far from dangerous. Land tortoises are more likely to be seen – there are more here than anywhere else in the world. Their unhurried, herbivorous habits permit excellent viewing for those with a little patience. Leaving land, Southern Africa's aquatic life alone could fill many books, but we've included a few

of the more obvious attractions: Lake Malawi's kaleidoscopic cichlids and, more visible here than anywhere else on earth, the great white shark.

Most people would rather not know about some of the smallest animals of the African bush, particularly those that bite. But unpleasant though some are, everything from lions to safari ants plays a role in the ecosystem, and the invertebrates, in particular, provide many crucial 'services'. Dung beetles use animal droppings for both food and nurseries, and clean up thousands of tons of the stuff daily. Termites convert cellulose into protein, becoming prey for hundreds of different predators, and their

FLAP-NECKED CHAMELEON

mounds provide dwellings for everything from ant-eating chats to spotted hyenas. Bees, wasps, flies and ants pollinate plants, and predatory species reduce the numbers of those insects we'd rather not encounter: spiders snag mosquitoes and velvet ants parasitise flies and bees.

Of course, invertebrates are, collectively, more dangerous than any other animal group – more so than large and dangerous mammals, with which we have extremely rare but dramatic clashes. Many species are harmless on their own, but act as hosts for disease-producing microscopic creatures: *Anopheles* mosquitoes transmit the malaria-causing organism, and tsetse flies are carriers of sleeping sickness. Others can kill outright: thick-tailed scorpions carry lethal doses of venom, and black-button spiders can immobilise a child. Less lethal but ubiquitous, cattle and bont ticks siphon the blood of mammals, and a human makes as good a meal as an impala.

Having said this, Africa's small fry are no more dangerous than those anywhere else in the world, and with a bit of common sense, the hazardous species can be avoided or even enjoyed. Scorpions on their nocturnal hunts are the lions of the invertebrate world, and the varied predatory strategies of spiders are as sophisticated as anything the mammalian arena has to offer. Even the instinctive migrations of ticks to the tips of grass to catch a passing herbivore are awe-inspiring in their own way. Whatever your feeling for the invertebrates, they've been around for 500 million years, and will be here long after our kind has departed.

OTHER CREATURES

RECOGNITION Grey-brown to olive-green with bands of yellowish spots. Up to 2.1m.

HABITAT Savanna, waterways.

BEHAVIOUR Solitary. Males fight for territory.

BREEDING Lays 20 to 60 eggs.

FEEDING Insects, crabs, small vertebrates and carrion.

VOICE Hisses if approached.

★ HOT SPOTS

- Hwange NP (p142)
- Lower Zambezi NP (p184)
  Kruger NP (p60)
- Moremi GR (p132)

NILE MONITOR

Southern Africa's largest lizard, the Nile monitor (locally known as the water leguaan), is a solitary reptile typically seen ambling through the savanna or lounging on a branch overhanging water. Watch early in the day for Nile monitors catching some rays on an exposed rock, sandbank or tree stump. Basking warms them up for the hunt, but like most reptiles they have low energy requirements and can go for long spells without eating. Normal locomotion is a slow, meandering gait (a large one sometimes drags its belly along the ground), but Nile monitors are proficient swimmers, and readily take to water if threatened.

Any nook or crevice is investigated for a morsel, which includes insects, birds and small mammals such as rodents; eggs are a favourite, and monitors readily dig up unguarded crocodile eggs, and climb trees to rob birds' nests. That long forked tongue constantly flicking in and out is completely harmless; in fact, it helps detect prey by transferring scent to an organ in the roof of the mouth (called the Jacobson's organ). Adult monitors have few predators, although they are sometimes taken by pythons, crocodiles and large raptors such as martial eagles; they inflate themselves impressively, and hiss at mammalian predators, which mostly leave them alone.

NILE CROCODILE

RECOGNITION Powerful jaws and tail. Olive or dull grey.

HABITAT Freshwater.

BEHAVIOUR Basks. Hunts by ambush and pursuit.

BREEDING Lays 30 to 40 eggs which hatch after 90 days.

FEEDING Strictly carnivorous.

VOICE Young yelp when hatching.

★ HOTSPOTS

- North Luangwa NP (p181)
- Chobe NP (p120)
- iSimangaliso Wetland Park (p80)
- South Luangwa NP (p178)

Africa's largest reptile, the Nile crocodile reaches a length of up to 6m and weighs over 1000kg. Smaller crocs eat mainly frogs and fish, or snatch swimming birds from the surface; for a large one, virtually any animal is fair game, including antelopes and even adult lions. Adult crocs take many wildebeests and zebras crossing rivers on migration, and are responsible for hundreds of human deaths every year. Submerged with only eyes and nostrils above the surface, it can wait up to six hours to ambush prey; shine a torch over a swamp at night and the reflected eyeshine will show just how abundant 'flat dogs' (what South Africans call them) can be. When prey gets within striking distance, the croc lunges with incredible power and speed, propelled by its massive tail, and drags its victim underwater to drown it. Several may gather at one floating carcass, clamping teeth on the flesh and spinning to rip off chunks; swallowing takes place at the surface to prevent water entering the lungs. Adults have no predators, though hippos will nudge them off a sandbank and even bite one in two if it threatens a calf; territorial disputes between crocodiles can cause serious injuries. But for a young croc to reach maturity it must first dodge birds, fish, monitors and larger crocodiles.

SNAKES

STRANGLERS & SPITTERS Although they universally provoke extreme reactions, it is actually quite a rare event to see even one of Southern Africa's 130 species of snake. Most of them are extremely shy, and disappear at the approach of people. Although snakes are generally diurnal to take advantage of solar power, Africa's warm climate allows nocturnal foraging by some of the most impressive species including numerous cobras and Africa's largest snake, the African rock python. Occasionally topping 6m, it crushes prey as large as adult impalas by wrapping it in muscular coils; the lethal embrace prevents circulation, and death is actually caused by cardiac arrest rather than suffocation. All snakes are carnivorous, and 34 Southern African species use venom to disable their prey; 14 of those are on record for human deaths, but normal prey for all includes rodents, lizards, frogs, nestlings, eggs and other snakes. Cobras (such as the Cape cobra), mambas and boomslangs are roaming hunters that actively search for prey, and stalk it like a cat before executing a lightning-fast bite. Two species of spitting cobras, the rinkhals and the Mozambique spitting cobra (or m'fezi), can spray venom up to 4m, usually reserved for enemies rather than prey. Spitting cobras aim for the eyes of aggressors, but in the case of people, modern fashion sometimes thwarts their aim; they occasionally hit lanyard-suspended sunglasses on walkers' chests. Rather

HORNED ADDER

than actively seeking out quarry, adders and vipers are generally sit-and-wait predators that ambush their prey. The superbly camouflaged Gaboon viper of evergreen forests is armed with the largest fangs of any snake, up to 5cm, but is extremely docile and rarely bites people. They wait hidden in leaf litter on the forest floor for small mammals to wander into striking range. More commonly encountered and armed with only slightly shorter fangs, puff adders are active at dusk, and are often found slowly crossing roads on their way to a suitable hiding place, or drinking from roadside puddles; although they can survive without standing water, many snakes drink when water is available. In the South West arid zone, Peringuey's and horned adders rely on coastal fogs (as well as the body fluids of prey) for moisture and lay their ambush in sand.

⭐ **HOTSPOTS**

- Namib-Naukluft Park (p104) Excellent for desert endemics including horned and Peringuey's adders
- Kosi Bay NR (p94) Gaboon vipers and many others including green mambas, forest cobras, Mozambique spitting cobras and boomslangs
- North Luangwa NP (p181) Many species including large rock pythons, puff adders, black mambas and numerous cobras

OTHER CREATURES

TORTOISES & TERRAPINS

The easiest way to differentiate between tortoises and terrapins is by where you see them: tortoises live on land, and terrapins inhabit fresh water (and turtles are marine dwellers). However, this rule of thumb does not indicate any taxonomic relationship.

Land holds the real attractions for chelonian-watchers in Southern Africa. There are more land tortoise species here than anywhere else on earth, 13 in all; unusually among reptiles, all are largely herbivorous, feeding on flowers, grass, succulents and leaves. Some occasionally take snails, insects or carrion and the ubiquitous leopard (or mountain) tortoise also chews bones and hyenas' calcium-rich droppings for the minerals. Most terrapins are more predatory; the widely distributed marsh terrapin sometimes even ambushes doves and sandgrouse that come to drink.

★ HOT SPOTS

- Etosha NP **(p100)**
- Addo Elephant NP **(p76)**
- Mkhuze GR **(p86)**
- Moremi GR **(p132)**

LIZARDS

Southern Africa has over 250 lizard species, but they're usually difficult to see; a few habitats hold the best chances. Koppies (isolated rock outcrops) are probably the best, where brightly coloured agamas and super-abundant flat lizards hunt insect prey or hang around people for handouts. Both agamids and flat lizards are highly sexually dimorphic: the males are brilliantly coloured to attract potential mates and intimidate rivals. The camouflage champion is the chameleon. While remarkable, their colour-changing abilities are often exaggerated, mostly restricted to shades of green, grey and brown, and take a few minutes to perform. However, some males flush swiftly with vivid colours when a female is spied or another male intrudes into his territory. Otherwise, chameleons' resting colours invariably match the environment beautifully; spotlighting sometimes picks out the most widespread species, the flap-necked chameleon. Other nocturnal lizards, the geckos, are more easily seen and often inhabit huts and lodges.

★ HOT SPOTS

- Augrabies Falls NP **(p78)**
- Namib-Naukluft Park **(p104)**

GREAT WHITE SHARK

PERFECT PREDATORS People flock to Southern Africa
to see its many terrestrial predators, but for equally
spectacular views of super-predators in action, its coastal
waters are unrivalled. Here, the great white shark patrols
massive Cape fur-seal colonies and, with a regularity
seen nowhere else, launches 'predatory breaches' on
its prey. Initiating their attack from deep water where
they're difficult to spot, the sharks accelerate vertically
towards seals on the surface, hitting – or missing – their
target with such explosive force that they erupt from the
water several metres into the air. At the premier site for
predatory breaching, Seal Island, great whites average a
kill in 48% of attempts, but some particularly proficient
individuals have a success rate of 80%. Young fur-seals
make up the bulk of kills; hefty quotas of body fat,
inexperience and helplessness (adult seals, in contrast,
can inflict damaging bites) combine to make them a far
superior target to adult seals.

Despite the dramatic behaviour, great whites in the region actually prefer fish, and their abundance in an area
depends on the movements of species such as yellowtail.
During the summer when yellowtails are plentiful, the
sharks largely ignore seals, and track the migratory fish
from east to west along the South African coast. Young
sharks have teeth and jaws more suited to a fish diet,
and seals probably only form an important part of their
diet once the sharks are mature. The dispersal of the
fish shoals in winter coincides with the first exploratory
swims of young seals (May to June), the best time to view
predatory breaching.

Great white sharks typically forage at the surface,
which explains why our knowledge is restricted largely
to their feeding behaviour. They are thought to live
between 30 and 40 years, and mature at around 12 to
15 years (females) and nine to 10 for males. Mating has
never been observed, and we still don't know where they
go to do it, but like many sharks, the male has prominent twin claspers used to flush sperm into the female;
if you're fortunate enough to see a shark breach (when
you're on a boat, not a surfboard…), it's the easiest way
to differentiate the sexes.

RECOGNITION Massive.
Swollen torpedo shape. Gun-
metal grey upperparts, white
below. Top size controversial
but males at least 6.4m and
2500kg (females larger).

HABITAT Tropical and temper-
ate coastal waters worldwide.
In the region, most visible off
South Africa's Cape coast.

BEHAVIOUR Mostly hunts
in coastal waters but can be
found hundreds of kilometres
from shore. Seminomadic,
tracking movements of fish
schools, but probably does
not make long-distance
migrations. Largely solitary,
sometimes congregating at
rich feeding grounds where
interactions seem largely
peaceful; they feed amicably
together on large carcasses.

BREEDING Largely un-
known. Females have litters
of seven to nine 'pups',
born swimming freely and
around 1.2, to 1.5m long.

FEEDING Carnivorous;
mostly fish, seals and sea
lions. Also carrion such
as whale carcasses.

VOICE None.

OTHER CREATURES

PLANNING YOUR SAFARI
EVERYTHING YOU NEED TO KNOW TO GET STARTED

SAFARI HAS TO BE ONE OF THE MOST EVOCATIVE words ever to infiltrate the English language. In the Swahili language, safari quite literally means 'journey,' though to eager visitors flocking to Southern Africa it means so much more. From inspiring visions of wildebeests fording raging rivers and lions stalking their heedless prey through the savanna grass, to iridescent flamingos lining a salty shore at sunset and the guilty thrill of watching vultures tear flesh and hyenas crunch through bone, a safari into the wild is untamed Africa at its finest.

From the bushveld of South Africa, which supports the region's greatest concentration of herd animals, to the deserts of Namibia and Botswana, which are inhabited by uniquely adapted creatures, Southern Africa presents a vast range of landscapes in which to watch wildlife. Varied topography and climatic influences have created a host of natural environments in which animals and plants have developed an extraordinary diversity, making the region's national parks and reserves among the best in the world for experiencing wildlife.

With such a choice at hand, and road conditions making efficient travel a challenge, it helps to do some planning before you set out. Fortunately, planning a safari to Southern Africa is a pleasure in itself: the region is so versatile that it's virtually a blank canvas, catering equally for thrillseekers and sunseekers, budget backpackers and high-end high rollers, those who like it tough and those who just want to get going.

Animals move around, seasons change and weather varies. There is no guarantee that you'll see absolutely everything you're after, but with the right directions you should see something amazing in just about any part of Southern Africa. And, while it may be stating the obvious, the more time you have to go on safari, the more you will see, and the richness of Southern Africa's wildlife diversity means that even after weeks you will encounter new species and new behaviours.

It's worth pointing out that there is absolutely no substitute for your own careful research: do as much reading as possible before you go, and concentrate on the areas with the key wildlife that matches your interests. Some safari-goers become quickly obsessed with the search for the Big Five, while others seek to tally massive birding checklists, though any specific wildlife-focused pursuit requires time spent in specialised habitats.

With that said, this chapter provides a useful general overview of the safari-planning process, from deciding where and when to go, to giving author-tested tips on how to book your trip. Whether you decide in the end to organise everything through a professional operator, or instead do everything yourself and have a memorable go at the self-drive safari experience, we'll help you organise each stage of your planning, and set essential priorities for your trip to come.

As an added bonus, we've outlined our favourite spots for everything from romance and adventure to luxury and family travel (see the boxed text, p302). We've also assembled some handy tables outlining which national parks offer what activities, as well as where to head if you want to spot some of Africa's most charismatic creatures. Hopefully, these features should help you jump-start your brainstorming sessions, and set you on a rapid trajectory for some of the most dramatic wildlife-watching this planet has to offer.

Safari njema. We wish you a rewarding journey.

WHERE & WHEN TO GO

SOUTHERN AFRICA: COUNTRY BY COUNTRY

SOUTH AFRICA

It's no wonder that South Africa draws more visitors than anywhere else in sub-Saharan Africa. World-class wildlife-watching, cosmopolitan cities, stunning natural panoramas and vibrant cultures make the country appealing to almost every taste and budget. Within the space of a day, you can journey from vineyard-clad hillsides in the Western Cape to the vast open spaces of the Kalahari, from Cape Town's waterfront chic to isolated Zulu villages, from elephant-spotting in Kruger National Park to the pounding surf and sublime seascapes of the coast. And, unlike many other areas of the continent, South Africa gives you the opportunity to do all this while still enjoying Western amenities and, for the most part, getting by speaking English.

Yet, while it's easy to travel around South Africa focusing on the glitz and developed-world infrastructure, you'll only get below the surface by seeking out the country's other face – most visible in the sprawling townships where far too many people live stalked by the shadows of hunger, poverty and one of the highest HIV/AIDS infection rates in the world. Behind its incredible natural beauty, South Africa is the stage for the daily drama of one of the world's greatest experiments in racial harmony. The intensity of this drama surrounds you wherever you go, and will likely be one of the most fascinating and challenging aspects of your travels. There's never been a better time to experience this than now, as the colours of the 'rainbow nation' finally begin to fuse.

INTERNET RESOURCES:

- **Eastern Cape Tourism Board** (www.ectb.co.za)
- **Free State Tourism Board** (www.dteea.fs.gov.za)
- **Gauteng Tourism Authority** (www.gauteng.net)
- **KwaZulu-Natal Tourism Authority** (www.kzn.org.za)
- **Limpopo Tourism Board** (www.golimpopo.com)

PLANNING YOUR SAFARI

WATCHING WILDLIFE – WHERE TO GO WHEN

ANIMAL	BEST PLACES TO SEE	BEST TIME TO VISIT
AFRICAN WILD DOG (P210)	KRUGER NP (P60)	MAY-OCT
	KAFUE NP (P182)	JUL-OCT
BLACK RHINOCEROS (P219)	ETOSHA NP (P100)	JUL-SEP
	MKHUZE GR (P86)	JUN-OCT
CHEETAH (P204)	KGALAGADI TRANSFRONTIER PARK (P68)	DEC-MAY
	NXAI PAN NP (P128)	DEC-MAR
CAPE FUR-SEAL (P215)	CAPE CROSS SEAL RESERVE (P110)	NOV & DEC
	SKELETON COAST NP (P108)	OCT-MAY
ELEPHANT (P216)	CHOBE NP (P120)	AUG, OCT, DEC-FEB
	ADDO ELEPHANT NP (P76)	SEP-NOV
FLAMINGO (P251)	ETOSHA NP (P100)	JUL-SEP
	ISIMANGALISO WETLAND PARK (P80)	OCT-MAR
LEOPARD (P203)	KRUGER NP (P60)	MAY-OCT
	SOUTH LUANGWA NP (P178)	JUN-OCT
LION (P202)	KRUGER NP (P60)	MAY-OCT
	CHOBE NP (P120)	AUG, OCT, DEC-FEB
SAMANGO MONKEY (P194)	NYIKA NP (P94)	OCT-APR
	ISIMANGALISO WETLAND PARK (P80)	OCT-MAR
WHITE RHINOCEROS (P218)	HLUHLUWE-IMFOLOZI GR (P64)	JUN-OCT
	PILANESBERG NP (P72)	SEP-JAN

- **Mpumalanga Tourism Authority**
  (www.mpumalanga.com)
- **North-West Province Parks & Tourism Board** (www.tourismnorthwest.co.za)
- **Northern Cape Tourism Authority**
  (www.northerncape.org.za)
- **Western Cape Tourism Board**
  (www.tourismcapetown.co.za)

NAMIBIA

Wedged between the Kalahari and the South Atlantic, Namibia enjoys vast potential and promise as one of the youngest countries in Africa. In addition to having a striking diversity of cultures and national origins, Namibia is also a photographer's dream – it boasts wild seascapes, rugged mountains, lonely deserts, stunning wildlife, colonial cities and nearly unlimited elbow room.

Running along the ocean coast is the Namib, one of the oldest and driest deserts in the world, which is comprised mainly of apricot-coloured dunes interspersed with dry pans. The barren and inhospitable landscapes of the Namib are markedly different from those of the Kalahari; its semiarid country is covered with thorny trees and criss-crossed by ephemeral rivers and fossil watercourses.

While wildlife is scarce in such extreme environments, spotting an oryx against a backdrop of towering sand is a dramatic and inspiring moment – and an incredible photo opportunity. Of course, Namibia isn't just about landscapes, especially given that Etosha National Park is regarded as one of Southern Africa's best safari parks. In the dry season, when herds of thirsty animals congregate around remote watering holes, well within the sights of hungry predators, wildlife-watching is unequalled.

INTERNET RESOURCES:

- **Namibian Tourism Board**(www
  .namibiantourism.com.na) A good-looking, user-friendly site providing a wide range of general travel information on Namibia. Also lists lots of useful links.
- **Namibian**(www.namibian.com.na) For up-to-date news, this is Namibia's main

English-language newspaper.

BOTSWANA

Botswana is an African success story. After it achieved democratic rule in 1966, three of the world's richest diamond-bearing formations were discovered within its borders. Today, the country enjoys a high standard of economic stability, education and health care that is unequalled elsewhere in sub-Saharan Africa (with the exception of South Africa). Its modern veneer, however, belies the fact that much of Botswana remains a country for the intrepid (not to mention relatively wealthy) traveller. This largely roadless wilderness of vast spaces requires time, effort and, above all else, lots of cash to enjoy it to its fullest.

Landlocked Botswana extends 1100km from north to south and 960km from east to west, making it roughly the same size as Kenya, France or Texas. Most of the country is covered with scrub brush and savanna grassland, though the Okavango Delta and the Chobe River provide a year-round water supply. As a result, nearly all Southern African mammal species are present. Herds of wildebeests, zebras and other hoofed mammals migrate annually in search of permanent water and stable food supplies, resulting in incredible displays of free-ranging wildlife that truly matches the Africa of your dreams.

INTERNET RESOURCES:

- **Botswana Gazette** (www.gazette.bw)
  The website of Botswana's leading independent newspaper, where you can catch up on local and regional headlines.
- **Government of Botswana** (www.gov
  .bw) The official government site with current news and links to businesses and government departments.

ZIMBABWE

Zimbabwe has its problems. Robert Mugabe has been in power for decades, and the opposition is only just starting to gain a foothold. Some of the world's poorest people are fighting to survive amid increasingly desperate conditions. Unemployment is above 80%, inflation is the highest in the world, and women die younger in Zimbabwe than anywhere else on the planet, according to the World Health Organisation. But, behind this grim data is one of Southern Africa's most beautiful – and today, untouristed – countries. And, despite their circumstances, Zimbabweans have not lost their humour or resolve. With so few visiting the country, those who do can expect royal treatment. They need you – and your foreign-currency reserves.

While the world's media focuses on the fall of Zimbabwe, visitors will see a Zimbabwe that continues to be a great place to visit, assuming you come with the right attitude. Richness in culture and colour remain, and local traditions alongside institutionalised reminders of British colonialism are still visible. Travelling in Zimbabwe will require more advanced planning than other destinations, and an intrepid and adventurous disposition will certainly serve you well, but the wildlife rewards awaiting you are rich, varied and poignant reminders of this once great country.

INTERNET RESOURCES:
- **Human Rights Watch: Zimbabwe** (www.hrw.org/en/africa/zimbabwe) Reports, background briefings, testimony, press releases and commentary on the human-rights situation in the country.
- **Zimbabwe Tourism Authority** (www.zimbabwetourism.co.zw) 'Africa's Paradise', at least according to the Zimbabwean government's Ministry of Tourism.

MALAWI
Flick through the glossy tourist brochures and the clichés come thick and fast. Malawi is 'the warm heart of Africa' or 'Africa for beginners', and its lake is 'the lake of stars'. It all seems too good to be true, but, with stunning and varied scenery and supremely friendly locals,

along with the relative ease of travel here, Malawi really does live up to the hype.

Malawi's big draw is the lake – a magnificent shard of crystal water stretching some 500km along Malawi's eastern border, separating it from the wild and mountainous coast of Mozambique and Tanzania. Isolated villages pepper the northern lakeshore, and the beautiful Liwonde National Park rests at its southern tip. Around 500 species of fish inhabit the lake, and the freshwater diving and snorkelling here are excellent. Dive and swim in the lake's warm waters, or simply soak up the vibrant local flavour and you're sure to find yourself seduced.

Malawi's not just for water babies and sun worshippers – there's plenty here to keep you active, and Malawi's landscape is surprisingly diverse. Head for the misty peaks of Mt Mulanje or to the Nyika Plateau, where you find sheer escarpments, dramatic peaks, endless rolling grassland and some of the most enjoyable hiking routes in the whole of Africa.

INTERNET RESOURCES:
- **Malawi Ministry of Tourism, Parks & Wildlife** (www.tourismmalawi.com) A comprehensive resource for all things tourism in Malawi.
- **Malawi.Com** (www.malawi.com) A glossy and informative site with some useful links.

ZAMBIA
Zambia is a diamond in the rough. The country boasts some of the continent's best wildlife parks, and is bordered by the Zambezi River, along which are three of the region's major highlights: Victoria Falls, Lake Kariba and Lower Zambezi National Park. Zambia's South Luangwa National Park is one of the best wildlife parks in the world, while the huge Kafue National Park (it's larger than Switzerland) boasts plenty of animals beyond the Big Five. Avid birders also flock to Zambia to glimpse a view of its fabulous diversity of birds, most notably the rare Chaplin's barbet.

Unfortunately diamonds don't come cheap (even if they are mined in Zambia), but the sparkle is mesmerising.

For independent travellers, Zambia can be a challenge: distances between major towns and attractions are long, and get-

ting around by car or public transport takes time and patience. But for many, this challenge is part of Zambia's appeal; this is 'real' Africa – which is becoming rare among the increasingly developed parts of the region – as well as 'safe' Af-

RECOMMENDED PARKS & RESERVES

No two wildlife-watching experiences in Africa are alike, which is why your choice of park should reflect exactly what it is you want out of your safari. Here are our top recommendations.

BEST FOR BIG FIVE
KRUGER NP (P60) You're going to have to scan every acacia tree if you want to spot a leopard, though black rhinos are present in small numbers, and lions, elephants and buffalo are fairly common.

BEST FOR ROMANCE
NAMIB-NAUKLUFT NP (P104) Looking to put some passion back into your lover's eyes? A hot-air balloon ride over the soft undulating dunes should more than do the trick.

BEST FOR LUXURY
MOREMI GR (P132) There are few experiences more lavish than fine dining in the middle of the African bush, only to retire for the night in the comfort and privacy of your own five-star safari tent.

BEST FOR ADVENTURE
HWANGE NP (P142) Although it remains one of Southern Africa's classic safari parks, negotiating the political and economic mess that is Zimbabwe will be an adventure in itself.

BEST FOR A HOLIDAY
LAKE MALAWI NP (P166) A cool and refreshing dip in the lake should provide plenty of relief from the tropical sun, while a mask and a snorkel should give you a new appreciation for the diversity of freshwater life.

BEST FOR FIRST-TIMERS
ETOSHA NP (P100) Home to a well-developed network of 2WD roads connecting wildlife-rich watering holes in the middle of the scenic desert, Etosha is a great training ground for honing your safari skills.

BEST FOR ROUGHING IT
CENTRAL KALAHARI GR (P124) If you're looking to eschew luxury in favour of bedding down on Mother Earth, this reserve has a rough-and-ready network of undeveloped camp sites.

BEST FOR GETTING WET
VICTORIA FALLS & ZAMBEZI NPS (P156) Standing before the mighty Victoria Falls should provide plenty of spray and mist, though watch where you swim in the Zambezi River as there are plenty of crocs and hippos about!

BEST FOR OFF-ROADERS
KAUDOM GR (P111) If you're bored of the pavement and looking to put your vehicle to the test, this remote and largely undeveloped game reserve provides some seriously challenging runs for 4WD enthusiasts.

BEST FOR KIDS
ADDO ELEPHANT NP (P76) This tiny safari park in South Africa packs in a whole bunch of elephants, which are sure to excite even the most finicky of children.

BEST FOR SOLITUDE
MAKGADIKGADI PANS & NXAI PAN NPS (P128) You will need superior navigation skills and a very reliable GPS unit before you even think about driving across these remote salt pans, especially since you won't meet a soul along the way.

rica, as Zambia is devoid of the harsh ethnic tensions that abound in its western, northern and eastern neighbours.

INTERNET RESOURCES:
- **National Tourist Board** (www .zambiatourism.com)
- **Zamnet** (www.zamnet.zm) Provides links to all major national newspapers and several other useful sites.

CLIMATE & SEASONS

Seasons in Southern Africa are rarely divided along conventional lines, and, broadly speaking, fall into a warm, dry period (usually May to October) and a hot, wet one (November to April). Rainfall – and the lack of it – is the single most important factor affecting wildlife behaviour and distribution in the region. However, don't assume this means a visit is always best timed to coincide with the arrival of the rains. Each season has its attractions and, regardless of when you go, excellent viewing is possible. However, certain attractions are more likely to be seen at particular times, which is crucial to keep in mind when planning a visit.

During the dry season, animals usually congregate around dwindling water supplies, making waterholes and permanent rivers productive areas. Carnivores, particularly lions, concentrate their hunting at these points, offering you good chances of seeing a kill. The undergrowth is dying off, and grass has been heavily grazed in this season, which makes spotting wildlife easier. On the flipside, it can be very dusty, and the scenery may look rather stark and barren. This is, however, the coolest period when days are clear, sunny and warm, which means getting around on sand or dirt roads is generally problem-free.

When rains arrive, there is a rapid flush of new life: new grass appears, trees flower and develop fruit, and insects proliferate. Birdlife tends to be best at this time with the arrival of migrants from

Eurasia as well as from elsewhere within Africa. Wildlife species disperse because they are no longer tied to restricted water-points, but this is usually when large herds of herbivores migrate into open savannas, with many species dropping their young. The wet season is the hottest period across most of the region, and temperatures and humidity can be extremely high. In some areas, particularly Zambia, the Okavango Delta and reserves along Namibia's Caprivi Strip, roads become impassable, and many lodges close down for the wettest period (usually December to February).

Remember that rainfall across different habitats in Southern Africa is highly variable, so a trip can take in elements of both the dry and wet seasons. For example, the period late in the dry season in Namibia's Etosha National Park, when animals congregate in the thousands at waterholes, may overlap with the arrival of rains in Savute in Botswana, prompting the return of huge herds of zebras. Plan your trip well, but don't expect to predict the timing perfectly. Speak to other travellers about destinations they have just left, and don't be afraid to change your itinerary when things happen unexpectedly.

BEFORE YOU BOOK

The majority of travellers prefer to get all the hard work done before they arrive in Southern Africa by booking from abroad, either through travel agencies or directly with safari companies. This fairly common practice also ensures that you'll be able to secure a spot at the more famous lodges, especially during peak seasons when places start filling up months in advance. However, while most safari operators will take internet bookings, making arrangements with anyone other than a well-established midrange or top-end operator can be a risky business. If you're going for a budget option, you should certainly wait and do your research on the ground when you arrive.

If you want to book a safari once you're in Southern Africa, a good starting point is to visit one of the travel agencies in Johannesburg, Cape Town, Windhoek or in any other large city or tourist town in the region. See p306 for important tips on getting the kind of safari you want.

For a list of tour operators, see p310.

COSTS & ACCOMMODATION

Most safari-operator quotes include park entrance fees, the cost of accommodation or tent rental, transport costs from the starting base to the park, and the cost of fuel plus a driver/guide for wildlife drives. However, this varies enough that it's essential to clarify before paying. Drinks (whether alcoholic or not) are generally excluded, and budget camping-safari prices usually exclude sleeping-bag rental. Prices quoted by agencies or op-erators usually assume shared (double) room/tent occupancy, with supplements for single occupancy ranging from 20% to 50% of the shared-occupancy rate.

If you are dealing directly with lodges and tented camps rather than going through a safari operator, you may be quoted 'all-inclusive' prices. In addition to accommodation, full board and some-times park fees, these usually include two 'activities' (usually wildlife drives, or sometimes one wildlife drive and one walk) per day, each lasting about two to three hours. They generally exclude transport costs to the park. Whenever accommodation-only prices apply, you'll need to pay extra to actually go out looking for wildlife. Costs for this vary considerably.

BUDGET SAFARIS
Most safaris at the lower end of the price range are camping safaris. In order to keep costs to a minimum, groups often camp outside national-park areas (there-

---

TRAVEL SAFETY

Visitors to Africa are understandably daunted by the continent's unenviable reputation as being a dangerous place, though it's a grossly naive to group 53 separate and unique countries into one broadly sweeping overgeneralisation. Each African country is as different from one another as any in Europe, Asia or the Americas, and offers a varied palette of urban and rural, young and old, traditional and modern, and rich and poor alike.

With that said, war and violence are indeed daily occurrences in some parts of Africa, and that the underlying social ills are unlikely to disappear in the near future. Tragically, cyclical poverty combined with diminishing natural resources can fuel crime based on opportunism, and tourists are sometimes perceived as being wealthy and easy targets.

However, government travel advisories tend to err on the side of extreme caution for Africa, and occasionally advise against travel to entire countries based on small areas of regional unrest. While these advisories are useful for tracking stability patterns and keeping up on current events, you should always balance these warnings against other sources.

Truth be told, the reality on the ground is almost always different from the international headlines, which means that your fellow travellers are often the best source of information. An excellent resource is Lonely Planet's own Thorn Tree, an engaging online forum where you can pose questions and get answers from a dynamic range of people.

Finally, it's worth taking comfort in the fact that the overwhelming majority of travellers in Africa never experience any kind of problem. In fact, the most likely annoyance for travellers is mere petty theft, which can occur anywhere in the world, and is easily preventable if you take the necessary precautions.

As a general rule, you should always take advantage of the hotel safe, and never leave your valuables out in the open. And – quite simply – when you're out and about, don't bring anything with you that you wouldn't want to lose. Exude confidence, practise street smarts, and never let fear get the best of you.

by saving park admission and camping fees) or stay in budget guest houses outside the park. Budget operators also save costs by working with larger groups to minimise per-person transport costs, and by keeping to a no-frills setup with basic meals and a minimum number of staff. For most safaris at the budget level, as well as for many midrange safaris, daily kilometre limits are placed on the vehicles.

MIDRANGE SAFARIS

Most midrange safaris use lodges, where you'll have a comfortable room and eat in a restaurant. Overall, safaris in this category are comfortable, reliable and reasonably good value. A disadvantage is that they may have something of a package-tour or production-line feel, although this can be minimised by selecting a safari company and accommodation carefully, by giving attention to how many other people you travel with (and who they are), and by avoiding the large, popular lodges during peak season.

TOP-END SAFARIS

Private lodges, luxury tented camps and even private fly-in camps are used in top-end safaris, all with the aim of providing guests with as 'authentic' and personal a bush experience as possible without forgoing creature comforts. For the phenomenal price you pay, expect a full range of amenities, as well as top-quality guiding. Even in remote settings without running water you will be able to enjoy hot, bush-style showers, comfortable beds and fine dining. Also expect a high level of personalised attention and an intimate atmosphere – many places at this level have fewer than 20 beds.

TIPPING

Assuming satisfactory service, tipping is an important part of a safari, especially to those whose livelihoods depend on tips. Many operators have tipping guidelines, and expectations increase substantially if you're on a top-end safari, if you're part of a large group or if an especially good job

has been done. Err on the side of generosity while tipping those who have worked to make your safari experience memorable. Other travellers follow you and the last thing anyone wants to find is a disgruntled driver/guide who doesn't care whether you see wildlife or not.

TYPES OF SAFARI

ORGANISED VEHICLE SAFARIS

The options here range from a couple of days up to a month, with a week or two being ideal. At least one full day in either direction will normally be taken up with travel, and after seven days you may well feel like a rest. If you pack too much distance or too many parks into a short period, chances are that you'll feel as if you've spent your whole time in transit, shuttling from place to place, rather than enjoying the destination.

Minivans are the most common option throughout most of Kenya and northern Tanzania, but if you have a choice, go for a good Land Rover–style 4WD instead. Apart from aesthetics, minivans accommodate too many people for a good experience, the rooftop opening is usually only large enough for a few passengers to use at once, and at least some passengers will get stuck in middle seats with poor views.

Whatever type of vehicle you're in, you should try to avoid crowding. Sitting uncomfortably scrunched together for several hours over bumpy roads, or squeezed into a middle seat, detracts significantly from the safari ambience. Most prices you will be quoted are based on groups of three to four passengers, which is about the maximum for comfort for most vehicles. Some companies put five or six passengers in a standard 4WD, but the minimal savings don't compensate for the extra discomfort.

DO-IT-YOURSELF SAFARIS

A DIY safari is a viable and enticing proposition in Southern Africa if you can get a group together to share the costs of renting a vehicle. Doing it yourself has several advantages over organised safaris: primarily total flexibility, independence and being able to choose your travelling companions. However, as far as costs go, it's generally true to say that organising your own safari will cost at least as much as, and usually more than, going on a cheap organised safari to the same areas.

Just remember to bring enough extra petrol in jerry cans (it's not available in most parks), as well as some mechanical knowledge and spare parts. Many park areas are quite remote, and if you break down you'll be on your own. On that note, it's certainly not a good idea to go on a DIY safari by yourself. Not counting the everyday risks of bush driving, if you have to change a tyre in lion country, you'll want someone to watch your back.

Apart from the cost and the risk of vehicle breakdowns, major issues are accidents, security and your lack of local knowledge. Maps are hard to find, particularly for remote areas, and whoever

---

WHICH SAFARI?

While price can be a major determining factor in safari planning, there are other considerations that are just as important:

- **AMBIENCE** Will you be staying in or near the park? (If you stay well outside the park, you'll miss the good early-morning and evening wildlife-viewing hours.) Are the surroundings atmospheric? Will you be in a large lodge or an intimate private camp?
- **EQUIPMENT** Mediocre vehicles and equipment can significantly detract from the overall experience, and in remote areas, lack of quality equipment or vehicles and appropriate back-up arrangements can be a safety risk.
- **ACCESS AND ACTIVITIES** If you don't relish the idea of hours in a 4WD on bumpy roads, consider parks and lodges where you can fly in. Areas offering walking and boat safaris are best for getting out of the vehicle and into the bush.
- **GUIDES** A good driver/guide can make or break your safari. Staff at reputable companies are usually knowledgeable and competent. With operators who are trying to cut corners, chances are that staff are unfairly paid, and are not likely to be knowledgeable or motivated.
- **COMMUNITY COMMITMENT** Look for operators that do more than just give lip service to ecotourism principles, and that have a genuine, long-standing commitment to the communities where they work. In addition to being more culturally responsible, they'll also be able to give you a more authentic and enjoyable experience.
- **SETTING THE AGENDA** Some drivers feel that they have to whisk you from one good 'sighting' to the next. If you prefer to stay in one strategic place for a while to experience the environment and see what comes by, discuss this with your driver. Going off in wild pursuit of the Big Five means you may miss the more subtle aspects of your surroundings.
- **EXTRACURRICULARS** It's not uncommon for drivers to stop at souvenir shops en route. While this does give the driver an often much-needed break from the wheel, most shops pay drivers commissions to bring clients, which means you may find yourself spending more time souvenir shopping than you'd bargained for. If you're not interested, discuss this with your driver at the outset, ideally while still at the operator's offices.
- **LESS IS MORE** If you'll be teaming up with others to make a group, find out how many people will be in your vehicle, and try to meet your travelling companions before setting off.
- **SPECIAL INTERESTS** If bird watching or other special interests are important, arrange a private safari with a specialised operator.

TYPES OF SAFARI

PARK OR RESERVE	NIGHT DRIVES	WALKING SAFARIS	BOAT SAFARIS	CAMEL/ HORSE SAFARIS	BALLOON SAFARIS
SOUTH AFRICA					
KRUGER NP	•	•	•		
HLUHLUWE-IMFOLOZI GR	•	•			
KGALAGADI TRANSFRONTIER PARK	•				
PILANESBERG NP	•	•			•
ADDO ELEPHANT NP	•	•		•	
AUGRABIES FALLS NP	•	•	•		
ISIMANGALISO WETLAND PARK	•				
ITHALA GR		•	•		
KAROO NP	•	•			
MKHUZE GR DE HOOP NR	•	•			
MALOTI-DRAKENSBERG TRANSFRONTIER AREA		•			
MOUNTAIN ZEBRA NP		•			
NDUMO GR		•			
PHINDA PRIVATE GR	•	•			
TEMBE ELEPHANT PARK		•			
NAMIBIA					
ETOSHA NP	•	•			
NAMIB-NAUKLUFT PARK		•		•	•
CAPE CROSS SEAL RESERVE		•	•		
MAMILI NP		•	•		
WATERBERG PLATEAU PARK		•			
BOTSWANA					
CHOBE NP	•	•			
CENTRAL KALAHARI GR		•			•
MAKGADIKGADI PANS & NXAI PAN NPS	•	•			
MOREMI GR	•	•	•		
MABUASEHUBE GR	•	•			
ZIMBABWE					
HWANGE NP	•	•			
GONAREZHOU NP		•			
MANA POOLS NP		•	•		
MATUSADONA NP		•			
VICTORIA FALLS & ZAMBEZI NPS		•	•	•	
MATOBO NP		•		•	
NYANGA NP		•			
MALAWI					
LAKE MALAWI			•		
LIWONDE NP	•	•	•		
NYIKA NP		•		•	
LENGWE NP		•			
VWAZA MARSH WR		•			
ZAMBIA					
SOUTH LUANGWA NP	•	•			
KAFUE NP	•	•		•	
LOWER ZAMBEZI NP	•	•	•		
BANGWEULU SWAMPS		•	•		
KASANKA NP		•	•		

is driving is going to be too busy concentrating on the road to notice much of the wildlife. However, there is a smug but well-deserved sense of total self-satisfaction that is inherent in any successful DIY adventure.

For more about off-road driving and self-driving safety tips, see p309.

For hiking or other safaris where you don't need a vehicle to get around once you're at the park, doing things yourself via public transport is much easier, with the main considerations being time, sorting things out with park fees, guides and other logistics, and finding some travelling companions. Generally speaking, allow up to a full day at the access town or trail head to organise food, equipment and guides.

SPECIALISED SAFARIS

In addition to the headings below, be sure to check out our coverage of specialised safaris – birdwatching, dolphin- and whale-watching and diving and snorkelling – on p318.

WALKING, HIKING & CYCLING SAFARIS

At many national parks, you can arrange relatively short walks of two to three hours in the early morning or late afternoon. The focus is on watching animals rather than covering distance, and walks like these are often included in organised vehicle-safari packages, especially at the top end of the scale. For keen hikers who want to minimise their time in safari minibuses, there is an increasing number of more vigorous options, usually involving point-to-point treks or longer circuits. Finally, cyclists who are in peak physical shape – and can tolerate the equatorial sun – have the option of criss-crossing the region with fellow road warriors.

DO IT AT...

» **De Hoop NR** (p88) » **Maloti-Drakensberg Transfrontier Area** (p89) » **Namib-Naukluft Park** (p104) » **Fish River Canyon Park** (p114)

BOAT SAFARIS

Boat safaris are an excellent way to experience the Southern African wilderness, and offer a welcome break from dusty, bumpy roads. They're also the only way to fully explore riverine environments, and they'll give you new perspectives on the terrestrial scene as you approach hippos or crocodiles at close range, float by a sandbank covered with birds, or observe animals on shore from a river vantage point.

DO IT AT...

» **Victoria Falls & Zambezi NPs** (p156)
» **Chobe NP** (p120) » **Moremi GR** (p132)
» **Lake Malawi NP** (p166)

GETTING AROUND

If you're not signing up for an organised tour, then you're going to need to plan out how to get around with your vehicle. Note that a vehicle is essential in most reserves, so even if you could get there by public transport, you won't be allowed in without a lift. Hire cars are readily available, but are expensive unless you share the costs among several people; most of the time you're better off hiring a driver/guide so you are free to watch animals instead of the road. You hire cars in cities, airports and towns, but you hire drivers at the entrance to the reserve, or at the park ranger station. Road conditions vary from good to abysmal; dry-season travel generally presents few problems, but in wet seasons a 4WD is advisable, and sometimes essential. You are allowed into reserves in your own vehicle as long as you pay the requisite entrance fees.

BUSH DRIVING

Although there is an extensive network of both tarred and gravel roads throughout Southern Africa, the thrill and adventure of bush driving is unequalled. Not surprisingly, the region is a favourite destination for off-roaders. However, just because you've read a survival manual doesn't mean that you're ready to head out into the wilds. 4WD driving is serious business, and tourists have died in the past due to careless mistakes. Remember – real (and safe) 4WD driving is nothing like you see on the TV. Following are some road-tested tips that should help you in planning a safe and successful 4WD expedition.

Although a good map and a compass may be sufficient for navigating in your own country, it is strongly advisable to invest in a good Global Positioning System (GPS) before travelling in Southern Africa. Although GPS units are *not* a substitute for a map and a compass, they are useful for establishing waypoints,

and helping you determine which direction you're heading. As a general rule, you should always be able to identify your location on a map, even if you're navigating with a GPS unit.

Stock up on emergency provisions, even if you're sticking to the main highways. Distances between towns can be extreme, and you never know where you're going to break down (and when someone is going to pick you up). Petrol and diesel tend to be available in most major towns, though it's wise to never pass a station without filling up.

TIPS FOR BUSH DRIVING

Still keen to give bush driving a go? If so, here are a few author-tested tips:

- Driving through high grass is a dangerous proposition as the seeds it disperses can quickly foul radiators and cause overheating. If the temperature gauge begins to climb, stop and remove as much plant material as you can from the grille.
- Keep your tyre pressure slightly lower than you would when driving on sealed roads.
- Try to avoid travelling at night when dust and distance may create confusing mirages.
- Keep your speed down to a maximum of 80km/h on gravel roads, much less so on dirt roads and tracks.
- Maximise your control by keeping both hands on the steering wheel.
- Follow ruts made by other vehicles.
- If the road is corrugated, gradually increase your speed until you find the correct speed – it'll be obvious when the rattling stops.
- Be especially careful on bends – slow right down before attempting the turn.
- If you have a tyre blowout, do *not* hit the brakes or you'll lose control and the car will roll. Instead, steer straight ahead as best you can, and let the car slow itself down before you attempt to bring it to a complete stop.
- You don't meet other cars very often, but when you do, it's like dust clouds passing in the night. When a vehicle approaches from the opposite direction, reduce your speed and keep as far left as possible. On remote roads, it's customary to wave at the other driver as you pass.
- In rainy weather, gravel roads can turn to quagmires, and desert washes may fill with water. If you're uncertain about the water depth in a wash, get out and check the depth (unless it's a raging torrent, of course!), and only cross when it's safe for the type of vehicle you're driving.
- Be on the lookout for animals. Antelope, in particular, often bound onto the road unexpectedly, resulting in an unpleasant meeting.
- Avoid swerving sharply or braking suddenly on a gravel road or you risk losing control of the vehicle. If the rear wheels begin to skid, steer gently into the direction of the skid until you regain control. If the front wheels skid, take a firm hand on the wheel and steer in the opposite direction of the skid.
- Dust permeates everything on gravel roads – wrap your food, clothing and camera equipment in dust-proof plastic or keep them in sealed containers. To minimise dust inside the vehicle, pressurise the interior by closing the windows and turning on the blower.
- In dusty conditions, switch on your headlights so you can be more easily seen.

If you're planning a long expedition in the bush, carry the requisite amount of fuel in metal jerry cans, and remember that engaging 4WD burns nearly twice as much fuel as highway driving. In terms of water and food, a good rule is to carry 5L of water per person per day, as well as a good supply of high-calorie, nonperishable emergency food items.

Garages throughout Southern Africa are surprisingly well stocked with basic 4WD parts, and you haven't truly experienced Africa until you've seen the ingenuity of a bush mechanic. The minimum you should carry is a tow rope, shovel, extra fan belt, vehicle fluids, spark plugs, baling wire, jump leads, fuses, hoses, a good jack and a wooden plank (to use as a base in sand and salt), several spare tyres and a pump. A good Swiss Army knife or Leatherman tool combined with a sturdy roll of duct tape can also save your vehicle's life in a pinch.

OPERATORS

Competition among safari companies is fierce these days, and corners are often cut, especially at the budget level. Some companies enter wildlife parks through side entrances to avoid park fees, while others use glorified minibus drivers as guides, offer substandard food and poorly maintained vehicles, or underpay and otherwise poorly treat their staff. Conversely, there are also many high-quality companies who have excellent track records, and provide truly memorable and high-quality safaris.

Following are some things to keep in mind when looking for an operator:

- Do some legwork (the internet is a good start) before booking anything.
- Be sceptical of price quotes that sound too good to be true, and don't rush into any deals, no matter how good they sound.
- Take the time to shop around at reliable outfits to get a feel for what's on offer; decide exactly what you want, then visit the various companies in person and talk through the kind of package you're looking for.
- Go through the itinerary in detail and confirm what is expected/planned for each stage of the trip.

One thing to look out for is client swapping. Quite a few companies shift clients on to other companies if they don't have enough people to justify running the trip themselves. This ensures that trips actually depart on time, and saves travellers days of waiting for a safari to fill up, but it does undermine consumer trust. Reputable companies will usually inform you before they transfer you to another company. In any case, it may not be the end of the world if you end up taking your safari with a different company from the one you booked with; just make sure the safari you booked and paid for is what you get.

The brochures for some safari companies may give the impression that they offer every conceivable safari under the sun, but in fact many companies also advertise trips run by other companies. While it's not the most transparent way to do business, again, it needn't be the end of the world. A reliable company will normally choose reliable partners, and you're only really likely to come unstuck at the budget end of the market.

Companies recommended in this chapter enjoyed a good reputation at the time of research, as do many others. However, we can't emphasise enough the need to check on the current situation with all of the listed companies and any others you may hear about.

SOUTH AFRICA

Africa Travel Centre (☎ 021-423 5555; www.backpackers.co.za) Books all sorts of tours and activities, including day trips, hire cars and extended truck tours of Africa.

African Routes (☎ 031-563 5080; www.africanroutes.co.za) Offers camping and overland itineraries for younger travellers, plus various tours for seniors.

BirdWatch Cape (☎ 021-762 5059; www
.birdwatch.co.za) A small outfit for
twitchers, focusing on Cape Town and
surrounding areas.

Bundu Safari Company (☎ 011-
675 0767; www.bundusafaris.co.za)
Budget-oriented tours ranging from
one to several days, focusing on Kruger
National Park and the surrounding area.

Cape Town Gourmet Adventure Tours
(☎ 083-693 1151; http://gourmet.cape
-town.info) Wining and dining, plus
'wellness' tours and other options in and
around Cape Town.

Day Trippers (☎ 021-511 4766; www
.daytrippers.co.za) Based in Cape Town,
many of the tours include cycling around
Cape Point and the Winelands as well as
whale-watching in season.

Eco-Ist (☎ 021-559 2420; www.eco
-tourisminvestments.co.za) Outdoor-
oriented 'biodiversity' tours around Cape
Town, plus longer itineraries taking in
Kruger National Park, the Garden Route
and other areas.

Grassroute Tours (☎ 021-706 1006;
www.grassroutetours.co.za) An
experienced operators of township tours.

Karoo Connections (☎ 049-892 3978;
www.karootours.co.za) Operates tours in
the Karoo Nature Reserve, and can also
arrange township walks, wildlife drives,
nature walks and city tours.

Rennies Travel (www.renniestravel.
co.za) Handles international and
domestic bookings and is the agent for
Thomas Cook travellers cheques. It can
arrange visas for other African countries.

Sani Pass Tours (☎ 033-701 1064; www
.sanipasstours.com) Based in
Johannesburg and offering tours up the
Sani Pass into Lesotho, as well as tailored
packages.

Springbok-Atlas (☎ 021-460 4700;
www.springbokatlas.com) One of the
major coach-tour operators, offering
midrange tours along popular routes,
including day tours. Aimed at older
tourists.

St Lucia Tours & Charters (☎ 035-590
1259; www.zululink.co.za) Specialises in
tours around the St Lucia Estuary.

Sunpath (☎ 072-417 6800; www
.sunpath.co.za) Offering a series of
fascinating tours and hikes around the
peninsula. Discover the ancient sunpaths
thought to have been used by the
indigenous people of the Cape.

Thompsons South Africa (☎ 031-201
3100; www.thompsonssa.com) Midrange
and top-end package tours and safaris,
including a two-week tour taking in
South Africa's main tourist spots.

Walks Tours (☎ 011-444 1639; www
.walktours.co.za) Offers regular weekend
walking tours around the greater
Johannesburg area.

Wilderness Safaris (www.wilderness
-safaris.com) Operator offering high-end
luxury safaris and special-interest trips;
also operates several luxury bush camps.

Wildlife Safaris (www.wildlifesaf.co.za)
Offers multiday panorama tours taking
in the Blyde River and Kruger National
Park.

NAMIBIA

Afro Ventures (☎ 064-463812; www
.afroventures.com) Afro Ventures offers several Namibian highlights tours,
focusing on fine lodges and 4WD tours.
The five- and seven-day Namib Desert
tours explore the desert coast and dunes.

Campfire Safaris (☎ 062-523946;
namibia@bigfoot.com) This
economically priced company offers
Kombi tours through a range of
Namibian highlights.

Cardboard Box Travel Shop (☎ 061-
256580; www.namibian.org) This friendly
agency offers bookings (including last-
minute options) for all budget safaris;
lodge, safari, car-hire and transport
bookings; national parks bookings; good
advice; and other travel services.

Chameleon Safaris (☎ 061-247668;
www.chameleonsafaris.com) This budget
safari company is geared to backpackers
and does a range of good-value safaris.

Crazy Kudu Safaris (☎ 061-222636;
www.crazykudu.com) One of Namibia's
friendliest and most economical safari
companies, Crazy Kudu does a variety of
package trips around the country, as well

as custom safaris to the Okavango Delta, Victoria Falls, Fish River and Kaokoland for the best possible price.

Enyandi Safaris (☎061-255103; enyandi@iafrica.com.na) This recommended company runs budget tours mainly in northwestern Namibia.

Felix Unite (☎061-255488; www.felix unite.com) This company runs river-rafting and canoeing adventures on the Kunene and Orange Rivers.

Kaokohimba Safaris (☎061-222378; www.kaoko-namibia.com) Kaokohimba organises cultural tours through Kaokoland and Damaraland and wildlife-viewing trips in Etosha National Park. A highlight is Camp Syncro, in remote Marienflüss.

Magic Bus Safaris (☎061-259485, 0811 298093; magicbus@iafrica.com.na) This small company runs budget trips from Windhoek to Sossusvlei, Etosha and other combinations.

Muramba Bushman Trails (☎067-220659; bushman@natron.net) This popular company, owned by Reinhard Friedrich in Tsumeb, provides a unique introduction to the Heikum San people.

Namib Sky (☎063-683188; www .namibsky.com) For those who dream of looming over the dunes in a balloon, this company offers Namib Desert balloon flights. The early-morning flight departs before sunrise, when not a breath of wind is stirring.

Okakambe Trails (☎064-40279; www .okakambe.iway.na) With Okakambe, you can ride on horseback along the Swakop River to a moon landscape; the company also organises a good variety of longer riding trips.

Outside Adventures (☎061-245595; www.namibia-adventures.com) These folks run excellent day tours from Windhoek: brewery tours, mountain biking in Daan Viljoen, Arnhem Caves, Katutura township and tours to see cheetahs, leopards and rhinos on private reserves in the capital area.

Turnstone Tours (☎064-403123; www .turnstone-tours.com) Turnstone runs 4WD camping tours around

Swakopmund, including Sandwich Harbour and Damaraland.

West Coast Safaris (☎061-256770; www.westcoast.demon.nl) Runs camping participation safaris averaging one week to a variety of destinations including Kaokoland, Etosha, Damaraland, Bushmanland and the Waterberg Plateau.

Wild Dog Safaris (☎061-257642; www .wilddog-safaris.com) This friendly operation runs Northern Namibia Adventures and Southern Swings tours and Etosha and Sossusvlei circuits as well as longer participation camping safaris and accommodated excursions.

BOTSWANA

Afro-Trek (☎686 0177; www.afrotrek .com) This Gaborone-based company specialises in midmarket safaris.

Audi Camp Safaris (☎686 0500; www .okavangocamp.com) This budget operator is run out of the popular Audi Camp in Maun and is an excellent place to book trips around the Delta area.

Bathusi Travel & Safaris (☎686 0647; www.info.bw/~bathus) Also in Maun, this company specialises in upmarket safaris around the Delta, particularly high fly-ins and luxury tented camps.

Crocodile Camp Safaris (☎686 0265; www.botswana.com) Budget operator located at the Crocodile Camp in Maun, and is a budget backpacker favourite.

Island Safari Lodge (☎686 0300; www .africansecrets.net/isl_home.html) Another popular budget operator in Maun; this operation is run out of a lodge of the same name.

Maun Rest Camp (☎686 3472; simonjoyce@info.bw) This budget operator specialises in mobile camping safaris, and is run out of a rest camp of the same name.

Ker & Downey (☎686 0375; www.ker downey.com) One of Botswana's – and the world's – most exclusive tour operators, Ker & Downey has an enviable reputation spanning decades of committed service to high-end customers.

Okavango River Lodge (☎ 686 3707; freewind@info.bw) Yet another popular budget operator run out of the Okavango River Lodge in Maun.

Okavango Tours & Safaris (☎ 686 1154; www.okavango.bw) This established operator specialises in upmarket lodge-based tours; good competition for some of the more famous players in the area.

Wilderness Safaris (☎ in Johannesburg 27-11 807 1800; www.wilderness-safaris .com) This Southern Africa–wide operator specialises in upmarket safaris of tremendous quality and service.

ZIMBABWE

Msuna Safaris & Travel (☎ 04-705716; musuna@mweb.co.zw) Can book any tour and lodge around the country.

Zimsun Leisure Group (☎ 04-737944, 735681; www.zimsun.com) Books large group trips and family-style hotels as well as bush retreats and lodges in the main destinations of Zimbabwe.

MALAWI

Barefoot Safaris (☎ 01-707346; www .barefoot-safaris.com) Budget and mid-range tours, mostly geared towards wildlife-watching in Malawi, Zambia and Tanzania. Also arranges walking tours of Lengwe National Park, Mt Mulanje, Liwonde National Park and Lake Malawi.

Jambo-Africa (☎ 01-823709; www .jambo-africa.com) Based Blantyre. Offers tours to Lengwe National Park and Mt Mulanje hiking packages.

Kayak Africa (☎ 09-942661; www. kayakafrica.net) Based in Cape Maclear, it offers guided one-, two- or three-night island-hopping kayak tours including tented accommodation, meals, snorkel gear and park fees. It also operates PADI open-water courses.

Kiboko Safaris (☎ 01-751226; www .kiboko-safaris.com) Specialises in budget tours; fully inclusive and four-day trips to South Luangwa are very reasonable and well worth the cash.

Monkey Business (☎ 01-352342; info@ njayalodge.com; Nkhata Bay) Offers excellent kayak excursions along the northern lakeshore. Itineraries include idyllic spots such as Usisya and Ruarwe, or spectacular trips to Likoma and Chizumulu Islands. Journeys are broken by stopovers at fishing villages and empty beaches, a great way to explore the area.

Nyika Safari Company (☎ 01-330180; www.nyika.com) Operates purely indulgent horse-riding safaris on the Nyika Plateau, which include all meals, rides and accommodation in luxury safari tents (hot showers and all!) or at the luxurious Chelinda Lodge. These tours only operate between May and October and last anywhere from two to 10 days.

Red Zebra Tours (☎ 01-263165; www .lakemalawi.com) Based in Senga Bay, it specialises in diving and lake safaris with an experienced guide.

Wilderness Safaris (☎ 01-771393; www .wilderness-safaris.com) Operates all accommodation and facilities in Liwonde National Park. It can also arrange flights, car hire and mid- to top-end safaris to South Luangwa National Park in Zambia.

ZAMBIA

Airmasters Travel (☎ 01-250000; www .zambiatourism.com/airmasters) This small shop in Lusaka books flights and hires cars and 4WDs.

Bush Buzz (☎ 01-256992; www.bush -buzz.com) This agency, also in Lusaka, is especially popular for trips to Kafue and Lower Zambezi National Parks

KNP Promotions (☎ 01-266276; www .knp-promotions.com) This agency is a booking agent for lodges and camps in and around Kafue National Park.

Steve Blagus Travel (☎ 01-227739; www.steveblagus.com) Also in Lusaka, this is the agency you go to for American Express transactions as well as to place bookings for over a dozen upmarket lodges and camps.

Voyagers (☎ 01-253048; www.voyagers zambia.com) Perhaps the most popular agency in Zambia, it arranges flights, hotel reservations and car hire.

ON SAFARI

MAKING THE MOST OF YOUR SAFARI EXPERIENCE

Up at first light, a quick gulp of coffee, and into the vehicle for an early game drive – few experiences compare with sunrise over the savanna, especially when it's teeming with African wildlife. While there's no way of knowing what each day will bring, you can be assured that each day will bring something special.

One of the finest prospects in the world for watching wildlife, a safari in Southern Africa ensures some spectacular viewing. Within the many parks and reserves, wildlife is not only abundant and diverse, it's also particularly habituated to the presence of people and vehicles. Visitors enjoy up-close encounters, and the chance of sightings normally reserved for specialists who live and work with animals.

Every scale of experience is here, whether you want to see epic seasonal migrations of huge herds, the prolonged grooming sessions of a meerkat colony, or a pair of beetles resolutely rolling a dung ball to their nest site. From giving tips on seeing as much variety as possible, to helping you get better acquainted with your old favourites, this chapter is aimed at maximising the quality of your safari experience.

THE SAFARI EXPERIENCE

WILDLIFE DRIVES

Wildlife drives (often called game drives) are the backbone of most safaris, with the idea being to spend as many hours as possible in the bush searching for animals. A wildlife drive can be done at any time of day, but early morning, mid-morning and late afternoon, with a break early on for breakfast and another in the middle of the day for lunch, is the usual plan. Night drives are also an excellent way to view nocturnal animals, though they're not permitted everywhere.

Most organised safaris begin with an early wake-up call – usually accompanied by a hot drink and the rising sun – and then a wildlife drive before breakfast. The same wisdom applies if you are doing it yourself: the importance of an early start cannot be stressed too highly. You will see large animals at virtually any time of day, but the earlier you set out, the better your chances of seeing nocturnal species still on the prowl, or predators gathered at a kill. There is also a greater chance of observing interesting interactions in the early hours and, practically speaking, it's usually cooler.

Savanna is an excellent environment in which to spot large animals, and you don't normally go far without seeing something. The basic technique is to drive along slowly, stopping for photos as you like. After an hour or two of driving around, it's back to camp or lodge for breakfast, time to freshen up, and then a mid-morning wildlife drive. Again, this is a good time of day: large raptors such as eagles and vultures are starting to take to the thermals as the land warms up, many grazers are still moving about, and primates have shaken off the night's chill. Activity wanes noticeably as noon approaches and animals seek shade and rest; primates also head for the shade, though they may remain active all day.

By late afternoon things are on the move again, and afternoon wildlife drives typically last from about 3pm until the park's closing time. Unfortunately, things tend to get most interesting just as the sun sets and it's time to leave. While darkness covers much wildlife activity normally hidden from people, in a handful of locales the night drives are usually the highlight of any safari, and offer all the thrills of a wildlife drive with a whole new suite of players.

An essential prerequisite for a night drive is a spotlight (preferably one that plugs into the vehicle's cigarette lighter) or a powerful torch, either of which is provided by your operator or vehicle rental company. While you're out and about, drive along slowly and look for eyeshine reflected in the light; even small animals can be detected using this technique.

VEHICLES & DRIVERS

Safari vehicles come in many permutations. You'll be spending quite a bit of time in a vehicle, and as a rule of thumb the more money you shell out – whether you're going along on a tour or renting your own vehicle – the more comfortable the ride. Most are Land Rovers or Land Cruisers, seating anything up to nine people, but most comfortably seat only four, with open sides, side windows or roll-back canvas flaps; the roof can be pop-top, flip-top or roll-back. A 4WD vehicle is the most desirable way to travel in the wet season, and essential in most wilderness areas.

Minivans – the target of much derision by 'serious' safari operators – are not usually 4WD, but are often driven as if they were. Again, they come in varying degrees of comfort, usually with a pop-top: those with a single, long pop-top provide the best viewing for all occupants; those with two or three smaller pop-tops offer less viewing flexibility and comfort. Those with a central aisle rather than bench seats give greater room for everyone to move around or take pictures. Minivans have the advantage of normally being cheaper than 4WDs (and most budget companies use them), but their use can be limited during wet seasons.

Your driver normally doubles as your guide, and is there to help you see wildlife and to get you back to camp safely. Most will do their utmost to make sure you enjoy your safari – after all, their livelihood depends on it. Establish a dialogue early on: if you want to stop, tell them, and make it clear if you want to take photos – they may have to be reminded to switch off the engine.

ON SAFARI

SPOTLIGHTING – LOOK THEN MOVE ON

A host of wildlife take advantage of darkness to move about and feed, and the best way to see it is by spotlighting. Unfortunately it's not allowed in many reserves, but where it is possible you should take the opportunity to get out after dark. The idea is to drive (or walk) along slowly, scanning the bush on either side of the vehicle for eyeshine (the telltale reflection from an animal's tapetum – a layer of reflective cells in the eye of a nocturnal animal). There's a knack to doing it effectively, and you must look directly along the light beam to see the eyeshine. Identification can be more difficult at night, with even the most familiar animal appearing quite different (although different coloured eyeshine gives a clue, eg antelope eyeshine is green-blue while bushbaby eyeshine is red). It's amazing what previously hidden wildlife and activity can be seen after dark: predators on the move; animals that hide in burrows during the day, such as aardvarks; birds such as owls and nightjars; and even large spiders and scorpions. Beware that extended exposure to bright lights can damage an animal's eyes and disturb its behaviour, so look then move on.

You are entitled to an early start if you want one, and to be at the reserve gates by opening time if necessary – arrange this the night before your wildlife drive. Also note that unless you direct otherwise, drivers tend to follow each other to a kill, pride of lions or whatever. If you don't want to be part of the 'minivan circus', let your driver know; likewise, if you are happy to spend hours watching a herd of something less glamorous, such as antelopes, just say so – you're the boss.

SPECIALISED SAFARIS

BIRDWATCHING

Southern Africa's bird tally is at least 1075 species, making it one of the prime birdwatching sites in the world. A well-planned trip covering half a dozen key sites can yield half this total, and many dedicated first-timers see 250 species in their first few days. All 10 of the uniquely African bird families or genera occur in Southern Africa, ranging from guaranteed-to-see secretary birds, hamerkops and guineafowl to local specials like nectar-eating sugarbirds found nowhere else. Many groups are particularly well represented including raptors, francolins, kingfishers and, for those who like a challenge, larks, warblers and cisticolas.

To ensure the best from a birdwatching trip, a little background research is invaluable. Work through any good field guide, and pay particular attention to the distribution maps: you'll rapidly see patterns of endemism emerging as well as which areas have the richest diversity. Identify key reserves within these areas where you should plan to spend

the most time. Remember that species with a very limited distribution in one country may be abundant in the next, so plan accordingly.

Binoculars are crucial, and pack some lens tissue to deal with the humidity and dust. Spotting scopes are more cumbersome, and require a tripod for easy use, but the many hides in Southern Africa present dozens of opportunities to make their inclusion worthwhile. Scopes are also excellent for wetlands or watching seabirds from the shore. Some hard-core birders also use a small tape player to call in elusive species like trogons. Scopes and tape players are standard equipment for specialist bird tours and some upmarket lodges, but pack your own if you're travelling independently.

Southern Africa is well covered by field guides. The original and still one of the best, *Roberts' Birds of Southern Africa* is almost 900 pages long, making it a little bulky for the field, but it has very detailed information and is excellent value. Less weighty, Newman's *Birds of Southern Africa: The Green Edition* and relative newcomer Sasol's *Illustrated Guide to Birds of Southern Africa* both feature slightly larger illustrations and a very helpful colour-coding system for rapid location of families and groups.

DO IT AT...
» **Kruger NP** (p60) » **Moremi GR** (p132) » **Liwonde NP** (p168) » **Table Mountain NP** (p95)

DOLPHIN- & WHALE-WATCHING

With at least 37 cetaceans (the order comprising whales and dolphins), Southern African oceans provide rich rewards for marine mammal lovers.

Warm currents and protected bays provide ideal habitat for whales and dolphins to breed, and for them to hunt the productive shallow waters close to shore. Although whale sightings are usually restricted to frustratingly brief glimpses, there are a few spots along the coast where quality sightings are virtually guaranteed at the right time of year.

Apart from patience and a pair of binoculars, cetacean spotting doesn't demand much in the way of specialised skills or gear. Shore-based watching is very rewarding, particularly in South Africa where natural cliffs and raised platforms provide excellent lookout posts. Watch for the characteristic 'blows' of whales and for hovering flocks of seabirds, such as Cape gannets, which indicate large fish shoals, irresistible to many dolphin species.

Since 1998, limited boat trips allowing close-up whale-viewing have been permitted in South Africa. Licensed boats are restricted from approaching any nearer than 50m, but whales often come closer of their own accord. Strict regulations ensure whales are not harassed, although policing originates mainly from tourists. By boarding only government-licensed boats, you can be fairly sure the operator abides by the rules. You'll also get a far superior experience – nonlicensed boats have to stay 300m away.

Whether you're viewing from land or boat, be sure to take a few layers of clothing. Weather is highly changeable along this coastline during the whale season (June through December), and cold sub-Antarctic winds bring fairly miserable conditions. A warm jacket and raincoat are highly recommended.

Guides on African cetaceans are scanty, but *A Guide to Whales, Dolphins and Other Marine Mammals of Southern Africa* by Vic Cockcroft and Peter Joyce includes information on identification, behaviour and where to go. *Whale Watching in South Africa: The Southern Right Whale* by Peter Best is a small but extremely useful booklet with practical tips and behavioural insights for viewing Southern Africa's most visible whale.

DO IT AT…
» **De Hoop NR** (p88) » **The South African coast**

DIVING & SNORKELLING

Long summers, warm seas and astonishing diversity make for superb diving conditions along Southern Africa's coastline. For scuba enthusiasts, dozens of reefs, shipwrecks, kelp forests and inland water-filled caves provide interest for all levels of expertise, while snorkelers are able to explore shallow-water reefs, protected bays and warm-water lakes. Some of the world's best diving occurs here, whether it's swimming alongside whale sharks on their annual migration, going eye-to-eye with great white sharks, or trying to distinguish between the hundreds of multicoloured cichlids in Lake Malawi.

You'll need internationally recognised certification for any scuba diving in the region. For nondivers looking for a course and experienced divers needing local knowledge and equipment, dive schools proliferate along the South African coast between Cape Town and KwaZulu-Natal's north coast. As well as providing instruction and gear for hire, many of them can arrange trips further afield to increasingly popular destinations. Instruction and gear is also available at Lake Malawi.

If you plan on snorkelling, you'll only need fins, mask and snorkel (and a wet suit in winter months), widely available

ON SAFARI

for hire at all dive centres. If you've never snorkelled before, it's hugely rewarding here, and extremely easy to learn. The key is to breathe normally through the snorkel; and anticipate a little resistance with the slight change in pressure even just a few inches below the surface. Also, don't panic when the snorkel fills with water as you submerge; simply blow it clear when you reach the surface.

The diver's bible for the region, *The Dive Sites of South Africa* by Anton Koornhof, lists attractions and technical information for more than 160 sites along the coast. If you're interested in identification, *Reef Fishes and Corals: East Coast of Southern Africa* (King) features illustrations of over 200 fish and 32 common coral species from the Kwa-Zulu-Natal and Mozambique coasts. *A Guide to the Fishes of Lake Malawi National Park* by Lewis Digby et al, is invaluable for the lake's 600-plus species. Though not a field guide, but an invaluable reference is *Two Oceans: A Guide to the Marine Life of Southern Africa*.

DO IT AT...
» **Lake Malawi NP** (p166) » **The South African coast**

HOW TO WATCH WILDLIFE

Animals are free to roam, and may not be where you want them to be, but the better informed you are, the more likely you are to see what you are after. If you are on a tour, your knowledge will complement that of the guide, and will often be in demand by other members of the party. Here are some vital tips:

TIME OF DAY
Arguably the most important factor in successful wildlife-watching. Learn what time of day your quarry is most active, how it spends other times, and how these might vary according to season and weather conditions – and plan your days to make the most of these factors. An early start may catch nocturnal predators still on the move; birds are most active in the early morning, although raptors ride thermals as the day warms up; and nocturnal animals may be active in overcast conditions. Activity dies off during the heat of the day, especially during the dry season (large mammals shelter under trees or shrubs, and birds rest in shade), picking up again in the late afternoon and peaking near sundown.

WEATHER
Daily, as well as seasonal, temperature and rainfall patterns also make a difference. For example, puff adders are often on the move after rain; lizards like to bask in early sunshine; and monkeys are more active when the day warms up. A storm can bring on a flurry of activity – swifts moving through on the front, termites swarming, and, in the aftermath, predators snapping up wind-blown insects and rodents swept about. And predators generally hunt into the wind – this helps guides predict where they'll be the next day.

FOOD SOURCES
Food availability can change with the season, and knowing your quarry's food preferences can help. Note what's about; for example, trees in flower attract birds, butterflies and bats; termite swarms are snapped up by many animals, from jackals to rollers; and some lions follow the wildebeest migration.

WATER
For many animals, daily access to water is essential and during dry seasons they will stay close to a ready source;

naturally the concentration of prey will attract predators. The daily ebbing and flowing of tides affects marine life, and the roosting and feeding of shorebirds on mudflats.

KNOW YOUR HABITAT

Some knowledge of where an animal lives will be of great value in finding it. Learn what to expect in each major habitat and by patiently waiting – sooner or later something will show. For example, a cliff face may harbour klipspringers, a leopard's den or an owl's nest. Once you make the link between species and habitat, your 'search pattern' will change and new things will reveal themselves. The area where one habitat merges into another is usually especially productive, eg woodland abutting grassland provides food and shelter to both grazers and browsers, and in the sunny woodland edge you find flowering plants that attract birds and butterflies. Check likely shelters, such as tree hollows, cliff overhangs or termite mounds, and dead trees and overhanging branches that are often used as lookouts or perches. Remember, habitats and their species composition also vary with altitude.

PUT IN THE HOURS

Don't rely on beginner's luck – the longer you spend observing, waiting and watching in the field, the more you will see. As the famous line goes, 'The more you practise, the luckier you get'.

SEARCHING & IDENTIFICATION

Prime your senses (especially sight and hearing), and keep quiet and look for clues. Watch for silhouettes against the sky in the forest canopy; body parts (a leg dangling from a branch, or twitching ears above long grass) and shadows; movement and moving vegetation; and shapes that don't fit. Look in both foreground and background; look at the ground and into the trees, and both upstream and downstream when crossing a river. Use your peripheral vision (especially at night) and watch where other creatures are looking, eg gazelles staring at a cheetah.

Listen for alarm calls (which themselves indicate that predators are nearby), rustling bushes, snorting breath, splashing water and changes in the activity of other creatures, eg monkeys screaming at a crowned eagle. Cupping your hands behind your ears helps to funnel sounds so you can detect faint calls (rotate your head to judge the direction of sounds). Many large animals give off a distinctive odour or attract insects. Relax, too – animals can detect tension; keep quiet and heed your own instincts, such as the feeling you're being watched, or the hair standing up on the back of your neck.

If on foot, learn to use the environment to your advantage: walk slowly, using cover such as bushes and trees; stay downwind of animals (keep the wind in your face); and avoid wearing strong artificial scents in the field which will help to give you away. Don't stare at an animal as you approach – this can be seen as a threat. Avoid making sudden movements and loud noises which startle mammals (birds are less concerned with noise than movement); and don't point at primates – they may feel threatened and retaliate. Don't sneak up on animals – they may think you're stalking them and react accordingly. Sit still awhile against a tree or termite mound (animals look for movement, and if you don't move they probably won't pay much attention). Stake out a burrow or den that appears to be in use – fresh droppings nearby are a promising sign.

ON SAFARI

And, perhaps most important of all, learn from the professional guides – listen to their stories, learn their techniques and ask questions.

The identification of animals is usually the first step towards finding out more about them. Most people categorise what they see without realising it; for example, a jackal is automatically recognised as a member of the dog family. But the finer points of identifying Southern Africa's species usually requires more than a cursory examination.

The first step, usually made with no conscious effort, separates things by shape; you recognise something as an elephant, or a cat, or some kind of antelope. Other basic indicators are pattern or colour (leopards and lions have a similar shape but different coloration) and size (both servals and leopards are spotted, but servals are much smaller). Looking for the basic differences will come naturally after a short time, and with practice the subtle differences attributable to sex, age and geographical variation will also become familiar. Bird identification is a science in itself (and, for birdwatchers, an abiding passion) with its own techniques and terminology.

For birds or mammals, nothing beats practice in the field, backed up by reading (field guides are a good place to start, as is the wildlife guide provided in this book, taking field notes and, if you have the talent or inclination, sketches or photos.

BEYOND LOOKING

For many people, the simple pleasure of looking at wildlife evolves into photography, writing, art or learning more about animal behaviour (plant behaviour happens much more slowly, but is no less fascinating). The realisation that a vast, milling mob of wildebeests is actually a structured, complex community of interacting animals opens up a whole new world of watching wildlife to complement the thrill of the chase. How does one bull react to another? Why are most females in the middle of the group? Follow one animal – what does it do? To which individuals is it submissive or dominant? Each observation can answer one question and pose several more.

But if you want to keep chasing new species, 'ticking', 'twitching' or 'listing' (ie keeping a list of what you have seen and pursuing those species that you haven't yet seen) can become a lifelong hobby. Listing is a reflection of the natural desire to collect and catalogue objects, and a harmless fulfilment of the hunting instinct. Should it need any justification, listing takes people to places they wouldn't otherwise visit, as they pursue the rare or unusual, or a new bird to complete the set; it hones the senses, powers of observation and skills of identification; and it leads to an appreciation of the diversity of life. Birds and, to a lesser extent, mammals are the usual targets of twitchers, but such is the stimulation of watching Southern African wildlife that it is easy to start ticking other diverse, conspicuous and colourful groups, such as butterflies and tropical fish.

ADVANCED TECHNIQUES

Mastered the basics? Here are advanced techniques for moving beyond the amateurs and playing in the same league as professional guides:

HIDES, OBSERVATION TOWERS AND BOARDWALKS

A hide (also called a blind) is any artificial structure that allows the watcher to remain hidden while wildlife behaves more or less as normal. Your safari vehicle is an effective hide, simply because most animals don't make the connection between vehicles and their occupants. Stationary hides are usually covered wooden shelters with horizontal openings through which wildlife can be observed or photographed; some are just fences, while others are more elaborate, such as game lodges that overlook waterholes. Bird hides are sometimes erected next to waterholes, and can be great places for wildlife photography. Wooden observation towers allow you to scan across vegetation from a height, and look at birds or monkeys at eye level (a great luxury). Boardwalks over water can also act as observation platforms by getting the observer deep into otherwise inaccessible habitat.

USING CALLS

Calls (vocalisations) are particularly important for locating birds and amphibians, but many mammals, including elephants, hippos and lions, also make loud or dramatic calls. Homing in on vocalisations is an important part of tracking primates, and an imitation of a bleating wildebeest can rouse a lion from slumber. Birdwatchers know that even a poor imitation of some calls can bring birds in for a closer look – a favourite trick is 'pishing', making a high-pitched kissing sound with the mouth to attract small birds (kissing the back of your hand can have the same effect). Similar sounds can be made with a 'squeaker' (available from birdwatchers supply shops), and by rubbing polystyrene foam against glass (eg a windscreen). High-quality MP3 players are available with microphones for recording a call and playing it back to attract the animal in question. Most birds respond well to playback, and it is

often the best way to locate and identify some species, such as flufftails, owls or nightjars.

However, always use discretion and restraint with any of these techniques. Animals attracted to your calls are having their normal routine disrupted, which can potentially have seriously adverse effects – a lion checking out your wildebeest-calf call may be missing a real opportunity to hunt. And a bird responding to what it perceives as a territorial challenge may be distracted from a real intruder; it may be deprived of valuable feeding time; or it may fail to notice the presence of a predator. If overused, the playback technique can also make individual mammals and birds so inured that they don't respond at all.

TRACKS AND SIGNS

Animal tracks (spoor) and droppings (scats) are a great way of finding out what's around, especially those hard-to-see nocturnal species, even if you don't see the beast in question. Some signs, such as those of elephants, are immediately recognisable (especially the droppings), but most others are also distinct and a few can be learnt quite quickly.

Experienced trackers can read a great deal from spoor and scats (such as where an animal has rested, whether it was hunting and so on). Spoor and scats change and disintegrate over time (owl pellets, for example, break down quickly in wet forests), and years of practice are needed to pick up the subtleties of the tracker's art.

Examples of signs to look for include fur on fences or acacia thorns; nests of squirrels (called dreys) or birds; burrows, such as those used by warthogs, in abandoned termite mounds; flattened grass where an antelope has been lying out; a smooth tree trunk where an elephant has been rubbing; animal trails leading to a waterhole, food source or shelter; 'whitewash' left by birds – especially raptors – on cliffs, rocks and termite mounds; and pellets of undigested material regurgitated by owls and hyenas. Carcasses can also be telltale signs of predators, such as a dead impala dragged into a tree by a leopard. Tracking rhinos offers an opportunity to get to grips with tracks and signs while on foot, where broken or flattened vegetation make an interesting detective story.

ON SAFARI

WATCHING RESPONSIBLY

Watching wildlife under natural conditions at such close range is a privilege, and with this privilege comes the responsibility to ensure wildlife continues to live unhindered, both for its own survival and so that other people can enjoy the same experience. Strict ethical codes exist for wildlife-viewing; visitors are usually briefed before setting out. Of course you'll want quick results for all the money you've forked out, but it is important for everyone to stick to the rules; should a serious breach occur, don't hesitate to report your (or someone else's) driver or guide – it's in their interests to keep their comparatively well-paid jobs. Immense benefits – personal, aesthetic, recreational, con-

servation and financial – stem from the wildlife-watching 'industry', and it is important for all concerned (especially the animals) to ensure that wildlife tourism is carried out responsibly. The following are a few particularly important points to consider.

CLOSE ENCOUNTERS
Accidental encounters with large and potentially dangerous animals are a distinct possibility, but with common sense and care, you will come to no grief. Most big animals move away as you approach, and little else can harm you. Wildlife-viewing from a vehicle is very safe, but more intimate encounters could be expected on a walking safari – it's part of the excitement, but remember to exercise extreme caution even when accompanied by an armed guide. Monkeys can become a pest around camping grounds – assert your dominance early on before they get too cocky. All snakes should be treated with extreme caution – a few are dangerous and on no account should you try to pick one up (injured snakes can be especially dangerous).

DRIVING
There's a strict curfew on driving at night in most reserves; outside the reserves it's not a good idea to be on the roads after dark because of the danger of hitting animals or of running into bandits. During the day, most of

THE NAME OF THE GAME

The word 'game' actually hails from hunting: originally the game was the thrill of the 'sport', but gradually the quarry itself came to be called game. Derivation notwithstanding, the term pops up regularly in Southern Africa when people refer to wildlife and doesn't necessarily mean that some poor beast is about to receive a lethal dose of lead poisoning. 'Game-viewing' is the most common local term for wildlife-watching and is usually done on a 'game drive', a guided tour by vehicle. 'Big game' is, of course, the Big Five, whereas 'general game' collectively refers to the diverse herbivore community, ranging from duikers to giraffes. Of course, while 'game' in its various forms is used widely, hunters also still employ the term, most often as 'Big Game' as well as 'Plains Game', their term for the herbivores; advertisements for the latter are usually for hunting.

your wildlife-watching will be inside reserves, where a speed limit of around 40km/h is usually enforced, and animals have right of way (if no speed limit is indicated, use 40km/h as a guide). The chances of getting bowled over by an elephant are pretty slim; however, if an elephant, buffalo or rhino charges you, it's a very good idea to get out of its way – drivers don't usually need to be told and will start the engine as soon as a large animal starts to look stroppy.

FEEDING WILDLIFE

Some lodges have feeding stations that attract birds and monkeys by day, and galagos and genets at night. However, for you there's one simple rule – don't feed wild animals. Artificial feeding can foster a dependence on handouts, change natural behaviour and, in the long term, even cause malnutrition (visitors' bags usually contain sugary foods, rather than beetle grubs). Monkeys and baboons are intelligent, opportunistic animals that quickly learn how to get a free feed; if one is suddenly denied a coveted morsel, it can turn ugly very fast. At best this will mean a tantrum that will convince you to deliver the goods, at worst physical aggression that you don't want to be involved with.

ANIMAL WELFARE

Most travellers are aware of the debate over buying souvenirs made from animal products such as ivory. It might be difficult to relate that innocent-looking souvenir to a real animal, but don't fool yourself: your purchases can be one more nail in the coffin of a species. And don't assume that a product openly on sale is legal – even if it is, it does not mean that it meets any standards for wildlife sustainability or the humane treatment of animals. Many countries have strict laws about quarantine and the importation of prohibited animal or plant products. Check your own country's regulations before wasting money on a potentially prohibited import – the penalties are sometimes severe.

DISTURBING WILDLIFE

In popular reserves, animals have become used to vehicles and often behave more or less naturally a few metres from camera-snapping tourists. This has had unfortunate side-effects, such as the spectacle of lions or cheetahs being literally surrounded by safari vehicles; cheetahs being so harassed that they cannot hunt effectively; the destruction of vegetation; and drivers churning up the countryside by cutting new tracks in their pursuit of animals. While it's understandably difficult not to join in the safari circus at times, especially if vehicles are swarming around a kill, resist the temptation and focus on finding your own discovery.

WHAT TO BRING

CLOTHING

Suitable clothing maximises comfort to the wearer, and minimises disturbance to wildlife. Subdued colours, eg greens or browns, make your presence in the landscape less obtrusive, but avoid camouflage clothing – in Africa it's for military use. Predawn departures can be chilly, especially in open vehicles with the wind whipping past, and be prepared for sudden storms during the wet season; dress in layers and peel off or add clothes as conditions dictate.

Cotton or cotton-synthetic blends are cooler in hot weather; wear synthetics that breathe and are waterproof in cool conditions. Sleeveless photographers' jackets have many pockets, which are very useful for carrying the paraphernalia necessary for wildlife-watching (like field guides and notebooks). A hat is important: light cotton protects your head against the sun, but opt for wool or synthetics in cold conditions; and a

ON SAFARI

ON SAFARI

wide brim cuts down glare and helps hide your eyes (looking directly at an animal can be taken as a threat).

FIELD GUIDES

Field guides are (usually) pocket-sized books that depict the flora and fauna of a specific area with photos or colour illustrations. Important identification pointers and a distribution map are usually provided for each species; sometimes there are also brief natural histories, summarising breeding, behaviour, diet and the like. Guides to animals are usually organised in taxonomic order, a system that shows evolutionary relationships between species and is generally consistent between guides. Plant guides often follow other systems, eg wildflowers may be ranked by colour.

Ideally you should combine your own observations, notes and sketches with what you read in field guides, but on safari the excitement and overwhelming variety often make this impractical. Don't assume that because the field guide says species X is found here, it must be species X. If you find something unusual – birds in particular often wander outside their usual range – take notes and refer to other books when you get a chance. Depending on how much you value the book's appearance, consider colour-coding the outside margin of the pages so you can flip to a section easily.

Field guides are handy tools that have made an incalculable contribution to the popularity of wildlife-watching. But rarely are they the last word on a subject, and further reading of weightier texts can provide valuable detail not covered in your field guide.

BINOCULARS & SPOTTING SCOPES

A good pair of binoculars is probably the most important piece of equipment on safari, and the best investment a wildlife-watcher can make. Any working pair is better than none at all: a rustle in the bushes can become a brilliant sunbird, and a cheetah at full pelt after an antelope can be brought close-up. Take your own (don't expect

DOS & DON'TS ON SAFARI

- Large animals can be dangerous; don't drive too close to animals and don't drive between a female and her young.
- Don't make loud noises, such as tooting the horn or banging the side of your vehicle, to attract an animal's attention.
- Stay well clear of a predator on the hunt – it or its young may starve if the hunt is unsuccessful.
- Leave things better than you find them. Pick up other people's rubbish and keep your own rubbish until you can dispose of it properly.
- Do not drive off designated tracks – it destroys vegetation and encourages erosion.
- Do not throw matches or cigarettes out of your car. Put all fires out completely.
- Do not collect souvenirs such as bones, horns, feathers, shells etc – they play a role in the natural environment.
- Move in towards an animal gradually or in stages; that way you'll eventually get closer without disturbing it.
- Respect your own life. Do not get out of the vehicle except at designated areas, and don't stand or sit on a roof or hang out a window – predators and primates can move very quickly.

someone else to share), but if you are serious about watching wildlife, it is worth investing in quality optics; prices range from US$100 to thousands of dollars. There's any number of brands on the market, and a few things are worth knowing before you buy.

Factors to consider are size (to suit your hands), weight (they could be hanging from your neck for hours at a time) and whether you wear glasses (special eyecups are available for spectacle wearers). Decent models also have a dial (diopter), which allows you to compensate for any focusing difference between left and right eyes. Good binoculars are hinged, allowing adjustment for the distance between your eyes.

Like cameras, with binoculars you get what you pay for. Top-end brands such as Zeiss, Leica, Bausch & Lomb and Swarovski offer superb optics, last for years, and are waterproof and dustproof. More affordable brands, such as Bushnell, and midrange to upper models from respected camera manufacturers (eg Pentax, Canon and Nikon) are perfectly good for most wildlife-watching. Good-quality compact models are worth considering, but don't be tempted by supercheap compacts or by binoculars with 'zoom' optics (they usually have poor light-gathering ability).

Your final choice of binoculars will depend on budget, likely amount of use, and desire for quality and comfort. But before you spend a lot of money, talk to people and test their binoculars in the field. Read manufacturers' brochures and product reviews in birdwatchers' magazines. Birdwatchers carry weight in the marketplace, and conduct exhaustive tests in the field; if a particular brand and/or configuration passes their (usually stringent) requirements it'll be good enough for use in Southern Africa. Recommendations usually come in different price categories. A useful website that tests new releases and has a host of background information, plus lists

of retailers and manufacturers, can be found at www.bettervie wdesired.com.

THE NITTY GRITTY

Numbers are usually stamped on every pair of binoculars, eg 10x50, 7x32. The first number refers to the number of times the image is magnified when you look through the eyepieces: at 10x, an object 100m away will appear as if only 10m away; at 7x, it will appear as if 14m away etc. The most useful magnifications for wildlife-watching are 7x, 8x and 10x. The second number, most commonly between 20 and 50, refers to the diameter in millimetres of the objective lens (the lens farthest from the eye); the wider the lens (the higher the number) the more light enters and therefore the brighter the image.

Larger objective lenses increase light-gathering ability, and hence image brightness. Higher magnification reduces brightness. Not only is a brighter image clearer, it is also more colour accurate – a sometimes crucial point for identification. Light-gathering ability can be estimated (it's not a perfect guide) by dividing the objective diameter by the magnification – the higher the result, the more light enters the binoculars. Thus, 10x50s and 8x40s perform similarly, but 7x42s often give a brighter image. Special interior coatings can also increase image brightness. Having extra light-gathering ability may not be all that useful during the middle of the day (your eye can take only so much light before your irises start to close), but in dim conditions, such as at dusk or in a rainforest, you'll want all you can get. As your irises can only open so far (and this decreases with age), opting for greater light-gathering power may be a waste. To check, test out different binoculars in dim light before you buy a pair.

Larger objective lenses also mean a larger field of view, ie the 'width' of the area (usually indicated in degrees) that fits into the image you see. Field of view is also a trade-off against magnification, ie higher magnifications reduce the field of view. The narrower the field of view, the harder it is to locate your target, especially if it is moving.

Internal lenses can also affect quality. Most binoculars have porro prism lenses, which are offset from each other to give the familiar 'crooked' barrels. Roof prism lenses are aligned directly behind each other and allow compact, straight barrels: cost is their only drawback. Good compromises of all factors are configurations such as 7x35, 7x40 and 8x40. Birders tend to favour 8x40 or 10x50 for the sometimes critical extra magnification.

Spotting scopes are essentially refracting telescopes designed for field use. Birders use 'scopes' most often in open habitats, such as when watching waterbirds and waders. Scopes offer higher magnifications than binoculars (usually starting at 20x or 25x), but must be mounted on a tripod or monopod to reduce shaking (not usually feasible in a vehicle). Disadvantages include weight and bulk; and a narrow field of view makes scopes difficult to use effectively in rainforests. Again, a quality scope will be expensive; Kowa, Leica, Celestron, Nikon and Bushnell are all excellent brands.

DIGITAL CAMERAS

Wildlife photography is a highly specialised field, but the quality of today's equipment – even modestly priced, non-professional gear – means that excellent results are possible for anyone.

If you're buying your first digital camera, the selection is mindboggling. Canon or Nikon are the choice of most professional wildlife photographers, largely because they offer formidable lens quality, but all established brands are good. Cameras essentially all do the same thing, though with varying degrees of complexity and technological assistance. Most digital SLRs have a full range of automatic functions, but you should select a model that also allows full manual operation. Once you've mastered the basic techniques, you'll probably find it limiting if you're unable to begin experimenting with your photography.

More important than camera bodies are the lenses you attach to them – and for wildlife, think long. A 200mm to 300mm lens is a good starting point, though bird portraits require something longer. Lenses of 400mm to 600mm focal length are probably out of the price range of most people, though 'slower' lenses (lenses with a relatively small maximum aperture) are reasonably priced and very useful. Dedicated (ie 'brand name') lenses have superb optical quality and are more expensive than generic brands (eg Tamron), but unless you're a pro, you'll probably notice only a slight difference.

Zooms are generally not as sharp as fixed focal length lenses (lenses which do not zoom), but the difference is only important if you're thinking about publishing your pictures. Many brands offer zooms around the 100mm to 300mm range which, when paired with a short zoom like a 35mm to 70mm, covers most situations for recreational photographers. Recently released 'super-zooms' – 55mm to 300mm and 100mm to 400mm – are worth investigating. None are cheap, but they yield excellent-quality results in one versatile package.

Hundreds of accessories can be used to enhance shots, but one that's vital is the tripod. Many shots are spoiled by 'camera shake', particularly when using longer lenses. Tripods can be cumbersome to include in your luggage, but sturdy, compact models can easily fit into a sausage bag. Collapsible monopods are light and easy to carry, but do not offer nearly as much stability as a tripod.

Most wildlife photographers in Southern Africa are restricted to a vehicle, where it is impractical to use a tripod. An excellent alternative for vehicle-based photography is a beanbag. A small cloth bag with a zip opening takes up almost no room, and can be filled with dried rice when you arrive at your destination. Simply roll down your window, lay the beanbag on the top of the door and rest the camera lens on it (or, if you're a passenger in a minivan, lay the beanbag on the roof if it opens).

IN THE FIELD

Before you go anywhere, know how your camera works. Visit the local zoo or park, and shoot a few dozen snaps to familiarise yourself with its controls and functions. Many good wildlife moments happen unexpectedly and pass in seconds; you'll miss them if you're still fiddling with dials and settings. For the same reason, when in reserves, leave your camera turned on (and pack plenty of batteries).

Most cameras in manual mode have shutter- and aperture-priority functions. In shutter-priority mode, you set the shutter speed, and the camera selects the appropriate aperture for a correct exposure; the reverse applies for aperture-priority. These two functions are probably the most valuable for wildlife photographers – but you need to know when to use them. Shutter priority is excellent for shooting action. If you want to freeze motion, select the highest shutter speed permitted with the available light, and the camera takes care of the aperture setting. On the other hand, if you're trying to emphasise depth of field in your shot, opt for aperture priority. Large apertures (low 'f-stops') reduce the depth of field – a useful trick for enhancing a portrait

shot by throwing the background out of focus. However, if you're shooting a scene where you want everything in focus, such as thousands of wildebeests on a vast plain, select a small aperture (high f-stops).

Composition is a major challenge with wildlife as you can't move your subject around; try different vantage points and experiment with a variety of focal lengths. If you're too far away to take a good portrait, try to show the animal in its habitat. A 400mm lens might give you a close-up of a seabird's face, while a 28mm will show the entire colony receding into the background – all from the same position. Try to tell a story about the animal or illustrate some behaviour. Jackal pups transfixed by grazing gazelles might be too shy for a decent close-up, but could make a lovely subject if you include the antelopes and surroundings.

Unless you're packing a very powerful flash, wildlife photography relies on the vagaries of natural light and the best shots are invariably those taken in the 'golden hour' – just after dawn and just before dusk. Where possible, get into position early, whether it's a bird hide, waterhole or scenic lookout you noted the day before. Don't always assume front-on light is the best. Side lighting can give more depth to a subject; back lighting, particularly when the sun is near the horizon, can be very atmospheric.

Above all else, when photographing wildlife, be patient. You never know what will appear at the waterhole next or when a snoozing predator will suddenly spot a chance for a kill. You cannot always anticipate when an opportunity will arise, but if you're willing to wait, you'll almost certainly see something worth snapping.

ON SAFARI

GLOSSARY

adaptation – physical or behavioural trait that helps an organism survive or exploit an environmental factor.

aestivate – to enter a state of dormancy in seasonal hot, dry weather, when food is scarce.

algae – primitive water plants.

alpha male or female – dominant animal in a hierarchy, eg primate troop (a sometimes tenuous position).

altricial – helpless at birth, requiring prolonged parental care, eg primates (*compare with* precocial).

amphibian – animal that lives part of its life cycle in water and part on land, eg frog.

annulated horns – ridged horns of some antelope species, eg oryxes, impalas.

aquatic – living in fresh water (*compare with* marine).

arboreal – tree-dwelling.

arthropod – invertebrate characterised by a segmented body and jointed legs, eg insects, spiders.

artiodactyl – an even-toed ungulate, eg hippo, pig, giraffe and antelope.

asynchronous – not occurring simultaneously, eg the hatching of eggs.

avian – characteristic of birds, eg avian behaviour.

bachelor group or herd – aggregation of nonbreeding adult and subadult males, eg antelopes.

big cat – the three largest cat species, ie lions, leopards and cheetahs.

Big Five – the five large animals (rhino, buffalo, elephant, lion and leopard) regarded as the most dangerous to hunt (and therefore the most prized) by colonial hunters.

binocular vision – vision with overlapping field of view to give a three-dimensional perception of space; best developed in cats and primates.

biodiversity – faunal and floral richness characterising an area.

biomass – total weight of living organisms in an ecosystem.

bipedal – standing or walking on two legs, eg humans.

bird party – a feeding party of birds, especially in forest, containing various species (also called bird wave).

birder – a birdwatching enthusiast.

blind – *see* hide.

bluff – behaviour to convince a predator or rival that the bluffer is stronger.

boar – male pig.

bolus – ball of food or dung.

boss – head covering that supports horns, eg on buffaloes.

bovid – a member of the antelope family (Bovidae).

bovine – cattlelike in appearance or behaviour.

brood – group of young animals produced in one litter or clutch.

browse – to eat leaves and other parts of shrubs and trees (hence browser).

bull – adult male of various large mammal species including buffalo, elephant, giraffe.

cache – (*noun*) a hidden store of food; (*verb*) to hide food for future use.

callosity – hardened area of skin, eg on knees of giraffes (also called callus).

camouflage – coloration or patterning that helps an animal blend into its surroundings.

canid – any a member of the family Canidae (dog, fox, jackal etc).

canine – doglike; also relating to or belonging to the family Canidae (dogs, foxes, jackals etc).

canines – the four large front teeth at the front of the jaw; well developed in carnivores for killing and in baboons for fighting.

carnassials – shearing teeth near the back of a carnivores' jaw.

carnivore – meat-eating animal.

carrion – dead or decaying flesh.

casque – prominent bony growth surmounting the bill of some hornbills and the head of guineafowl.

cellulose – component that strengthens plants' cell walls, supporting them and forming stems.

cetacean – whales and dolphins.

cheek pouch – extension of cheeks for the temporary storage of food, eg in monkeys.

class – a major division of animal classification, eg mammal, birds, reptile etc.

climax forest – mature forest.

colony – aggregation of animals (eg birds) that live, roost or breed together (hence colonial).

commensalism – relationship between two unrelated animal species in which one species benefits from the interaction and the other is unaffected.

contiguous – adjoining, eg woodland spanning two adjacent reserves.

convergent evolution – evolution whereby unrelated species develop similar characteristics, usually seen among geographically separate species occupying similar niches, eg bushbabies and possums (also called convergence).

coursing – to run down prey along the ground mainly by sight, eg African wild dog.

courtship – behaviour (often ritualised) associated with attracting a mate.

crèche – young birds or mammals gathered for safety and play.

crepuscular – active at dawn and dusk.

crustacean – arthropod with gills, which can breathe underwater or survive in damp conditions on land.

cryptic – behaviour, appearance or lifestyle that helps conceal an organism from predators.

cud – partly digested plant material regurgitated and chewed by resting ruminants.

decurved – downward-curving.

dewlap – loose skin (eg in eland) or feathers hanging under the chin.

digit – finger or toe.

dimorphism – having two forms of colour or size, eg spotted and black leopard (*see* sexual dimorphism, polymorphism).

dispersal – movement of animals (eg after breeding or rains) or plants (eg seeds) across a geographic area (*compare with* migration).

displacement activity – behaviour performed out of normal context, eg grooming when an animal is stressed.

display – behaviour transmitting information from the sender to another, often associated with threat, defence of territory, courtship etc.

diurnal – active during daylight hours (opposite of nocturnal).

diversity – variety of species or forms in an area.

dorsal – upper (top) surface, ie the back on most animals (opposite of ventral).

down – loose, fluffy feathers that cover young birds and insulate plumage of adults.

drey – squirrel nest.

dung – animal excrement (faeces).

dung midden – accumulation of dung as a territory marker, often accompanied by scent-marking (*see* latrine).

ear-tuft – wispy hairs extending beyond ear-tips (eg, caracal) or erectile feathers near ears (eg some owls).

ecology – scientific study of relationships between organisms, their environment and each other.

ecosystem – community of living organisms and their physical environment.

ecotone – *see* edge.

edge – transition zone between two habitats, eg savanna and forest; hence edge species (also called ecotone).

endangered – in danger of imminent extinction if trends causing its demise continue.

endemic – found only in a certain area, eg louries are endemic to Africa.

environment – physical factors that influence the development and behaviour of organisms.

epiphyte – plant growing on another for support, eg orchids on a tree.

equatorial – living on or near the equator.

erectile – can be erected, eg hair or feathers erected in defence or courtship displays.

estrus – *see* oestrus.

evolve – to change physical and/or behavioural traits over time to exploit or survive changing environmental constraints.

faeces – excrement.

family – scientific grouping of related genera, eg Felidae (the cat family).

farrow – litter of pigs (*also verb*).

feline – catlike; also related to or belonging to the Felidae (cat family).

feral – running wild, especially escaped domestic stock.

fledgling – young bird able to leave the nest, ie to fledge.

flight distance – distance at which an animal will flee from a perceived threat.

flight feathers – large wing feathers (also called primary feathers).

flock – group of birds, sheep or other herbivores (*also verb*).

foliage – leafy vegetation, eg on trees.

folivore – a leaf-eating animal.

fossorial – adapted for digging.

frugivore – a fruit-eating animal.

gallery forest – forest growing along watercourses, which thus may extend into an adjoining habitat (also called riverine forest).

game – wild animals, especially mammals and birds, hunted by humans for food and sport.

genera – plural of genus.

genus – taxonomic grouping of related species.

geophagy – eating rock or soil.

gestation – period that young mammals develop in the womb before birth.

glaciations – periods during ice ages when glaciers covered large areas of the earth's surface.

gland – *see* scent gland, inguinal gland, interdigital gland, preorbital gland.

granivore – grain-eating animal.

gravid – pregnant or bearing eggs.

graze – to eat grass (hence grazer).

gregarious – forming or moving in groups, eg herds or flocks.

guano – phosphate-rich excrement deposited by seabirds and bats, usually accumulated over generations.

habitat – natural living area of an animal; usually characterised by a distinct plant community.

hackles – long, loose feathers or hairs on nape or throat, often erectile.

harem – group of females that mate with one male; the male defends his harem against other males.

hawk – (*verb*) to fly actively in search of prey such as insects, usually caught in the open mouth.

helper – animal, usually from a previous brood, which helps parents raise subsequent brood or broods.

herbivore – a vegetarian animal.

herd – social group of mammals, usually applied only to herbivores.

hide – artificial construction, usually of wood, for the observation of animals while keeping the observer hidden (also called blind).

hierarchy – order of dominance among social animals, usually with a dominant individual or caste and one or more tiers of power or function, eg termites, primates.

hive – home of bees or wasps.

holt – otters' den.

home range – the area over which an individual or group ranges over time (*compare with* territory).

host – organism on (or in) which a parasite lives; bird that raises young of parasitic species.

immature – stage in a young bird's development between juvenile and adult.

incisors – front (ie cutting) teeth.

incubate – to hatch eggs using warmth.

inguinal gland – scent gland in groin area.

insectivore – an insect-eating animal.

interdigital gland – scent gland between toes or hooves, eg on cats and antelopes.

invertebrate – an animal without a spinal column or backbone, eg insects, worms.

iridescence – metallic sheen on many insects and birds, eg sunbirds.

jinking – moving jerkily or with quick turns to escape a predator.

juvenile – animal between infancy and adulthood (mammals) or with first feathers after natal down (bird).

koppie or **kopje** – outcrop of rock on savanna plains.

lamellae – comblike plates in the bill of some birds (eg flamingos) that filter food particles from water.

latrine – site where mammals habitually deposit dung or urine (*compare with* dung midden).

lek – communal arena for mating and territorial sparring (antelopes) or courtship displays and mating (birds).

loaf – to laze about, especially used in describing bird behaviour.

localised – found only in a small or distinct area.

lying-out – remaining motionless with head flat on the ground to avoid danger (eg antelopes).

mammal – warm-blooded, usually furred or hairy animal (except cetaceans) that gives birth to and suckles live young.

mandible – lower part of beak or jaw.

mantle – shoulder or upper back area on birds or mammals.

marine – living in the sea.

matriarchal – female dominated.

matrilineal – relating to kinship or descent among related

females.

melanism – naturally occurring excess of dark-brown pigment that produces black forms of some animals, eg leopards and servals.

midden – *see* dung midden.

migration – regular movement, often en masse, from one location to another, eg wildebeests, shorebirds (hence migrant, migratory).

miombo – fire-resistant deciduous woodland, especially that dominated by Brachystegia.

mob – to harass a predatory animal (eg small birds mobbing an owl); often in response to a distress call.

monogamy – having one reproductive partner for life or breeding season, eg bat-eared fox.

montane – living or situated on mountains.

moult – to shed and replace all or selected feathers, skin or fur, usually prompted by seasonal or behavioural changes, eg courtship.

musth – a frenzied state of sexual readiness in certain large male mammals, particularly elephants (also spelt must).

mutualism – interaction between two species where both benefit.

natal – pertaining to birth.

nestling – young bird until it leaves the nest (*compare with* fledgling).

nest parasitism – laying eggs in the nest of another bird species and taking no further part in rearing the offspring (also called brood parasitism).

niche – specialised ecological role played by an organism.

nictitating membrane – semitransparent membrane that draws across eyes of most birds and some mammals and reptiles.

nocturnal – active at night.

nomadic – wandering in search of resources, eg food or water.

oestrus – period when female mammal is ovulating and therefore sexually receptive (also spelt estrus).

omnivore – an animal that eats both plant and animal matter.

order – grouping of one or more

animal families, eg cats and dogs into Carnivora/carnivores.

pair bond – social ties that keep mates together, reinforced with grooming, calls etc.

parasite – plant or animal that obtains nourishment during all or part of its life from another life form, usually to the detriment of the host.

pelagic – living at sea, ie in or above open water.

perissodactyl – an odd-toed ungulate, eg rhino, horse.

photosynthesis – process whereby plants convert sunlight, water and carbon dioxide into organic compounds.

pioneer – the first species of animal or plant to colonise an area.

piscivorous – fish-eating.

plantigrade – walking with whole foot on the ground, eg elephant, humans.

plumage – birds' feathers, often used to describe total appearance, eg drab plumage.

polyandry – female having access to more than one reproductive male.

polygamy – having access to more than one reproductive mate.

polygyny – male having access to more than one reproductive female.

polymorphism – having more than one adult form, size or colour.

precocial – being able to walk or run (eg wildebeest), forage (eg ostrich) or swim shortly after birth or hatching (*compare with* altricial).

predator – animal that kills and eats others.

prehensile – flexible and grasping, eg tail, fingers.

preorbital gland – scent gland in front of the eyes, especially in antelopes, used to mark territory.

present – to show genital region as appeasement (eg apes) or to indicate readiness to mate.

prey – animal food of a predator.

pride – collective term for lions.

primary feathers – *see* flight feathers.

primate – a monkey, prosimian or ape.

primitive – resembling or representing an early stage in the evolution of a particular group of animals.

pronk – see stot.

prosimian – 'primitive' primate, eg bushbaby.

prusten – loud huffing sound made by female leopard to call cubs.

pug – footprint or other imprint left on the ground by an animal.

quadruped – a four-legged animal.

quarter – to systematically range over an area in search of prey, eg jackals, birds of prey.

race – see subspecies.

raptor – bird of prey, eg hawk, falcon, vulture.

recurved – upward-curving, eg bill of avocet.

regurgitate – to bring up partly digested food from crop or stomach, particularly when feeding young.

relict – remnant of formerly widespread species, community or habitat, now surrounded by different communities.

reptile – a scaly, cold-blooded vertebrate, eg turtle, crocodile, snake, lizard.

resident – an animal that remains in an area for its entire life cycle.

rinderpest – disease of cattle that can affect related animals, eg antelopes.

riparian – see riverine.

riverine – living or occurring near or in rivers or streams (also called riparian).

rodent – type of mammal characterized by two continuously growing incisors, eg rat, mouse, squirrel.

roost – area where mammals (eg bats) or birds gather to sleep, sometimes in large numbers (also verb).

ruminant – ungulate with four-chambered stomach (rumen) that chews the cud (hence ruminate).

rump – upper backside of mammal or bird, often distinctively marked, eg antelopes.

rut – (antelopes) the mating season (also verb).

saddle – mid to lower back area on mammals and birds.

sagittal – pertaining to the prominent upper seam of skull, eg sagittal crest on male lion.

savanna – vegetation zone characterised by contrasting wet and dry seasons where grassy understorey grows with scattered trees and shrubs.

scavenger – animal that feeds on carrion or scraps left by others.

scent gland – concentration of special skin cells that secrete chemicals conveying information about the owner's status, identity, reproductive state etc.

sedentary – animal remaining in one area for all or part of its life cycle (see resident).

selection – process whereby traits that are detrimental to an organism's reproductive success are weeded out by environmental or behavioural pressures.

semidesert – semiarid area with more rainfall, and hence more vegetation and biodiversity, than true desert.

sexual dimorphism – differences between males and females of the same species in colour, size or form, eg the lion's mane and many spectacular examples in birds.

sibling – related offspring with the same parents (hence foster sibling in brood parasites).

signal – movement or trait that conveys information, eg danger, from one animal to another.

skein – collective term for geese.

slough – to shed skin when growing, eg reptiles, amphibians.

sounder – group of pigs.

sow – female pig.

spawn – eggs of fish and amphibians, usually laid in water (also verb).

speciation – the process whereby species are formed.

species – organisms capable of breeding with each other to produce fertile offspring; distinct and usually recognisable from other species, with which the majority don't interbreed.

spoor – the track or tracks of an animal.

spraint – otter urine, used as territorial marking.

spur – horny growth on some birds, eg on forewing (lapwings) or 'heel' (francolins).

spy-hop – to jump above vegetation such as grass, or water's surface (whales and great white sharks) to check bearings, threats etc.

stage – level in development of an organism.

stalk – to pursue prey by stealth.

stoop – powerful dive of bird of prey.

stot – stylised high leap while bounding, especially by young antelopes in play and adults when fleeing (also called pronk); thought to display fitness to would-be predators.

streamer – long tail feather, eg of swallows.

subadult – last stage of juvenile development, usually characterised by near-adult coloration, size or plumage.

subordinate – an animal that is ranked beneath another in a social hierarchy, eg baboons.

subspecies – population of a species isolated from another population (eg by landforms) that has developed distinct physical traits (also called race).

succulent – fleshy, moisture-filled plant, eg euphorbias, aloes.

sward – grass or a stretch of grass.

symbiosis – see mutualism.

talon – hooked claw on bird of prey.

taxonomy – scientific classification of organisms according to their physical relationships (also called systematics).

tectonic – pertaining to changes in the earth's crust caused by movement below its surface.

temporal gland – facial glands between the eyes and ears of elephants that secrete temporin.

termitarium – earthen mound constructed by a termite colony (also called termitary).

terrestrial – living on the ground.

territory – feeding or breeding

area defended against others (usually unrelated) of the same species (*compare with* home range).

thermal – rising column of air; used by large birds to gain height.

troop – group of monkeys or baboons.

tropical – found within the tropics, ie between Tropics of Cancer and Capricorn.

tsetse fly – biting, blood-sucking fly.

tusker – large elephant or boar.

tusks – greatly enlarged canine teeth, used as tools, or in defense and ritual combat, eg in elephants.

ungulate – a hoofed animal.

vent – the urogential opening of cetaceans, birds, reptiles and fish (occasionally applied to female mammals).

ventral – lower (under) side of an animal (opposite of dorsal).

vertebrate – an animal having a backbone, ie bony fish, amphibians, reptiles, birds and mammals.

vestigial – small, nonfunctional remnant of a feature formerly present, eg vestigial horns.

vocalisation – sound made orally by an animal as a signal.

volplane – steep, controlled dive on outstretched wings, eg by vultures to a kill.

waders – shorebirds and related families, eg plovers.

warm-blooded – maintaining a constant body temperature by internal regulation, eg birds and mammals (also known as homoiothermic).

warren – network of holes used as shelter and nursery.

waterfowl – water-dwelling bird with webbed feet, eg swan, goose, duck.

wattle – fleshy, sometimes brightly coloured growth often prominent in courtship, eg on birds.

yearling – a mammal in its second year of growth.

INDEX

GLOSSARY

INDEX

INDEX

BEHIND THE SCENES

THIS BOOK

This book was commissioned and produced in Lonely Planet's Melbourne office.

Publisher Chris Rennie
Associate Publisher Ben Handicott
Commissioning Editor Janine Eberle
Project Manager Jane Atkin
Designers Mark Adams, Nic Lehman
Layout Designer Yukiyoshi Kamimura
Assisting Layout Designer Indra Kilfoyle
Coordinating Editor Andrew Bain
Assisting Editors Daniel Corbett, Kate James
Coordinating Cartographer Sam Sayer
Assisting Cartographer Ross Butler
Prepress Production Ryan Evans
Print Production Manager Graham Imeson

Thanks to Yvonne Kirk, Shahara Ahmed, Julie Sheridan, Wayne Murphy, Sally Darmody, Melanie Dankel, Darren O'Connell. Special thanks to James Hardy.

TITLE PAGE IMAGES BY LONELY PLANET IMAGES

Highlights Andrew Parkinson p10-11, Environement & Conservation Ariadne Van Zandbergen p32-33, Destinations Luke Hunter p54-55, Wildlife Mason Florence p188-9; Planning Andrew Parkinson p296-7, On Safari Mitch Reardon p314-5.

SOURCES

Common names for many wide-ranging African mammals and birds vary across the continent; and no two references agree completely on names (scientific or common). Mammal names used in this book follow *Mammals of the Southern African Subregion* by Skinner and Smithers. For birds we followed the *Illustrated Guide to the Birds of Southern Africa* by Sinclair, Hockey and Tarboton, and *Collins Illustrated Checklist – Birds of Southern Africa* by van Perlo.

THE LONELY PLANET STORY

Fresh from an epic journey across Europe, Asia and Australia in 1972, Tony and Maureen Wheeler sat at their kitchen table stapling together notes. The first Lonely Planet guidebook, *Across Asia on the Cheap,* was born.

Travellers snapped up the guides. Inspired by their success, the Wheelers began publishing books to Southeast Asia, India and beyond. Demand was prodigious, and the Wheelers expanded the business rapidly to keep up. Over the years, Lonely Planet extended its coverage to every country and into the virtual world via lonelyplanet.com and the Thorn Tree message board.

As Lonely Planet became a globally loved brand, Tony and Maureen received several offers for the company. But it wasn't until 2007 that they found a partner whom they trusted to remain true to the company's principles of travelling widely, treading lightly and giving sustainably. In October of that year, BBC Worldwide acquired a 75% share in the company, pledging to uphold Lonely Planet's commitment to independent travel, trustworthy advice and editorial independence.

Today, Lonely Planet has offices in Melbourne, London and Oakland, with over 500 staff members and 300 authors. Tony and Maureen are still actively involved with Lonely Planet. They're travelling more often than ever, and they're devoting their spare time to charitable projects. And the company is still driven by the philosophy of *Across Asia on the Cheap:* 'All you've got to do is decide to go and the hardest part is over. So go!'